Corporate Social Responsibility?

Corporate Social Responsibility?

Human Rights in the New Global Economy

EDITED BY
CHARLOTTE WALKER-SAID
AND JOHN D. KELLY

THE UNIVERSITY OF CHICAGO PRESS   CHICAGO AND LONDON

CHARLOTTE WALKER-SAID is a historian of modern Africa and assistant professor of Africana studies at the John Jay College of Criminal Justice at the City University of New York. JOHN D. KELLY is professor of anthropology at the University of Chicago, where he serves on the faculty board of the Human Rights Program. He is the author or coauthor of several books and, most recently, coeditor of *Anthropology and Global Counterinsurgency*, also published by the University of Chicago Press.

The University of Chicago Press, Chicago 60637
The University of Chicago Press, Ltd., London
© 2015 by The University of Chicago
All rights reserved. Published 2015.
Printed in the United States of America

24 23 22 21 20 19 18 17 16 15   1 2 3 4 5

ISBN-13: 978-0-226-24427-3 (cloth)
ISBN-13: 978-0-226-24430-3 (paper)
ISBN-13: 978-0-226-24444-0 (e-book)
DOI: 10.7208/chicago/9780226244440.001.0001

Library of Congress Cataloging-in-Publication Data

Corporate social responsibility? : human rights in the new global economy / edited by Charlotte Walker-Said and John D. Kelly.
      pages cm
   Includes bibliographical references and index.
   ISBN 978-0-226-24427-3 (cloth : alkaline paper) — ISBN 978-0-226-24444-0 (ebook) — ISBN 978-0-226-24430-3 (paperback : alkaline paper)   1. Social responsibility of business.   2. Human rights.   I. Walker-Said, Charlotte, editor.   II. Kelly, John Dunham, 1958– editor.
   HD60.C6936 2015
   658.4′08—dc23

                                                                                    2015006380

Publication of this book has been aided by a grant from the University of Chicago Pozen Family Center for Human Rights.

♾ This paper meets the requirements of ANSI/NISO Z39.48-1992 (Permanence of Paper).

Contents

Preface

John D. Kelly

We hope this book will make a difference. There are many books on human rights: histories, philosophy, legal studies, sociological and anthropological studies. Ethnographies are myriad, and human rights are mentioned in a remarkable range of studies of contemporary politics in the complex discipline called political science. Economists, global health scholars, and public policy scholars of almost every focus make contributions. But still, it is difficult to get a topic such as corporate social responsibility into focus, to find the perspective, comprehensive and practical, necessary to reach informed judgments.

There is something curiously problematic about what scholars tend to contribute to human rights theory and practice. By and large they do what they do well. Many studies considered individually, including stellar monographs by contributors here, make major contributions in their own terms—their own disciplinary terms. As Charlotte Walker-Said might put it—in fact as she does, in the introduction here, when talking specifically about legal studies of corporate social responsibility—scholarship is all too often "siloed." I want to say something complicated about this simple situation.

To discuss the purpose of human rights scholarship, and its failures as well as its successes, I want to start with a short overview of the politics of human rights in practice. Human rights as a political issue has emerged at particular moments in mostly Western political history. Historians and political theorists often identify three moments: First, there were the liberal revolutions of the eighteenth century, especially American and French. An American declaration in 1776 located its defense of

radical political decisions "in the course of human events," and spoke
of the propriety of clarifying its motives before the opinion of mankind.
This profound relocation of once-divine rights of sovereigns within a
universe of human events and opinion was fundamental to revolutionary America's legitimacy—and it was still uncertain, as Lincoln saw it
eighty-seven years later, whether "any nation so conceived and so ded-
icated can long endure." And it was also a powerful inspiration to the
revolutionary French, and specifically to the French declaration of 1789
that found rights of "man and citizen." French visionaries saw nations as
the only sovereigns, and the necessity and propriety of both liberty and
law, and yet could not stop appalling terror from emerging as a price of
freedom. Scholars still debate these events, their meanings, and the lessons to be drawn from their astonishing trajectories. Research with a human rights focus has added to efforts to track the consequences of doctrines, declarations, discoveries, and adjudications through the maze of
events. It has brought new insights and no promise that the basic questions are closed.

Second, in the twentieth century, there was the strange public debate between the Americans and the Nazis, Adolf Hitler pitting his
own new truths of Volk right against what he saw as Woodrow Wilson's
false promises and anti-German fictions. This conflict began as the Ger-
mans metamorphosed antidemocratically, against the onerous terms of
the Versailles treaty, and organized Axis powers against a coalition that
came to call itself the "United Nations." It ended not with a synthesis but
with one side's triumph, with global repudiation of Nazi racism and all
racism, and a remarkably American reassertion of the self-determining
nation-state as the global vehicle for sovereign order in 1945. At the San
Francisco Conference in 1945, Harry Truman declared a new world free
from the fear of war, chopping the air with his hands to emphasize each
word. This vindication of the American vision of democracy, equality,
and self-determination via separate but equal nation-states began with
this final concord but also with its own coercion. Truman's speech came
just weeks before mushroom clouds at Hiroshima and Nagasaki ended
the Second World War and claimed to end all legitimate war between nations and states, by way of required unconditional surrender. The resolution of this war was not a treaty but a new global architecture for nation-
state sovereignty. Exactly how a new universal grammar of sovereign
interrecognition via global coordination of nation and state could end war
and certify peace with justice was clearly seen as the overarching prob-

lem for the new "United Nations," as the alliance against the German-Italian-Japanese Axis metamorphosed in San Francisco into an embodiment of a once-utopian American plan for new world ordering.

Accelerated at the Bandung Conference in 1955, this vision of sovereignty and its new doctrine of nation building, opposite of the Nazi Volk destinies, became the recipe for decolonization. Even the rise of the Cold War could not derail decolonization, but rather it transformed the doctrine of self-determination, at Bandung, into a cardinal moment of choice of governmental system, at the moment of nation building and state building, as a destiny-setting exercise of the free political right. Again, scholarship tracking human rights doctrines and influences through this maze of events is well under way. Books from Mary Ann Glendon's *A World Made New* to Erez Manela's *The Wilsonian Moment* illuminate the process by which Western and even specifically American human rights ideas become global realities. And we still have much to discuss.

And finally, the third moment, and the true explosion of human rights as political discourse and practice, begins with the end of the Cold War, begins among the forces accelerating the collapse of that power politics and the delineation yet again of new world order and political possibilities. This large-scale moment is our own, its critical events still unfolding, its new debates about sovereignty, self-determination, legal orders of right and duty still under way. The plain fact that it is too soon to know with certainty which developments are most important of course does not stop scholarship from seeking to frame, to explain, and all the more—and we come to my point—to participate in events. In their usual, almost necessary fashion, scholars come in after the facts, in pursuit of the meanings, trying to organize, clarify, and judge, questing for perspective and insights that might be useful. Some points of order can be clearly discerned. NGOs, as we call them, have risen to a prominence in events rivaling that of states and nations. Many allege that revolutions of new kinds, especially in information technology, must be reckoned with. Environmental questions vie with all others for priority. The future of sovereignty is questioned, and global connections, flows, and mediations are thought to be more significant than at any prior time.

It is entirely possible that observers a century or more from now will look back on our times and emphasize emergent things, trends, and relationships largely different from those we now take as the signs of our times, even as our own fashions in self-estimation vary by discipline and now global location. Cognizant of this complex situation, I wish to recall the problem of discussions of human rights that, however well informed and insightful, are "siloed," both by disciplines and often, I think, by location.

In fact, for scholarship such silos are vital. Without strong criteria for evidence, analysis, criticism, argument, and judgment, subtle problems can go unnoticed and major problems can be misunderstood via useful but flawed partial truths. Such discussions as those in and for a national legal academy, or debates between schools of ethnographic theory, to speak of two disciplinary modalities dominant in this volume, can be important for development of a science of anthropology and for schools of jurisprudence, even the training therein of practitioners. They may go far down the road of self-understanding, embracing and operationalizing, each in their own way, the agenda of enlightenment.

By their nature they do not, directly, address the questions that Weber taught us to call "Tolstoy's Questions," not *what is true?* or even *who are we?* but rather *what is to be done? how shall we live?* Weber agreed with Tolstoy but not with his condemnation of social science. Weber argued that social sciences, of and for themselves, cannot answer Tolstoy's questions, because the questions involve value judgments as well as matters of fact and its assessment, conception, and criticism of concepts. Tolstoy's questions are irreducibly political regardless of their possible connection, also, to fruits of sciences, social and otherwise. Weber's point was that Tolstoy's impatience for final truths, for answers to his value-oriented questions, led him to miss what kinds of enlightenment social sciences could by their nature provide.

Generations of scholars have been as troubled as Weber was by the implications of these arguments. Weber's clear moral vision of the enlightenment foundations of all sciences made him avid to give, when invited by Munich University, what has become his famous 1917 lecture "Science as a Vocation," which includes his reflections on Tolstoy. Munich had wanted him to address politics as a vocation, and Weber had insisted on science as his first topic. But Munich University was persistent. Weber was cajoled and compelled, in fact, by repeated suggestions that he would be replaced by Spartacist Rosa Luxemburg or, after her assassination, by Socialist Kurt Eisner, until he agreed to give the now equally famous lecture "Politics as a Vocation." The lecture was given in January 1919 at Munich University, which was then within the Bavarian Soviet Republic; in his lecture Weber correctly predicted that this republic would be short-lived. The German word traditionally translated, for these lectures, as "vocation" is the same word, *Beruf*, which we know in his conceptual analysis in *The Protestant Ethic and the Spirit of Capitalism* as the all-important idea of "calling." Politics as a calling. Weber composed his lecture on politics in the same year that he advised the German delegates at Versailles. And what, exactly, did he advise? While French and English delegations sought reparations and imperial advantage, and tailored themselves to Wilson's plans for extension of democratic self-determination, Weber advised Germany to use the moment to plan a future of constitutional democracy for Germany. Weber sought a German state including a strong bureaucracy to insure the centrality of legal rationality, but also direct election of the Reich president (what he saw as the American model) to give charisma, ironically, an instituted role and power to redirect the ship of state. Weber was willing to pass judgments and give advice about political practices, and to take the risk that he could be wrong—and he was later blamed for instituting the führer principle, opening the door to Hitler, notably by Wolfgang Mommsen in 1959—but he saw politics and science as problematic in conjunction. To Weber, politics always requires the prophet and her opposite, the person called to the responsibilities intrinsic to politics, as well as those temperamentally called to pursuit of truth, justice, and self-knowledge, science and scholarship.

Scholars address human rights in myriad ways in myriad locations and disciplines. And not merely from Weber's day but also from long before it has been recognized that it is not always wise to ask them to do things they are less good at, such as render political judgments, let alone interventions. However, this complex conceptual and practical area we know as human rights demands more from us than the fine-tuned engines of disciplinary insight. There is a reason why so much great scholarship on human rights can simultaneously feel empty, hollow, as something vitally missing. Considered as individual contributions, we submit, each paper in this volume, in its disciplinarily informed strengths, can show symptoms of such limits. The ethnographers of CSR in practice see so much more going on, have such better-informed judgment about actual motives and outcomes, ironies of doctrine in practice and complexities of heterogeneous situations, that their skepticisms of law and code can seem to overwhelm the mere tinkering of lawyers, bureaucrats, and managers. But then, when the anthropologists conclude, how often do they call upon authorities to somehow, some way, intervene with a wiser code or law or practice? The acuity of their diagnoses (I say *they*, but I too am an anthropologist and ethnographer) is wholly matched by the utopian vagary of their moments of prescription. Consider then the other most dominant voices in this volume: enter the lawyers. Their desire for manageable facts follows from their need, the legal utility of a settled set of facts, and the ethnographers with their uncontrolled comparisons provide accounts much richer, more complex and humanly believable. But when it comes to plotting, and tracking, and assessing, and criticizing, and debating, and repairing, actual remedies, including long, real histories of institutions of intervention and their successes and failures, the lawyers know things the ethnographers only dream about, in the calls for state and legal intervention and their actual prospects and consequences.

So can codes of corporate social responsibility work? Can corporations, the infamous joint stock companies of predatory, neocolonial, and globalizing capitalism, the famous engines of prosperity that we all require to do their work well—can corporations become the vehicle not for the undermining of state protections of society but rather for the extension, definition, and development of regimes of human rights in practice? What is to be done with codes of corporate social responsibility? Our claim, speaking here for Charlotte Walker-Said and myself, is not that we know, or that we are sure, or even that we have in these pages a single piece of advice. It is that we have assembled the best interdisciplinary discussion of the issues we can assemble, for discussion of this, Tolstoy's questions applied to a key dimension of human rights controversy for our times. We have to get the scholarship out of the siloes and into conversations like this, to make the works of science and scholarship more relevant in real time, to actual political questions for our age.

The Pozen Family Center for Human Rights at the University of Chicago is sponsoring this volume, *Corporate Social Responsibility? Human Rights and the New Global Economy.* This volume draws on lectures, reading groups, a major conference on CSR and human rights, and a series of workshops and editorial interactions that have brought this discussion into this shape, all made possible by the generosity of Anne and Richard Pozen. I hope that this is the first of many such intense collaborations to be sponsored by our center, books gathering scholarship that is collectively focused on bringing scholarship to bear on political questions of our age, addressing the major global institutions that bring human rights theory into practice.

CHAPTER ONE

Introduction

Power, Profit, and Social Trust

Charlotte Walker-Said

Translating Human Rights and Corporate Social Responsibility: Shifting Terrains

In the new world order that emerged in the wake of the Second World War, Hannah Arendt argued that the nation-state had become the necessary guarantor of human rights and their greatest potential threat. Now, in our global economy infused with new modes of governance, ascendant market forces, and competing value hierarchies, the same paradox has another institutional home: the corporation. Is the corporation a crucible or an obstacle for the global human rights order? A benefactor or nemesis? The time has come for serious inquiry into the understudied but critical relationship between corporations and human rights and the trend toward codes and practices of corporate social responsibility.

Corporate social responsibility (CSR) is a burgeoning arena of corporate activity and academic research and reflects the growing integration of business and market-oriented strategies in the day-to-day activities of government, civil society, development practice, and humanitarian intervention. Among its many aims and positions, it claims to quantify and qualify the "social impact" as well as the environmental and social corollaries of business in a particular space. CSR is both a conceptual framework of operation, strategy, and human relations and a corporate culture movement with a focus on ethical standards. These standards are a broad and largely self-defined set of devotions, with some corporations emphasizing environmental stewardship, some underscoring their humane labor conditions, and others highlighting their business's contributions to achieving human flourishing in poor or marginalized communities. The World Business Council for Sustainable Development qualifies CSR as "the continuing commitment by business to contribute to economic development while improving the quality of life of the workforce and their families as well as of the community and society at large."[1] Many scholars simply consider CSR a framework for conceptualizing the business and society interface.[2] Its critics argue that CSR constitutes a legitimizing discursive domain that implies an inclination toward ethics and humane standards, but in reality safeguards capitalist imperatives against critique and regulation.[3] What is incontrovertible is that corporate social responsibility has become a prevailing mandate for multinational corporations and is transforming the role of business in global politics and social relations. It is also conceptually altering human rights law, policy, and theory.

Human rights scholars, to date, have attended more to nation-states and international law, and to nongovernmental organizations (NGOs) and their redressive intervention systems. But corporations have greater weight, not only in economies but also in society and governance globally. Here we are interested in theories but first of all in reality, and we study actual interventions. This volume has invited experienced ethnographers, political scientists, legal scholars, historians, and other expert social scientists to inform current deliberations on two key questions: can codes and practices of corporate social responsibility solve fundamental human rights problems? And what happens when CSR becomes a new vehicle of the progressive politics that characterize the human rights movement?

Serious evaluation of corporate social responsibility is timely for several reasons. First, recent decisions in the realm of "hard law" have questioned the use of national and international laws to prosecute human rights violations by corporations.[4] This has had the effect of transforming corporate respect for human rights from a government-enforced public commitment to one of private choice. Second, human rights have assumed a central position in the discourse surrounding international development, and rights institutions have embraced a progrowth stance in regard to national and global economies.[5] As capitalist expansion becomes increasingly embedded in global human rights movements, corporations have gained considerable authority as economic as well as humanitarian leaders. In light of these cultural shifts, international human rights institutions are transitioning away from antiglobalization, anticorporate discourses toward global initiatives to *increase*, rather than decrease, the role of corporations in developing economies and markets so that they might foster more positive outcomes for the world's societies.

International human rights activism has also undergone a significant philosophical transition that privileges economic concerns and the human condition of poverty rather than social and political rights. This marks a shift from post-World-War-II-era human rights milestones, such as the Universal Declaration of Human Rights, which emphasized the fulfillment of fundamental freedoms, including freedom of thought, conscience, religion, and belief, as well as civil rights such as nondiscrimination, political equality, and self-determination. International preoccupation with suffering as a result of material want has spawned two dimensions of the current human rights agenda that this volume will examine in depth: the use of human rights to interpret, intervene in, and manage the specific human rights catastrophe of poverty, and the promotion of the Right to Development, passed as a United Nations charter in 1986, which takes as given that to accomplish the provision of freedoms and opportunities for individuals, there must be a universal escalation of entitlements that are borne through increases in wealth.[6]

Critics of human rights in their late twentieth-century expression have cited the turn toward humanitarian crisis and underdevelopment as an apolitical or antipolitical gesture. Rather than institution building and coordinated government action on matters of paramount human importance, such as erecting safeguards to secure peace and guarantee justice, humanitarian praxis mobilizes response to catastrophes and does little to transform the causes of emergency.[7] Corporate social responsibility can be interpreted either as another iteration of the minimalist, "rescue" approach of humanitarian outreach or a novel undertaking that seeks to redirect human rights considerations toward a framework that allows individuals to achieve their social and political capabilities through just economic practices and is thus rights affirming from the outset.

In November 1999, John Ruggie, assistant secretary-general of the United Nations, and Georg Kell, executive director of the United Nations Global Compact, publicly admitted the failure of postwar global economic institutions to advance human rights and promote universal well-being. Drawing from examples of extreme poverty and the state of human vulnerability worldwide, Ruggie and Kell argued that the financial gains attained from connecting networks of production and finance in the late twentieth century were unevenly distributed, which isolated economic growth from human development and the achievement of human rights. Ruggie and Kell then called on the world's corporations and financial institutions to commit themselves to adopting governance principles derived from the Universal Declaration of Human Rights in order to embed the economic sphere in broader frameworks of shared values and ensure the positive human corollaries of the expansion of wealth.[8] The tangible outcome of this declaration was the creation of the UN Global Compact, the world's largest corporate citizenship initiative launched in 2000, in which corporations voluntarily commit to align their operations with human rights principles.[9] Ruggie has recently attested that the Global Compact is intended to remedy a state-based system of global governance and demonstrate that international protocols can guide and promote business as well as human rights.[10]

The impact of this endeavor and others like it, and their future as models for what Anne-Marie Slaughter terms the "new world order," in which suprastate, substate, and nonstate actors balance multiple allegiances and have global reach, is explored in this volume. As critical partners in the new world order, corporations have considerable incentive to contribute to effective governance, since—in the words of Kofi Annan—"unless the global market is held together by shared values, it will risk serious global instability, conflict, and insurmountable risk to both business and economic security on a macro level."[11] Ruggie has echoed Annan's warning to corporate entities to consider human rights in the name of self-preservation, urging corporations to reform business practice so they can "survive and thrive."[12]

Ruggie, Kell, and Annan's arguments for a new institutional equilibrium managed by agents of capital communicate a faith in corporations and markets to align their goals with humanitarian priorities. Other UN representatives have stated that they believe there is an emerging "global consensus" regarding what concerted efforts are required to reform corporate policies and link business and human rights concerns.[13] However, despite enthusiasm across governance sectors, what this volume will demonstrate is that no such collective unanimity exists on what CSR ultimately endorses and promotes, even within distinct fields of action.

The Organization for Economic Cooperation and Development (OECD) proposes that business reform should take the form of promoting business concern for the welfare of society, which can be realized in part by freeing business-sector capacity and further opening markets, which can "empower poor people."[14] Alternative CSR approaches seek to establish guidelines of conduct rather than modes of market expansion in distressed regions.[15] These and other parallel initiatives illustrate the rise of competitive and converging transnational campaigns to advise the private choice to protect human rights, which are critical in an era of nonexistent regulatory mechanisms.

In the legal discipline, human rights lawyers and policy advocates have demonstrated a greater desire to move current international CSR initiatives toward establishing enforceable international law, as well as human rights treaties regulating corporate activity in developing countries, particularly in those countries whose commitment to human rights in national law and governance practice is feeble or nonexistent. However, as this volume demonstrates, this dimension of CSR is in fundamental tension with other current ideologies. The CSR movement that promotes corporations as partners in humanitarian outreach and economic growth resists to some degree demands for greater accountability for corporations who abuse human rights.[16] As a corollary of the growing consensus to develop business sectors, invest in market systems, channel finance to underdeveloped countries, and deliver development impacts, arguments for a regulatory model of CSR have been marginalized from many institutional discussions. Even the United Nations declared it is unambiguously against establishing a form of CSR that would create a transnational judicial system of redress for human rights violations committed by corporations.[17] The UN Guiding Principles on Business and Human Rights and John Ruggie's "Protect, Respect, and Remedy" framework attest to the successful pairing of corporate and human interests and stop well short of imposing a regulatory framework that could address corporate malfeasance.[18] Nevertheless, many legal practitioners are often skeptical of relying on "soft law" and ethical voluntarism to protect human rights and are critical of the benevolence expected of corporate agents.

In addition to competitive fields of action with disparate visions for CSR, there are also contentious philosophical dimensions: how and why is business practice politicized and socially inscribed, and why are institutions that govern private activity called to have a function for the public good?[19] Despite continued efforts and grand claims by major human rights actors like the United Nations, current iterations of CSR lack a truly universal set of normative ethics and practices. Thus the theme of "responsibility" in this volume is conceptualized along various political-economic and sociocultural lines. In this way, this work mirrors CSR themes in practice throughout the world, which claim participation in a global movement, but in fact are highly distinctive, autonomous, and require contextualization.

Corporate Social Responsibility Proponents and Critics

Growing approval of the role of corporations in development as well as social and political life has numerous critics. Many critique sanguine conceptualizations of the current global economic system and distrust its corporate leaders.[20] Some argue that CSR is a "hegemonic accommodation" that reflects the dominant cultural, economic, and political role of business in society, and the permeation of the discourse of competitiveness and free markets into state and social structures.[21] They are joined by other critics of the neoliberal economic model who make broad claims that corporations, as the engines of liberal market expansion, deregulation, and declining state authority, cannot be rightly harnessed and have no real capacity to transform conditions of poverty, inequality, and injustice.[22] The world of human rights blogs, mass media, and activism largely echoes and intensifies scholarly criticism of corporate engagement with human rights and development.[23]

As allies of this critique, an active community of human rights litigators, legislators, and legal advocates is seeking mechanisms for corporate *accountability* rather than expressing enthusiasm for corporate collaboration. The legal history of Alien Tort Statute (ATS) jurisprudence in the United States points to renewed attention to the question of corporate liability for violations of international human rights law. Many are concerned with the growing power of corporate agents to not only avoid remedial justice mechanisms but also to go as far as to influence the provisions of national legislation and international trade treaties to serve their private interests.[24] Select legal scholars of this volume demonstrate that a strong tradition of civil remedies that have been able to address serious wrongs is a critical foundation for building greater accountability through litigation as a complement to the more preventive and cooperative focus of CSR that is embedded in multilateral initiatives and transgovernmental regimes. Among lawyers and human rights litigators, however, there is acknowledgment that few tools exist to file lawsuits against corporate defendants in cases of violations of human rights. Alternative instruments, including voluntary networked agreements, meaningful stakeholder engagement, and the entrenchment of corporate policies that are compliant with human rights, will be critical in preventing, reporting, and rectifying human rights abuses by corporations in the future.[25]

For its part, the corporate world has been developing multifaceted approaches to solve the challenges posed by growing international humanitarian concern for corporate abuse of human rights. At the leadership level of corporations, CSR has become a prevailing operational mandate, which is evident in the substantive fields of research on corporate strategy, corporate governance, and corporate citizenship.[26] Academic work on CSR has initiated serious discussion as well as strategy shifts among executives regarding the role of the corporation in the world. Certain business scholars point to the fact that the theme of "global citizenship" has impacted corporate initiatives by "shifting the mentality" toward considering transnational human rights regimes as the framework for global strategic operation. As multinational corporations engage with a larger number and greater variety of stakeholders, including suppliers, manufacturers, consumers, indigenous groups, landowners, nongovernmental organizations, and shareholders from across the economic, social, and political spectrum, their operational landscape has become decidedly more complex and unstable.[27] Hence, the CSR of the future will have to address increasingly complex human and environmental concerns while securing a durable and protected domain of possibilities for business in the world.

There is no doubt that CSR as a form of business regulation and capitalist expansion that identifies and is responsive to human rights is a potential new source of global governance. The question remains, however, of whether duties of corporations should be directly linked to their capacity to harm human dignity, or rather be based on broad conceptions of duty related to the improvement of economic life for all.[28] But are corporations morally responsible for broad economic growth and social welfare? Amartya Sen understands the rights-duty relationship via a Kantian perspective of "imperfect obligations": instead of perfectly linking rights to exact duties of identified agents, he argues the mandate for growth and well-being "is addressed generally to anyone who can help."[29] Scholarship on CSR has largely struggled to define the moral responsibility of corporations based on legal or historical precedent. However, what is irrefutably present in the current literature on CSR is that the "will to do right" has departed its origins in altruistic sentiment and is considered a marketable strategy, a survival tactic in an era of corporate criticism, and a method of putting corporate initiatives to work for a broader and more complex set of constituencies. As such, CSR is no longer viewed simply as a form of window dressing or rhetorical maneuver.[30]

This volume presents CSR as a series of economic and political strategies that are currently shifting the focus of international human rights activism and signaling the rise of new forms of global governance. In some cases, not only is the realization of human rights possible through corporate engagement, but also substantive corporate reform and accountability is achievable in cases where corporations have not answered the call to encourage livelihood creation, and instead have capitalized on a globalized economic system that has few formal prohibitions against exploitation.

Engaging Current Debates

The authors here are in conversation with the broad literature that analyzes neoliberalism and its manifestations in law, policy programs, economic agendas, and intellectual positions. The breadth of work on this topic—much of it polemical—frames the position of neoliberalism as a contest between market economies and nonmarket values. Recent scholarship has noted that the earliest neoliberal policies that freed capitalism to pursue global ambitions were concurrent with the ascendance of coordinated transnational human rights movements.[31] Neoliberalism and human rights' "historical companionship" is worthy of debate because their power to influence agents of capital, governance, and security continues to grow, often in coordination with one another.[32] Global economic liberalization has fostered the privatization of powers previously held by states, including regulating industry; determining taxation; deciding employment and wage rates; and, increasingly, determining environmental, social, and civil rights.[33] This undeniably has caused the erosion of state capacity in social service and security provision and the regulation of economic production, which many argue are the primary vehicles of human rights protections.[34] And there is daily evidence of corporate malfeasance, particularly in the form of human rights abuse as a result of unfettered power, as this volume will also show. However, the enlargement of corporate "rights" and even corporate abuse of power have often been followed by public demands for corporate "responsibility" rather than corporate restraint. Responsibility denotes authority and power, and gives a specific function to corporations in the realm of human welfare.

Scholars of corporate activity and international monetary cooperation as well as human rights have recently been more carefully scrutinizing the transformation in corporations' motivations and constraints over the past half century. Many have argued that the financialization of the American domestic economy and the burgeoning power of the logic of the common stock structure gradually forced the American economy to detach itself from business and reattach to a new global rule of finance.[35] The social corporatism and welfarist capitalism that thrived in the immediate postwar era in the United States and Europe underpinned national and international growth that broadly impacted society and strengthened access to higher standards of living and social security. However, the 1973 oil crisis, concerns about economic "shocks" through the global financial system, and the turn toward monetarism and deregulation each contributed to the triumph of finance over business, or, as Mark Mazower describes: forced a world of producers and consumers to accept the new rules of creditors and debtors.[36] As a result, contemporary business decisions are not made in the best interests of employees, stakeholders, suppliers, distributors, clients, or even leaders, but rather in the best interests of shareholder value, "the standard of business performance."[37] Understanding the origins of neoliberal engineering is not only crucial for locating the simultaneous beginnings of international human rights activism but also for identifying when corporate practices marked by impaired moral judgment were codified and transmitted internationally.

Inasmuch as this volume demonstrates the limitations of CSR and offers a critical perspective on corporate techniques of market domination, it also posits a future for CSR within the human rights movement. The scholars in this work aim to grant specific agency to the "neoliberal position" and identify *whose* capitalist imperatives have defeated or promoted human rights ideals. This volume's contributors engage directly with the conduct and objectives of corporations, moving beyond discussions of markets and economic policy to examine how particular corporate agents have shaped realities on the ground. The work as a whole demonstrates that there are precise conditions that discipline when corporate and noncorporate values can come into conflict, as well as when they can and will align. These conditions are often determined by corporations as well as financial institutions and stock markets, national governments, multilateral governance bodies, and smaller agents such as human rights NGOs, civil society organizations, and activists, all of whose loyalties and duties lie with a larger number and greater variety of stakeholders.

As corporations, multilateral institutions, and states integrate CSR into the international human rights agenda, they are transforming the essence and philosophy of human rights. Global convergence around human rights in the 1970s revealed that rights discourse could be deployed as "a set of moral trump cards."[38] Today, human rights have achieved near-universal legitimacy as an ethical regime, to the point where critics such as Boaventura de Sousa Santos have declared that it usurps all ethical language.[39] In recent decades, various initiatives have demonstrated interest in making CSR the new focus of global idealism. As CSR continues to snowball in the form of movements for sustainability, fair trade, renewable energy, transparency, poverty alleviation, triple bottom line (TRL), socially responsible investing (SRI), private sector development (PSD), as well as the UN Global Compact, it positions itself as an unassailable framework for organizing ethical priorities, improving the human condition, and achieving social progress while simultaneously protecting economic expansion, thus superseding human rights in its stated aims and correcting its shortcomings.

Making Inroads: The Structure of the Volume

Part I of this volume, "Corporate Social Responsibility as Controlled Negotiation: The Hierarchy of Values," explores CSR as a set of relations of communication and coercion. In the first chapter, Peter Rosenblum sketches the broad terrain of CSR movements, moving between activist claims and corporate governance initiatives and examining the latter as response, counternarrative, or preemption. He describes the "patchwork" effect of the concatenation of efforts for corporate reform in the area of human rights, but ultimately places coercive power in the hands of activists rather than corporations. The next three chapters by Peter Benson, Anna Zalik, and Stuart Kirsch challenge Rosenblum's assessment. These authors provide evidence for the gap between CSR codes and reality, and how such codes construct a "value hierarchy"—as described by Benson—to diffuse mobilized activism, a trend Rosenblum also identifies. The value hierarchy not only communicates but also has coercive power, and as Kirsch, Zalik, and Benson argue, it remains in the hands of corporations. Stated values and codes also bond corporations with stakeholders and shareholders, as is evident in public trust of the corporation as the steward of development and modern life.

The first section of the volume analyzes the CSR discourses of extractive and toxiferous industries, revealing strategic mass communication as political lobbying that involves and engages states, markets, and civil society. Kirsch explores political economy transformed into discourse—a discursive convergence surrounding the use of CSR and human rights codes in corporate settings to control institutional and activist counterclaims. Zalik analyzes the discursive convergence surrounding transparency, looking in particular at audit culture and relations between activist rhetoric, corporate response, and ethical outcomes. In analyzing how CSR theories can function alongside free market doctrines as well as satiate activist demands, Zalik joins Amelia Evans in the second section of the work, who elucidates the possibilities as well as dangers of multistakeholder initiatives (MSIs) as mechanisms for preventing and remedying human rights abuses, rooted as they are in voluntarism and negotiating activist petitions. Zalik and Evans take the logics of discourse discussed by Kirsch and Benson and recount how actors in the CSR universe identify each other using language and play set roles to influence and determine the moral economy of the corporation using vocabularies with various powers and meanings. Evans discerns the power of communication within CSR frameworks by examining how nomenclature brings words into strong institutional form. As part of this, she seeks a transition in the modes of communication employed by MSIs to enlarge the possibilities of their goals.

The chapters in part I portray CSR as coordinated mobilization—as Rosenblum states, a force "which compels systematic responses," which is, itself, the result of the "confrontation and cooperation" Evans describes and will be highlighted in the second segment of this work. Kirsch, Zalik, and Benson present this coordinated mobilization not as reformative but rather as contributive to the dynamics of corporate abuse. They present corporate social responsibility rather as a discourse of representation—in which corporations, institutions, organizations, academia, and citizenries participate—that produces social consent. On the whole, the first part of this book demonstrates that CSR is at once discursive, material, and economic, and that it deploys particular knowledge systems. The question that is unresolved at the end of this section is what will become of the future state of human rights as it joins with CSR practice. Benson and Zalik propose that the production of knowledge, audits, ethics, and responsibility codes take place outside of the realm of the corporation and be relegated to independent actors. However, Kirsch determines that even the university has been drawn into the "discursive nexus" of the political ethics of CSR without comprehension of their roots or corollaries. Rosenblum gestures toward the arguments of the legal practitioners in the next section, who envision yet-unrealized mechanisms for greater corporate accountability that are produced without corporate consent. Thus we turn to the two subsequent sections of this book to determine how CSR can function within the human rights movement without controlled negotiation.

In part II, "Corporate Social Responsibility and the Mandate to Remedy: Between Empowerment and Mitigating Vulnerabilities," legal scholars articulate various global visions for the improvement of the human condition via robust assessments of responsibility. Jonathan Bush historicizes the corporate social responsibility precedent set at Nuremberg and reveals its work in generating human rights victories as well as human rights failures as part of the historical trajectory of international human rights law. He demonstrates that particular kinds of human rights standards for corporations have concomitantly forwarded justice and cemented corporate personhood in transnational legal regimes. Whether corporate personhood presents a fundamental threat to prospects of guarantees for the full range of human rights entitled to the world's citizens remains to be seen, but Bush's chapter reveals that CSR as law and as an ethical movement is both extensive and mature—existing in a continuum of development agendas, international legal remedies, and postconflict rehabilitation—that forms part of transnational governance ideologies. Like the scholars in part I, Bush demonstrates that corporate responsibility has developed as a moralistic discourse using universalistic language, and that particular attention must be paid when such discourse enters the realm of international law.

David Scheffer and Scott Gilmore present current-day initiatives of the CSR movement for corporate regulation and accountability led by lawyers, human rights activists, and political institutions. Scheffer's model demonstrates how "corporate responsibility" can attain the force of law as corporate "criminal liability." This proposal echoes the established conceptual framework of human rights envisioned in the Universal Declaration of Human Rights, that is, an international set of norms for human freedoms and entitlements secured through treaties, consti tutions, and national laws. He offers a solution to the dilemmas posited in part I, in particular that CSR negotiates human rights pressures so that they sustain, rather than challenge, corporate power. Scheffer's proposed shift in the regulatory framework demands institutional cooperation, the vigilant enforcement of human rights treaties and laws, and strong state institutions, and in the case of weak states, transnational human rights courts to impose a higher degree of accountability on corporate agents. Scheffer's approach does not seek corporate consent but rather confrontation in order to fully realize the ideals of international human rights.

Building on Scheffer's confrontational schema, Scott Gilmore illustrates the interaction between corporate liability and CSR by drawing an analogy with the regimes for military compliance under the laws of war. Gilmore argues that both corporate accountability and command responsibility seek to impose ethical norms, for example, humanitarian concerns, on hierarchical organizations whose missions seem opposed or indifferent to these norms, for example, profit maximization and war fighting, respectively. The international laws of war, however, have developed a powerful legal regime for securing compliance. This regime has a proactive, preventive component, which seeks to acculturate humanitarian concerns through training, best practices, and oversight. And it also has a reactive, punitive component: commanders may be prosecuted for failing to prevent or punish war crimes committed by subordinates, and those subordinates may not rely on superior orders as a defense. For the military, these acculturation and sanctions regimes are fully complementary and mutually reinforcing. The CSR project, however, has yet to achieve this symmetry. While CSR is developing an acculturation regime for corporate entities, the sanctions regime for human rights abuses—resting on civil tort liability—has been gutted by three recent US Supreme Court decisions and is slow to emerge in other jurisdictions. The history of military command responsibility suggests that CSR cannot sustain a corporate ethos of human rights compliance without effective sanctions.

Presenting an alternative vision for vigorously compelling corporations to behave responsibly, Caroline Kaeb, as well as Ursula Wynhoven and Yousuf Aftab, argues the vulnerabilities of the "hard law" approach—an approach elucidated in the section note by Kaeb. Kaeb terms her model for promoting responsible corporate practice "incentive compatibility," which demonstrates that proper moral incentives can "steer corporate behavior toward responsibility" in a way that exogenous liability litigation cannot. In her chapter, she locates the limitations as well as the institutional difficulties of Scheffer's and Gilmore's criminal liability frameworks, demonstrating that corporations have proven themselves adept at managing the regulatory landscape. Wynhoven and Aftab present an alternative perspective on the discursively formed "hierarchy of values," examining the potential of "voluntarism" to emerge as a standard value of CSR that guarantees genuine responsibility mechanisms at the heart of corporate responsibility as a movement. Wynhoven and Aftab argue the philosophical distinctions between compliance and responsibility, championing voluntarism as an ethos that deeply engages with the incentive structure of the market, into which human rights are woven. Wynhoven and Aftab and Kaeb argue the vulnerability for human rights in a compulsory compliance framework, which they believe discourages a true integration of human rights into long-term strategic-management plans and encourages nominal or basic compliance.

The chapters in part II each engage in some regard with the economic and humanitarian values present in what the business literature terms "the market for virtue." Also known as "the business case for CSR," this principle argues for corporate strategy that pursues profit-generating avenues that correspond with positive social and human rights outcomes. Social cause-related marketing, corporate social marketing, and socially responsible business practices are part of the "reputation capital" approach to CSR, and this approach is the most popular as it has proven to positively affect profits. When human rights are interwoven into markets, corporations are forced to respond—as Peter Rosenblum argues. However, as Anna Zalik and Peter Benson illustrate, there are broader and more troubling ramifications and vulnerabilities for the rule of law, as well as human rights within the expansion of "marketable ethics" as a guiding principle of corporate practice.

The "business case" for CSR is an example of a new ethical dilemma posed by the human rights and CSR dialectic. Perhaps the greatest risk within the voluntary, self-actualized process of developing CSR frameworks discussed by Kaeb and Wynhoven and Aftab is the corporations' ability to choose which human rights "come first." In this case, CSR becomes less of an ethical judgment than a market evaluation, which creates incentives for companies to attend to human rights risks that capture the market's attention rather than the most critical human rights issues that affect stakeholders. Scheffer and Gilmore seek to reduce the influence of markets and intensify the influence of law on corporate behavior regarding human rights. Law, unlike markets, argue these scholars, provides a framework for assessing and implementing human rights philosophies according to human concern, social interest, and national sovereignty rather than return on investment.

The dilemma that undergirds Kaeb's and Wynhoven and Aftab's chapters has also been presented by Amartya Sen, who engages with rational choice theory in the context of freedom. Sen warns against reliance on an overinvolved state or judicial apparatus to compel responsible action. He advocates for an understanding of the distinction between "nannying" an actor's choices and creating more opportunity for choice and for substantive decisions to act responsibly.[40] Sen's framework demands that such a commitment to freedom must not operate only through the state but must also involve other institutions such as political and social organizations, nongovernmental agencies, the media and public communication, and institutions that allow the functioning of markets and contractual relations. Sen's position that freedom is a precondition of responsibility is clearly evident in Kaeb's and Wynhoven and Aftab's chapters. Scheffer, along with Gilmore, posits that freedom from regulation defines the current state of corporate behavior, which threatens human rights as well as the proper functioning of states and markets, broadly. Through the enlargement of the sphere of human rights litigation and the role of legal action in negotiating corporate accountability, Scheffer and Gilmore assert that that formal legal proceedings would reorganize the global hierarchy of values by injecting established human rights law, written by states and government institutions, which is historically and operationally independent from CSR discourses. However, these scholars also concede that human rights litigation against corporations faces substantial obstacles—most commonly in the form of political ideologies that oppose the interference of government in the sphere of business activity.[41]

Part II of this volume frames a critical debate that is central to the subsequent section: does CSR as an emergent force within international human rights strengthen the power of the nation-state to legislate human rights and regulate economic activity or does it seek to diminish

the state vis-à-vis the power of the "New World Order" of global capital and transgovernmental systems?[42] And furthermore, is the nation-
state still even a salient framework for guaranteeing rights and should
state sovereignty still be considered a measure of human security in the
international system? As liberalization has fostered the privatization of
powers previously held by states, should private enterprise then be considered a new locus of human rights authority? Or is the answer the return to stronger nation-states that can push against global governance
structures?

This dilemma is particularly present in the final part of this book.
While CSR is intended to be a corrective to the challenges that deregulation and liberalization pose to the sovereignty of the nation-state, as
a corrective it also marginalizes the involvement of the state—seeking
mandates and frameworks provided by the international system, or, al-
ternatively, autonomous, voluntarist action. As the international human
rights movement shifts toward formal assessments of corporate responsibilities, liabilities, and duties, it reveals itself as a process with bifurcated ambitions. Human rights scholarship and activism increasingly
laments the phenomenon of "state weakness" or "state failure," which
leads to abuses by private individuals and rogue agents of the state, as
well as dysfunctional and feeble economies. However, inspired in part by
thinkers like Hannah Arendt, international human rights—as a body of
thought and practice—contains within it an attack upon the concept of
unrestricted state sovereignty. Corporate social responsibility—whether
mandated by law or self-imposed by business—requires heightened involvement of corporations in social life and even advances philosophies
of "corporate personhood," the doctrine that forms the basis of the legal
recognition that corporations are rights-bearers and free to exercise autonomy and influence as lawful entities.[43]

Thus part III, "Africa as CSR Laboratory: Twenty-First-Century
Corporate Strategy and State Building," reassesses the claims and proposals made in earlier sections by examining dilemmas and possibilities
for the future of CSR as it addresses state sovereignty and human rights.
It explores the nation-state in Africa and how CSR strategies connect
the African state to international markets and new systems of political
ordering. All four chapters explore possibilities for achieving human
rights for populations for whom corporate activity is a significant determinant (if not the primary determinant) of well-being. These chapters
also address and contradict oft-repeated discourses on the "failed state"

in Africa as well as claims of how CSR impulses emerge from neoliberal frameworks that seek to diminish state power.[44] These scholars eschew the analytical category of the "failed state" and rather choose to adopt characterizations similar to that of Janet Roitman, who uses the term "reconstituted state."[45] This grounding counters claims of "failure" by demonstrating that many African governments have restructured their authority through networks that have emerged in the interstices of the state system and by no means have disappeared as formidable forces in commanding coercion, violence, as well as economic initiatives from within and outside the state. Much like Roitman, William Reno, Charlotte Walker-Said, Lauren Coyle, and Richard Joseph, Kelly Spence, and Abimbola Agboluaje describe how private investment, corporate-led development, and a large informal sector do not "gut" the state but rather force the state to negotiate with increasingly complex actors and claims, as well as restructure itself to respond to local and international institutions and citizenries.

These authors contextualize the experience of African nation-states and African nonstate actors in the age of nongovernmental politics.[46] Charlotte Walker-Said presents the CSR mandate of sustainability as an ideology that signals the end of a certain kind of politics—specifically, the politics of civil and political rights—and the emergence of the politics of a new social compact for human rights defined by compromise between a wide variety of local and global actors. She argues for the enduring salience of the African nation-state and its reconstitution as a result of endogenous and exogenous pressures to deliver material security. Africa has historically been a staging ground for new idealizations of human, ecological, and economic management and continues to be in the present day under new CSR mandates, which are transforming human rights from a revolutionary—and hence destabilizing—force to a force for compromise, endurance, and peace. The CSR policies of sustainability assume that African postcolonies have overcome their greatest civil and political struggles and what remains is a battle over resources. Within her chapter is a deeper exploration of the way in which consensus is achieved to determine when the past is completed and what the present demands of the nation-state in Africa.

Lauren Coyle and Will Reno examine the issue of social trust in postcolonies where local and global confidence in the nation-state is shifting and reconstituting new policies that favor certain agents. Both of their chapters reveal that global governance frameworks bluntly deny the relevance of the local by privileging nation-state orthodoxies and denying access to justice to nonsovereign entities. Using a novel line of inquiry, Reno and Coyle analyze corporations who join in productive undertakings with nonstate actors such as rebels and regional groups and comply with particular kinds of law that are produced and upheld by popular consent rather than national legislatures. Coyle and Reno demonstrate that corporations in Africa are establishing new baselines for human rights adherence, attempting to negotiate the supremacy of the nation-state as the exclusive authority overseeing human rights agendas and global governance as well as corporate guidelines for operation.

These chapters demonstrate that as much as the world's societies and organizations find human rights compelling and employ them to demand particular kinds of justice or redress, the current state of many of the world's nation-states makes it difficult to see how they can attain accountability, especially regarding human rights claims that are politically destabilizing, such as indigeneity, heritage rights, and customary law status. Reno illustrates how rebel groups in Africa, as parties to armed conflicts, learn to manipulate emerging efforts to prosecute corporations for war crimes. As the nation-state is simultaneously weak and the backbone of the international system, global networks of governance act in accordance with national priorities rather than in the best interests of human rights and social and economic conditions on the ground when interpreting corporate behavior. Coyle describes the complex formation of "shadow states" that create new forms of legitimacy through the work of corporations who fulfill certain rights claims. This consequently transfers dependence away from formal national bureaucratic structures toward informal constitutions of contractual relations. In these cases, corporate operations establish social trust through popular (i.e., neither false nor coerced) consent. This evidence provides a counterexample to the warnings of the authors in part I, who believe consent to corporate practice is often obtained through force. These chapters reveal the possibilities as well as the vulnerabilities inherent in human dependence on corporate agents for human rights guarantees, as corporations expand and assist in the formation of new "state-like" entities that challenge established orders of law and governance.

Joseph, Spence, and Agboluaje depict the Nigerian state as a powerful bureaucracy, capable of assembling the forces of productivity and development through networks based on ethnicity, regional alliance, client base, labor unions, and social class. However, Nigeria remains a state where "traditional" elites and "modern" merchants exchange influence and productive capacity to harness the power of the private sector—a sector that is at once distinct from and controlled by the Nigerian public sector. Joseph, Spence, and Agboluaje illustrate the Nigerian state's dependence on private business activity to create pathways to achieving human capabilities, but their focus on local business incentives and promoting regional industrial leaders signals an important shift away from seeking foreign direct investment that is very often accompanied by corruption and little redistribution. Joseph, Spence, and Agboluaje join Kaeb in demonstrating the limits of a CSR movement that would be rooted only in visions of bolstering a countervailing legal force to corporate power.

Joseph, Spence, and Agboluaje's chapter refutes critiques that condemn capitalist expansion and segregate the social from the transactional, as if these spheres existed separately at some moment in history. Not only have markets influenced human societies (including those in the global South) since premodern times, they have the potential to yield enormous opportunity, and such critiques exhibit a low-minded sentimentality for mythic notions of marketless societies.[47] As Amartya Sen states, "We have good reasons to buy and sell, to exchange, and to seek lives that can flourish on the basis of transactions."[48] Evidence presented throughout the last section of this book illustrates that simultaneously with their unencumbered pursuit of profit, corporations are engineering their own CSR platforms that are transforming the terms and capacities of transaction for the world's citizens and, at the behest of world leaders, cooperating in the development logics of states.

Moving Forward

This volume presents a series of discussions on the practice of corporate social responsibility in the twentieth and twenty-first centuries and its relation to the state of human rights for the world's populations. Each chapter demonstrates how networks of activists, institutions, and corporations are created and how they shape discourses on rights and freedoms, which in turn establish visions for a certain kind of order. While each chapter addresses CSR as practice, the work as a whole demonstrates that CSR as theory has become deeply embedded in global governance principles and is primarily aimed at the social and political legitimization of corporations through the establishment of *social trust*. This trust enables far more than freedom from restrictive parameters; it underpins corporate authority, gives license to operate, and—crucially for the future of human rights—entrusts the world's resources and the management of human beings' entitlements to them to corporate agents. Social trust allows for the penetration of markets and the transformation of economies within an atmosphere of controlled negotiation.[49] It also is the key to success in twenty-first-century global endeavors as it allows for the social and political harmony that is the prerequisite of major enterprise.[50]

Corporate social responsibility is an outgrowth of the current market mechanism as well as a countervailing force against it. Ultimately, corporations form an essential component of international economic development and continue to intensify their role within that global mandate. This is at once empowering and enriching for corporations, but it also forces them to engage with established governance and human rights frameworks, treaties, and laws. By assuming responsibilities to individuals and groups, corporations have the capacity to deliver returns as well as improve social conditions, but in the process inevitably attain enormous authority. Some evidence suggests that with the assumption of significant responsibilities to develop economies, reduce human rights emergencies, and defeat poverty, corporations demand as much control and stability as is possible and can only guarantee economic rights advancements in a context of repressed political and social rights.[51] While there is no foreseeable future where humans will cease their interactions with markets, there remains the question of how those who control markets will establish or maintain equitable returns to society as a result of economic expansion, and what the political corollaries of that will be. The proceeding chapters seek to answer this question by illustrating when and how human necessity and the free exercise of human rights can guide the market and when the market can shape the contours of human rights thought and practice and thereby define what a human rights victory is.

Notes

1. Phil Watts and Lord Holme, "Corporate Social Responsibility: Meeting Changing Expectations," World Business Council for Sustainable Development Report, 3.

2. Andrew Crane, Abagail McWilliams, Dirk Matten, Jeremy Moon, and Donald Siegel, *The Oxford Handbook of Corporate Social Responsibility* (Oxford: Oxford University Press, 2009), 4.

3. See K. Ravi Raman and Ronnie D. Lipschutz, *Corporate Social Responsibility: Comparative Critiques* (New York: Palgrave Macmillan, 2010); Volker Rittberger, Martin Nettesheim, and Carmen Huckel, *Authority in the Global Political Economy* (New York: Palgrave Macmillan, 2008); J. George Frynas, "The False Developmental Promise of Corporate Social Responsibility: Evidence from Multinational Oil Companies," *International Affairs* 81, no. 3 (2005): 581–98; John Roberts, "The Manufacture of Corporate Social Responsibility: Constructing Corporate Sensibility," *Organization* 10, no. 2 (2003): 249–65.

4. Kiobel v. Royal Dutch Petroleum Co., 133 S.Ct. 1659 (2013). American jurisprudence has also recently significantly curtailed laws that regulate corporate activity in the social and political spheres. See Citizens United v. Federal Election Commission, 558 U.S. 310 (Docket No. 08–205).

5. Notable works on this include Jeffrey Sachs, *The End of Poverty: Economic Possibilities for Our Time* (New York: Penguin, 2005); Paul Collier, *The Bottom Billion: Why the Poorest Countries Are Failing and What Can Be Done about It* (Oxford: Oxford University Press, 2008); Arhit Bannerjee and Esther Duflo, *Poor Economics: A Radical Rethinking of the Way to Fight Global Poverty* (New York: PublicAffairs, 2011); Amartya Sen, *Development as Freedom*, 1st ed. (New York: Knopf, 1999).

6. Craig Calhoun, "The Imperative to Reduce Suffering: Charity, Progress, and Emergencies in the Field of Humanitarian Action," in *Humanitarianism in Question: Politics, Power, Ethics*, ed. Michael Barnett and Thomas G. Weiss (Ithaca, NY: Cornell University Press, 2008), 73–97.

7. Robert Meister, *After Evil: A Politics of Human Rights* (New York: Columbia University Press, 2011), 273–84; Mahmood Mamdani, *Saviors and Survivors: Darfur, Politics, and the War on Terror* (New York: Pantheon Books, 2009), 260–303; Didier Fassin, *Humanitarian Reason: A Moral History of the Present* (Berkeley: University of California Press, 2012); Michel Agier, *Managing the Undesirables* (New York: Polity Press, 2011).

8. Georg Kell and John Gerard Ruggie, "Global Markets and Social Legitimacy: The Case of the 'Global Compact,'" paper presented at York University, Toronto, Canada, November 4–6, 1999.

9. See the United Nations Global Compact's Blueprint for Corporate Sustainability Leadership, http://www.unglobalcompact.org/docs/news_events/8.1/Blueprint.pdf; for an example of the implementation of the Global Compact guidelines into corporate governance, see BASF The Chemical Company, "Reference to the UN Global Compact Blueprint for Corporate Sustainability Leadership," http://www.basf.com/group/corporate/us/en/sustainability/global-compact/blueprint.

10. John G. Ruggie, "Business and Human Rights: The Evolving International Agenda," *American Journal of International Law* 101, no. 4 (2007): 819–40.

11. Kofi Annan, "Address to World Economic Forum in Davos, Switzerland," United Nations, United Nations Press, 1999.

12. Kell and Ruggie, "Global Markets and Social Legitimacy."

13. Faris Natour, "UN Council Endorses Principles on Business and Human Rights," *Business Ethics*, June 16, 2011, http://business-ethics.com/2011/06/16/un-council-endorses-principles-on-business-and-human-rights/.

14. An example of this is private sector development (PSD), which seeks to reform the business environment to "make the market work for the poor" (M4P). See OECD, *Business for Development: Fostering the Private Sector—A Development Centre Perspective* (Paris: OECD, 2007); Mark Langan, "Private Sector Development as Poverty and Strategic Discourse: PSD in the Political Economy of EU-Africa Trade Relations," *Journal of Modern African Studies* 49, no. 1 (2011): 83–113.

15. One such strategy is the Extractive Industries Transparency Initiative (EITI), in which corporations adhere to international standards set by supporting countries; international and domestic oil, gas, and mining companies; civil society members; and investor representatives that ensure transparency around natural resource governance in nation-states. See Anwar Ravat and Sridar P. Kannan, *Implementing EITI for Impact: A Handbook for Policymakers and Stakeholders* (EITI International Secretariat with the Oil, Gas and Mining Unit [SEGOM], Sustainable Energy Department [SEG], Sustainable Development Network Vice-Presidency [SDN] of the World Bank, 2013).

16. See Surya Deva and David Bilchitz, *Human Rights Obligations of Business: Beyond the Corporate Responsibility to Respect?* (Cambridge: Cambridge University Press, 2013).

17. Interim report of the Special Representative of the Secretary-General on the issue of human rights and transnational corporations and other business enterprises, E/CN.4/2006/97.

18. For an extensive critique, see Álvaro J. de Regil, "Business and Human Rights: Upholding the Market's Social Darwinism: An Assessment of Mr. John Ruggie's Report: 'Protect, Respect and Remedy: A Framework for Business and Human Rights,'" Jus Semper Global Alliance, Human Rights and Sustainable Human Development essay, October 2008.

19. Morten Ougaard, "Instituting the Power to Do Good? The CSR Movement and Global Governance," in *International Political Economy Yearbook*, ed. Christopher May, vol. 15 (New York: Lynne Rienner Publishers, 2006), 227–47. The best-known opponent of the claim that corporations should have a function for the public good is Milton Friedman. See Milton Friedman, "The Social

Responsibility of Business Is to Increase Its Profits," *New York Times Magazine*, September 13, 1970.

20. Jean Comaroff and John L. Comaroff, *Millennial Capitalism and the Culture of Neoliberalism* (Durham, NC: Duke University Press, 2001), 14.

21. Rami Kaplan and David L. Levy, "Corporate Social Responsibility and Theories of Global Governance: Strategic Contestation in Global Issue Arenas," in *The Oxford Handbook of Corporate Social Responsibility*, ed. Andrew Crane, Abagail McWilliams, Dirk Matten, Jeremy Moon, and Donald (Oxford: Oxford University Press, 2008), 432–51.

22. Noam Chomsky and Robert W. McChesney, *Profit over People: Neoliberalism and Global Order* (New York: Seven Stories Press, 1999); Daniel Yergin and Joseph Stanislaw, *The Commanding Heights: The Battle for the World Economy* (New York: Free Press, 2002); David Harvey, *A Brief History of Neoliberalism* (Oxford; New York: Oxford University Press, 2005).

23. Nicholas Robson, "Human Rights for All: Transatlantic Free Trade Agreement, a Corporate Power Grab That Must Be Stopped," Human Rights for All, October 4, 2013, http://global-human-rights.blogspot.com/2013/10/transatlantic -free-trade-agreement.html; George Monbiot, "It's Business That Really Rules Us Now," *The Guardian*, November 11, 2013, http://www.theguardian.com/ commentisfree/2013/nov/11/business-rules-lobbying-corporate-interests; George Monbiot, *Captive State: The Corporate Takeover of Britain* (London: Pan, 2001); Vandana Shiva, "How Economic Growth Has Become Anti-Life," Common Dreams, accessed April 1, 2014, https://www.commondreams.org/view/2013/ 11/01-2; "Arundhati Roy Explains How Corporations Run India and Why They Want Narendra Modi as Prime Minister," Straight.com, March 30, 2014, http:// www.straight.com/life/616401/arundhati-roy-explains-how-corporations-run -india-and-why-they-want-narendra-modi-prime-minister.

24. Bruno Simma, "Foreign Investment Arbitration: A Place for Human Rights?" *International and Comparative Law Quarterly* 60, no. 3 (2011): 573– 96; Daniel J. Ikenson, *A Compromise to Advance the Trade Agenda: Purge Negotiations of Investor-State Dispute Settlement* (Washington, DC: Cato Institute, March 4, 2014); George Monbiot, "This Transatlantic Trade Deal Is a Full-Frontal Assault on Democracy," *The Guardian*, November 4, 2013.

25. Jonathan Drimmer, "Jonathan Drimmer on Kiobel v. Royal Dutch Shell Petroleum Co. and the Alien Tort Statute," LexisNexis Legal Newsroom: International Law, December 14, 2010, http://www.lexisnexis.com/legalnewsroom/ international-law/b/commentry/archive/2010/12/14/jonathan-drimmer-on-kiobel -v-royal-dutch-shell-petroleum-co-and-the-alien-tort-statute.aspx.

26. See C. K. Prahalad and Yves Doz, *The Multinational Mission: Balancing Local Demands and Global Vision* (New York: Free Press, 1999); Michael Porter and Claas van der Linde, "Toward a New Conception of the Environment-

Competitiveness Relationship," *Journal of Economic Perspectives* 9, no. 4 (1995): 97–118. The Porter and Linde article is now widely referred to as the "Porter hypothesis," and is the subject of substantial debate. Porter's theories on the complementarity of environmental stewardship and economic performance are now gaining wide acceptance and are guiding corporate practice and regulation. See also Philip Kotler and Nancy Lee, *Corporate Social Responsibility: Doing the Most Good for Your Company and Your Cause* (New York: Wiley, 2004); Dean Karlan and Jacob Appel, *More Than Good Intentions: How a New Economics Is Helping to Solve Global Poverty* (New York: Dutton, 2011); Edward Humes, *Eco Barons: The Dreamers, Schemers, and Millionaires Who Are Saving Our Planet* (New York: HarperCollins, 2009).

27. See Nancy J. Adler, "Global Companies, Global Society: There Is a Better Way," *Journal of Management Inquiry* 11, no. 3 (2002): 255–60; Nancy J. Adler, *From Boston to Beijing: Managing with a World View*, 1st ed. (Cincinnati, OH: Cengage Learning, 2001).

28. Stephen Ratner, "Corporations and Human Rights: A Theory of Legal Responsibility," *Yale Law Journal* 111 (2001): 461–546; Mahmood Monshipouri, Claude Welch Jr., and Evan Kennedy, "Multinational Corporations and the Ethics of Global Responsibility," in *Human Rights in the World Community: Issues and Action*, ed. Richard Pierre Claude and Burns Weston (Philadelphia: University of Pennsylvania Press, 2006), 434–45.

29. Sen, *Development as Freedom*, 227–31.

30. "Corporate Social Responsibility Is Evolving, and Becoming a Little Less Flaky," *The Economist*, May 19, 2012, Schumpeter column.

31. Susan Marks, "Four Human Rights Myths," LSE Legal Studies Working Paper, London School of Economics and Political Science (LSE), September 4, 2012; Naomi Klein, *The Shock Doctrine* (London: Penguin, 2007), 126–30.

32. Samuel Moyn, "Human Rights and 'Neoliberalism,'" Humanitarianism and Human Rights, December 9, 2013, http://hhr.hypotheses.org/215.

33. See Joel Bakan, *The Corporation: The Pathological Pursuit of Power* (New York: Penguin, 2004); James Ferguson, "Seeing Like an Oil Company: Space, Security, and Global Capital in Neoliberal Africa," *American Anthropologist* 107, no. 3 (2005): 377–82; Kim Fortun, "Remembering Bhopal, Refiguring Liability," *Interventions: International Journal of Postcolonial Studies* 2, no. 2 (2000): 187–98; John Gledhill, *The Enron Scandal: Global Corporation against Society* (New York: Berghahn Books, 2004); Lawrence E. Mitchell, *Corporate Irresponsibility: America's Newest Export* (New Haven, CT: Yale University Press, 2001); Harvey, *A Brief History of Neoliberalism*.

34. Cyril K. Daddieh and Kidane Mengisteab, *State Building and Democratization in Africa: Faith, Hope, and Realities* (New York: Praeger, 1999); James Howard Smith, *Bewitching Development: Witchcraft and the Reinvention of De-*

velopment in Neoliberal Kenya (Chicago: University of Chicago Press, 2008); Louis Althusser, "Ideology and Ideological State Apparatuses: Notes Towards an Investigation," in *The Anthropology of the State: A Reader*, ed. Aradhana Sharma and Akhil Gupta (Oxford: Blackwell, 2006), 86–111.

35. Mark Mazower, *Governing the World: The History of an Idea, 1815 to the Present* (New York: Penguin, 2012), 346–48; Harold James, *The Creation and Destruction of Value: The Globalization Cycle*, 1st ed. (Cambridge, MA: Harvard University Press, 2009); Rawi Abdelal, *Capital Rules: The Construction of Global Finance* (Cambridge, MA: Harvard University Press, 2009); Greta R. Krippner, *Capitalizing on Crisis: The Political Origins of the Rise of Finance* (Cambridge, MA: Harvard University Press, 2012); Lawrence E. Mitchell, *The Speculation Economy: How Finance Triumphed over Industry*, vol. 2 (San Francisco: Berrett-Koehler, 2007).

36. Mazower, *Governing the World*, 346.

37. James M. McTaggart, *Value Imperative: Managing for Superior Shareholder Returns* (New York: Free Press, 1994), 7.

38. Michael Ignatieff, *Human Rights as Politics and Idolatry* (Princeton, NJ: Princeton University Press, 2001), 21.

39. Boaventura de Sousa Santos, ed., *Another Knowledge Is Possible: Beyond Northern Epistemologies* (New York: Verso, 2007); Boaventura de Sousa Santos, *Democratizing Democracy: Beyond the Liberal Democratic Canon* (New York: Verso, 2007).

40. Sen, *Development as Freedom*, 284.

41. Friedrich Hayek, *The Road to Serfdom* (Chicago: University of Chicago Press, 1944); Milton Friedman, *Capitalism and Freedom* (Chicago: University of Chicago Press, 1962).

42. Anne-Marie Slaughter, *A New World Order* (Princeton, NJ: Princeton University Press, 2005). Will Reno (this volume) applies the term "state interlocutors."

43. Corporate personhood was first legally enshrined in the 1819 case *Dartmouth College v. Woodward*. Subsequently, the 1886 US Supreme Court decision in *Santa Clara County v. Southern Pacific Railroad Company* was instrumental in laying the foundation for modern laws regarding corporate personhood, ruling that the Fourteenth Amendment equal protection clause granted constitutional protections to corporations as well as to natural persons. The 2010 Supreme Court decision in *Citizens United v. Federal Election Commission* further cemented civil and political freedoms of corporations and reflects the ascendance of corporate personhood as a governing ideology. See Clay Calvert, "Freedom of Speech Extended to Corporations," in Paul Finkelman, *Encyclopedia of American Civil Liberties*, vol. 1 (New York: CRC Press, 2006); Carl Mayer, "Personalizing the Impersonal: Corporations and the Bill of Rights," *Hastings Law*

Journal 41 (March 1990): 577–667; Thom Hartmann, *Unequal Protection: How Corporations Became "People"—and How You Can Fight Back* (San Francisco: Berrett-Koehler, 2010).

44. See Robert Bates, *When Things Fall Apart: State Failure in Late-Century Africa* (Cambridge: Cambridge University Press, 1998); Daron Acemoglu and James Robinson, *Why Nations Fail: The Origins of Power, Prosperity, and Poverty* (New York: Crown Business, 2012); Noam Chomsky, *Failed States: The Abuse of Power and the Assault on Democracy* (New York: Holt, 2007); James C. Scott, *Seeing Like a State: How Certain Schemes to Improve the Human Condition Have Failed* (New Haven, CT: Yale University Press, 1999).

45. Janet Roitman, *Fiscal Disobedience: An Anthropology of Economic Regulation in Central Africa* (Princeton, NJ: Princeton University Press, 2005).

46. Michel Feher, Yates McKee, and Gaëlle Krikorian, *Nongovernmental Politics* (New York: Zone Books, 2007). See also Gregory Mann, *The End of the Road: Nongovernmentality in the West African Sahel* (Cambridge: Cambridge University Press, 2015).

47. Valerie Hansen, *Negotiating Daily Life in Traditional China: How Ordinary People Used Contracts, 600–1400* (New Haven, CT: Yale University Press, 1995); M. Małowist, "The Social and Economic Stability of the Western Sudan in the Middle Ages," *Past and Present* 33 (April 1, 1966): 3–15; Neeraj Hatekar, "Farmers and Markets in the Pre-Colonial Deccan: The Plausibility of Economic Growth in Traditional Society," *Past and Present* 178 (February 1, 2003): 116–47; Fernand Braudel, *The Structures of Everyday Life: Civilization and Capitalism, Fifteenth to Eighteenth Century*, vol. 1 (New York: Harper and Row, 1982); Irfan Habib, "Potentialities of Capitalistic Development in the Economy of Mughal India," *Journal of Economic History* 29, no. 1 (1969): 32–78.

48. Sen, *Development as Freedom*, 112.

49. Business management leaders and scholars delineate two forms of relationship building with stakeholders: formal trust and informal trust. Formal trust includes adhering to the rule of law, upholding transparency, and building public openness. Informal trust is defined by the values and norms that allow people to communicate and deal with others who share those values. See Michael B. Goodman, "Restoring Trust in American Business: The Struggle to Change Perception," *Journal of Business Strategy* 26, no. 4 (2005), 29–37.

50. Francis Fukuyama, *Trust: The Social Virtues and the Creation of Prosperity* (New York: Free Press, 1995).

51. Bill Moyers and Michael Winship, "Chevron's 'Crude' Attempt to Suppress Free Speech," *Huffington Post*, May 14, 2010, http://www.huffingtonpost.com/bill-moyers/chevrons-crude-attempt-to_b_576595.html; Timothy Mitchell, *Carbon Democracy: Political Power in the Age of Oil* (New York: Verso, 2011).

PART I

Corporate Social Responsibility as Controlled Negotiation

The Hierarchy of Values

Charlotte Walker-Said

This section analyzes corporate social responsibility as a powerful set of practices that aims to position the corporation as a particular kind of human rights agent in society and the world. The scholars in this section present the CSR and corporate governance strategies of controversial industries who face of serious public skepticism. They also illustrate the approaches of human rights activists, regulators, and civil society representatives who seek to restrain the practices of such industries. In this operational environment, CSR is an essential strategy that permits critics to delineate and demand performance standards and allows corporations to represent and reconnect themselves to the human world and shape mentalities about corporate practice. Thus CSR is analyzed here as a means of negotiation and as a struggle of political economy that extends beyond particular business practices to include the determination of the role of corporations in assuming responsibility for global economic development that reconciles growing human needs with increasingly demanding business imperatives.

The "responsibility" dimension lies at the center of this section's critical inquiry, as it seeks to analyze the potential human rights outcomes of CSR for the world's citizens, who, as the authors of this section remind us, are entitled to the fulfillment of human rights *duties* rather than informal "responsibilities" in the achievement of their capabilities. Through

investigating the meanings and execution of responsibility in two separate but interdependent spheres—business and humanitarianism—these
scholars also engage with the concept of "corporate rights" and their interface with human rights.

Corporate rights have foundations in early twentieth-century American philosophies of "corporate personhood," which were realized in
landmark judicial decisions that paved the way for greater freedoms for
business around the world.[1] The last quarter century in world history has
seen the unprecedented enlargement of the rights of the corporation,
and consequently, in many parts of the developing world, their power
and control over territory, property, human productivity, and profit exceed that of the nation-state.[2] Even the world's foremost superpower, the
United States, has overseen the enlargement of the rights of corporations in its own political sphere.[3] Corporate influence on national governments, international capital flow, local social and labor relations, and
the conditions of human life around the world are a result of the expansion of corporate rights to control the functioning of markets and contractual relations.

In the opening chapter, Peter Rosenblum examines the possibilities
of mass political engagement for human rights in an atmosphere where
corporations are simultaneously political and economic agents asserting
their own claims. Rosenblum reveals the history of CSR activism as a
significant force in inducing moral revision of corporate practice.[4] Peter Benson takes the opposite stance, asserting that the corporate rights
and responsibility movements largely forward a "mythical vision of the
corporation as a person," which have created a fiction of a moral aspect
to corporate practice. Anna Zalik similarly refutes the theoretical possibilities inherent in CSR frameworks, arguing that CSR reflects particular "constitutions" of economic development as humanitarian assistance, which exclusively recognize the vast potential of multinational
corporations to renovate and reinvigorate both society and economy and
disregard evidence of corporations' involvement in diminishing health,
security, stability, wealth, and social life in many regions of the world.
Stuart Kirsch describes how CSR is strategically deployable, responding
to shifting political and economic pressures and maximizing the utility
of virtuous language.

Each chapter eliminates any doubt that CSR is a new form of global
governance that has profound implications for the state of human rights
outcomes for the world's populations as well as for the moral and ide-

ological direction of the international human rights agenda. As corporate social responsibility rapidly integrates itself into transnational strategies for economic and social development, standards for institutional legitimacy, and everyday forms of communication, it gains credence as a moral movement and increasingly positions itself as the principle determinant for improving the human condition around the world.[5]

Notes

1. Carl Mayer, "Personalizing the Impersonal: Corporations and the Bill of Rights," *Hastings Law Journal* 41 (March 1990): 577–667.

2. See James Ferguson and Akhil Gupta, "Spatializing States: Toward an Ethnography of Neoliberal Governmentality," *American Ethnologist* 29, no. 4 (2002): 981–1002; Peter Utting, "CSR and Equality," *Third World Quarterly* 28, no. 4 (2007): 697–712.

3. The 2010 US Supreme Court decision in Citizens United v. Federal Election Commission granted the corporation new freedoms of advocacy and influence in the American political sphere. "Summary Citizens United v. Federal Election Commission (Docket No. 08–205)," Cornell University School of Law. See also Justin Levitt, "Confronting the Impact of Citizens United," *Yale Law and Policy Review* 29 (2010): 217–26.

4. Specific responses include James Heckman, Alan B. Krueger, and Benjamin Friedman, *Inequality in America: What Role for Human Capital Policies?* (Cambridge, MA: MIT Press, 2005); Douglas Irwin, *Free Trade under Fire* (Princeton, NJ: Princeton University Press, 2009).

5. David Mosse, *Cultivating Development: An Ethnography of Aid Policy and Practice* (London: Pluto Press, 2004); David Hopkins, *Corporate Social Responsibility and International Development: Is Business the Solution?* (London: Routledge, 2008); Alastair Greig, David Hulme, and Mark Turner, *Challenging Global Inequality: Development Theory and Practice in the 21st Century* (New York: Palgrave Macmillan, 2007); Matthew Kiernan, *Investing in a Sustainable World: Why GREEN Is the New Color of Money on Wall Street* (New York: Amacom, 2008).

Two Cheers for CSR

Peter Rosenblum

As corporate social responsibility has risen to center stage, it has become increasingly discredited in the eyes of a large segment of the engaged public. CSR has become a "dirty word." It signals co-optation and the derailing of mobilized activism into countless soft initiatives. Internal compliance departments, voluntary codes, and multistakeholder mechanisms absorb the energies of civil society into interminable processes. The voluntariness, vagueness, and uncertainty of enforcement—not to mention blatant propagandizing by many companies—overwhelm any good intentions and spread cynicism about the enterprise. In the guise of improvement, many argue, CSR diverts attention while helping to erode national laws and international agreements.[1]

At the other end of the spectrum, advocates of CSR celebrate the new norms and processes that are emerging under its broad umbrella. In their view, it is part of a new paradigm that is breaking the stranglehold of shareholder value understood as short-term profits. At the very least, CSR facilitates efforts to constrain corporate behavior, internalize systematic responses, and stigmatize outliers. Voluntariness is relative. When nested in institutional mechanisms and multilayered stakeholder commitments, noncompliance is costly; exit becomes nearly unthinkable. For some advocates, CSR and its adjuncts have the potential to transform the corporate model, to introduce a range of "stakeholders" and their issues into the governance of the corporation. For others, the soul of the corporation may not be changing, but the changes are nevertheless profound, creating further expectations that will be hard to reverse.[2]

The truth, in this case, does not lie somewhere "in between" so much as on both sides. While they can't all be right—especially about the more extreme claims—there is considerable evidence for the most pessimistic views and startling examples to support the optimists. CSR has been a battleground where every element, including language, is part of a campaign. As long as CSR remained controversial within the corporate world, advocates were not terribly concerned about the language. But with its "phenomenal success" after 1990, they have come up with "competing labels that cover the same or similar territory."[3] Advocates deployed the language of corporate "accountability" as a challenge to "voluntariness," "business and human rights" as an effort to bring business into a recognized field of international accountability for destructive human impacts, and "sustainability," as a new consensus term that offers companies and advocates a positive ground for reimagining (and perhaps repackaging) the company's social obligations. The terms may present themselves at times as alternatives to CSR, but that is largely rhetorical in that they fit firmly within the ongoing struggles to define the extent of the company's obligations, the mechanisms of accountability, and the limits of voluntariness. And in the end they all land in corporate CSR reports.

The results of these battles are a shifting patchwork of success and failure. Even as some trends such as codes of conduct, independent monitoring, stakeholder engagement, and social certification spread across industries and find their place in multisector arrangements, CSR cannot be fully understood without particular attention to the forces at work in particular sectors. Without it, the generalizations overwhelm the reality. For example, the apparel and extractive sectors are dense with initiatives, and though they developed at roughly the same time, very different factors were at work, including different perceived harms, advocacy goals, constituencies, and constraints. Their successes and failures reflect these differences. Supply chain monitoring in the apparel sector may miss routine problems, but apparel companies are paying compensation to workers mistreated by unrelated factories. NGOs are bogged down in troubled multistakeholder initiatives (MSIs) dealing with conflict diamonds and abusive security forces, but companies and governments are disclosing more information than ever about the deals they make and the money they pay. As the tools and tactics of each sector are carried over into other fields like food production, electronics, and infrastructure, each poses new challenges.

In the first part of this chapter, I draw out aspects of the apparel and extractive sector struggles, both because of their centrality to the evolution of CSR and for what they suggest about strengths and weaknesses in the system. One of those weaknesses is that despite all the effort to create systems of monitoring, policing, and enforcing standards, they don't actually work on their own. When they do work, it is because of external forces like local law enforcement, worker organizing, or the continuing efforts of gadfly journalists and NGOs. In the second part, I draw on these examples and others to address the arguments for and against CSR, highlighting how much has been accomplished in light of how awful the obstacles. I also consider the merits of the extremes: that CSR is a weak tool that serves to legitimize a massive expansion of global capitalism, on the one hand, or that we are on the road to a new form of "stakeholder"-driven corporate governance, on the other. Both have their place, but neither provides a sufficient explanation for current developments.

Apparel and Extractives

The struggles in the apparel (including footwear) and extractive sectors figure prominently in the history of CSR.[4] Over nearly a quarter century, these sectors have grown to be dense with CSR initiatives, frequently serving as models for other sectors. They provide some of the most developed programs in certification, supply chain monitoring, community engagement, and transparency. They emerged at effectively the same time in the mid-1990s, employing related, consumer-based tactics to name and shame their way to establishing new principles of corporate accountability. But their similarities also mask significant differences that are related to the sectors, the problems they were confronting, and the constituencies they could mobilize. The different dynamics of each sector, more than any global advances in CSR, continue to drive their successes and failures.

It is no coincidence, of course, that the phenomenal rise of CSR coincides with the end of the Cold War and the tremendous acceleration of globalization, including diminished tariffs, unrestricted movement of capital, and World Bank–led reforms to promote private investment in the developing world. As Gerard Hanlon argues, CSR is "not a driving force of change, but rather an outcome of changes brought on by other forces."[5] Worse, in responding to destructive changes, it serves primarily to legitimize them, replacing confrontation with dialogue. The examples from apparel and the extractive sector suggest that this is true and not so true. While the advocacy movements reacted to global economic shifts, they also took advantage of the tactics globalization enabled to pursue other goals. This is where the distinction between the apparel and extractive sectors is helpful. It may be an exaggeration, but useful nevertheless, to say that apparel activism was driven by failures brought about by globalization, while extractive advocacy found an opportunity to use new tools to address existing problems. Both have been willing to engage in collaborative multistakeholder processes, but in neither case has dialogue entirely replaced confrontation.

The apparel sector best reflects the reasons for Hanlon's skepticism. For apparel, globalization meant loss and, for advocates, CSR solutions were always second best. In the 1980s and '90s, brands were outsourcing—giving up manufacturing in favor of designing and marketing products produced by unrelated contractors in the developing world. The North American Free Trade Agreement passed in 1994 with labor's opposition, spurring the expansion of maquiladoras on the border. What were lost were jobs in the United States and direct accountability from the company to the worker who produced the product. What advocates wanted initially was protection for jobs and later some degree of the vertical accountability that had been lost. They largely succeeded in the latter, though the loss of apparel jobs was never reversed.

The difference between two companies, Levi Strauss and Nike, targeted by campaigners during the 1990s, illustrates the preeminence of globalization's economic impacts and also highlights how insignificant the internal ethics of the company—a main focus of traditional CSR—were in the face of those economic impacts.[6] Until the 1990s, Levi Strauss was a manufacturer of clothes with an extraordinary commitment to social responsibility. It had defied segregation in its southern factories, deliberately reached out to underserved communities, and, in 1985, privatized the company, in part to insulate its social commitment from market forces. It fought the pressure to close factories in the United States and outsource production into the 1990s, resisting far longer than many other American companies. But the company eventually gave in. By 1997, Levi Strauss no longer had employees manufacturing clothes. In their production, they were now like Nike, a company that relied on outsourcing from the start and which only briefly dabbled in domestic production with two factories in the United States.

In principle, there remained a major difference between the two companies. Levi's developed one of the first codes of conduct and clearly took human rights in the supply chain seriously. Nike did not. But Levi's still found itself caught in scandals related to work conditions, and Nike's recalcitrance provided essential fuel to the rise of a hugely successful public advocacy campaign. The campaign was launched in 1992 by Jeff Ballinger, a labor organizer and activist, with a *Harper's* magazine article annotating the pay stub of an Indonesian worker. Nike fought back at every step, initially dismissing responsibility and eventually engaging in a public relations battle, using proxies like Andrew Young, the former UN ambassador and mayor of Atlanta. But the public relations campaign backfired spectacularly, providing more fodder to activists. In 1998, the CEO of Nike, Phil Knight, effectively threw in the towel, acknowledging that Nike had "become synonymous with slave wages, forced overtime and arbitrary abuse." As Jeff Ballinger said, the campaign would never have succeeded without Nike's help.[7]

The Nike campaign was one of several that targeted well-known clothing and footwear brands. During the same period, another gadfly activist, Charles Kernaghan, identified child labor in the manufacture of clothes sold under the label of Kathie Lee Gifford, a daytime television personality. Like the resistance from Phil Knight, her public battle and eventual recognition of problems further magnified awareness in the United States. As brands began to look for a way out, the Clinton administration offered a platform, the Apparel Industry Partnership, which led eventually to the creation of the Fair Labor Association (FLA), a multistakeholder initiative (MSI) to provide social certification to brands. The absence of firm obligations related to a living wage and right to organize led to a split in the initiative and the eventual creation of the Workers Rights Consortium (WRC), a monitoring organization with strong union and student ties, that focused on products licensed by universities. Relying on its strong internal culture, Levi Strauss initially refrained from joining any of the MSIs, but eventually they, too, gave in to the need for broader legitimacy offered by the FLA.

The movement continued to lose the bigger battles against globalization, including struggles for legal protection at the national and international level. In 1996, the World Trade Organization rejected the proposal for a "social clause" that would have recognized the right to link free trade to improved labor protection.[8] At the national level, many countries suspended labor rights in export processing zones, and by the end of 2004, multifiber export quotas were phased out, largely eliminating the last significant reason that brands had to produce in countries with higher labor costs or better protections.

In the shadow of these losses, there was nevertheless "real" progress in CSR. European MSIs like the Fair Wear Foundation, organizations like Clean Clothes Campaign, and individually targeted corporate campaigns continued to extend the reach of advocates. Despite differences in specific codes of conduct and mechanisms for enforcement, supply chain accountability spread through the sector. It moved from public relations to increasingly competent compliance departments inside of global brands. Individual companies began to use increasingly sophisticated methods of engagement as they came to understand in a more nuanced way the reasons why their sourcing methods were leading to problems like unpaid overtime, undisclosed subcontracting, or abusive floor conditions.[9]

Finally, other industries have borrowed the mechanisms or entered them directly, suggesting that gains could be translated without similar struggles. The electronics industry also turned to outsourcing in the 1980s, but companies like HP only shut down North American factory production in the late 1990s. HP and others then launched an industry-based initiative, Electronics Industry Citizenship Coalition, in 2004 with a code of conduct and weak monitoring provisions. When Apple computer was targeted for violations at Foxconn, in late 2011, it very quickly joined the Fair Labor Association, the first technology company to do so.[10]

It is unlikely that any of this "progress" matches the rights that workers could have achieved in direct employment relations with major brands or through strong legal protections, including the right to organize. In fact, what little empirical evidence there is suggests that the compliance mechanisms are not effective on their own. Richard Locke and colleagues have produced extensive empirical analysis of Nike and HP production that is extremely critical of what "private voluntary regulation" can achieve on its own. In Locke's view, the legitimacy and support of national law is essential to enabling CSR mechanisms to play a more effective role. He also identifies circumstances where gadfly activism triggered effective enforcement of the law through the private mechanisms.[11] This is where traditional naming and shaming by people like Charles Kernaghan, Jeff Ballinger, and their successors around the world continue to play a role. Having accepted accountability, companies can no longer rely on the absence of a legal relationship to the workers.

But with all its limits, apparel advocacy has crossed a significant and unlikely divide. In a number of cases, for example, brands are paying compensation to workers who were dismissed or left unpaid by factories producing for them. The number is small but the ramifications quite important. Some of this has resulted from remediation provisions in the WRC code of conduct. In 2010, Nike agreed to pay $1.54 million after student groups pressured universities into threatening action on behalf of 1,800 workers who lost their jobs to a subcontractor in Honduras.[12] In 2013, Adidas agreed to make severance payments to 2,700 Indonesian workers after the factory producing for them shut down without paying wages.[13] What was exceptional about this case is that the University of Wisconsin actually sued Adidas for a breach of its licensing agreement. In most cases, companies have sought to avoid any appearance of contractual or other obligation. Nike had already paid $1.2 million as its share of the severance.[14] The Rana fire in Bangladesh brought out some of the best and worst of reactions from companies. While there is still considerable dispute about long-term engagements, a number of companies have paid compensation to workers and others have reportedly made commitments to future safety investments.[15]

The battles over extractive companies were as well known as those that led to innovations in apparel, but of a very different nature. The problems predated globalization. Campaigners initially targeted complicity by corporations with repressive regimes engaged in long-standing human rights violations. Later campaigns began to address issues associated with the "resource curse"—poor governance, corruption, and destruction of the local environment. The tactics used global corporations and global capital to break the hold of developing states—bypassing traditional notions of sovereignty in which the sovereign made the decisions, with the goal of subjecting the government to local accountability and rules of human rights. The success of those campaigns has led to significant institutionalized structures of disclosure and compliance.

The worldwide campaign against Shell Oil that began in 1995 targeted the company for complicity with the government of Nigeria in the execution of Ken Saro Wiwa and other activists from Ogoniland, where Shell was active.[16] In addition to issues of complicity with repression, it

brought attention to massive destruction of the environment and livelihoods in the oil region of the Niger Delta. In other parts of the world,
campaigners targeted the gold mining operations of Freeport McMoRan
for similar complicity with Indonesian officials in West Papua[17] and the
operations of a Unocal/Total pipeline project in Burma.[18] All of these
campaigns fit within long-standing struggles for democracy and human
rights that were a product of the Cold War era. By alleging complicity,
campaigners built on a model that was at least as old as the 1970s antiapartheid struggle, linking it to a more contemporary focus on accountability for human rights violations.

The campaigns against extractive companies led to a series of innovative lawsuits under the Alien Tort Statute in the United States.[19] In addition, two significant if contested MSIs emerged, the "Voluntary Principles on Security and Human Rights" (VP), which primarily addresses
the relationship of extractive companies to security forces and local security, and the "Kimberley Process," which is intended to eliminate
"conflict diamonds" through certification and tracing.[20] These have been
extremely prominent, with high-level participation of governments and
endorsement by the United Nations. On the other hand, their continuing
effectiveness has been challenged by NGOs who complain about dom-
inance by governments and industry, as well the participation of ques-
tionable NGOs. In the view of some NGO activists, these are two of the
MSIs that threaten to consume the resources of qualified NGOs while
yielding increasingly uncertain results. In 2011, Global Witness, a UK-
based NGO whose pioneering work elucidated the problem of conflict
diamonds, broke from the Kimberley Process.

In the late 1990s, advocates also began to focus on the extractive sector in an innovative way to address a broader range of issues related
to the "resource curse"—the corruption, poor governance, and lack
of growth associated with resource wealth in many parts of the world.
Again, the problems had little specifically to do with globalization,
though the tools that were used did. Some of the issues came into focus
in 1998 when the World Bank's planned support for an oil pipeline from
Chad to Cameroon became a source of contention.[21] Exxon Mobil had
turned to the bank for financing, leading to an international campaign
among development and environmental groups who followed the work
of the bank. While the project went through despite pleas for a moratorium by NGOs, the bank attached unprecedented conditions on transparency, disclosure, oversight, and even how revenues could be spent.

The government of Chad eventually undermined the conditions, but they set in motion new demands for transparency and oversight. In response, the World Bank president, James Wolfensohn, launched the Extractive Industry Review, a worldwide consultation on investment in the extractive sector. The process articulated some clear conditions for investment and helped extend civil society mobilization even further.

The process was furthered by international human rights and development NGOs that began to report on corruption and mismanagement of resource wealth in the late 1990s and early 2000s. Some were already well known for other work, like Human Rights Watch, Oxfam. and Catholic Relief Services. In 2003, Amnesty International published an entire "human rights" report about an oil pipeline contract through Azerbaijan, Georgia, and Turkey. One of the most significant NGOs to engage was Global Witness, which took, as its exclusive mandate, the multiple dimensions of natural resource issues. Global Witness coined the phrase "publish what you pay" in a report about companies operating in Angola.

There was also a burst of mobilizing on the funding side. The Open Society Institute, funded by George Soros, launched the Revenue Watch Institute in 2002. With the support of the Hewlett Foundation and the Norwegian Oil for Development Program, it became an independent funding and research organization in 2006. With this as background, the "Publish What You Pay" coalition (PWYP) was launched in 2002, demanding that companies publish what they pay to governments and, later, adding disclosure of investor contracts. Among other things, the PWYP coalition serves as the civil society component of the MSI launched at around the same time, the Extractive Industries Transparency Initiative (EITI), which organizes the process for companies and countries to disclose extractive industry revenues.[22]

The influence of EITI and PWYP has been extremely significant. All of the major Western extractive companies are involved in EITI, as are a growing number of resource producing nations. The international financial institutions and bilateral funders have implemented EITI through aid and development programs. Nevertheless, the reach of EITI has been limited by resistance from some of the major oil-producing countries and a certain collusion from companies that are not eager to confront them or disclose too much detail about payments.

Then, in 2010, the US Dodd-Frank Financial Reform Act changed the game, launching a new phase of legally required financial disclosure that then spread quickly to Europe and Canada.[23] Section 1504 of Dodd-Frank requires all listed oil and mining companies to publish what they pay to governments, everywhere in the world. Meanwhile, another section of Dodd-Frank, Section 1502, attacked the problem of "conflict minerals" from the Democratic Republic of Congo, effectively requiring brands to police their supply chain and publish the results. Both provisions built on obligations that major companies had already accepted, at least in principle. Section 1504 tracked the disclosure requirements of EITI and Section 1502 built on a due diligence framework that the OECD was developing in a multistakeholder process. As discussed below, without the process of voluntary, private regulation that preceded it, it is hard to imagine that the wave of laws would have been possible.

Evaluating the Claims

The examples from the apparel and extractive sectors should give a strong sense of why the "truth" about CSR lies on both sides of the argument. There are accountability mechanisms that have led to improved enforcement and others that are mired in contention and consume needed resources. Twenty years ago, a company like Nike denied any legal obligation to the workers who produced its shoes; now it may pay compensation to those workers when the factories fail them. Yet routine monitoring and sophisticated compliance departments are not redressing the best-known problems. Returning to the contentions from both sides, the next section draws on these examples and others to some of the specific contentions raised at the outset, including (i) propaganda and obfuscation, (ii) voluntariness, and (iii) whether CSR crowds out the law and other enforcement. Finally, I return to the arguments at the extremes, whether CSR is essentially a fig leaf to capitalist expansion or whether it is the gateway to a new form of corporate governance.

Propaganda and Obfuscation

While researching this chapter, the Internet search phrase "corporate social responsibility" always yielded advertisements. For much of the time, Chevron appeared to own the phrase on Google, "Corporate Responsibility—learn about Chevron's Dedication to Local Communities & the Environment." Its advertising campaigns and logo were ubiquitous where CSR was discussed, at the same time that the company was fighting multifront battles to avoid legal obligations related to social responsibility around the world.[24] These propaganda campaigns are galling to activists and fuel cynicism about the CSR project. But as the apparel story emphasizes, they don't always win. In fact, they can also backfire and become the engine for expanded accountability. As discussed above, Phil Knight of Nike and Kathie Lee Gifford of daytime television propelled the CSR movement toward enforceable standards.

At the same time, the rise of CSR has led to the proliferation of organizations whose motivations and funding sources are mixed. Referring to the early 2000s, Jem Bendell writes, "the fact that CSR had become a popular acronym attached to a growing industry made it a target for those who were focused more on the economic and political dimensions of business practice."[25] In supply chain monitoring alone, a huge range of not-for-profit and for-profit companies are now involved. Some are very credible, professional organizations that may rely on business funding but depend on transparency and objective standards for legitimacy. On the other hand, the proliferation of civil society organizations relativizes the role of those NGOs and activists who were responsible for bringing to light the problems that launched the initiatives. The well-intentioned debates over process and participation in MSIs, rather than focusing on facts and reporting, have served to further dilute the role of those NGOs. It is less surprising that an MSI like the Voluntary Principles has been mired in contention when the NGO members include not only Human Rights Watch, which regularly reports on rights violations by corporations, but also PACT, a Chevron-funded NGO that regularly collaborates with extractive companies.[26]

Voluntariness

Voluntariness is a feature of the corporate definition of CSR and a constant target of attack by advocates. For corporations, CSR is framed in terms of corporate policy—often in terms of the "caring" company.[27] It typically incorporates everything from charitable contributions to participation in MSIs, but it ends at the point that legal compliance takes over.

Many advocates argue that voluntariness is relative, that CSR mechanisms are voluntary up to the point of joining—and even that is often constrained or effectively forced by public campaigns or socially responsible investors.[28] Jem Bendell dates the change from when advocates moved from "brand bashing" in the 1990s to focusing on mechanisms of accountability. By 2003, he writes, "there was a broad range of groups involved in specific corporate accountability initiatives" that involved serious governance constraints on business. MSIs like Fair Labor Association, Workers' Rights Consortium, Extractive Industries Transparency Initiative, and Voluntary Principles for Security and Human Rights in the Extractive Sector are all "voluntary" but make serious demands for disclosure, monitoring, and training.[29]

In addition, some CSR commitments, including MSIs and certification, are embedded in normative arrangements with investors, lenders, and even brands, often going as far as to make them binding as a matter of contract. Bilateral donors and the World Bank have taken on EITI and the Voluntary Principles, raising the normative status and increasing the social cost of withdrawal. In lender agreements with the private lending arm of the World Bank (the International Finance Corporation or IFC), IFC's own social conditions, the "Performance Standards," are incorporated into the contractual relationship with the borrower.

While companies may cling to voluntariness, advocates have grown savvy about building a chain of accountability. One appealing example came in the course of the Coalition of Immokalee Workers' (CIW) long struggle for a "penny a pound" wage increase for Florida tomato pickers. In order to circumvent growers who claimed economic hardship the CIW began to single out big brands that purchased the tomatoes. They started with Taco Bell—not because it was a dominant purchaser of tomatoes but because it had a product associated with tomatoes and a significant presence on college campuses. Three years into its groundbreaking boycott, the parent company, Yum Brands, sent the CIW a $110,000 check, corresponding to the "penny a pound" increase, and promised to help work toward an industry-wide agreement to increase payments. CIW returned the check.[30] In the decade since, CIW has successfully obtained commitments from Yum Brands, McDonald's, and most recently, Walmart, among other sellers of tomatoes, effectively breaking the stranglehold of the growers.

Crowds Out Law / More Demanding Standards

One of the most contentious arguments about CSR is that it crowds out other options, including new laws and regulations. It is true that corporate efforts to occupy the field with voluntary commitments and to use them in an effort to delegitimize legal constraints are widespread and unconcealed.[31] But as in the case of other CSR battles, they are not necessarily winning. The example of lenders and companies incorporating CSR into contracts shows the spread of "private" legal obligations.[32] There is also evidence of increased state regulation and enforcement. In the labor rights field, Richard Locke documents what others have described as a "regulatory renaissance," in the developing and developed world.[33] While recognizing the appearance of a paradox, Doreen Mc-Barnet also notes: "Law is playing an increasing role in enforcing 'voluntary' CSR policies."[34] She and her colleagues detail the complex and multiple levels at which public and private law interconnect with CSR.[35]

One of the oft-overlooked points that Locke notes is that strong laws typically exist, already.[36] While specifically discussing workers and workplace safety, the point is true of many other areas of law. The broad protections of the 1951 Indian Plantations Labor Act extend, for example, to the housing, education, health care, and nutrition of workers and their families. With possible carve-outs for "export processing zones" or other promotional mechanisms, most developing countries have extensive protective legislation; the historic problem has been enforcement. There is evidence that CSR can provide a pretext for government inaction as well as a trigger for enforcement.[37]

In contrast to the argument that CSR crowds out law, there is evidence to suggest that voluntary mechanisms can actually facilitate new laws. Locke does not make this argument for the "regulatory renaissance," but it is plausible. The recent example of Dodd-Frank's extractive industry regulation shows how this might be true. During the drafting phase for sections 1502 and 1504, the major mining and oil companies were in shocking disarray, unable to come up with a shared position. Their room to maneuver was constrained by having already agreed to the principles in the two sections as well as significant aspects of their implementation. Their response afterward exposed extreme rifts among companies. Big oil companies organized a concerted attack, individually and through the American Petroleum Institute, but many mining companies and a few smaller oil companies embraced the financial disclosure law as a shield against corrupt officials and insurance against less reputable operators. Meanwhile, the US law induced European and Canadian versions that are extending its reach, even as the oil industry succeeded in delaying US implementation. The conflict minerals provision has shown similar divisions though, there, the legal challenges failed and the regulations are going into effect.[38]

Arguments at the Extremes: Evils of Capitalism or Transformation of Governance

The incidental, anecdotal stories of success don't respond to some of the biggest claims for and against CSR—that it has legitimized and provided social cover for a massive expansion of global capitalism, or that it is part of a reconceptualizing of corporate governance away from short-term shareholder value toward a stakeholder model. The former argument pits an appealing radical critique against the meliorist activism of NGOs and unions that are working within the system rather than trying to bring it down. It serves as, at least, a note of caution for those who overstate the progress of CSR, including those who would make the latter argument for the transformation of the shareholder model. While a variety of forces are exercising influence over companies, forcing them to attend to consumers, workers, and communities, it is still mediated through the shareholders who own the companies. In the United States, in particular, the shareholder model of governance remains largely unscathed, and mainstream investors view CSR as a niche activity.

Many of those who denounce CSR are calling for stronger measures that are less voluntary and more accountable. As I have argued in this chapter, the difference is rhetorical rather than substantive. Effectively binding, accountable processes are now a routine part of the CSR menu and will find their way into the corporate CSR report, whatever its name. But there is a more radical critique that assaults CSR as not just a fig leaf but also an integral feature of global capitalism at its worst. As Gerard Hanlon writes, "CSR represents a further embedding of capitalist social relations and a deeper opening up of social life to the dictates of the marketplace."[39] In this view, CSR legitimates the expansion of the global corporation at the expense of labor and the state. "CSR is not a driving force of change but rather an outcome of changes brought on by other forces," he writes.[40]

There is much to support Hanlon's arguments, though more for some sectors than others. As discussed above, while apparel activism responded to new problems created by market changes, the extractive sector activism took advantage of those changes to address preexisting problems. Still, both responded to the weakness of national governments and their susceptibility to corporate interests by inventing processes that circumvented the state, at least in part. To the extent that the radical critique regrets this, it hints at nostalgia for a model of the state, and self-determination, that was largely chimeric. Sovereignty over natural resources was a major claim and important victory for the nonaligned states during the Cold War. But control by unaccountable leaders accentuated the resource curse and allowed for repressive labor conditions in factories. Cold War ideas of sovereignty are what made the relationship between Shell Oil and the government of Nigeria entirely reasonable for its time. The new initiatives in the sector trounce those rules with the goal of increasing accountability to citizens and communities affected by extraction.

Still, by suggesting that CSR merely compensates for market changes with inferior solutions, privileging "pluralism" and "discussion" over the confrontation that enabled labor to achieve significant goals in the West, the radical critique touches on all the fears of activists concerned with legitimizing a system with which they disagree. The relative absence of empirical evidence to measure the impact of CSR combined with the few studies there are, including those of Richard Locke, which ultimately declare private mechanisms to be a failure without a significant state role, highlight how little is known and how great the risks[41] Yet, it would be hard to argue that refusal to participate in such "meliorative" initiatives would have produced better results. The forces for free trade, unfettered investment, and global deregulation had few counterweights. In 1994, when US labor opposed the North American Free Trade Zone, it failed to stop the process and ended up with a weak labor side agreement rather than strong labor guarantees. Even if I am wrong about the capacity of CSR to facilitate news laws and regulations, it is hard to imagine that CSR initiatives have made prospects for renewed regulation any worse.

The optimistic arguments about changing corporate governance posit a new vision of corporate governance, a stakeholder model, to replace exclusive reliance on shareholders. "As a concept," writes Kevin Campbell and Douglas Vick, "CSR directly challenges the dominant Anglo-American paradigm of corporate governance, which emphasizes profit maximization for investors as the most efficient way of promoting wealth for the society as a whole."[42]

CSR has certainly become an element of "governance" in a broad sense that is consistent with the current literature of "new governance" or "global governance" that explores the myriad normative forces acting on institutions in the absence of strong government regulation.[43] However, this approach to "governance" stands in stark contrast to the "corporate governance" taught in business and law schools and enforced in the West. While corporations were once perceived to have larger obligations to the public welfare, the trend of the last hundred years has definitely been in the other direction. It is only a slight exaggeration to write that, "Corporate governance systems throughout the world are converging on a shareholder-centric ideology."[44] As Katharina Pistor, a strong critic of mainstream corporate law, characterizes the dominant scholarship, "the only relevant criteria for corporate decision making is and should be the maximization of shareholder value."[45] Among the United States, United Kingdom, and Germany, only Germany legally recognizes something that could be called "multistakeholder governance," in the form of co-determination with worker bodies. For the rest, interests have to be channeled through shareholders in the United States, or, with slightly more leeway, through board members in the United Kingdom.

In fact, despite the rhetoric, the practice of corporations and CSR activists effectively supports the dominant shareholder model. Advocates channel their activism through investors and corporations treat "stakeholders" without a sense of accountability or continuing obligation. In their 2005 survey and analysis of CSR practice, including linguistic analysis of CSR reports, John Conley and Cynthia Williams, note that "companies are treating both stakeholder dialogue and CSR reporting as opportunities to shape and control the debate over their conduct. . . . Rather than redressing the imbalance between corporations and civil society, these processes may be reinforcing it in subtle but effective ways."[46] The "mainstream," as Conley and Williams note, still treats CSR as "fringe." Having worked in law schools for most of my career, I can only stress how few mainstream corporate lawyers would recognize the stakeholder governance claims.

Conclusion

In 2000, the *New York Times* correspondents Nicholas Kristof and Sheryl WuDunn wrote "Two Cheers for Sweatshops," a long opinion piece castigating westerners for their naive and destructive campaigns against sweatshop production for American brands. "For all the misery they can engender, sweatshops at least offer a precarious escape from the poverty that is the developing world's greatest problem," they wrote. The couple fretted that Western pressure to increase wages would lead to premature mechanization, putting more people out of work. They overstated the risk of boycotts—which were never a major part of campaigns—and concluded that the solution to the problem of sweatshops was to "buy more" from them.[47]

While antisweatshop activists may have undervalued the development contribution of globalization, Kristof and WuDunn certainly misunderstood the potential of antisweatshop activism in forcing companies to take responsibility for the workers in their supply chain. Luckily for the evolution of CSR, few enough people joined in the cheering.

Still, even for activists, there were strong reasons for skepticism. The antisweatshop campaigns and their CSR successors are disproportionately dependent on brands that are susceptible to consumer pressure and publicly traded companies in which investors are willing to assert social obligations. Corporate propaganda and the proliferation of CSR businesses put even the best efforts in doubt. Not all products are branded, not all brands are equally susceptible to social pressures, and the reach of socially responsible investors has been relatively limited.

It would have been reasonable to imagine that, at best, CSR would create a virtuous network, a kind of not-in-my-backyard option for particular consumers. A company like Walmart succeeded on prices, not work conditions. Oil companies were fungible and had to get the oil wherever they could, including in corrupt and repressive regimes. Underpaid workers like the tomato pickers in Immokalee were employed by hundreds of private farmers whose names were unknown to the public. There was little reason for optimism that CSR could close the gaps. Any effort to do so was immediately met with claims that business would just be lost to less scrupulous competitors.

But those limits were all overcome. It is a measure of success that CSR has reached Walmart, Big Oil, and Florida tomato pickers, as well as similar companies in other sectors. The results shouldn't be overstated, but the change over the past decade has been dramatic. It is a modest success. CSR is not transforming corporations, but in fits and starts it is yielding surprising results.

So two cheers for CSR! It opens the door to advocates and has led to some genuine and surprising improvements. In some cases, it might be creating conditions for new laws and better enforcement. Even in the face of willing hypocrisy, it can restrain a corporation. Its limits aren't yet defined, but the alternatives are still not feasible. Embrace it, engage it, but don't trust it.

Notes

1. This is a composite of many shared views. For one strong characterization by a prominent NGO, see Christian Aid, *Behind the Mask: The Real Face of Corporate Social Responsibility*, Global Policy Forum 2004, www.globalpolicy .org/socecon/tncs/2004/0121mask.pdf.

2. This is similarly a composite. See Deborah Spar, "The Spotlight and the Bottom Line: How Multinationals Export Human Rights," *Foreign Affairs* 77, no. 2 (1998): 7–12.

3. Andrew Crane, Abagail McWilliams, Dirk Matten, Jeremy Moon, and Donald Siegel, "The Corporate Social Responsibility Agenda," in *The Oxford Handbook of Corporate Social Responsibility*, ed. Andrew Crane, Abagail Mc-Williams, Dirk Matten, Jeremy Moon, and Donald S. Siegel (Oxford: Oxford University Press, 2008), 3–18.

4. The story of the apparel sector is recounted and critically explored in many sources. Richard Locke reviews some of the literature in Richard Locke, *The Promise and Limits of Private Power* (Cambridge: Cambridge University Press, 2013). Randy Shaw provides an advocates' perspective in Randy Shaw, *Reclaiming America: Nike, Clean Air, and the New National Activism* (Berkeley: University of California Press, 1999). Karl Schoenberger gives a detailed and sympathetic account of the experience of Levi Strauss in Karl Schoenberger, *Levi's Children: Coming to Terms with Human Rights in the Global Marketplace* (New York: Grove Press, 2001). For a more detailed discussion of the resource curse and advocacy efforts to confront it, see Macartan Humphreys, Jeffrey D. Sachs, and Joseph E. Stiglitz, *Escaping the Resource Curse* (New York: Columbia University Press, 2007); Paul Collier, *The Bottom Billion: Why the Poorest Countries are Failing and What Can Be Done about It* (Oxford: Oxford University Press, 2008); Mabel van Oranje and Henry Parham, "Publishing What We Learned," 2009, a thoughtful internal review of the Publish What You Pay campaign; and Peter Rosenblum and Susan Maples, *Contracts Confidential: Ending Secret Deals in the Extractives Industry* (New York: Revenue Watch Institute; 2009).

5. Gerard Hanlon, "Rethinking Corporate Social Responsibility and the Role of the Firm," in *The Oxford Handbook of Corporate Social Responsibility*, ed. Andrew Crane, Dirk Matten, Abagail McWilliams, Jeremy Moon, and Donald Siegel (Oxford: Oxford University Press, 2008), 157, 169.

6. For details allowing a comparison of Nike and Levi Strauss, see Karl Schoenberger, *Levi's Children*; Shaw, *Reclaiming America*; Donald Katz, *Just Do It: The Nike Spirit in the Corporate World* (Avon, MA: Adams Media, 1995).

7. Shaw, *Reclaiming America*, 25.

8. Virginia A. Leary, "The WTO and the Social Clause: Post-Singapore," *European Journal of International Law* 8, no. 1 (1997): 118–22.

9. See Locke's discussion of "Capability Training and Its Limitations," in Locke, *Promise and Limits of Private Power*, 78–104.

10. See Keith Bradsher and Charles Duhigg, "Signs of Change Taking Hold in Electronics Factories in China," *New York Times*, December 16, 2012, available at http://www.nytimes.com/2012/12/27/business/signs-of-changes-taking-hold-in-electronics-factories-in-china.html?pagewanted=all.

11. Locke, *Promise and Limits of Private Power*, 163–66.

12. Stephen Greenhouse, "Pressured, Nike to Help Workers in Honduras," *New York Times*, July 26, 2010.

13. See http://www.business-humanrights.org/Categories/Lawlawsuits/Lawsuits regulatoryaction/LawsuitsSelectedcases/adidaslawsuitreuniversityofwisconsin.

14. Worker Rights Consortium, Assessment of PT Kizone (Indonesia): Findings, Recommendations and Status, January 18, 2012.

15. See University of California, Santa Barbara, professor Richard Appelbaum's response to the New York University report on Alliance for Bangladesh Worker Safety, http://business-humanrights.org/media/joint-letter-re-stern-bangladesh-report.pdfl.

16. The focus on Saro Wiwa followed on a campaign led by Greenpeace that focused on sinking a European oil platform.

17. See Simon Handelsman, "Human Rights and the Minerals Industry— Challenges for Geoscientists," lecture, MINE 583—Mining and Society, University of British Columbia, Vancouver, Canada, February 2010, for a summary of issues with Freeport. See also material connected with the largely unsuccessful Alien Tort lawsuit against Freeport at http://www.business-humanrights.org/Categories/Lawlawsuits/Lawsuitsregulatoryaction/LawsuitsSelectedcases/Freeport-McMoRanlawsuitsreWestPapua.

18. The campaign culminated, in the United States, in the first significant Alien Tort case against a corporation. See http://www.business-humanrights.org/Categories/Lawlawsuits/Lawsuitsregulatoryaction/LawsuitsSelectedcases/UnocallawsuitreBurmaformaterialconcerningtheAlienTortlawsuitagainstUnocal.

19. Ibid.

20. http://www.voluntaryprinciples.org/ and http://www.kimberleyprocess.com.

21. For a contemporaneous description, see Peter Rosenblum, "Pipeline Politics in Chad," *Current History* 99, no. 637 (2000): 195–99.

22. Much of the background is described in van Oranje and Parham, "Publishing What We Learned." See also the EITI website at http://eiti.org/eiti/history.

23. See Michael Goldhaber, "Will the US Get Back on the Transparency Train?" *Litigation Daily*, July 16, 2013.

24. In particular, Chevron has been managing a multinational battle to avoid paying a judgment to Ecuador for environmental damage by Texaco and participating in oil industry efforts to block application of Dodd-Frank Section 1504. For a collection of articles by advocates, critically assessing Chevron, see A. Juhasz, M. Anderson, N. Bassey, A. Chicaia, V. Clark, S. E. Cotton, C. Cray, D. Cullen, P. Donowitz, S. Dotlich, D. Herriges, M. Klinman, L. Livoti, M. Langlois, B. Olson, A. Suzara, and J. Tovar, "The True Cost of Chevron: An Alternative Annual Report," 2009, http://truecostofchevron.com/2011-alternative -annual-report.pdf.

25. Jem Bendell, "Barricades and Boardrooms: A Contemporary History of the Corporate Accountability Movement," United Nations Research Institute for Social Development, Paper no. 13, Geneva, 2004, 34.

26. See http://www.voluntaryprinciples.org/for-ngos/ for names of NGO members and http://pactworld.org/partnerships for details about PACT funding.

27. John M. Conley and Cynthia A. Williams, "Engage, Embed, Embellish: Theory versus Practice in the Corporate Social Responsibility Movement," UNC Legal Studies Research Paper no. 05-16, 2005, 25.

28. See Doreen McBarnet, Aurora Voiculescu, and Tom Campbell, eds., *The New Corporate Accountability* (Cambridge: Cambridge University Press, 2007). The object of this 2007 collection is to detail the complicated ways that "voluntary" comes to merit the quote marks in CSR, particularly with regard to the role of law. As McBarnet writes in the introduction, "From the very start, 'voluntary' CSR has been socially and economically driven." In McBarnet, Voiculescu, and Campbell, *The New Corporate Accountability*, 1.

29. Bendell, "Barricades and Boardrooms," 30.

30. Mireidy Fernandez, "Farmworkers Reject $110,000 Check from Yum! Brands," *Naples News*, Friday, June 18, 2004, reproduced at http://www .naplesnews.com/news/2004/jun/18/ndn_farmworkers_reject__110_000_check _from_yum__br/.

31. Jem Bendell writes: "As partnerships and voluntary corporate responsibility morphed from a methodology to an ideology, it became clear that some participants in and commentators on partnerships were using them to pursue a neoliberal political agenda." Bendell, "Barricades and Boardrooms," 33. Richard Locke reviews what he refers to as the "displacement hypothesis," that "private voluntary regulation . . . displaces and undermines more thorough government regulation." See Locke, *Promise and Limits of Private Power*, 156.

32. Doreen McBarnet and Marina Kurkchiyan document an expanding world of supply chain arrangements, in particular, in which CSR standards are contractually required. Doreen McBarnet and Marina Kurkchiyan, "Corporate Social Responsibility through Contractual Control? Global Supply Chains and 'Other Regulation,'" in *The New Corporate Accountability*, eds. Doreen McBarnet, Aurora Voiculescu, and Tom Campbell (Cambridge: Cambridge University Press, 2007), 59–92.

33. Locke, *Promise and Limits of Private Power*, 169–70, attributing the expression to Michael Piore and Andrew Schrank. One of the principal conclusions of his multiyear empirical study of private compliance mechanisms is that law is nearly essential to the success of such mechanisms. Even where NGOs have played a critical role in identifying problems, systemic change depends on their ability to channel their knowledge through the state-sanctioned mechanisms.

34. McBarnet, introduction, in McBarnet, Voiculescu, and Campbell, *New Corporate Accountability*, 31.

35. Ibid.

36. Locke, *Promise and Limits of Private Power*, 169.

37. Locke describes how a "standard naming and shaming" campaign by a Mexican NGO, CEREAL, brought meaningful implementation to legal standards that were otherwise unenforced. Locke, *Promise and Limits of Private Power*, 163–66. Columbia Law School's three-year study of tea plantations controlled by the Tata Group shows how a sophisticated company, together with the IFC, was able to claim the highest levels of CSR without any attention to long-standing gaps in legal compliance. Peter Rosenblum and Ashwini Sukthankar, "'The More Things Change . . .' The World Bank, Tata, and Enduring Abuses on India's Tea Plantations," January 2014, Columbia Law School Human Rights Institute Report. Once the problems were exposed, however, the company and the IFC began to address the problems of legal compliance for the first time. See Nita Bhalla, "World Bank Probes Tata Tea Project over Worker Abuse," *Reuters*, February 14, 2014, available at http://in.reuters.com/article/2014/02/14/india-tata-tea-humanrights-idINDEEA1C0GG20140214, and "Tata Tea to Look into Rights Violation Charge," *Assam Tribune*, April 17, 2014, available at http://www.assamtribune.com/scripts/detailsnew.asp?id=apr1814/at08.

38. Goldhaber, "Will the US Get Back on the Transparency Train?"

39. Hanlon, "Rethinking Corporate Social Responsibility and the Role of the Firm," 157.

40. Ibid.

41. Locke, *Promise and Limits of Private Power*, 174–81.

42. Kevin Campbell and Douglas Vick, "Disclosure Law and the Market for Corporate Social Responsibility," in *The New Corporate Accountability*, ed. Doreen McBarnet, Aurora Voiculescu and Tom Campbell (Cambridge: Cambridge

University Press, 2007), 278. While stating the broad claim, I would not associate the authors with the extreme position. Their arguments about the current state of corporate governance are nuanced and informed.

43. John M. Conley and Cynthia A. Williams discuss CSR in the context of what they call the "new governance." Conley and Williams, "Engage, Embed, Embellish," 31–36. The literature includes, for example, important discussions of multinational corporations as, themselves, norm creators and enforcers, often in a manner more significant than nation-states.

44. Ann K. Buchholtz, Jill A. Brown, and Kareem M. Shabana, "Corporate Governance and Corporate Social Responsibility," in *The Oxford Handbook of Corporate Social Responsibility,* ed. Andrew Crane et al., 328.

45. Katharina Pistor, "On the Plasticity of Corporate Form," *Complexity and Institutions: Markets, Norms, and Corporations* (2012): 177.

46. Conley and Williams, "Engage, Embed, Embellish," 37.

47. Nicholas Kristof and Sheryl WuDunn, "Two Cheers for Sweatshops," *New York Times*, September 24, 2000.

CHAPTER THREE

Assessing Corporate Social Responsibility in the Tobacco Industry

Peter Benson

In the invitation to participate in this edited volume, contributors were encouraged to consider the ethics of corporate social responsibility (CSR) and the effects of new business practices on human rights and local worlds without devolving into a spirit of condemnation—invited, in other words, to go beyond questions of good and evil. The nineteenth-century German philosopher Friedrich Nietzsche is a surprising starting point for inquiring about CSR. In his late works, *Beyond Good and Evil* (1886) and *On the Genealogy of Morals* (1887), Nietzsche repudiated traditions of philosophy, religion, and science for naturalizing doctrines of sin, principles of reason, and laws of nature. While he is often misinterpreted as saying anything goes, the call to go "beyond good and evil" is about assessing ethics in light of the contingencies and vagaries of actual existence. Human action must be diagnosed from the perspective of life—not good and evil as pregiven Platonic forms, but rather questions of how particular interests shape the very notions of what is good and what is evil. For Nietzsche, the issue of morality is a matter of historical and sociological interpretation. This hermeneutical approach focuses on what the French philosopher Gilles Deleuze, in his reading of Nietzsche's work, calls "forces."[1] A symptomatology of how power works, this approach examines how particular actors and institutions construct, appropriate, dominate, and exploit meanings and values associated with morality in relation to the production of a social ordering and a regime of truth.

A whole trajectory of ideas—what Paul Ricoeur calls the "hermeneutics of suspicion"[2]—derives from this cynical view of morality as a sordid politics of public relations. Think of Freud's critical take on virtue, bourgeois culture, and the unconscious, the existentialist concepts of bad faith and authenticity, Foucault on the politics of freedom and hypocritical institutions, and the Marxist literature on ideology and hegemony. There is a common concern with the tendency of forces to don masks, say one thing and do another, and reference truth and morality to tame critique and conflict. This lineage, the hermeneutics of suspicion, shapes how I think about CSR. I am suspicious of the timing of the whole thing; the very corporations that benefit from harmfulness now claim to advance a new business ethics aligned for the common good. Not a matter of good or evil, my interest in assessing CSR reflects a concern with strategies, motivations, and effects. Admittedly, my skepticism of CSR derives from the fact that I study a most harmful industry, tobacco, where questions of "evil" loom indeed.

Tobacco has been a visible part of daily life in large parts of the world for hundreds of years. Profound changes in tobacco's prevalence and effects occurred in the twentieth century. The modern commercial cigarette and multinational tobacco corporations proliferated.[3] Smoking is now the single greatest cause of preventable disease and death worldwide. In the last century, there were one hundred million tobacco-related deaths. Although smoking declined and tobacco-control measures took hold in several countries, it is now widely recognized that the unabated global demand for cigarettes will kill one billion people in the current century.[4] The majority of these deaths will be in developing countries, where the industry continues to infuse smoking with positive social meanings, recruit adolescent smokers, maintain free-market environments for harmful products, and leverage political influence to limit public health efforts, including implementation of the international Framework Convention on Tobacco Control of the World Health Organization.[5]

Tobacco companies now claim to work with and for the public health and in the promotion of human well-being. They developed CSR platforms and talk the talk. Although some might argue that this transformation indicates evilness, my aim is to analyze the industry beyond the personification of force as having some essential moral character. It is precisely this mythical vision of the corporation as a person that helps to constitute the force of CSR as a timely business strategy and an effective means for corporations to position themselves as moral actors. My concern is with how corporations respond to critique or increased public awareness about the environmental and health problems related to their business. In tracking a dialectics of corporate response, I explore some of the economic and ethical paradoxes that define Big Tobacco's stated commitment to "social responsibility."

The Dialectics of Corporate Response

Regarding smoking as gravely threatening to the nation would have been a plausible response to the scientific evidence about smoking and health in the last half century. But this is not what happened. Tobacco's legitimacy and legality were not initially questioned, even though tobacco killed more Americans in the last century than the country's combined military operations. The federal government was not going to take bold action with tobacco products ubiquitous throughout the culture. In contrast to the temperance movement's somewhat religious focus, postwar regulatory approaches were more secular. The emphasis on sin and moral ruination shifted to a concern with a scientific understanding of health in terms of epidemiological risk factors.[6] The landmark Surgeon General's Report of 1964 did not lead to a call for prohibition or even the wholesale restructuring and regulation of the tobacco industry. The report led to new government interventions designed to enhance public awareness of risk and improve individual decisions, mainly by mandating warning labels on cigarette packs and beginning to regulate tobacco advertisements. The project of eliminating tobacco from society, an approach characteristic of the prohibition movement, was replaced by a biopolitics linking accumulated knowledge about smoking to the development of techniques for managing risk at the population level and promoting behavior management and modification at the individual level. While prevention has been part of the official public health response to the epidemiological transition, characterized by an increased chronic disease burden and disease problems linked to consumption and lifestyle issues, the dominant approach has favored health promotion over prevention, making consumers the locus of intervention (as in the case of warning labels) and upholding distinctive American beliefs in individual autonomy and responsibility and the cultural framing of freedom in terms of the marketplace.[7]

Tobacco companies never simply responded to a problem that existed apart from their involvement in shaping the terms of debate. The tobacco problem was constructed out of the back and forth between the intensified criticism of the industry in the last half century and the responses and justifications the industry provided. In the 1960s and 1970s, the tobacco industry and the federal government worked collaboratively to develop potentially reduced-risk tobacco products. The US Department of Agriculture funded studies in search of less toxic tobacco leaf varieties. The American Cancer Society and the American Heart Association pushed for the removal of "high-tar" cigarettes from the market. Leading public health officials formed the Less Hazardous Cigarette Working Group (later renamed the Tobacco Working Group to appease the industry) and contracted with scientific laboratories and industry scientists to develop less risky products. Meanwhile, the federal Public Health Service cautioned that the promotion of supposedly reduced-risk products "might lull the consumer into believing that he could smoke this kind of cigarette without *any* accompanying risk."[8] The relationship of government and industry is not so starkly posed if one considers the institutional complicities that influenced how tobacco was reckoned a problem and that drove responses that were frankly nonchalant given the public health impact. The tobacco industry is illustrative of how corporations and industries effectively engage with governments, criticism, and public awareness about harms to sustain marketability, manage the scope of regulation, and maintain legitimacy.

The proliferation of doubt as a key strategy was pioneered by the tobacco industry and has since become standard practice across a range of industries.[9] Beginning in the 1950s, the tobacco industry sponsored its own scientific studies and funded nongovernmental organizations, most infamously the Tobacco Institute, to disseminate favorable reports presented as though they were the product of neutral scientific research. Clear knowledge of the dangers of smoking was sequestered. As recently as the 1990s, the tobacco industry continued to deny that there is a direct causal link between smoking and disease and that nicotine is a powerfully addictive drug. The industry has also used marketing campaigns to discourage smokers from being concerned about health issues, most notably in Philip Morris's Marlboro Man campaign, which linked smoking to images of individual autonomy and defiance about risk and government.[10]

In the process of raising doubts about the relationship between smoking and disease, the tobacco industry used marketing to address specific concerns about risk and harm. During the 1950s and 1960s, the industry introduced a series of products, such as filtered cigarettes, that were purported to be safer than conventional cigarettes. These new products were marketed as a form of what one company called "health protection,"[11] implicitly acknowledging that tobacco products were causing harm. Subsequent advertising used misleading product descriptors like "light" or "low-tar" to allay consumer anxieties.[12] However, it was well known within the industry that these new products provided a false sense of security. Aggressive marketing perpetuated dependence on tobacco as smokers switched to the new products en masse in the mistaken belief that they were less risky.[13]

In the late 1980s and 1990s, the threat of litigation against the tobacco industry in the United States intensified. These lawsuits are an example of a tipping point, when the problems an industry faces become potentially unmanageable, raising questions about its continued existence.[14] It became clear that the cost of defending themselves against simultaneous class-action lawsuits in multiple municipalities would cripple tobacco companies. Industry consultants began to speak of a "litigation time bomb." Institutions such as universities divested from tobacco stock. Public image and legal liability were impacting the market value of tobacco companies, while tobacco control was gaining as a movement with several strong national organizations, a widespread network of public health activists and researchers, and an approach that now included more forceful strategies of litigation, excise taxes on cigarettes, clean air ordinances, and other public health regulations.[15] These factors combined to push the industry into a phase in which denial is no longer a feasible response to criticism and in which the adoption of a CSR campaign is a strategic means of counterbalancing critical and regulatory impulses.

Project Sunrise

In the late 1980s, Philip Morris considered quitting the cigarette business because mounting legal pressures threatened the company's food and beverage subsidiaries. Certain executives wanted to gradually move away from tobacco by focusing on immediate profits from cigarette sales rather than long-term growth or strategic political engagement. They believed that this "controlled retreat" would probably accelerate "into an abrupt end" and suggested that "fighting back" was not preferential since a large proportion of the corporation's revenues came from the other businesses. "I think we all believe that our future lies outside tobacco," an executive said in the late 1980s, "I certainly believe this."[16]

After analyzing public opinion data, inspecting lessons from historical cases of industry collapse, and holding numerous executive planning sessions, the company's management decided to redefine the company's public image and create a legal shelter by incorporating its tobacco businesses as separate entities.[17] Focus groups showed corporate officials that standard concepts like size and power, which work well inside the company, are not as appealing to tobacco consumers or the general public as concepts like trustworthiness and caring about consumer health. They also showed that notions of community commitment and providing choice worked particularly well, boosting company likability by 30 percentage points.[18]

The resulting campaign, called "Project Sunrise," also known as "PM21," meaning "Philip Morris in the 21st Century," was launched in 1995. Most of what the public has seen involves positive images of social responsibility and the corporation's investments in certain public health issues like youth smoking prevention. But archived company documents—openly available to researchers and the public as a result of court rulings against the tobacco industry—make it clear that management's goal all along was to "ensure the social acceptability of smoking."[19]

Since the 1990s, Philip Morris has invested $1 billion in an internal Youth Smoking Prevention department, which creates communications and resources aimed at encouraging parents to "talk to their kids about not using tobacco products," as the company's website states. The department provides schools and youth organizations with grants to support the development of "healthy lifestyles" and funds programs to inform tobacco product retailers about smoking laws.[20] This selective public health focus is strategic. Internal company documents reveal that Philip Morris executives have long believed that philanthropic engagement with youth health issues is an especially effective way of demonstrating that the company "is acting reasonably and responsibly," one memo states, while shaping the public debate about health behaviors to focus on parents and kids rather than industry. In one memo from the early 1990s, corporate officials strategized about how to tilt the balance of "youth smoking versus prohibition" trends in public health.[21] They sought to reconfigure the smoking problem as a problem of law enforcement related to age limits and youth access. The narrowing of tobacco governance to focus on adult choice, law enforcement, and family matters are choreographed effects of what appear on the surface to be noble investments in public health on the part of a responsible corporate citizen.

The $100 million television campaign launched by the Youth Smoking Prevention department in the early 2000s, called "Think. Don't smoke," is the largest antitobacco campaign ever undertaken by the industry. Apart from the fact that youth education programs are a less impactful means of controlling tobacco use than regulatory measures, public health research finds that effective youth smoking prevention programs must include comprehensive information about smoking disease and the nature of addiction, and also critical anti-industry perspectives that discuss how tobacco companies market products to underage populations and prey upon young people in order to turn a profit.[22] Not surprisingly, Philip Morris steers clear of these issues and favors an emphasis on parenthood. Sociological studies of how viewers respond find that regular viewers of this campaign believe that tobacco companies are "more responsible" socially than in the past and are not culpable for smoking harms.[23]

While Philip Morris openly claims to support efforts to reduce the youth smoking rate, this claim about responsibility arises in tandem with corporate activities that seem ethically ambiguous and interested in expanding the cigarette market. Philip Morris has since the 1980s systematically sought to undermine smoke-free legislation around the world by paying scientists and consultants who are usually affiliated with academic institutions and who conduct research on secondhand smoke to attend international symposia without acknowledging their corporate sponsorship. These researchers and consultants are hired to disseminate "accurate" (proindustry) information concerning smoking regulation in public places, with the goal of influencing policy makers, media, and the public.[24] Along with this opposition to public smoking bans, Philip Morris vigorously opposes the other truly effective means of reducing smoking prevalence: taxation. It opposes public health measures—smoke-free environment laws and excise taxes on tobacco products—that have been proved time and again to reduce the size of the smoking population. Meanwhile, the philanthropic focus on youth smoking is only one part of PM21. We also learn from internal company documents that as part of this campaign, Philip Morris actively conducts social research on smoking and smokers with the aim of tailoring products and programs to promote social acceptability and reinforce smoking rituals. The multi-sided PM21 campaign also involves what Philip Morris calls the "accommodation" strategy—namely, efforts to assure that smoking remains permitted in public places. Here the company invests in cigarette butt litter reduction programs; research to promote the use of ventilation systems in restaurants, bars, and other public places as an alternative to smoking bans; and the design of cigarettes said to be less toxic or to emit less secondhand smoke.[25]

Philip Morris has also been involved in amassing a database on the composition and objectives of different tobacco-control groups, as well as their relationships to one another and to funding sources. According to internal documents, company executives have believed that this "competitive intelligence" would improve the company's ability to respond in "proactive" and "offensive" ways to the tobacco-control movement. The identification of more "moderate" groups would facilitate efforts to "disrupt" the movement's "cohesion," executives stated. From the beginning this database of information was imagined as a political resource for shaping public health intervention and regulation, forging partnerships with groups deemed moderate, and casting other tobacco-control perspectives as, in the words of the internal memos, "extreme" and "prohibitionist." Through this kind of engagement, the memos disclose, managers aimed to reposition Philip Morris as "reasonable," acknowledging some element of risk or harm while claiming to work with the public health to "expand the debate over tolerance for lifestyle choices and freedoms." The company determined through focus groups that this message is effective with younger generations and taps into a larger "pro-choice/tolerance" ethos in the culture.[26]

FDA Legislation

As another part of its makeover into a "responsible corporate citizen,"[27] Philip Morris aligned itself with the leading public health groups (for example, National Campaign for Tobacco-Free Kids, American Lung Association, American Heart Association, and American Cancer Society) in the United States in supporting sweeping tobacco-control measures—namely, legislation granting the Food and Drug Administration (FDA) authority to regulate cigarettes and other tobacco products. Passed in 2009, a landmark bill, the Family Smoking Prevention and Tobacco Control Act ("Tobacco Control Act"), empowered the FDA to ban the sale of any tobacco product not approved by the agency and to curtail tobacco marketing in important ways. The positive trade-offs for Philip Morris, which supported the legislation, is that it may limit corporate liability from legal claims and forbid the FDA from banning tobacco sales to adults or requiring that nicotine levels be reduced to zero. The bill's language may also make it difficult for the FDA to substantially reduce nicotine levels at all.[28] As critics of the Tobacco Control Act have inveighed, these legislative provisions effectively ensure an adult's "right" to smoke addictive cigarettes.[29]

One of the most important critiques of the Tobacco Control Act concerns harm reduction. Interestingly, the FDA had already been regulating nicotine since the mid-1980s, when nicotine gum and other medicinal therapies were approved as short-term treatments for nicotine dependence. FDA approval of such products for over-the-counter sale in 1996 signaled a shift in the medical meaning of nicotine dependence. The first clinical-care guidelines were developed that same year and classified nicotine dependence and withdrawal as disorders and included the use of medicinal nicotine as recommended treatment. The clinical and personal use of medicinal nicotine products as a harm reduction or smoking cessation strategy[30] has been taken by the tobacco industry as an opportunity to extend safe cigarette myths. Whereas medicinal devices deliver controlled levels of nicotine, tobacco companies have introduced a spate of new tobacco products, such as smokeless cigarettes, that claim to reduce harm for consumers who do not want to or cannot quit. Medicinal nicotine products can potentially benefit large numbers of smokers. But harm reduction remains a controversial concept in public health and medical communities because "the tobacco industry would like the public health tobacco control movement to adopt a harm reduction strategy so that the industry could use it to promote its alternate nicotine delivery systems that include tobacco."[31] In fact, there have been very few verified or replicated scientific data about the new tobacco products.[32]

While the Tobacco Control Act grants federal regulators new powers to control the tobacco industry's pattern of deceptive marketing, it
remains unclear exactly how the agency will regulate harm reduction
claims for modified tobacco products. Public health critics worry that tobacco companies will be able to legitimately market products that make
assertions about reduced toxicity, even though such products may not reduce health risks.[33] As Philip Morris recently commented, the bill will
"create a framework for the pursuit of tobacco products that are less
harmful than conventional cigarettes."[34] It is possible that tobacco companies will be able to continue to treat risk as a selling point by promoting improved product design, using anxiety about health risks to enhance the marketability of their products and increase their share of the
nicotine dependence market.

One of the ways in which the tobacco industry continues to legitimize its operation is by promoting an ideology of individual risk assumption that dovetails with a broader acceptance of consumer choice. The
idea that consumers choose to smoke permits an industry that causes extensive harm to continue to operate as long as it is regulated. However,
FDA regulation does nothing to address the worldwide smoking epidemic, and by reducing the serious threat of litigation against the industry at home, it may actually help sustain the international market.[35] In
effect, Philip Morris has been pursuing a strategic trade-off, accepting
domestic regulations in order to limit liability and ensure the company's
long-term profitability and survival. These paradoxes are not news to the
public health community. The Tobacco Control Act can be seen largely
as a case of pragmatic resignation; antitobacco groups were willing to
broker the best deal possible, given the tacit acceptance of tobacco's legality, an outcome of decades of industry influence in the culture.[36]

The Global View

In 2005, the World Health Organization (WHO) established the Framework Convention on Tobacco Control (FCTC), the organization's first
multilateral treaty. This framework encourages individual nations to
adopt a set of universal recommendations: to impose significant excise
taxes on tobacco products, restrict access for adolescents and educate
them about health behavior, strongly regulate tobacco advertising; in-

centivize alternative livelihoods for tobacco growers, prohibit smoking in public places, and pursue litigation against tobacco companies.[37]

When the WHO adopted this treaty, Philip Morris talked the talk. "What we hope and expect is that this treaty can be a catalyst in every country that signs on for meaningful and effective treatment of tobacco," a Philip Morris lawyer said.[38] But as the treaty was being developed in Geneva, Philip Morris portrayed it as paternalistic. "A clumsy pursuit of global standards can become a form of moral and cultural imperialism, based on assumptions that 'west is best,'" a spokesperson from the firm said. "Imposing western priorities, or 'global solutions' that force the values and priorities of any one country on another, can become a new form of colonialism." The company said that its opposition is based on a "respect for cultural diversity."[39] In spite of claims about respect and autonomy, throughout the process in which the FCTC was being developed, Philip Morris pressured the US government to limit the treaty's scope and strength, asking for US officials to demand that key recommendations, especially the recommendation to tax cigarettes and to prohibit public smoking, be left out.[40]

Part of the reason why Philip Morris in practice sought to weaken the FCTC is that the globalization of the tobacco-control movement—the framework convention being evidence of a new degree of international collaboration and of a powerful antitobacco consensus—poses a threat to its business. As the tobacco-control movement becomes more and more globalized, multinational tobacco companies face new kinds of public scrutiny and regulatory pressures that are related to tobacco production in poor countries. Tobacco companies, concerned with economic performance, often negotiate such low prices that production requires child labor and debt servitude, while the tobacco production process involves heavy chemical use, water depletion, and deforestation.[41]

The FCTC, namely Article 17, addresses policies of crop diversification and alternative livelihoods for growers and workers and calls for governments to provide "support for economically viable alternative activities for farmworkers and growers," while Article 18 calls for environmental health and safety protection with respect to tobacco cultivation.[42] The WHO acknowledges that a holistic framework is required to address all aspects of tobacco and health, including the economic dependence of farming and manufacturing communities and social and health problems related to tobacco work. The WHO's position builds on several years of engagement of global tobacco-control advocates with grower and farmworker issues. The most promising collaborations so far have been seen in emerging alliances in developing countries, such as collaborations between public health groups and trade unionists in Malawi that demand tobacco worker rights.[43] Public health groups have also been involved in addressing the problems of child labor, deforestation, agrochemical exposure, and debt servitude by building on research by anthropologists and other social scientists in South America, South Asia, and southern Africa, where tobacco farming is an important contributor to poverty. The creation of the Human Rights and Tobacco Control Network in 2008 is another example of the integration of global health groups and tobacco grower and worker issues. It pulls together disparate advocates and groups that have been working to improve the rights of farmworkers and growers while simultaneously promoting tobacco control.

Recent anthropological studies by Marty Otañez and Stanton Glantz critically examine the CSR initiatives of Philip Morris and, another of the world's leading tobacco manufacturers, British American Tobacco. The strategic creation of international supply chains in the 1990s by these companies allowed them to improve production, procure tobacco leaf more efficiently, and control access to markets and profits. These supply chains have since been adapted and "greened" by integrating environmental and labor considerations to serve CSR campaigns "in an effort," Otañez and Glantz write, "to legitimize portrayals of tobacco farming as socially and environmentally friendly, while keeping actual practices essentially unchanged."[44]

Looking at tobacco industry documents, Otañez and Glantz show how in 2000 Philip Morris hired a consulting firm, Business for Social Responsibility, to study its CSR reputation from the perspective of environmental groups, among other stakeholders, and identify external partners. The conclusion that environmental groups respect companies that put a high value on supply chain management was integrated into Philip Morris's CSR approach. Philip Morris's chairman stated that the company's "goal is to redefine the role of a corporation in American society. . . . To deal with our product issues and figure out how to deliver social value on a large scale." Subsequently, the company used external social reports to disseminate information on reductions in environmental emissions and child labor and improvements in worker safety.[45]

Multinational tobacco companies attempt to present themselves on the world stage as socially and environmentally responsible in various ways. British American Tobacco created the Eliminate Child Labor in Tobacco (ECLT) foundation in 2000 in response to criticism of its child labor practices in Malawi and elsewhere, and Philip Morris joined ECLT shortly thereafter. The group's mission statement claims it is guided by "a new understanding that tobacco production is not just about products and the marketing, but also about corporate citizenship and about the whole value chain." The foundation invests in programs in primary education, in vaccination and screening programs, and in sewage and water in southern African countries. It insists that the main way to prevent child labor is increasing access to education and vaccination coverage in poor countries. In some publications it indirectly blames the HIV epidemic in those countries for the problem of child labor. It also invests in microcredit loans to tobacco growers to help them mechanize, become more efficient, and grow their businesses as a means of alleviating child labor, a dynamic that makes tobacco growers deeply dependent on the tobacco industry for basic livelihood and infrastructural and health care needs. While the tobacco industry has now been involved in these CSR campaigns in southern Africa for about a decade, anthropological reporting in recent years reveals that tobacco growing in the region is still characterized by child labor, debt servitude of tobacco farmers due to high debts to tobacco companies, and powerful downward pressure on prices.[46]

To further foment loyalties and dependencies and expand political influence in poor countries, tobacco companies are helping to train cohorts of future ministries of agriculture by funding agronomy programs at major universities around the world and establishing and funding a variety of nongovernmental organizations in southern Africa and in Asia to focus on reforestation projects in ways that do not challenge or displace tobacco agriculture but serve its needs. Nearly all of the reforestation projects introduce nonnative trees that grow more rapidly than native trees, and the quantification of the number of trees replanted as a claim to civic virtue embeds the hidden economic calculus of optimizing leaf curing and economies of scale in reforested areas. These industry-funded projects make it more difficult for public health advocates and officials to argue for crop diversification and alternative livelihoods for tobacco farmers. Meanwhile, national and local officials have become reluctant to criticize the tobacco industry out of fear of disrupting the cash flow and external funding for economic and environmental projects.[47]

Conclusions

On July 8, 2012, amid yet another heat wave sweeping the United States, the weekly news talk program *Up with Chris Hayes* aired a segment focusing on the role of the oil and gas industry in climate change and the obstruction of more sustainable, cleaner energy systems. The host, Chris Hayes, drew a parallel with the tobacco industry.

> There has been a well-documented, highly resourced, concerted effort, often funded by the fossil fuel industry, that has with evil determination sought to sow doubt among Americans about the basic scientific consensus that our carbon emissions are warming the planet. It's reminiscent of a decade-long battle the tobacco industry waged to discredit the robust and sustained medical evidence that smoking causes cancer and kills tens of thousands of people every year.

The parallels are indeed striking. Because many industries are implicated in global health crises and significant environmental problems, corporations employ elaborate, expensive, multinational campaigns for evoke CSR principles. Big fossil fuel companies like Chevron and BP claim that through research and development they play an effective role in helping to resolve the climate crisis. Walmart now makes public claims about its efforts to maintain consistently low prices while improving the nutritional quality of its food products by pressuring its suppliers to reduce levels of fat, sodium, and sweeteners. This shift arose in direct response to public health research that shows that Walmart's food sales alone account for 10 percent of the increase in obesity prevalence in the United States.[48] Looking at Pepsi and Coca-Cola, a recent article from the public health literature shows how the soda beverage industry is also adopting CSR campaigns to promote through philanthropy healthy lifestyles and decisions.[49] As in the case of Philip Morris, a focus on educating consumers and improving lifestyles is perhaps comfortable for corporations because it meshes with a wider neoliberal ethos that emphasizes rational choice and individuality.

Returning to the conceptual issues with which I opened this chapter, CSR campaigns are in this analysis the strategic means by which certain corporations facing criticism and regulatory pressures construct a public morality, defining the terms and limits of good and bad, defining themselves as responsible actors, and localizing responsibility for health outcomes on individual consumers. In the wider culture, obesity, like smoking, is reckoned a private issue, addressed as a feat of individual overcoming on the television show *The Biggest Loser*, tapped as a market opportunity by the massive dieting industry, and ultimately construed publicly as a personal flaw, not the result of industrial calculation— sweetness and power. Quitting smoking and dieting and losing weight are truly difficult feats, in many cases impossible, but tobacco dependence and obesity are made to seem like states that individuals choose to inhabit. These states are publicly framed as problems of health promotion and behavior rather than the results of a certain kind of capitalism, a political economy of massively profitable industries, their public relations campaigns, and claims about social performance.

When it comes to the handling of the growing burden of chronic diseases, business plans and marketing strategies across various industries are developed in light of public health concerns and take advantage of a dominant governmental approach that emphasizes corporate and consumer agency rather than industry regulation. Warning labels, instructions for use, and ingredient disclosures are legal apparatuses that safeguard corporations from liabilities related to consumption and underwrite individual risk assumption, while corporations are strengthened through their development of and participation in markets in civic virtue. Corporations redefine their own value as actors and the value of their products in the process of molding the scope of an emergent problem or responding to critique. "The meaning or sense of something is its relation or affinity to the possessing force," Deleuze writes, "and the value of something is the hierarchy of forces which are expressed in the thing as a complex phenomenon."[50] CSR is usefully thought about in these terms. CSR is a complex phenomenon, a set of talking points, organizing concepts, and practical activities, appropriated and used by corporate actors in order to manage a location within a global hierarchy of value. It is a means of eschewing labels of evilness and attributing to the corporation a kind of personality that is good, not bad, productive, not destructive, responsible, not rampant, socially concerned, not committed to basic motives.

The corporate adoption of CSR indicates publicly a stark contrast between the past and the present, evil and good. Through public relations, philanthropic activities, and other indexes of CSR values corporations seek distance from the "evil determination" of the past, as Chris Hayes describes the tobacco industry's history of malfeasance and wrongdoing. But in common across time is a predictable tendency to act in ways that are strategic, tactical, and interested—which is, of course, not surprising given the corporate profit motive. CSR represents not a new phase of corporate capitalism as much as an unprecedented level of corporate engagement with the regulatory agencies and public debates that impact their business functions and bottom lines. Although the tobacco industry is remarkable in its capacity for causing harm, it is not an "evil" outlier or exception; it reveals fundamental dynamics of corporate power. However well intentioned corporate actors may be, their CSR agendas are beholden to the fiduciary responsibility to shareholders, which often entails continuously legitimizing and expanding harmful industrial processes. This structural feature of capitalism can confound business ethics and encourages an understanding of capitalism in historical and practical terms as a field of strategy and rhetoric in which meanings of responsibility are constructed as much as invoked, a Nietzschean world of language games and charitable giving.

Anthropology and history, involving research on how industries influence the culture, rightly belong on the list of essential resources in international tobacco control and the understanding of business ethics. Field reporting in the underbellies of industries exposes health and social problems for which industries like tobacco can be held accountable. Claims about social performance can be scrutinized in light of the backstage intentions of corporations revealed in internal documents and anthropological research with key stakeholders that are part of industries or are impacted by them. There are likely to be discrepancies between what companies say and what their activities actually do to populations and environments. Not only is such research helpful for understanding how the politics of health and civic virtue shapes capitalism, it also reveals the underappreciated role of corporations in shaping what the ethics and politics of life mean, how significant health and social problems are strategically structured and governed, how supply chains that bring harm to humans and environments are maintained even in the face of substantial criticism, and how corporations influence the public meanings of good and evil.

Notes

1. Gilles Deleuze, *Nietzsche and Philosophy* (New York: Columbia University Press, 1983).

2. Paul Ricoeur, *Freud and Philosophy: An Essay on Interpretation* (New Haven, CT: Yale University Press, 1970).

3. Allan Brandt, *The Cigarette Century: The Rise, Fall, and Deadly Persistence of the Product That Defined America* (New York: Basic Books, 2007).

4. Robert N. Proctor, "Tobacco and the Global Lung Cancer Epidemic," *Nature Reviews Cancer* 1, no. 1 (2001): 82–86.

5. World Health Organization, *WHO Report on the Global Tobacco Epidemic, 2008: The MPOWER Package* (Geneva: World Health Organization, 2008).

6. Allan Brandt, "The Cigarette, Risk, and American Culture," *Daedalus* 119 (1990): 155–76.

7. Brandt, *Cigarette Century*, 442–45.

8. Amy Fairchild and James Colgrove, "Out of the Ashes: The Life, Death, and Rebirth of the 'Safer' Cigarette in the United States," *American Journal of Public Health* 94, no. 2 (2004): 192–204, 193–95.

9. Brandt, *Cigarette Century*; Robert N. Proctor, *Golden Holocaust: Origins of the Cigarette Catastrophe and the Case for Abolition* (Berkeley: University of California Press, 2012).

10. Brandt, *Cigarette Century*, 263–64.

11. Ibid., 244.

12. R. W. Pollay and T. Dewhirst, "The Dark Side of Marketing Seemingly 'Light' Cigarettes: Successful Images and Failed Fact," *Tobacco Control* 11 (2002): 18–31.

13. Fairchild and Colgrove, *Out of the Ashes*.

14. Peter Benson and Stuart Kirsch, "Capitalism and the Politics of Resignation," *Current Anthropology* 51, no. 4 (2010): 459–86.

15. Elizabeth A. Smith and Ruth E. Malone, "Thinking the 'Unthinkable': Why Philip Morris Considered Quitting," *Tobacco Control* 12 (2003): 208; Patricia A. McDaniel, Elizabeth A. Smith, and Ruth E. Malone, "Philip Morris's Project Sunrise: Weakening Tobacco Control by Working with It," *Tobacco Control* 15 (2006): 216.

16. Smith and Malone, "Thinking the 'Unthinkable.'"

17. Elizabeth A. Smith and Ruth E. Malone, "Altria Means Tobacco: Philip Morris's Identity Crisis," *American Journal of Public Health* 93, no. 4 (2003): 553–56; Smith and Malone, "Thinking the 'Unthinkable.'"

18. Smith and Malone, "Thinking the 'Unthinkable,'" 210.

19. McDaniel, Smith, and Malone, "Philip Morris's Project Sunrise," 215.

20. Philip Morris USA, Helping Reduce Underage Tobacco Use, http://www

.philipmorrisusa.com/en/cms/Responsibility/Helping_Nav/Helping_Reduce _Underage_Tobacco_Use/default.aspx?src=top_nav, 2010.

21. McDaniel, Smith, and Malone, "Philip Morris's Project Sunrise," 217.

22. J. F. Thrasher, J. Niederdeppe, M. C. Farrelly, K. C. Davis, K. M. Ribisl, and M. L. Haviland, "The Impact of Anti-Tobacco Industry Prevention Messages in Tobacco Producing Regions: Evidence from the US Truth Campaign," *Tobacco Control* 13 (2004): 283.

23. Glen Szczypka, Melanie A. Wakefield, Sherry Emery, Yvonne M. Terry-McElrath, Brian R. Flay, and Frank J. Chaloupka, "Working to Make an Image: An Analysis of Three Philip Morris Corporate Media Campaigns," *Tobacco Control* 16 (2007): 344–50; Lissy S. Friedman, "Philip Morris's Website and Television Commercials Use New Language to Mislead the Public into Believing It Has Changed Its Stance on Smoking and Disease," *Tobacco Control* 16, no. 6 (2007): e9.

24. Joaquin Barnoya and Stanton A. Glantz, "The Tobacco Industry's Worldwide ETS Consultants Project: European and Asian Components," *European Journal of Public Health* 16, no. 1 (2006): 69–77.

25. McDaniel, Smith, and Malone, "Philip Morris's Project Sunrise," 215–16.

26. Ibid., 217–18.

27. Brandt, *Cigarette Century*, 444.

28. Michael Siegel, "Food and Drug Administration Regulation of Tobacco: Snatching Defeat from the Jaws of Victory," *Tobacco Control* 13 (2004): 440.

29. Patricia A. McDaniel and Ruth E. Malone, "Understanding Philip Morris's Pursuit of U.S. Government Regulation of Tobacco," *Tobacco Control* 14 (2005): 193–200; Michael Givel, "FDA Legislation," *Tobacco Control* 16 (2007): 217–18.

30. Dorothy K. Hatsukami, Jack E. Henningfield, and Michael Kotlyar, "Harm Reduction Approaches to Reducing Tobacco-Related Mortality," *Annual Review of Public Health* 25 (2004): 377–95.

31. John P. Pierce, "Harm Reduction or Harm Maintenance?" *Nicotine and Tobacco Research* (supplement) (2002): S53.

32. Saul Shiffman, Joe G. Gitchell, Kenneth E. Warner, John Slade, Jack E. Henningfield, and John M. Pinney, "Tobacco Harm Reduction: Conceptual Structure and Nomenclature for Analysis and Research," *Nicotine and Tobacco Research* 4, supplement 2 (2002): S121–22.

33. Givel, "FDA Legislation."

34. Brian Montopoli, "Tobacco Bill's Big Winner: Philip Morris?" *CBS News*, June 11, 2009.

35. Givel, "FDA Legislation"; Siegel, "Food and Drug Administration Regulation of Tobacco."

36. *Wall Street Journal*, "Washington's Marlboro Men: Congress Loves Big Tobacco Enough to Regulate It," June 13, 2009.

37. World Health Organizations, Framework Convention, World Health Organization website, http://www.who.int/fctc/en, 2009.

38. Brandt, *Cigarette Century*, 482.

39. Ibid., 484.

40. Ibid.

41. Marty Otañez and Stanton A. Glantz, "Social Responsibility in Tobacco Production? Tobacco Companies' Use of Green Supply Chains to Obscure the Real Costs of Tobacco Farming," *Tobacco Control* 20 (2011): 403–11.

42. World Health Organizations, Framework Convention.

43. Marty G. Otañez, Hadii Mamudu, and Stanton A. Glantz, "Global Leaf Companies Control the Tobacco Market in Malawi," *Tobacco Control* 16 (2007): 261–69.

44. Otañez and Glantz, "Social Responsibility in Tobacco Production?"

45. Ibid.

46. Ibid.

47. Ibid.

48. Charles Courtemanche and Art Carden, "Supersizing Supercenters? The Impact of Wal-Mart Supercenters on Body Mass Index and Obesity," *Journal of Urban Economics* 69, no. 2 (2011): 165–81.

49. Lori Dorfman, Andrew Cheyne, Lissy C. Friedman, Asiya Wadud, and Mark Gottlieb, "Soda and Tobacco Industry Corporate Social Responsibility Campaigns: How Do They Compare?" *PLoS Medicine* 9, no. 6 (2012): e1001241.

50. Deleuze, *Nietzsche and Philosophy*, 8.

CHAPTER FOUR

Transparency, Auditability, and the Contradictions of CSR

Anna Zalik

In her recent 2009 book on competitive strategy in business, Mia de Kuijper, global business consultant, dean of the Duisenberg School of Finance in Amsterdam, and former Royal Dutch Shell executive, identifies what she calls a new "star driver" shaping the global economy: the rapid and unstoppable decrease in the cost of information, also known as the "vanishing cost of information." This she calls *transparency*—"a state in which the cost of information is approaching zero or, equivalently, in which cheap connectivity is so abundant and easy, one might consider it infinite."[1] From the perspective of critical geography, the concept of "transparency" is illusory.[2] On this point de Kuijper's own caveat, immediately following, is suggestive:

> My use of the word transparency is meant to emphasize the fact that information will travel instantly and without obstruction, equally clear and perceptible to everyone. I am not describing the sort of transparency that is demanded when critics insist that windows into business or government operations be held open in order to enforce accountability.[3]

One might ask why the term *transparency* is used so prominently here, and this disclaimer made so forthrightly, given that public understanding of the term clearly corresponds to the second sentence. Indeed, key international bodies claiming to promote regulation of the oil and gas industry, an industry with which de Kuijper is closely associated, use the term prominently. International organizations embracing the concept—Transparency International and the Extractive Industries Transparency Initiative—employ the term in the form that she does not.[4] Why, arguably, does she use the term *transparency* at all? Perhaps because the decreasing cost of information is important to firm strategy, and because she is also interested in what she describes as "interdependent decision making," which is to occur, according to the model, even under a context of vicious competition. That is, the nature of competition between firms will change due to this improved access to information. It would seem, however, that while there is immediate availability and connection to such information, so-called accessibility is still largely confined to competing firms, not to society as a whole. Perhaps, also, and as will be discussed below, the second use of the term—the "sort of transparency that is demanded when critics insist that windows into business or government operations be held open in order to enforce accountability"—is not in fact a key objective of those international institutions that claim to endorse it. Thus transparency has come to be increasingly conflated with audit practices, offering a marker of corporate social responsibility (CSR) intended to secure the financial-industrial value of private firms.

Over the past ten years my research has concerned the mutual constitution of the oil and gas industry's political economy with the social claims it faces. This work has examined, in part, how the implementation of a range of corporate social interventions in local/global governance regimes manifest a kind of merging of industrial security and "humanitarian" practice. Forming part of a long social project of colonialism pursued by the joint stock company,[5] imperial practice by the transnational enterprise has relied on cultural authority structures alongside divide and rule.[6]

Today, audit practices associated with flexibilized capitalism aim to imbue social trust into operations physically distanced from the loci of control (arising from the shifting investments characteristic of financialization). As recent scholarship has underlined, transparency and audit is a cultural practice that extends to the constitution of economics and finance as discipline and practice,[7] holding imperial weight through the international financial institutions and agencies that champion it. Through the lens of a critique of ideology, one sees how transparency covers for the role of private capital in shaping socioecological practice at the site of operations as well as in global governance.[8] Applied to oil, gas, and mining, the formal auditability that these practices achieve frequently runs counter to substantive access to information in key extractive regions, both in global North and South.[9] This leads to increasingly compromised regulatory regimes. Below I examine how intensified oil and mining activity over the past decade has been accompanied and facilitated by the pursuit of such auditability. The "audit" of the corporation has in no form entailed substantive transparency in industrial practice. As Michael Power argues:

> Auditing is not merely a collection of technical tasks but also a programmatic idea circulating in organizational environments, an idea which promises a certain style of control and organizational transparency. Auditing threatens to become a cosmetic practice which hides real risk and replaces it with the financial risk faced by auditors themselves. Where the audit process is defensively legalized there is a risk of relying too heavily on an industry of empty comfort certificates. The audit society endangers itself because it invests too heavily in shallow rituals of verification at the expense of other forms of organizational intelligence. In providing a lens for regulatory thought and action audit threatens to become a form of learned ignorance.[10]

The discussion takes up some of my research experiences regarding the oil and gas industry's security dealings and social interventions. The first, which concerns the Voluntary Principles on Security and Human Rights (VPs), revisits some earlier research in light of a recent expert survey regarding the VPs' effectiveness. A second set of experiences concerns constraints on access to information, archives, and communication from industry insiders, with a focus on a number of cases involving Shell Oil. Finally, I place these experiences with careful control of information in the context of new ecological governance regimes in the Gulf of Guinea. These regimes, constructing marine ecological knowledge and baseline data for environmental management, may be understood as a precondition for auditability in a regional context of deepening hydrocarbon extraction.

Security, CSR, and the Constitution of Auditability: The Voluntary Principles on Security and Human Rights

The adoption of voluntary codes has been a trend since the new millennium, reacting to social critiques of industry while evading formal regulation. The formation of the UN Global Compact in 2000, alongside other parallel codes, marked and legitimated these practices among institutions external to private business. The Voluntary Principles on Security and Human Rights, established in that same period, exemplify these moves toward the privatization of decision making on industry's harmful social practices. Initially the VPs were piloted to apply to Nigeria, Indonesia, and Colombia—locations considered particularly contentious for US business groups due to armed violence at sites of operations.[11] In earlier work I argued that the merging of private and public security described in the Voluntary Principles is conjoined in practice with the redefinition of citizens as shareholders, and—in the context of the Nigerian state governed by bifurcated rule[12]—the redefinition of the community members who experience subject rule as stakeholders. The "stakeholder," or the local resident at the site of extraction, is significant to firm valuation under financialization primarily to the extent that this stakeholder's well-being threatens *shareholder* value, that is, profit. The stakeholder's identification with the firm is solidified through a number of social practices associated with CSR and permitted by the VPs, for instance, community development tied to particular industrial projects as well as the practice of contracting private security guards from surrounding locales. In the past decade the establishment of private firms assessing the relationship between social practices and financial risks manifests the further penetration of this logic, where participation in CSR and auditability helps to protect share price.[13]

Although a late 1990s initiative of government through former British foreign secretary Robin Cook and led by Bennett Freeman of the Clinton State Department, the Voluntary Principles were written through a closed-door process that remains in place. A group of private actors from the human rights NGO and business community, as participant-signatories, established and continue to consult on these corporate rules of engagement for private and public security. The initial negotiations involved seven oil and mining companies, including the "big five": Texaco, Chevron, Conoco, Shell, and BP; the first two subsequently merged.

Although Exxon Mobil did not accept the invitation to the original process, it ultimately became a signatory to the Principles. From the NGO
sector, Amnesty International, the Prince of Wales Business Leaders Forum, and Human Rights Watch were involved in their establishment, and Oxfam and Global Rights are more recent signatories, in 2006
and 2012 respectively. The 2011 *Implementation Guideline Tool*, a set of
modules for VP signatories, sets reasons for implementing the VPs that
make the relationship between CSR, risk reduction, and financial stability eminently clear. These reasons are: "reduction in production delays;
maintenance of the 'Social License to Operate'; access to financing—
for example, via Equator Principles financial institutions or the International Finance Corporation; mitigation of litigation risk; maintenance/
enhancement of company reputation and; confidence in operating successfully in complex business environments."[14] Collectively they express
a widely held position in liberal business scholarship that promotes CSR
as a strategy for building value[15] as conventionally understood by business agents, the so-called business case for CSR.

My 2002–3 Nigeria research demonstrated that sections of the Voluntary Principles are conducive to the redefinition of citizen as share/
stakeholder and the merging of public and private at the site of extraction
just as they are at the scale of the global economy. The violence in the
Western Niger Delta in this period (the Warri crisis), while directly tied
to election disputes over ward boundaries, emerged from competitive intercommunal claims to territory on which oil industry installations are
sited.[16] In the invocation of the VPs in the 2003 violence in Warri, I identified three phenomena that illustrate the merging of public and private
(capital) interests at the extractive site and that typify oil industry–social
relations in southern Nigeria and elsewhere. These are: the construct of
the "host community" by the oil industry that plays out in local ethnically inflected struggles over territory—where the identity of subject
communities becomes shaped by their role as physical sites for corporate
extraction/production; the engagement of "community guards," that is,
the local public, as private security to the oil companies shaping conditions wherein local residents must engage in self-surveillance and impose
collective punishment; and finally, the merging of humanitarian and security concerns—central to the Voluntary Principles—exemplified in
Warri in 2003 by the provision of relief supplies by USAID and Chevron-
Texaco alongside security apparatus from the US government.[17]

Eight years following that work, companies with highly controversial human rights records, such as the Canadian mining giant Barrick Gold, have becomes signatories to the VPs, and Canada, which is now a target for global social movement criticism both with relation to tar sands extraction and the activities of its mining industry overseas, is a major player in its implementation.[18] Barrick Gold in fact cited membership in the Voluntary Principles as some form of assurance that the company was protecting local human rights following the sexual abuse and killing of community members by security forces at its North Mara, Tanzania, operations.[19] In 2009–10 Barrick and the Canadian mining industry, through the Prospectors and Development Association of Canada, actively lobbied Canadian parliamentarians against a private members bill (Bill C-300) that aimed to promote ethical practice by Canadian mining firms overseas.[20] Similarly Total, another recent signatory to the VPs, has been associated with human rights violations in the vicinity of its Burma operations. Significant criticism for violence against communities at sites of operation has been leveled against other recent signatories, including Inmet[21] mining and AngloGold Ashanti.[22] Indeed, six out of the ten most controversial 2011 companies identified by Zurich-based RepRisk are Voluntary Principle participants.[23] RepRisk's 2010 report on the ten most environmentally and socially controversial companies included five additional VP participants not among the aforementioned six mining companies. These are all oil companies: Shell, Chevron, BP, BG, and Exxon Mobil. Total was also identified as one of the five most controversial global oil companies in a 2010 RepRisk report.

The involvement of local security forces (private and public) in industrial operations continues to characterize the activities of the VPs most controversial participants. As currently framed, the only mandatory reporting for Voluntary Principles membership is on a firm's *efforts* to meet the guidelines, a requirement itself clouded in qualifications. As written, participants are required to disclose to other participants "subject to legal, confidentiality, safety, and operational concerns . . . timely responses to reasonable requests for information from other Participants with the aim of facilitating comprehensive understanding of the issues related to implementation or assistance in implementation of the Voluntary Principles." Currently, then, the monitoring potential that the VPs offer is confined to corporations and member NGOs, who themselves are subject to confidentiality rules in the negotiations. The VPs thus remain explicitly nonbinding and as such offer auditability without formal disciplinary outcomes.

According to neoliberal ideology, changes in corporate social behavior should emerge from "market forces." As per de Kuijper's position regarding the "vanishing cost of information," knowledge of a firm's negative social practice should become widely available, impacting firm value, and thereby encouraging better social practice. Yet human rights abuses around extractive operations are ubiquitous, and the outright criminalization of protest at the site of extraction, and among protesters at national and global scales, has also accompanied the era of corporate "self-regulation."[24] Signing on to the VPs, in the context of overall industrial impunity, serves as a means of protecting corporate liability while promoting a set of practices that promote auditability and procedural consistency. Indeed, as made plain in the de Kuijper quote, this is not the sort of transparency requiring governments or businesses to open their files to critics in order to enforce accountability.

Auditability, Transparency, and the Protected Archive

Information generated through the VPs is restricted to participating firms and organizations, thus the information does not stimulate public sanction against firms, one form of popular regulatory control under global information capitalism. This brings us to the second research area of note. In a 2002 interview I conducted, a senior Shell CSR manager stated in response to my request to examine their archives, "we do not think like an archive; we look toward the future rather than the past." In the context of my research at that time, the archival record of the corporation was of interest, particularly as it pertained to the Nigerian Civil War (Biafran War) that emerged postindependence and in which the British and French supported opposing sides; the British sided with the Nigerian federation—General Gowon; the French with Biafra (Ibo secession) and Colonel Ojokwu. In 2003 and 2006 I collected material related to this period and the role of the British oil industry at the UK Public Records Office at Kew. This included secret correspondence from 1969 between the Oil Department of the Foreign and Commonwealth Office and the British High Commission in Luanda, Angola. While it concerned both UK and Shell activities during the Biafran War, it focused upon UK and Shell military and/or financial support to the Nigerian Federal Forces to ensure protection of British oil operations, including Shell's.

A good portion of this correspondence pertains to the British Foreign and Commonwealth Office and concerns arms being supplied to the Nigerian federal forces. This includes communication from a certain John Wilson of the High Commission (1969) to Foreign and Commonwealth Office staff:

Shell/B.P. and Nigeria

Shell/B.P. have now given me the following details of an understanding they have reached orally with Chief Awolowo in Lagos following the Federal Government's request for a loan of 10 mn (pounds) by which they have been somewhat embarrassed.

2. Their Manager in Nigeria, Mr. Stanley Gray, was authorised to tell Chief Awolowo that Shell/B.P. guaranteed to take from Nigeria up to an average of 730,000 barrels a day in 1970. This undertaking would result in an increase of revenue for the Nigerian authorities of some 5–6 mn pounds.

3. The offer was made subject to two very firm conditions:

    (a) that the Federal Government should take all necessary steps to guarantee the safety and security of Shell/B.P. operations in Nigeria;

    (b) that the Federal Government would ensure that the effective depth of the channel at Bonny should be kept satisfactory for normal tanker usage.

4. Shell/B.P. said that Awolowo accepted this proposal as very reasonable and promised to put it to his colleagues in the Federal Government. If they too agree this will commit Shell/B.P. to taking off a higher level of oil from Nigeria which they should be able to do provided their installations can be secure from Biafran attack while they will be saved having to support the Federal Government directly by a loan which they are reluctant to do for obvious reasons. Shell have informed Gulf of the principle of their agreement but they have not given Gulf the figures which are commercially confidential.

There are other references, also in letters signed by John Wilson, of a phone call received from Shell's own intelligence regarding arms being provided to the Biafrans by groups of Swedish mercenaries led by one Van Rosen. But the most controversial part of these files, in the view of this author, discusses Shell's sale of fuel to gunrunners to the Biafran forces (the opponents of the Nigerian federal forces), as a form of "money spinner," to use the term employed by staff at the British Consulate General in Luanda.[25] The letter from Luanda to London, of May 1969, reads in part:

> You will, I imagine, already be aware from your close relations with Shell in the context of the Nigerian war, that Shell are also fuelling the planes carrying the airlift into Biafra from Sao Tome. This presents them with a minor conflict of interest.
>
> 2. As far as I can make out Shell are the only company who have been supplying aviation fuel at Sao Tome. When the war began they supplied the few planes staging there with fuel. This represented a small amount. As the war continued the amounts became larger, and in a modest way represented what appeared to be a money spinner for Shell. One of their customers was the American gun-runner, Wharton, who a year or so ago was flying arms into Biafra via Portugal and Sao Tome. Shell were apparently unwise enough to give him credit and he has left them with the bad debt of 5 million escudos (say 75000 pounds).
>
> 3. According to the local and newly arrived Shell manager here his head office told him in London that the less they knew about the Shell operations in Sao Tome the better. They are evidently willing to do business there as long as this does not attract unfavourable publicity. Should they now cease to supply aviation fuel at Sao Tome this would presumably attract unfavourable comment about Shell in the world press for having deliberately held up the relief supplies being flown in by the church organisations. It would also be badly regarded by the Portuguese to whom Shell, some months ago, applied for a large oil concession in Southern Angola and, I believe, permission to expand their activities in metropolitan Portugal.

In 2004, I published some of this correspondence at length in an article in the *Review of African Political Economy*. When I returned to the archives in 2006 I found this material no longer indexed, so that without the box number I would have been unable to find the pertinent pages using the search terms I had originally employed. My colleague Ike Okonta later reported that he found all of the material on the Nigerian Civil War disorganized when compared to his previous visits. Archive staff indicated that I should make a copy of all the materials in that particular box and suggested that this was unlikely accidental. Notable is that this occurred at a period in which a number of major cases against Nigerian oil operators were being tried overseas, namely *Wiwa v. Shell* and *Bowoto v. Chevron*, which concerned complicity of the transnational corporation in judicial murder and assassinations in Nigeria. In both of these cases a longer corporate record of war profiteering in the country would not sit well for the firm, if not in the courtroom then in the court of public opinion and media.

But the protection of firm reputation-as-value under conventional economic logic is not confined to activities of extractive industries in countries of the South. More recently a colleague–graduate student and I sought specific information on Canadian oil and gas company activities in the United States supported through Export Development Canada (EDC). The EDC is a Canadian government ("Crown") corporation that helps Canadian firms respond to international business opportunities—as the byline on its website reads, "minimize risk, maximize opportunity with help from EDC." Our research here focused on firms involved in two controversial pipeline projects, the Northern Gateway and the Keystone. We sought information on significant financing through the EDC in support of the sale and delivery of pipeline transmission equipment to particular locations in the United States; here the EDC discloses no geographical specifics. Our requests were made via freedom of information legislation (Access to Information and Privacy as the Canadian act is known) to gain more detail. We were informed in advanced by EDC staff that most likely the requested material would not be disclosed as it is subject to confidentiality and nondisclosure agreements with the corporate client. Indeed, when our access-to-information requests were ultimately returned, we received hundreds of pages of redacted information, with no detail on the locations or activities to which the monies were being directed. Elsewhere we have documented the millions of dollars received by these corporations from Export Development Canada, formally a federal government agency, and the nondisclosure of the majority of associated environmental reviews for these projects. As we point out, the legal nondisclosure of this information flies in the face of any notion of substantive transparency in liberal democratic procedure.[26]

That a Canadian government agency will not provide basic information on the private sector activities it finances should not be especially surprising, particularly in the case of extractive industry. Indeed, this experience clearly squares with the fact that the Canadian government claims to be a supporter, but *is not an implementer* of the Extractive Industries Transparency Initiative (EITI). As explained on the Natural Resources Canada (government) website:

Canada is an EITI supporting country which means that it helps promote more effective resource revenue management by providing policy advice and technical assistance to host country governments. It encourages Canadian multinational companies to participate in EITI and disclose company payments by country of operation. Canada also gives support to The EITI Multi-Donor Trust Fund which provides technical and advisory support to countries seeking to implement EITI.

Canada is not an implementing country. There are existing regulations and financial disclosure requirement in place in Canada that support the transparency in taxation, royalties and other natural resource revenues.[27]

As a major natural resource exporter with a booming and controversial tar sands mining industry, choosing not to implement the EITI would seem to run counter to international interests. A fall 2011 piece in the business pages of Canada's major daily, the *Globe and Mail*, took exception to Canada's decision not to implement the EITI on this basis. As Barrie McKenna put it:

It is perplexing Canada has shown zero interest in implementing the 2002 Extractive Industries Transparency Initiative. The voluntary international code is based on a simple premise: convince countries to disclose the revenue they collect from oil, gas and mining assets, and then get resource companies to report those royalties.

On the surface, at least, Canada is all for EITI. Prime Minister Stephen Harper has publicly endorsed the initiative, Canadian tax payers have sunk millions of dollars into the process and a top Canadian government bureaucrat sits on the organization's international board of directors. Five major Canadian companies are also EITI signatories: Barrick Gold Corp., Goldcorp, Talisman Energy, Dundee Precious Metals and Kinross Gold.

And yet Ottawa refuses to embrace EITI at home. On its website, Natural Resources Canada offers a lengthy explanation why implementing the agreement is a bad idea. The department says its royalty disclosure standards are already higher and the initiative is really about helping developing countries out of poverty. The department concludes that implementation would be "detrimental to the vitality of EITI.[28]

McKenna continues with the point that EITI's current director, the former British Labour MP Clare Short, practically "begged" Canada to implement the agreement the week prior to the writing of his piece. He also stresses that Norway has implemented the EITI, that the EU recommends that member countries force disclosure of payments to governments by "extractive" companies, and that even the United States, under the Dodd-Frank act, requires the US stock exchange to disclose payments to foreign companies. This would include Canadian companies listed in the United States. As this chapter goes to print, some steps have been taken toward greater corporate disclosure in Canada. In March 2014, the federal government announced a commitment to implement legislation requiring extractive sector payment disclosure by April 2015.[29] The terms of these negotiations remain distinct from the requirements of the EITI, and, as we have seen, EITI compliancy is itself applied to the state, not the private firm.

What McKenna presents, that Northern firms have largely remained protected from EITIs requirements, should not come as a surprise. Norway is to date alone in the global North in its implementation of the EITI. Indeed, despite Clare Short's "begging" Canada to implement the EITI, the United Kingdom has yet to commit to implement it either. As Sarah Bracking underlines, the EITI applies to so-called host countries for industry in the global South, but not to the home countries of the corporation from which they hail:

> It is important not to evaluate EITI for what it is not. It is not a Fair Reward mechanism, or Fair Trade standard, which has at its centre any discussion over the distribution of rents. Thus, the procedural values—of transparency and accountability—are the end in and of themselves in the official EITI formulation. It does not go on to say that then consideration will occur of whether the distribution of benefits is equitable and necessary adjustments will be actioned to ensure that the country's poor and natural owners of subsoil resources are properly compensated for their extraction. That poverty reduction or sustainable development might occur is an add-on, which is not built into the process of EITI. This is simply a process of high-level meetings, the appointment of an administration, and the publication of some accounts. . . . it is a top-down process of applying a "global" standard in a "local" context.[30]

While Canada has taken steps toward greater disclosure in the period since this chapter was first drafted, and legislation is anticipated in 2015, the country has yet to comply with the EITI domestically.[31] Concurrently, Canada's own environmental regulations were further eroded in

2012 by a major overhaul to legislation under an omnibus budget bill. Within the international context, one Canadian expert described this as "a particularly extreme example of regressive changes with important lessons for participants in law reform initiatives elsewhere."[32]

As reflected in experiences recounted here, transparency is illusory and the practices develop to ensure it hide more than they reveal. Consequently, transparency as per de Kuijper's "second usage," the opening of public books for accountability, is not deducible even in those initiatives that on the surface seek to espouse it. What is important, rather, is the *procedural value* of transparency and accountability. This is the audit, or rather audit culture, a peculiarly late-capitalist phenomena.

Auditability as Securitization: Ecological Regimes

Transparency, it is suggested here, is largely reducible to auditability and certainly does not encompass substantive access to information on corporate activities. Auditability is the direction of new ecological governance initiatives, which collect information on ecosystem health in the context of deepening corporate activities. In the Gulf of Guinea, such initiatives are part of a set of projects to establish regional management initiatives in highly sensitive regions and produce environmental data that facilitates ecological valuation.

Tracking the constitution of the Gulf of Guinea as a site of extraction and environmental management suggests how transparency and audit regimes are imbued with imperial power, constituting particular regions as socioecologically governable. Governability, from the standpoint of liberal practice, justifies "penetrability" while also providing the mechanisms that mark the extractive industry's activities as legal, fundamental to shaping the contours of a liberal market. As a metaphor, *penetrability* clearly points to gendered and sexualized accounts of colonized space. It is also related to those suppositions in the business world that de Kuijper highlights that, through flattened information payments, could level the playing field among large global enterprises with regard to transaction costs.

Key international institutions have facilitated this flattening of the cost of information, related to the production of information concerning ecological "assets." The Global Environmental Facility (GEF) of the World Bank has served as a formal mechanism to address Southern nations' concerns over the undue burden that climate change, and a global regime on CO_2 emissions, would have on their economies. GEF's mandate is in part to compensate for the industrialization foregone through emissions reduction,[33] and also to create the conditions for valuation of ecology—sometimes called "environmental services." In 1995, the GEF funded a six-country pilot project concerning water pollution in the Gulf of Guinea via what is called the Guinea Current Large Marine Ecosystem (LME) as part of broader transnational initiatives to demarcate and evaluate marine areas globally. Coastal pollution is particularly salient to the area, as 40 percent of the region's 300 million inhabitants live in coastal areas and depend on its ecosystem for food security and exports. Additionally 60–80 percent of all the industrial production occurs near shore.[34] In part due to the legacy of colonial trade routes, coastal cities thus remain key centers. Since major infrastructure, airports, harbors, and other developments are sited near coastal cities, much industrial production—and pollution—occurs in marine zones. Population density near the oceans has only increased, as rural dwellers migrate to these urban areas. The pilot project identified expected problems as key issues in ecosystem health in the Gulf of Guinea: degraded water quality, loss of critical habitats for migratory and nonmigratory species, effluents in rivers flowing into the LME, the risk of offshore spills, marine debris and beach pollution, industrial and solid waste, as well as the impact of pollution from oil and gas on coastal fisheries and human settlements. A key outcome of the 1995 GEF project was the 1998 Accra Declaration calling for the development of integrated coastal areas management.[35] This was followed by a second phase of the LME project encompassing the sixteen countries whose exclusive economic zones (EEZs) form part of the larger Guinea Current LME.

The constitution of ecological governance through this process occurred alongside securitization of natural resources in the form of US Africom as well as the British government's increasing focus on Africa in the post-9/11 security climate.[36] Both ecological and economic security projects were supported through bilateral and multilateral channels, and both were significant regional initiatives on resource governance. After 9/11, the US and UK security establishments put significant emphasis on the securing of the Gulf of Guinea region. Over the past five years this securitization process has accelerated through a range of antipiracy initiatives. Marine piracy in the Gulf of Guinea has increased. In 2013 and 2014 the EU and the US government passed resolutions directed specifically at supporting the Gulf of Guinea council in securing these regions.[37] While the security of port workers is invoked by anti-piracy initiatives examining the region, the working conditions faced by marine workers does not receive such scrutiny.[38]

The political and spatial challenges associated with offshore petroleum regulation are magnified due to industrial nondisclosure agreements and contracts, as paid employees are inhibited from revealing risks due to their employment contracts, and whistleblower protections are absent or inadequate. Industry produces its own intelligence, data products that are beyond the means of most noncapitalist entities. For instance, the business research service GlobalData published a report in 2008 titled *The Gulf of Guinea Commission and the Developmental Prospects for the Region's Petroleum Industry*. Now available for $500 on Amazon.com, the report no longer appears on a quick search of their website; it is replaced by new products on liquefied natural gas prospects in Equatorial Guinea whose prices range from $2,500 to $3,500. Douglas-Westwood's single user price for its World Deepwater Market Forecast 2014–18 is priced at £3,250 (US$5,466). While certain NGOs report on planned projects in the region, the oil and gas industry in West Africa, and elsewhere, is a closely guarded and elite activity. Limited public access to information on the development of, or pollution resulting from, particular offshore projects in the region illustrates a breach in any functional transparency for marine regulation.

Thus we have seen that a set of global market trends toward information availability alongside transnational disclosure initiatives are heralded by industry insiders as movement into a period of perfect transparency. Industry pronouncements of growing transparency, however, remain one sided. In the case of the EITI, the activities of *home states* and private firms are not subject to the same scrutiny as the global South exporters; Northern exporters, like Canada, are not economically pressured to the same degree to join this initiative. Additionally, because the organizational relations between private firms and states are frequently concealed, and access to records blocked by proprietary information clauses, scholars meet roadblocks in trying to analyze the political sociology and political economy of the industry, a problem increasingly apparent in Canada via the muzzling of federal scientists critical of tar sands.[39] As the experience of many commentators with access to information and our recent experience with Export Development Canada illustrates, private firms still largely control data and information on operations, thus limiting open discussion on questions of safety, ecology, and production figures.

Eight years prior to the 2008 financial crisis, critical sociologist Laureen Snider wrote an article titled "The Sociology of Corporate Crime: An Obituary, or Whose Knowledge Claims Have Legs?" in which she writes "even where stock market fraud seems poised to destroy the system of exchange that is the foundation of capitalism, the neo-liberal religion of deregulation retains its hold on financial elites. Massive frauds continue unabated, unpunished and largely unremarked in the world's press."[40] The article documents how neoliberal regulatory reforms of the 1990s weakened the possibility of stringent environmental monitoring in Canada and how sociological critique of corporate malfeasance has been overshadowed by industry-funded science. While audit practice and corporate social responsibility have partially filled the social confidence gap created by repealing enforceable legislation, they have certainly not raised regulatory standards or promoted substantive access to information. An effective transnational disclosure regime, meant to promote meaningful social responsibility, would ensure consequences for corporate criminals. It would also require greater national level legislation to facilitate that firms be held liable in their home country for human rights abuses associated with their activities in their so-called host countries.

Notes

Many thanks to Kimia Ghomeshi and Ujunwa Nwachukwu for research assistance and the Social Sciences and Humanities Research Council of Canada and York University for financial support for this research.

1. Mia de Kuijper, *Profit Power Economics: A New Competitive Strategy for Creating Sustainable Wealth* (Oxford: Oxford University Press, 2009), 42.

2. While not used in the sense of this particular discursive application, the notion of transparent space—as per Lefebvre's work—is comparable to various elements of socialized space that obscure the material relations undergirding the *appearance* of transparency or perceptibility.

3. De Kuijper, *Profit Power Economics*, 42.

4. Ibid., 46.

5. Timothy Mitchell, *Carbon Democracy: Political Power in the Age of Oil* (New York: Verso, 2011).

6. Tania Murray Li, *The Will to Improve: Governmentality, Development, and the Practice of Politics* (Durham, NC: Duke University Press, 2007); Mahmood Mamdani, *Citizen and Subject: Contemporary Africa and the Legacy of Late Colonialism* (Princeton, NJ: Princeton University Press, 1996).

7. See Michael Power, *The Audit Society: Rituals of Verification* (Oxford: Oxford University Press, 1997); Marilyn Strathern, "The Tyranny of Transparency," *British Journal of Educational Research* 26, no. 3 (2000): 309–21; Costas Lapavitsas, "Financialised Capitalism: Crisis and Financial Expropriation," *Historical Materialism* 17, no. 2 (2009): 114–48.

8. Nikolas Rose, *Powers of Freedom* (Cambridge: Cambridge University Press, 1999).

9. Marieme Lo, "Revisiting the Chad-Cameroon Pipeline Compensation Modality, Local Communities' Discontent, and Accountability Mechanisms," *Canadian Journal of Development Studies* 30, no. 1–2 (2010): 153–74.

10. Power, *Audit Society*, 122–3.

11. See Bennett Freeman's testimony: "Former US Deputy Assistant Secretary of State—Democracy, Human Rights and Labor and Voluntary Principle initiator, to the Senate Judiciary Sub-Committee on Human Rights and Law," September 2008, http://www.calvert.com/sri-SAGE-extracting-natural-resources.html.

12. Mamdani, *Citizen and Subject*.

13. Examples of the socially responsible investment (SRI)–risk reduction trend here include Jantzi Sustainalytics, arising from the merger of Canada-based Jantzi Research and the European Sustainalytics in 2010. The Jantzi Social Index, created in 2002, is a list of firms that meet social, environmental, and governance criteria. RepRisk, established in 2006 according to its own website in response to needs of a major banking client, emerged from the firm ECOFACT formed in 1998, renaming itself in 2010. See www.sustainalytics.com and www.reprisk.com.

14. International Council on Mining and Metals et al., *Implementation Guideline Tool*, 2011, 9. The consultant firm Stratos, based in Ottawa and Calgary, which engages in risk management and sustainability strategy in the private sector, prepared the tool. The involvement of the Canadian mining sector in the VPs in the recent past is notable and reflects the rising fortunes—and criticism—leveled at the Canadian mining industry since 2007.

15. Here the term refers to the transnational firm's conceptualization of share value and returns under financialized global capitalism. Further exploration of this notion of value alongside a definition of value emerging from Marxist analysis, based on abstract social labor, would require an extended essay.

16. Through a range of types of relationships to particular oil and gas industry installations, local residents access various kinds of legislated and informal

payments by company agents—both in cash and social project form, however meager.

17. The clauses contained in the Voluntary Principles are discussed at greater length in Anna Zalik, "The Peace of the Graveyard: The Voluntary Principles on Security and Human Rights in the Niger Delta," in *Global Regulation: Managing Crises after the Imperial Turn*, ed. Libby Asassi, Kees vanderPijl, and Duncan Wigan (London: Palgrave, 2004), 111–27.

18. The current chair of the board is a Canadian diplomat, formerly posted to Nigeria. Notable recent signatories are Canadian mining companies, and the consulting company that produced the one-hundred-page implementation guideline report (Stratfor) is based in Calgary and Ottawa.

19. See http://www.barrick.com/News/PressReleases/PressReleaseDetails/2011/North-Mara-Mine-Tanzania. The relationship between artisanal mining and such incidents at Barrick's Tanzania operations has been the subject of various reports. Barrick is Canada's largest mining company. Peter Munk, the company's founder and CEO, has encountered criticism in public talks in Canada. Media coverage has become critical in part as a result of this outcry. See protestbarrick.net and munkoutoftoronto.wordpress.com.

20. S. Rennie, "Mining Industry Lobbied Nine of 24 MPs Who Helped Kill Ethics Bill," *Canadian Press*, November 11, 2010. PDAC's opposition to that bill is at http://www.miningwatch.ca/bill-c-300-corporate-accountability-activities-mining-oil-or-gas-corporations-developing-countries ghttp://www.pdac.ca/pdac/publications/na/pdf/090812-bill-c-300-position-statement.pdf.

21. For controversy surrounding Inmet activities in Panama, see http://www.miningwatch.ca/sites/miningwatch.ca/files/Petaquilla_background.pdf and http://www.miningwatch.ca/news/investment-agreement-between-inmet-mining-corporation-and-koresls-nikko-cobre-inc-violates. A recent Canadian Broadcasting Corporation documentary highlighted debates over Canadian mining in Panama, in which Inmet is a key player.

22. In 2011, NGOs meeting at Davos awarded AngloGold the "Shame" award for "corporate irresponsibility" in Ghana. The selection of the company to carry out a health program through the Global Fund for HIV was heavily criticized by Ghanaian Health NGOs. AngloGold Ashanti's activities in Colombia have been the subject of critical documentation in reports by a coalition of Canadian NGOs. See http://www.interpares.ca/en/publications/pdf/Land_and_Conflict.pdf.

23. These are Newmont Mining, BHP Billiton, Freeport McMoran, Rio Tinto, Barrick Gold, and Anglo-American.

24. See, for instance, the case of Steven Schnoor, a Canadian photographer and filmmaker accused of fabricating footage, and interview of local reactions to the destruction of a village by security contractors at a mining site in El Salvador. Schnoor ultimately won a legal suit against the Canadian ambassador (see http://

www.schnoorversuscanada.ca/), but assassination of those engaged in protest against the mining industry has continued through this period. See, for instance, a detailed reporting on the murder of Mariano Abarca Roblero in the Blackfire case in Chiapas, Mexico, http://www.miningwatch.ca/news/two-years-canadian -government-silent-blackfire-case-corruption-and-murder-chiapas-mexico, and the recent assassination of an antimining activist in Oaxaca, Mexico.

25. See Anna Zalik, "The Niger Delta: Petro-Violence and Partnership Development," *Review of African Political Economy* 31, no. 101 (2004), 407–8, for extended citation from this correspondence.

26. Ghomeshi and Zalik 2013, available at http://antipodefoundation .org/2013/10/23/corporate-privacy-and-environmental-review-at-export -development-canada/.

27. See http://www.nrcan.gc.ca/extractive-industries/canadas-role/2286.

28. It should be noted that this statement seems no longer to be present on the website.

29. See March 3, 2014, Publish What You Pay Canada press release at pwyp.ca.

30. Sarah Bracking, "Hiding Conflict over Industry Returns: A Stakeholder Analysis of the Extractive Industries Transparency Initiative," Brooks World Poverty Institute/University of Manchester, 2009, 4.

31. For details see Publish What You Pay Canada at pwyp.ca.

32. Robert B. Gibson, "In Full Retreat: The Canadian Government's New Environmental Assessment Law Undoes Decades of Progress," *Impact Assessment and Project Appraisal* 30, no. 3 (2012): 180.

33. Isaac Osuoka, "Paying the Polluter? The Relegation of Local Community Concerns in 'Carbon Credit' Proposals of Oil Corporations in Nigeria," in *Upsetting the Offset: The Political Economy of Carbon Markets*, ed. Steffen Bohm and Siddartha Dabhi (London: Mayfly Books, 2009).

34. C. N. Ukwe and C. A. Ibe, "A Regional Collaborative Approach in Transboundary Pollution Management in the Guinea Current Region of Western Africa," *Ocean and Coastal Management* 53 (2010): 493–506; P. A. Scheren, A. C. Ibe, F. J. Janssen, and A. M. Lemmens, "Environmental Pollution in the Gulf of Guinea—a Regional Approach," *Marine Pollution Bulletin* 44, no. 7 (2002): 633–41; N. A. Chukwuone, C. N. Ukwe, A. Onugu, and C. A. Ibe, "Valuing the Guinea Current Large Marine Ecosystem: Estimates of Direct Output Impact of Relevant Marine Activities," *Ocean and Coastal Management* 52, no. 3 (2009): 189–96.

35. Full text available at http://gefgclme.chez.com/english/accra.htm.

36. Jeremy H. Keenan, "Chad-Cameroon Oil Pipeline: World Bank and ExxonMobil in 'Last Chance Saloon,'" *Review of African Political Economy* 32, no. 104–5 (2005): 395–405; Jeremy Keenan, "Demystifying Africa's Security," *Review of African Political Economy* 35, no. 118 (2008): 634–44; Rita Abra-

hamsen, "Blair's Africa: The Politics of Securitization and Fear," *Alternatives: Global, Local, Political* 30, no. 1 (2005): 55–80; Godwin Onuoha, "Energy and Security in the Gulf of Guinea: A Nigerian Perspective," *South African Journal of International Affairs* 16, no. 2 (2009): 245–64.

37. See Council of the European Union, *EU Strategy on the Gulf of Guinea*, March 17, 2014; and US Senate Resolution 288, November 6, 2013.

38. Kaija Hurlburt, Conor Seyle, Cyrus Mody, Roy Paul, Jon Bellish, and Bridget Jankovsky, "The Human Cost of Piracy," Oceans beyond Piracy, 2012.

39. See Verilyn Klinkenborg, "Silencing Scientists?" *New York Times*, September 21, 2013; *CBC*, "Could Muzzling Federal Scientists Be Illegal?" at http://www.cbc.ca/news/technology/could-muzzling-federal-scientists-be-illegal-1.1341021, February 20, 2013.

40. Laureen Snider, "The Sociology of Corporate Crime: An Obituary," *Theoretical Criminology* 4, no. 2 (2000): 169–206, at 175.

CHAPTER FIVE

Virtuous Language in Industry and the Academy

Stuart Kirsch

Several years ago I attended a symposium at my university on how to integrate sustainability into the curriculum, a topic of interest to me as an anthropologist who works with indigenous peoples affected by mining.[1] We were told that the university and the corporate world are now aligned in their shared commitment to sustainability. But I wondered why no one mentioned the BP oil spill in the Gulf of Mexico, which was making headlines at the time. British Petroleum's confident assertion that "we will make this right" seemed to contradict scientific uncertainty about the long-term environmental consequences of the spill. I also wanted to know what it meant that the business community and the academy were suddenly using the same vocabulary. I was not the only one in the audience with these concerns, but the presentation left us tongue-tied. It is difficult to criticize sustainability, as the environmental values it promotes are widely shared. Yet it is possible to acknowledge the need for sustainability while contesting some of the claims made in its name.

This experience leads me to question the discursive convergence of industry and the academy, which might be taken to imply mutual understanding and commitment. But the recourse to shared language can conceal all manner of difference. Sustainability and corporate social responsibility are examples of what linguistic anthropologists call *strategically deployable shifters*.[2] Ordinary shifters are words or phrases that lack standardized lexical meanings because their referential value depends on the context in which they are employed. Shifters are therefore simultaneously symbolic and indexical.[3] The adverbs *here* and *now* are examples of shifters, as are pronouns. Consider, for example, what have been called the "slippery pronouns" of nationalism, the third-person plural that alternately incorporates or excludes particular categories of persons.[4]

Strategically deployable shifters allow people to communicate across social boundaries and political vantage points.[5] The participants in these conversations understand themselves to be "'talking about the same thing,' when, pragmatically they are not, or are doing so only up to a point."[6] This can be seen in the different ways that people mobilize the concept of sustainability. Contemporary use of the concept can be traced back to the UN Conference on the Human Environment held in Stockholm in 1972, which defined sustainability as the need to "maintain the earth as a place suitable for human life not only now but for future generations."[7] Sustainability was subsequently integrated into discussions about economic growth, including the argument that "for development to be sustainable, it must take account of social and ecological factors, as well as economic ones."[8] For the mining industry, however, sustainability and sustainable development have come to mean something quite different. Thus the website of BHP Billiton, one of the world's largest mining companies, asserts that "sustainable development is about ensuring that our business remains viable and contributes lasting benefits to society."[9] Similarly, despite a historical legacy of destructive environmental impacts, the mining industry now claims to practice what it calls "sustainable mining." Such corporate oxymorons are "intended to ease the mind of an otherwise critical" public by pairing a harmful or destructive practice or commodity with a positive cover term.[10] In the discourse of the mining industry, the relationship between sustainability and the environment has been completely elided, "emptying out" the original meaning of the term.[11]

The differences in how environmentalists and the mining industry define sustainability are more than simply rhetorical. Its status as a strategically deployable shifter allows BHP Billiton to claim that its commitment to sustainability is its "first value" despite the negative impacts of its operations on the environment. This includes its responsibility for catastrophic damage downstream from the Ok Tedi copper and gold mine in Papua New Guinea, where I have conducted research since the mid-1980s.[12] BHP Billiton's environmental record did not prevent the university where I teach from appointing the company to the external board of advisors of its new institute on sustainability.[13] Nor did it prevent the university's school of engineering from prominently displaying the company's logo on its solar car, a prominent symbol of its commitment to the environment. These examples illustrate how sustainability operates as a strategically deployable shifter that provides mining companies with symbolic capital.

The recognition that sustainability is a strategically deployable shifter leads me to ask what is being accomplished socially, politically, and discursively when such terms are invoked to describe, categorize, reform, valorize, or criticize corporate practices. This question is part of a larger study of the dialectical relationship between corporations and their critics.[14] Sustainability is one of a series of concepts that corporations deploy under the general rubric of corporate social responsibility. The virtuous language of responsibility, sustainability, and transparency has become an important resource for corporations in their response to criticism. That these discourses enhance corporate reputations is not simply a corollary of their use, but central to their invocation. Despite their appearance of political neutrality, these discourses also promote market-based solutions to social and environmental problems as an alternative to government regulation. As strategically deployable shifters, the discourses of corporate social responsibility and sustainability facilitate conversations across a range of perspectives while concealing important political differences.[15]

The discourse of corporate social responsibility has also become a subject of academic research in programs on business and management. This literature plays an essential role in "consolidating, validating, and even celebrating" claims about corporate social responsibility.[16] Academic research on CSR is "not external to its object of study," but central to its formulation and legitimation.[17] The promotion of the discourses of corporate social responsibility and sustainability within the academy enhances their credibility and complicates efforts to analyze these terms by conveying the impression that their definitions are well established and widely recognized rather than contested. However, my research on the relationship between the mining industry and its critics provides a productive vantage point from which to ascertain whether the discourse of corporate social responsibility reflects changes in how corporations and markets operate, as its proponents suggest, rather than changes in how corporations market themselves.

These preliminary observations lead to the four questions that I address in this essay. First, why did the discourse of corporate social responsibility emerge at this particular historical moment? I answer this question with reference to the relationship between the mining industry and its critics since the 1990s. This follows the anthropological inclination to study language within specific social contexts. Second, what are the intended audiences of the discourse of corporate social responsibility? Attention to reception helps to identify the goals of the speaker. Third, which actions are identified as demonstrating corporate social responsibility and how might we distinguish between them? Here I contrast philanthropy and reform, both of which are represented as examples of corporate social responsibility. My final question has to do with academic discussion about corporate social responsibility and sustainability. How does the identification of these discourses as strategically deployable shifters help us to understand their promotion and reception within the academy?

The Origins of CSR in the Mining Industry

Why do corporations and industries seek to enhance their reputations by invoking claims to social responsibility? Research on the relationship between the mining industry and its critics since the 1990s offers a historical perspective on the two dominant narratives invoked to explain the emergence of the discourse of corporate social responsibility. The first argument refers to corporate recognition of the need to raise industry standards. For example, one of the goals of the International Council of Mining and Metals is "to act as a catalyst for performance improvement in the mining and metals industry."[18] The alternative "business case" for social responsibility emphasizes the economic rationale or competitive advantage that can be gained by enhancing corporate reputations. The mining company Rio Tinto expresses this view in very specific terms: "Our contribution to sustainable development is not just the right thing to do. We also understand that it gives us business reputational benefits that result in greater access to land, human, and financial resources."[19] Policy changes are presented as a response to internal concerns. In contrast, historical evidence suggests that pressure from external critics was responsible for the mining industry's adoption of the discourse of corporate social responsibility and sustainability in the late 1990s.

For decades, the mining industry managed to maintain a low profile. The industry's lack of visibility is related to the remote locations in which most mines operate, affording them considerable freedom from oversight or interference. In many cases, opposition to mining is suppressed by state or private security forces, reducing the need to respond to their critics.[20] The relative anonymity of most mining companies is also a consequence of the way metals are sold to other businesses rather than directly to consumers. This can be contrasted with branding in the petroleum industry, in which consumers engage directly with corporations at the pump.

The spread of neoliberal economic policies during the 1990s, including the promotion of foreign direct investment, opened up new regions of the world to minerals extraction. Many of these projects are located in marginal areas in which indigenous peoples retained control over lands not previously seen to have economic value and where development has historically been limited or absent. Neoliberal reforms also dismantled state regulatory regimes designed to protect labor, the environment, and the rights of persons displaced or otherwise negatively affected by mining. Consequently, much of the responsibility for monitoring international capital has shifted from the state to NGOs and social movements.[21] Critics of the mining industry increasingly deploy new technologies ranging from the Internet and mobile phones to satellite imaging, enabling them to monitor and report on corporate activity in approximately real time wherever it occurs. They also participate in transnational action networks that forge horizontal ties to their counterparts in other regions of the world and partner with NGOs concerned with social justice, the environment, and financial accountability.[22]

One of the iconic mining conflicts of the 1990s was the political campaign and international litigation against the Ok Tedi copper and gold mine in Papua New Guinea. Since 1986, the mine has discharged more than one billion metric tons of tailings and waste rock into local rivers.[23] Although the people living downstream from the mine faced a steep learning curve, they eventually forged strategic alliances with international NGOs who helped them call attention to the environmental problems caused by the mine. In 1994, thirty thousand indigenous people affected by pollution filed a lawsuit against Broken Hill Proprietary, Ltd. (BHP), the managing shareholder and operating partner of the Ok Tedi mine, in the Australian courts.[24] The case was settled in 1996 for an estimated $500 million in compensation and commitments to tailings containment.[25] When the Ok Tedi mine continued to discharge tailings into the river system, the plaintiffs returned to court in 2000. Pressure from the second case forced BHP to transfer its 52 percent share in the project to a development trust that has already accumulated $1.4 billion in re serves, although only a fraction of these funds reaches the communities affected by the mine.

The Ok Tedi campaign was an example of the politics of space, which links together a variety of actors in different locations. The resulting networks are comprised of individuals, communities, nongovernmental organizations, experts, lawyers, and others. They benefit from the complementary mobilization of resources, discourses of persuasion, access to power, and forms of leverage deployed by their members.[26] The ability to enroll participants in multiple locations makes these networks especially effective in challenging transnational corporations wherever they operate. The decade-long campaign against the Ok Tedi mine helped to usher in a new era in which mining companies acknowledge the need to negotiate with the communities affected by their projects in contrast to the prevailing assumption that the state has the sole authority to represent their interests.[27] It also served notice to the industry that it could no longer afford to ignore its critics, prompting a "crisis of confidence" among mining executives that led to unprecedented collaboration among companies that previously viewed each other as fierce competitors.[28]

However, the politics of space has a critical shortcoming: the length of time required to diagnose the problem, mobilize a network of supporters, and mount an effective intervention. In the Ok Tedi case, the response to the environmental problems downstream from the mine came too late to save the river. More recent protests against the mining industry have shifted their attention to earlier in the production cycle before the onset of mining. These social movements seek to limit the environmental impact of mining by opposing the development of new projects. I refer to this strategy as the *politics of time*. Relatively small mining projects may require investments of several hundred million dollars, and the budget for a large mine may be as much as ten or twelve billion dollars. Investments on this scale generate substantial political inertia, especially after they begin to earn revenue for the state. Consequently, political opposition to mining is more likely to be successful when it addresses proposals for new projects, jeopardizing the ability of the mining company to raise the capital required for construction.

An important example of the politics of time is the burgeoning so-

cial movement across Latin America in which communities undertake popular votes—known as *consulta* or referenda—that express support or opposition to proposed development projects, especially new
mines.[29] These votes contest the authority of the state to grant mining
licenses. The participants generally view these referenda as expressing
their rights to democratic participation and their sovereignty over land
and territory rather than their participation in a larger social movement
based on the politics of time. Nonetheless, the organizers of these actions are familiar with their history in the region. A recent survey identifies sixty-eight consultas on mining projects in Latin America, including Argentina, Colombia, Ecuador, Guatemala, Mexico, and Peru, over
the last decade.[30]

   The first consulta to vote on a major mining project was held in the
town of Tambogrande in northwest Peru in 2002; 98 percent of the eli-
gible voters opposed the mine.[31] Three years later in Esquel, Argentina,
the members of the largely middle class community voted overwhelm-
ingly against a proposed open pit gold mine located seven kilome-
ters upstream from the town, blocking its development.[32] The first referendum against a mining project in Guatemala was held in Sipacapa
in 2005; since then, there have been votes on mining projects in fifty-
four municipalities, almost all of which were negative.[33] These referenda
demonstrate widespread opposition to mining, although they also seek
to limit state interference in local affairs. In addition, they express the
rights of individuals and communities to make important decisions concerning their land, territories, and access to water, as well as local livelihoods and health. Although earlier social movements based on the politics of space influenced debates about mining and indigenous peoples,
new strategies based on the politics of time represent a more hopeful
turn given their potential to prevent other environmental disasters from
occurring.

   The promotion of indigenous rights to free, prior, and informed consent, or FPIC, is a key resource in the politics of time. FPIC was first established in binding international treaty law by the International Labour
Organization (ILO) convention 169 in 1989.[34] The World Bank initially
refused to recognize the principle of indigenous consent, arguing that it
was too difficult to operationalize and ran counter to established principles of eminent domain.[35] Employing the same acronym but representing a much weaker standard, the World Bank adopted a policy of free,

prior, and informed *consultation*. Many other international financial institutions followed suit.[36]

Some of the participants in the mining industry prefer the alternative concept of a "social license to operate," which refers to the existence of broad-based community support. The expression was previously used by the American pulp and paper industry to indicate its need to gain the trust of the public and thereby avoid "costly new regulations."[37] It first entered conversations about the mining industry in 1997, at a time when the mining industry was under pressure from the legal action against the Ok Tedi mine.[38] It is treated as a kind of shorthand for those aspects of relationships between mines and communities that are not directly addressed by government contracts and permits.[39] A key difference between a social license to operate and free, prior, and informed consent is that the purpose of the former is to reassure potential investors that a project meets certain baseline criteria, reducing their exposure to risk, whereas the latter is based on the recognition of indigenous rights and addresses the interests of those communities. The acquisition of a social license to operate is also a voluntary practice rather than a legal requirement.

Lobbying by NGOs and indigenous peoples at the United Nations led to the passage of the Declaration on the Rights of Indigenous Peoples in 2007, which mandates the principle of free, prior, and informed consent. Such "soft law" standards, while not legally binding, may give rise to new international norms. Even the World Bank has begun to take heed; in May 2011, it announced a new policy recognizing the higher standard of consent for certain projects affecting the rights of indigenous peoples.[40] BHP Billiton's most recent statement of operating principles stakes out a position in the middle ground: "New operations or projects must have broad-based community support before proceeding with development. Free Prior and Informed Consent (FPIC) is only required where it is mandated by law. Evidence demonstrating support or opposition to the project must be documented."[41] According to industry observers, although "the debate over FPIC will continue . . . the realization that the game has changed is sinking in. The goal posts are shifting."[42] Paradoxically, however, there is a risk that the protocols for implementing the new standard may result in the transfer of political authority from communities recently empowered to speak on their own behalf to private sector consultants who implement assessments on behalf of corporate sponsors, potentially turning free, prior, and informed consent into the check-box compliance of audit culture.

Thus in contrast to corporate narratives about internal recognition of the need to improve performance and the business case for responsibility, evidence from the study of social movements critical of the mining industry suggests that changes in corporate practice are hard won. Reform should be seen as the achievement of indigenous and NGO critics rather than a consequence of the spontaneous enlightenment of industry executives. Nor is there evidence to support the mining industry's assertion that it has internalized important lessons from its past mistakes and incorporated them into their decision making.[43] Instead, corporate claims to practice sustainable mining should be seen as attempts to reassure critics that their efforts and interventions are no longer required.

The Audiences for CSR Discourse

The next question is concerned with potential audiences for the discourse of corporate social responsibility. In recent decades, reputational risks have become increasingly important to the corporate bottom line. This is related to the rise of shareholder capitalism, which emphasizes share value at the expense of corporate relationships to labor, consumers, and communities.[44] Shareholder capitalism is closely associated with the financial collapse of the last decade, during which attention to share value took precedence over economic performance. It is also driven by increased participation in the stock market by individual investors, which has been spurred by the dismantling and privatization of pensions and retirement plans.[45] Managing shareholder confidence has become an essential component of doing business for publically traded companies. Corporations seek to reassure both shareholders and potential investors by adopting policies on corporate social responsibility.

Another potential audience for the discourse of corporate social responsibility is the consumer. One of the ways corporations seek to reassure consumers is through certification programs that provide commodities with the stamp of public approval.[46] Certification consists of a set of rules or guidelines and a mechanism for monitoring or self-reporting that indicates compliance.[47] But participation is voluntary, compliance is not enforceable, and the sanctions that do exist tend to be informal, including dialogue, peer pressure, and the threat of expulsion.[48] An example of a certification regime in the mining industry emerged in response to concern about the trade in "blood diamonds" from conflict zones in Africa. Corporations may also envision the possibility of competitive advantage in addition to enhancing their legitimacy through participation in these initiatives; for example, support for the Kimberley Process that imposed restrictions on diamond trading had strategic value for De Beers, which controls the bulk of the world's diamond trade and benefited from the resulting reduction in supply, which keeps diamond prices high. The Kimberley Process has gradually been weakened as various parties find ways to circumvent its restrictions. But the anonymity of most metals—as it is impossible to identify the source of the copper wire in our computers or the gold in our jewelry—means that the mining industry is largely immune to consumer politics.

As the history of mining conflicts suggests, another potential audience for the discourse of corporate social responsibility is nongovernmental organizations. The language of CSR helps corporations persuade many NGOs to move from confrontation to collaboration in what the mining industry likes to call "win-win" relationships.[49] NGOs increasingly join arm in arm with CEOs in the boardroom rather than subaltern peasants manning the barricades. This has led to the fragmentation of the NGO community according to their willingness to collaborate with industry. One example of these new collaborations is the way that conservation organizations increasingly align themselves with mining companies, endorsing their projects in return for financial support for conservation set-asides.[50] These partnerships have led indigenous peoples in many areas of the world to regard conservation organizations as their enemies rather than potential allies or partners in the protection of local biodiversity.[51] The proliferation of relationships between mining companies and NGOs has also made it easier for the industry to marginalize organizations that reject corporate collaboration and are skeptical of market-based solutions to environmental problems.

Finally, the discourse of corporate social responsibility may also be addressed in part to labor. For example, Jessica Smith Rolston found that CSR messages at a gold mine in Washington State were directed primarily at its own employees, as the mining company sought to overcome stereotypes about the industry in a region in which much of the labor pool possesses strong environmental values.[52] The multiple audiences of

the discourse of corporate social responsibility illustrate the way strategically deployable shifters facilitate interactions that conceal important
contradictions.

The Varieties of CSR Work

It is possible to distinguish between two kinds of CSR work: "doing
good" through corporate philanthropy and "doing better" by improving
corporate practices. A distinguishing feature of CSR is the link between
corporate philanthropy and public relations. American businesses have
long made important charitable contributions: sponsoring a local sports
team, for example, or participating in fund-raising for nearby hospitals.
These were seen as demonstrations of the corporation's role as a good
neighbor.[53] More recently, corporations have also begun to donate employee labor in charitable undertakings such as house building for Habi-
tat for Humanity, which enhances employee loyalty while building community ties.

Even when operating overseas, local philanthropic contributions have
been perceived as a demonstration of corporate responsibility. Given
that these donations are not readily visible from a distance, raising corporate profiles in the international arena requires new forms of philanthropy. In particular, global public health has become a key focus for
corporate donations. In the last decade, the companies that comprise the
Fortune 500 have contributed to campaigns against some of the world's
major health threats, most notably HIV/AIDS, malaria, and tuberculo-
sis. These campaigns are often announced in full-page ads in the *New
York Times*, such as the two-page ad from Chevron on June 1, 2011, with
the caption: "Fighting Aids Should be Corporate Policy. We Agree." A
similar ad from the Global Business Coalition on HIV/AIDS, Tubercu-
losis and Malaria, which lists a number of mining companies as patrons,
salutes the winners of the 2007 Awards for Business Excellence with
the headline: "Fighting AIDS, TB and Malaria Is Our Business." These
contributions help corporations "gain access to new kinds of moral and
social resources" that can be mobilized "in pursuit of their economic
goals."[54]

The mining industry's attention to malaria is of particular interest.
The mining giants Anglo American and BHP Billiton are two of the
key corporate funders of Africa Fighting Malaria, an NGO that seeks

to overturn the ban on DDT use. Africa Fighting Malaria is also supported by the American Enterprise Institute, a conservative organization not ordinarily known for its involvement in Third World humanitarian causes. Widespread public concern about DDT can be traced to the publication of Rachel Carson's *Silent Spring* in 1962, which described the threats posed to humans and the environment by the use of chemical pesticides in industrial agriculture.[55] Carson's work provoked widespread criticism of the chemical industry, leading to the establishment of the US Environmental Protection Agency, which subsequently banned DDT. The recognition that DDT and other insecticides enter the food chain and accumulate within certain organisms was already well established in the scientific community prior to the publication of her work.[56] The toxic effect of DDT on songbirds provided Carson with the evocative image of a "silent spring" in which "no birds sing," galvanizing popular understandings of the harms caused by industrial pollution. This opened up a critical space for political intervention that facilitated the emergence of the environmental movement in the 1970s and the subsequent efflorescence of environmental NGOs during the 1980s, suggesting one reason why Carson's work remains a target for the conservative movement so long after its publication.

Criticism of the ban on DDT might also be seen as an attempt to put the genie of public participation in science back in the bottle, returning policy making to scientists and their corporate employers. If it could be demonstrated that NGO opposition to DDT use for malaria prevention was misguided, this would discredit NGOs on the very grounds through which they claim legitimacy, the protection of vulnerable populations. The assertion that millions of people have needlessly died as a result of Carson's work seeks to reverse the shift toward public participation in scientific decision making.[57] It may also help to explain why the American Enterprise Institute and the mining industry support Africa Fighting Malaria.

A second focus of the mining industry in promoting its contribution to society is poverty reduction, which is increasingly invoked by mining industry executives as a key objective. For example, the mining industry was determined to make a strong presentation at the 2002 World Summit on Sustainable Development (WSSD) in Johannesburg, South Africa, in order to preempt civil society's ability to advocate for stronger regulatory control over its operations.[58] To this end, the industry commissioned a ten million dollar study of the challenges facing the mining industry.[59] When the final report of the Mines, Minerals, and Sustainable Development project was presented at the Johannesburg summit, Brian Gilbertson, the CEO of BHP Billiton, invoked John F. Kennedy's call to "abolish all forms of human poverty" and Nelson Mandela on the need to fight against "poverty and lack of human dignity" in relation to the industry's contribution to sustainable development.[60] Gilbertson also argued that "the real challenges of Sustainable Development arise when a major project goes awry, when one stares into an environmental abyss. For BHP Billiton, that abyss was Ok Tedi." He praised BHP Billiton's "solution" to the problems downstream from the Ok Tedi mine, the transfer of the company's share in the project to a development trust, but failed to mention the alternative option of staying in Papua New Guinea to clean up the polluted river system. Gilbertson also commended the Mines, Minerals, and Sustainable Development project for having "brought much self-examination throughout the industry."[61]

In contrast to corporate philanthropy, or "doing good," are reform efforts that result in the reduction of corporate harm, which might be described as "doing better." Despite the self-congratulatory tone of Gilbertson's speech in Johannesburg, the mining industry largely failed to raise its operating standards in the decade following the 2002 summit. There are several important exceptions, such as BHP Billiton's pledge not to discharge tailings into the river system in any new project. Its chief competitors, however, refused to follow suit. Rio Tinto, for example, argues that it is counterproductive to make general policy decisions on tailings disposal and continues to address these issues on a case-by-case basis. The problem with voluntary reforms is that noncompulsory measures create free rider problems when corporations that decline to follow the new standard gain a competitive advantage over companies operating according to the higher standards. Given the high cost of environmental mitigation in the mining industry, only the lowest cost producers can afford to operate during an economic downturn, which discourages participation in voluntary reforms.

The mining industry is also largely insulated from shareholder preferences. This is especially true for gold, which serves as an important hedge against the volatility of the stock market because the price of gold is countercyclical with the market's economic performance. Mining company stocks are also relatively immune from the pressures of the "shareholder democracy" in which investors use their voting power to promote corporate reform.[62] One of the most significant innovations in shareholder activism over the last two decades was the establishment of social and green choice investment funds. These funds have generally outperformed the market average due to their popularity and the resulting supply of capital. Consequently, rather unlikely corporations and industries have lobbied for membership, often invoking industry awards for sustainability and corporate social responsibility as their rationale.[63] During the period between the Kyoto accord on global climate change in 1997 and the 2011 Fukushima crisis, when nuclear power received the reluctant endorsement of mainstream conservation organizations concerned about greenhouse gases emanating from carbon-based energy sources, the uranium mining industry sought inclusion in green choice funds. These efforts were subsequently delegitimized by the tsunami that brought Japan's nuclear industry to the brink of disaster. Ironically, stock fund managers invoke green and social choice funds as a rationale for blocking shareholder resolutions by arguing that individuals who do not wish to invest in particular corporations have the option of investing in these more specialized funds. For example, a 1999 shareholder initiative to force TIAA-CREF, the major pension fund for American professors and schoolteachers, to divest its shares in Freeport McMoRan, which owns and operates the controversial Grasberg mine in West Papua, Indonesia, was rebuffed by the management of TIAA-CREF.[64]

CSR in the Academy

Finally, how does the discourse of corporate social responsibility affect academic debates? The issue arises at a historical moment when corporations and the market are influencing the academy in a variety of ways. Universities are increasingly adopting new business models, including the application of "audit culture" to assess research performance.[65] Public universities are required to justify their activities in terms of contributions to local economic growth, with implications for course offerings and academic positions. This includes a shift in resources from the humanities and social sciences to the STEM fields of science, technology, engineering, and mathematics. These changes are accompanied by the proliferation of corporate-academic partnerships in the life sciences and other fields, resulting in new research priorities and accountabilities.[66]

Even within the field of anthropology, there has been a rise in demand for our skills by corporations. In the arena in which I work, anthropolo-

gists may choose to collaborate with the participants in indigenous political movements, work with NGOs and lawyers, provide expert testimony to multilateral organizations, and so forth.[67] But my colleagues
are more likely to consult or work for mining companies than criticize
or oppose them. They argue that they are better able to effect positive
change by working within these organizations than by addressing problems and concerns from the outside, ignoring corporate mechanisms for
neutralizing internal dissent and disciplining employees.[68] This includes
the threat of legal action or the termination of their contracts, which pre-
vents anthropologists from making the results of their research available
to the public.[69]

Neoliberal confidence in the ability of the market to solve complex
problems also influences the role played by the study of business and
management in universities, especially in relation to the environment.
No one at my university objected when the business school established a
new institute to foster sustainable business practices. But the proponents
of market-based solutions to environmental problems have not been content with greening their own institutions. The establishment of a joint
master's degree program between the business school and the school
of natural resources prompted criticism and concern, even though this
might be seen as a return to the school's original mission, which was to
make more efficient, rational, and productive use of the state's natural
resources in contrast to the environmental values that have influenced
the school since the 1970s. The advocates of market-based reforms have
also sought to promote their views across the campus by helping to establish a new institute for sustainability. The external board of advisors
appointed to this institute included a number of corporations with controversial environmental track records, including Dow Chemical, Duke
Energy, Shell Oil, and BHP Billiton, the mining company responsible
for the Ok Tedi disaster. The acting director of the institute defended
the decision to include BHP Billiton on the board to the *Chronicle of
Higher Education*: "'There's no pure company out there,' he says. 'I have
no reason to doubt that this company has really screwed a lot of people,'
just as nearly every other company is 'unjust to people' at one point or
another. . . . 'These organizations are part of the problem, and they're
also part of the solution.'"[70] In these transformations of the academy,
critical attention to the ways in which market forces are responsible for
environmental problems risk being elided in favor of promoting the ability of the market to offer solutions, much like the way the environment is

no longer seen as a crucial element of sustainability. Such claims are also presented as though they were politically neutral.

Conclusion

In this chapter, I argue that the discourse of corporate social responsibility is a strategically deployable shifter that claims to represent values we all support. CSR discourse extends the power of corporations to achieve their goals through the use of virtuous language. It assigns positive value to one side of political debates about the role of corporations and markets in society at the expense of a critique that calls for greater regulation or other interventions. Nonetheless, the discourse of corporate social responsibility conveys the impression that it is technocratic, professional, fair, innovative, optimistic, and open-minded, whereas the critics of CSR risk being scolded for their "low-minded sentimentality" for believing the worst about corporations and their motives.[71]

It is the task of scholars in the social sciences and the humanities to analyze discursive claims and to study how, when, why, and by whom these discourses are mobilized. But strategically deployable shifters like sustainability and corporate social responsibility have the potential to neutralize their critics, limiting their ability to question these claims. Indeed, this may be the primary objective of the discourse of corporate social responsibility. The only way to demystify such virtuous language is to examine its history, and in particular the concrete struggles through which it emerges in contrast to "just so" stories of corporate enlightenment or the economic rationalization of the business case for social responsibility, the audiences to which it is directed, what it claims to accomplish, and the consequences of its deployment in both industry and the academy.

Acknowledgments

I am grateful to Charlotte Walker-Said, John Kelly, and the contributors to this volume for an engaging set of conversations. I also thank the linguistic anthropology lab at the University of Michigan, including Alaina Lemon, Michael Lempert, and Bruce Mannheim, for their helpful comments. Bonnie Urciuoli generously provided feedback on an earlier version of the paper presented at a Sawyer Seminar at Indiana University on "Neoliberal Regimes and Institutions of Knowledge Production" co-organized by Ilana Gershon and Rebecca Lave. Wes Shumar and Ilana Gershon also made particularly helpful suggestions at the Bloomington workshop.

Notes

1. Stuart Kirsch, *Reverse Anthropology: Indigenous Analysis of Social and Environmental Relations in New Guinea* (Stanford, CA: Stanford University Press, 2006); Stuart Kirsch, *Mining Capitalism: Dialectical Relations between Corporations and Their Critics* (Berkeley: University of California Press, 2014).

2. Bonnie Urciuoli, "Excellence, Leadership, Skills, Diversity: Marketing Liberal Arts Education," *Language and Communication* 23 (2003): 385–408; Bonnie Urciuoli, "Skills and Selves in the New Workplace," *American Ethnologist* 35, no. 2 (2008): 211–28; Bonnie Urciuoli, "Entextualizing Diversity," *Language and Communication* 30 (2010): 48–57.

3. Michael Silverstein, "Shifters, Linguistic Categories, and Cultural Description," in *Meaning in Anthropology*, ed. Keith Basso and Henry Selby (Albuquerque: University of New Mexico Press, 1976), 29.

4. Danilyn Rutherford, *Laughing at Leviathan: Sovereignty and Audience in West Papua* (Chicago: University of Chicago Press, 2012).

5. Urciuoli, "Entextualizing Diversity," 55.

6. Ibid.

7. Barbara Ward and René J. Dubos, *Only One Earth: The Care and Maintenance of a Small Planet* (New York: W. W. Norton, 1972), xviii.

8. International Union for the Conservation of Nature (IUCN), "World Conservation Strategy," 1.

9. BHP Billiton. "Our Sustainability Framework," September 2010, www.bhpbilliton.com/home/aboutus/Documents/ourSustainabilityFramework2010.pdf.

10. Peter Benson and Stuart Kirsch, "Corporate Oxymorons," *Dialectical Anthropology* 34, no. 1 (2010): 47.

11. Antonio Negri, "The Specter's Smile," in *Ghostly Demarcations: A Symposium on Jacques Derrida's Specters of Marx*, ed. Michael Sprinker (New York: Verso, 1999), 9.

12. BHP Billiton, corporate website, 2012; Kirsch, *Reverse Anthropology*; Kirsch, *Mining Capitalism*.

13. Goldie Blumenstyk, "Mining Company Involved in Environmental Disaster Now Advises Sustainability Institute at U. of Michigan," *Chronicle of Higher Education* 54, no. 15 (2007): A22.

14. Kirsch, *Mining Capitalism*.

15. Urciuoli, "Entextualizing Diversity," 49.

16. Ronen Shamir, "Capitalism, Governance, and Authority: The Case of Corporate Social Responsibility," *Annual Review of Law and Social Science* 6 (2010): 545.

17. Ibid.

18. International Council on Mining and Metals (ICMM), home page.

19. Rio Tinto, corporate website.

20. Denise Leith, *The Politics of Power: Freeport in Suharto's Indonesia* (Honolulu: University of Hawai'i Press, 2003); James Ferguson, *Global Shadows: Africa in the Neoliberal World Order* (Durham, NC: Duke University Press, 2006).

21. Stuart Kirsch, "Anthropology and Advocacy: A Case Study of the Campaign against the Ok Tedi Mine," *Critique of Anthropology* 22, no. 2 (2002): 175–200; Kirsch, *Mining Capitalism*; Suzana Sawyer, *Crude Chronicles: Indians, Multinational Oil, and Neoliberalism in Ecuador* (Durham, NC: Duke University Press, 2004); David Szablowski, *Transnational Law and Local Struggles: Mining, Communities, and the World Bank* (Portland, OR: Hart Publishing, 2007).

22. Margaret E. Keck and Kathryn Sikkink, *Activists beyond Borders: Advocacy Networks in International Politics* (Ithaca, NY: Cornell University Press, 1998); Arjun Appadurai, "Grassroots Globalization and the Research Imagination," *Public Culture* 12, no. 1 (2000): 1–19; Stuart Kirsch, "Indigenous Movements and the Risks of Counterglobalization: Tracking the Campaign against Papua New Guinea's Ok Tedi Mine," *American Ethnologist* 34, no. 2 (2007): 303–21.

23. Kirsch, "Anthropology and Advocacy"; Kirsch, *Reverse Anthropology*; Kirsch, *Mining Capitalism*.

24. John Gordon, "The Ok Tedi Lawsuit in Retrospect," in *The Ok Tedi Settlements: Issues, Outcomes, and Implications*, Pacific Policy Paper 27, ed. Glenn Banks and Chris Ballard (Canberra: National Centre for Development Studies and Resource Management in Asia-Pacific, the Australian National University, 1997), 141–66.

25. Nikki Tait, "Ok Tedi Copper Mine Damage Claim Settled," *Financial Times*, June 12, 1996, 19.

26. Keck and Sikkink, *Activists beyond Borders*; Kirsch, "Indigenous Movements and the Risks of Counterglobalization"; Anna Lowenhaupt Tsing, *Friction: An Ethnography of Global Connection* (Princeton, NJ: Princeton University Press, 2004).

27. Chris Ballard and Glenn Banks, "Resource Wars: The Anthropology of Mining," *Annual Review of Anthropology* 32 (2003): 287–313.

28. Luke Danielson, *Architecture for Change: An Account of the Mining, Minerals, and Sustainable Development Project*. Berlin: Global Public Policy In-

stitute, 2006. http://info.worldbank.org/etools/library/view_p.asp?lprogram=107 &objectid=238483, 7.

29. Kirsch, *Mining Capitalism*; Brant McGee, "The Community Referendum: Participatory Democracy and the Right to Free, Prior, and Informed Consent to Development," *Berkeley Journal of International Law* 27, no. 2 (2009): 570–635.

30. Katherine Fultz, "Local Referendums on Mining Projects in Latin America," unpublished report in the possession of the author, 2011.

31. McGee, "The Community Referendum," 604–10.

32. Ibid., 615–18.

33. Ibid., 618–26.

34. Ibid., 585.

35. Ted Downing, "Why Comment on the World Bank's Proposed Indigenous Peoples Policy?" *Anthropology News* 42, no. 9 (2001): 23–24.

36. Maurice Bridge and Angus Wong, "Consenting Adults: Changes to the Principle of Free, Prior, and Informed Consent Are Changing the Way in Which Firms Engage Communities," *Mining, People, and the Environment* (July 2011): 12–15.

37. W. Henson Moore, "The Social License to Operate," *Paper Industry Manufacturing Association (PIMA) Magazine* 78, no. 10 (1996): 23.

38. Ian Thomson and Robert G. Boutilier, "Social License to Operate," in *SME Mining Engineering Handbook*, ed. P. Darling (Littleton, CO: Society for Mining, Metallurgy, and Exploration, 2011), 1179; Colin Filer, Glenn Banks, and John Burton, "The Fragmentation of Responsibilities in the Melanesian Mining Sector," in *Earth Matters: Indigenous Peoples, Extractive Industries, and Corporate Social Responsibility*, ed. Ciaran O'Faircheallaigh and Saleem Ali (Sheffield, UK: Greenleaf, 2008), 163–79.

39. Colin Filer, personal communication, 2012.

40. Bridge and Wong, "Consenting Adults," 15.

41. BHP Billiton, "Our Sustainability Framework," 2010.

42. Bridge and Wong, "Consenting Adults," 15.

43. See Andrew J. Hoffman, *From Heresy to Dogma: An Institutional History of Corporate Environmentalism* (San Francisco: New Lexington Press, 1997).

44. Karen Ho, *Liquidated: An Ethnography of Wall Street* (Durham, NC: Duke University Press, 2009).

45. Marina Welker and David Wood, "Shareholder Activism and Alienation," *Current Anthropology* 52, no. S3 (2011): S57–S69.

46. Szablowski, *Transnational Law and Local Struggles*.

47. Ibid., 63.

48. Ibid., 63–64.

49. Dinah Rajak, *In Good Company: An Anatomy of Corporate Social Responsibility* (Stanford, CA: Stanford University Press, 2011).

50. Business and Biodiversity Offsets Programme, "Compensatory Conservation Case Studies." Washington, DC: Business and Biodiversity Offsets Programme, 2009. http://content.undp.org/go/cms-service/stream/asset/?asset_id=2469112; Caroline Seagle, "Inverting the Impacts: Mining, Conservation, and Sustainability Claims Near the Rio Tinto/QQM Ilmenite Mine in Southeast Madagascar," *Journal of Peasant Studies* 39, no. 2 (2012): 447–77.

51. Mac Chapin, "A Challenge to Conservationists," *Worldwatch Magazine* (November/December 2004): 17–31.

52. Jessica Smith Rolston, "What Are Good Intentions Good For? Corporate Social Responsibility in the Mining Industry," unpublished paper presented at the American Anthropological Association meeting, 2010.

53. Roland Marchand, *Creating the Corporate Soul: The Rise of Public Relations and Corporate Imagery in American Big Business* (Berkeley: University of California Press, 1998).

54. Rajak, *In Good Company.*

55. Rachel Carson, *Silent Spring* (New York: Houghton Mifflin, 1962).

56. James E. McWilliams, *American Pests: The Losing War on Insects from Colonial Times to DDT* (New York: Columbia University Press, 2008).

57. Naomi Oreskes and Erik M. Conway, *Merchants of Doubt: How a Handful of Scientists Obscured the Truth on Issues from Tobacco Smoke to Global Warming* (New York: Bloomsbury Press, 2010), 216–39.

58. Darryl Reed, "Resource Extraction Industries in Developing Countries," *Journal of Business Ethics* 39 (2002): 199–226, at 218.

59. Luke Danielson, *Architecture for Change: An Account of the Mining, Minerals, and Sustainable Development Project.* Berlin: Global Public Policy Institute, 2006. http://info.worldbank.org/etools/library/view_p.asp?lprogram=107&objectid=238483.

60. Brian Gilbertson, speech to the World Business Council for Sustainable Development / International Institute for Economy Development, Mining, Minerals, and Sustainable Development meeting. World Summit on Sustainable Development, Johannesburg. August 30, 2002, http://www.qni.com.au/bbContentRepository/Presentations/ WorldSummit.pdf.

61. Gilbertson, speech to the World Business Council for Sustainable Development.

62. Robert L. Foster, *Coca-Globalization: Following Soft Drinks from New York to New Guinea* (London: Palgrave McMillan, 2008).

63. Rajak, *In Good Company.*

64. Social Funds, "Merrill Lynch Fund Participant Pioneers Divestment Resolution," July 27, 2000, http://www.socialfunds.com/news/save.cgi?sfArticleId=321.

65. Marilyn Strathern, "Introduction: New Accountabilities," in *Audit Cultures: Anthropological Studies in Accountability, Ethics, and the Academy*, ed. Marilyn Strathern (New York: Routledge, 2000), 1–19.

66. Stephen Bocking, *Nature's Experts: Science, Politics, and the Environment* (New Brunswick, NJ: Rutgers University Press, 2004), 37.

67. Kirsch, *Mining Capitalism*.

68. Thomas D. Beamish, *Silent Spill: The Organization of an Industrial Crisis* (Cambridge, MA: MIT Press, 2002).

69. Catherine Coumans, "Occupying Spaces Created by Conflict: Anthropologists, Development NGOs, Responsible Investment, and Mining," *Current Anthropology* 52, no. S3 (2011): S29–S43.

70. Blumenstyk, "Mining Company Involved in Environmental Disaster Now Advises Sustainability Institute."

71. Charlotte Walker-Said (this volume) citing Amartya Sen, *Development as Freedom* (Cambridge, MA: Harvard University Press, 1999), 280.

PART II

Corporate Social Responsibility and the Mandate to Remedy

Between Empowerment and Mitigating Vulnerabilities

Caroline Kaeb

When construing corporate social responsibility (CSR) as either business or as humanitarianism, a critical analysis of the role of the law is indispensable. The legal dimension of CSR is determined largely by the fiduciary duties owed by corporate directors and officers to the corporation. In the United States, the principle of "shareholder primacy," according to which management decisions need to be in the best interest of shareholders (in terms of profit maximization) in order to avoid a breach of fiduciary duties, has been prevailing as classical theory.[1] Jurisdictions in Europe and Asia, on the other hand, have embraced stakeholder-centric governance structures and have construed fiduciary duties more broadly as to extend to stakeholder interests as well.[2] Regardless, the question of the legitimacy of public interest decisions by corporate managers, especially when those decisions are profit sacrificing, is determined on the basis of corporate law. As a consequence, premises of human rights law and philosophy are not sufficiently accounted for when delineating the scope of CSR. However, since CSR is at the intersection of law, business, ethics, and development, a serious attempt must be made to construe and structure CSR in an integrated manner rather than promoting a siloed treatment of the issue under separate disciplines. As early as 1979, Archie Carroll acknowledged the multidimensional nature of CSR by stating the social responsibility of business "encompasses the economic, legal, ethical, and discretionary expectations that society has of organizations at a given point in time."[3]

By examining the different stages CSR has embodied over the decades and its interaction with the law, it becomes clear that the quest for the best methodology to make CSR effective and "give it teeth" has been long. Still, to date, locating the right balance of soft law and hard law responses to the CSR compliance challenge is a task for legal scholars, law practitioners, and government officials alike. This section of the volume critically assesses the existing regulatory and self-regulatory attempts in different country contexts and across industries, the lessons learned, and the risks and opportunities of the different methodologies. The contributions in this section aim to provide a fresh perspective on the interaction between CSR and the law and demonstrate how soft law and hard law can be structured to ensure positive compliance results on the part of corporations in a way that is consistent with human rights, upholds the legal deterrence theory, and accounts for system inefficiencies. The implications of soft and hard law methodologies for human rights in terms of empowerment of victims or reinforcement of their vulnerabilities are still largely unknown and require further examination.

Early theories construed CSR as a moral responsibility, thereby relying on corporate self-regulation and on soft law standards.[4] In this vein, CSR often took the form of philanthropic efforts that focused mainly on charitable giving as a response to vulnerabilities rather than true rights empowerment.[5] Many soft law standards, addressing the corporate responsibility for human rights and other areas of CSR (among others, labor, anticorruption, and environment), were set by the intergovernmental system. Prominent examples are the ILO Tripartite Declaration of Principles Concerning Multinational Enterprises and Social Policy and the OECD Guidelines for Multinational Enterprises.[6] CSR was mainly framed as the "right thing to do" in pursuit of being a good corporate citizen within the global economic structure, an effort that was at the discretion of corporate actors.[7] CSR in this form has had potentially sensitive implications for the philosophical underpinnings of human rights, framing the human being as the holder of natural rights. However, neither the international community nor the scholarship has traditionally assessed CSR conceptually through the lens of human rights. More recently, some soft law intergovernmental initiatives have added internal mechanisms to enhance accountability for corporate compliance in the form of nonjudicial review mechanisms, such as the network of national contact points for the OECD guidelines.[8] These developments for enhanced review structures within soft law mechanisms have introduced a hybrid model that increasingly blurs the boundary between self-regulation and accountability.

Conceptually, a significant turn came in the last decade, when CSR has increasingly been framed as a human rights issue by intergovernmental organizations (such as the UN Global Compact), corporations (such as Yahoo!'s Business and Human Rights Program within their legal department), and civil society organizations (such as the Business and Human Rights Resource center tracking corporate-related human rights abuses of over five hundred companies across various industry sectors and in over 180 countries of operation).[9] The "business and human rights" understanding of CSR initially marked a vivid departure from the mere soft law premises to a hard law approach with regard to the corporate responsibility toward society. In 1998 the United Nations (through the United Nations Sub-Commission on the Promotion and Protection of Human Rights) spearheaded an effort to adopt a set of universal norms that would impose human rights duties on companies directly under international law. Known as the "U.N. Norms on the Responsibilities of Transnational Corporations and Other Business Enterprises with Regard to Human Rights,"[10] these measures were never adopted by the UN Human Rights Council and proved futile.[11] The main conceptual challenge that the Sub-Commission's Working Group faced during the drafting process of the Norms was the difficulty of delineating state and corporate responsibilities with regard to human rights.[12] Critiques of the Norms have been voiced, arguing that corporate responsibilities for human rights cannot simply mirror the responsibilities of states, since, while states have a "general" human rights responsibility, corporations have a "specialized" one.[13] As an answer to the failure of adopting binding universal standards on the subject, the UN Human Rights council appointed John Ruggie as the UN general-secretary's special representative on business and human rights.[14] The goal of Ruggie's UN mandate has been to identify and assess existing practices in the field and provide a "common conceptual and policy framework" to guide the relevant actors involved in economic globalization. The UN effort under Ruggie has deviated from aiming to regulate corporate behavior through hard law norms and instead provides a more accessible "policy framework" as "a foundation on which thinking and action can build" and that corporations can use as a reference point when structuring their very own specific human rights policies and mechanisms.[15]

John Ruggie's work during his two terms as UN special representative on business and human rights has pointed to some difficult conceptual challenges when framing social expectations toward corporations as human rights issues. One of the major challenges has proven to be developing a framework that integrates hard and soft law elements in a way that accounts for the "specialized" role of corporations (as nonstate actors) under an international law system where traditionally states have been the duty holders with regard to human rights.[16] Aside from accommodating companies as nonstate actors under the original international human rights system, many questions still remain as to the right balance between soft law and hard law dimensions of the framework. This hard law versus soft law debate can be considered a function of the complex relationship between law and ethics in the field of human rights, which is further amplified by the corporate context of the violations. The fact that even within quite coherent regional systems, such as the European Union, there is ambiguity about the appropriate methodology for CSR implementation illustrates just how far from settled the issue is. Thus, whereas the European Commission embraces a strictly voluntary approach to CSR, the European Parliament favors a mixed approach combining soft law as well as legal regulation and adjudication of CSR-related issues.[17]

Ruggie's "business and human rights framework" rests on distinct yet complementary state and corporate responsibilities with regard to human rights—namely, "the State duty to protect against human rights abuses by third parties, including business: the corporate responsibility to respect human rights; and the need for more effective access to remedies."[18] The framework is an attempt to delineate the role and responsibility of states and corporations with regard to the society and to identify the status quo of such responsibilities under international law. Thinking along the lines of a hard law–soft law dichotomy, it becomes apparent that currently under international law, states have a *duty* to protect human rights, whereas corporations merely have a *responsibility* to respect human rights. It is coherent under international law, as a state-centric system, that states remain the primary obligation holders in relation to human rights and that a corporate responsibility in this context "does not diminish those [state] obligations."[19]

Ruggie stresses the current soft law nature of the corporate responsibility for human rights. At the same time, however, he points toward the sensitive relationship of this soft law responsibility with hard law standards by emphasizing that corporate responsibility "exists over and above compliance with national laws and regulations protecting human rights."[20] It seems that after past efforts to develop a set of universally binding norms, the international community through the United Nations has refocused on the benefits of soft law, namely, its normative effect and its aspirational goals that can (and ought to, according to Ruggie) go beyond mere law. This last point resonates with the position of the European Commission as pronounced in its 2001 Green Paper on CSR, which states: "By stating their social responsibility and voluntarily taking on commitments which go beyond common regulatory and conventional requirements, which they would have to respect in any case, companies endeavor to raise the standards of social development environmental protection and respect of fundamental rights."[21] Other scholars have argued that "the province of law is always and properly limited, since . . . governments 'can't legislative morality' particularly in the most challenging ethical areas."[22] However, the current UN framework on business and human rights does not suggest going back to a mere philanthropic or voluntary understanding of CSR. Rather, it features a mixed implementation approach that leverages the potential of soft law but aims to strengthen judicial and nonjudicial accountability mechanisms in the long run.[23] This accounts for and mitigates the reality that in some instances soft law standards and self-regulation might be pursued by some corporations to avoid having more binding measures gain political momentum and thus escape the realm of legally binding and enforceable standards.[24] The fact remains that soft law initiatives that lack accountability measures run the risk of merely mitigating crisis rather than upholding human rights.

Despite the fact that under current international law and human rights law no corporate legal duty yet exists with respect to human rights, there have been increasing, yet sporadic, efforts to provide effective legal remedies for corporate infringements, particularly those amounting to international crimes, at the domestic level both in the United States under the Alien Tort Statute (ATS) and in Europe.[25] While human rights litigation targeted at corporations has been most prevalent in US courts under the ATS, there has been an increasing number of civil law systems, including in Europe, that in theory provide for corporate liability for in-

ternational crimes.[26] Even though such cases have not been brought on
a broad scale outside of the United States to date, there is an emerging
and "expanding web of liability for business entities implicated in international crimes."[27] The increasing number of domestic laws prescribing
corporate liability for international crimes traces back, in part, to the increase in international and regional agreements relating to transnational
crimes that mandate states adjust their domestic legal system accordingly.[28] In Europe, liability venues for such cases have slowly but steadily
developed in domestic legal systems since the Council of Europe in 1988
urged member states to change their domestic criminal codes to include
corporate criminal liability.[29] Moreover, civil courts in Europe can potentially accommodate tort claims related to the different CSR issue areas under the so-called Brussels I Regulation.[30] However, despite increasing enforcement and accountability venues for CSR-related issues,
new laws have only focused on regulating the most egregious violations
and thus have only set an obligatory minimum standard in the form of a
baseline criterion. This still leaves a significant field of unregulated activities, which therefore will be governed by soft law initiatives and self-
regulatory efforts on the part of corporations.

This volume aims to make a contribution to finding a differentiated
approach for corporations in modern-day economic globalization in a
way that empowers vulnerable groups and incentivizes corporations to
set aspirational goals for human rights on a voluntary basis that go beyond mere prescriptions of the law. Revisiting and potentially redefining
CSR in light of past lessons requires striking a balance between soft and
hard law implementation that is effective as well as sensitive to the implications for the philosophical underpinnings of human rights theory.

In an effort to deliver on their social and particularly human rights
responsibility, corporations have increasingly subscribed to multistakeholder initiatives as hybrid and inclusive forms of soft law mechanisms
that have great potential bridging the gap between the state and corporate responsibilities for society in general, as Amelia Evans demonstrates in this section. To date there have been some prominent examples
of such initiatives that have enjoyed broad engagement with industry,
governments, and civil society, namely, the Voluntary Principles on Security and Human Rights for the extractive and mining sector, the Kimberley Process Certification Scheme on conflict diamonds, and the
Global Network Initiative to promote freedom of expression and privacy
protection in information communication technologies.[31] However, since

multistakeholder initiatives are a recent occurrence and are few in number, many questions still have to be addressed and their structures to be refined in order to generate sustainable impact that is aimed as self-sufficiency and empowerment rather than mitigation of vulnerabilities.

The authors of this section focus on the practicability of successful CSR law implementation and its underlying implications for human rights ideology in terms of individual empowerment. Caroline Kaeb, Amelia Evans, and Ursula Wynhoven and Yousuf Aftab delve deeply into the philosophies of the "business case for CSR"[32] and the role of morality and law in the compliance game; the recognition that there are multiple drivers for corporate behavior has become a significant component of effective and sustainable treatment of contemporary CSR. At the same time, however, several authors acknowledge that justice and human rights also require empowered individuals who play an active and integral role in the society they live in. David Scheffer and Scott Gilmore's respective chapters delineate past strategies and potential future capabilities for the law's reach and its potential for shaping responsibility by corporations through direct enforcement. Jonathan Bush's chapter historicizes the economic and political consequences of setting legal precedent in the realm of corporate responsibility and provides a critical insight into the foundations of our current debates, laid out by the section's other scholars.

All of this section's chapters—whether directly or indirectly—contend with the ramifications of private victims' litigation under the US Alien Tort Statute against businesses for extraterritorial human rights infringements. Human rights litigation under the ATS has snaked through the last decades of experimentation with soft law and hard law implementation in the area of CSR. In its ancient statutory form (it was originally adopted to provide redress merely for violations of safe passage, infringement of the rights of ambassadors, and piracy), the ATS has been used to address and remedy contemporary human rights–related problems in the context of global business.[33] In its decision in *Kiobel v. Royal Dutch Petroleum* handed down in April 2013, the US Supreme Court severely constrained the extraterritorial reach of the ATS, which has undeniably diminished its role of the United States as the primary venue to hold corporations accountable and induce compliance.[34] This recent development has changed the CSR debate significantly by requiring some creative thinking about alternative effective venues of CSR implementation. It has also provided momentum to critically assess the high-level implications of the respective approaches and methodologies. The question remains, what is the relationship between ethics and the law in the contemporary CSR debate? At the current stage of CSR, many lessons have been learned and best practices distilled. Yet there are still many connections that merit a more detailed and in-depth treatment by the scholarship. This section and this volume aim to contribute to this debate.

Notes

1. Milton Friedman, *Capitalism and Freedom* (Chicago: University of Chicago Press, 1962); see also Dodge v. Ford Motor Co., 204 Mich. 459, 170 N.W. 668 (S.C. Mich. 1919). A common law deviation from a strict "shareholder primacy" exists in the United Kingdom, where the law requires corporate directors since 2006 to take into account interests of other stakeholders beyond shareholders (U.K. Companies Act 2006, Art. 172 (1)).

2. See Michael Kerr, Richard Janda, and Chip Pitts, *Corporate Social Responsibility: A Legal Analysis* (Ontario: LexisNexis, 2009), 113–14, 162.

3. Archie Carroll, "A Three-Dimensional Conceptual Model of Corporate Performance," *Academy of Management Review* 4 (1979): 500.

4. Thomas Donaldson and Thomas Dunfee, *Ties That Bind: A Social Contracts Approach to Business Ethics* (Cambridge, MA: Harvard Business Press, 1999); Archie Carroll, "The Pyramid of Corporate Social Responsibility: Toward the Moral Management of Organizational Stakeholders," *Business Horizons* (July–August 1991): 39–48.

5. See Mark Schwartz and Archie Carroll, "Corporate Social Responsibility: A Three-Domain Approach," *Business Ethics Quarterly* 13 (2003): 505–6.

6. International Labour Organization (ILO), Tripartite Declaration of Principles concerning Multinational Enterprises and Social Policy, Governing Body of the ILO, 204th Sess. (1977), last amended 295th Sess. (2006); OECD, *The OCED Guidelines for Multinational Enterprises* (Paris: OCED, 1976).

7. See Dirk Matten and Andrew Crane, "Corporate Citizenship: Toward an Extended Theoretical Conceptualization," *Academy of Management Review* 30 (2005): 168; Schwartz and Carroll, "Corporate Social Responsibility," 505–7.

8. See John Ruggie, *Business and Human Rights: Mapping International Standards of Responsibility and Accountability for Corporate Acts*, report of the Special Representative of the Secretary-General on the issue of human rights and transnational corporations and other business enterprises, A/HRC/4/35, at para. 50 (February 19, 2007).

9. United Nations Global Compact, "Human Rights, Principles 1 and 2,"

http://www.unglobalcompact.org/issues/human_rights/; Yahoo!, "Business and Human Rights Program," http://www.yhumanrightsblog.com/blog/; Business and Human Rights Resource Center, "A brief description," http://www.business-humanrights.org/Aboutus/Briefdescription.

10. Draft Norms on the Responsibilities of Transnational Corporations and Other Business Enterprises with Regard to Human Rights, E/CN.4/Sub.2/2003/12 (2003).

11. John Ruggie, *Guiding Principles on Business and Human Rights: Implementing the United Nations "Protect, Respect and Remedy" Framework*, report of the Special Representative of the Secretary-General on the issue of human rights and transnational corporations and other business enterprises, A/HRC/17/31, at para. 3 (March 21, 2011).

12. See Weissbrodt and Kruger, "Norms on the Responsibilities of Transnational Corporations and Other Business Enterprises with Regard to Human Rights," 911–12.

13. See John Ruggie, Interim Report of the Special Representative of the Secretary-General on the Issue of Human Rights and Transnational Corporations and Other Business Enterprises, U.N. Doc. E/CN.4/2006/97, para. 66 (2006).

14. Commission on Human Rights, U.N. Doc. E/CN.4/RES/2005/69.

15. John Ruggie, A/HRC/8/5, at para. 5, 8, April 7, 2008.

16. The UN framework on business and human rights rests upon the corporate responsibility to respect human rights, as reflected in soft law mechanisms, while also stressing the need for more effective access to remedies in the form of judicial and nonjudicial grievance mechanisms. John Ruggie, *Protect, Respect, and Remedy: A Framework for Business and Human Rights*, report of the Special Representative of the Secretary-General on the issue of human rights and transnational corporations, A/HRC/8/5, at para. 23, 53, 82 (April 7, 2008).

17. Commission Green Paper (EC) COM (2001) 366 final on Promoting a European Framework for Corporate Social Responsibility, at 8 (July 18, 2001); Parliament Resolution (EC) of April 1999 on EU Standards for European Enterprises Operating in Developing Countries: Towards a European Code of Conduct, 1999 O.J. (C 104/180), Recital F.

18. Parliament Resolution (EC) of April 1999 on EU Standards for European Enterprises.

19. John Ruggie, A/HRC/17/31, Principle 11 (March 21, 2011).

20. Ibid.

21. Commission Green Paper (EC) COM (2001) 366 final on Promoting a European Framework for Corporate Social Responsibility, at para. 3 (July 18, 2001).

22. Kerr, Janda, and Pitts, *Corporate Social Responsibility: A Legal Analysis*, 80.

23. See John Ruggie, A/HRC/4/35, at para. 47, 76 (February 19, 2007). See also John Ruggie, A/HRC/8/5, at para. 82 (April 7, 2008).

24. John Ruggie, A/HRC/4/35, at para. 45 (February 19, 2007).

25. See Peter Muchlinski, *Multinational Enterprises and the Law* (New York: Oxford University Press, 2007), 517.

26. Many legal systems around the world have domestic legal provisions to assert jurisdiction extraterritorially over international crimes committed outside of their territory; see R. C. Thompson, A. Ramasastry, and M. Taylor, "Translating Unocal: The Expanding Web of Liability for Business Entities Implicated in International Crimes," *George Washington International Law Review* 40 (2009): 856.

27. Beth Stephens, "Judicial Deference and the Unreasonable Views of the Bush Administration," *Brooklyn Journal of International Law* 33 (2008): 773; Thompson, Ramasastry, and Taylor, "Translating Unocal: The Expanding Web of Liability for Business Entities Implicated in International Crimes," 856.

28. See Bert Swart, "International Trends towards Establishing Some Form of Punishment for Corporations," *Journal of International Criminal Justice* (2008): 949.

29. Celia Wells, *Corporations and Criminal Responsibility* (New York: Oxford University Press, 2001).

30. Council Regulation (EC) No. 44/2001 of December 22, 2000, on jurisdiction and the recognition and enforcement of judgments in civil and commercial matters, O.J. (L 12/1) ("Brussels I Regulation"). The Brussels I Regulation confers jurisdiction on European courts over corporate misconduct that occurred abroad provided that the corporate defendant is domiciled in the forum jurisdiction (Art. 2 (1) Brussels I Regulation) or the "event giving rise to the damage" occurred in the forum jurisdiction even if the damage has been suffered outside of the European Union (EU) by non-EU nationals. (Art. 5 (3) Brussels I Regulation; European Court of Justice, Case 21/76, Bier v. Mines de Potasse d'Alsace [1976] ECR 1735).

31. Voluntary Principles on Security and Human Rights, http://www.voluntaryprinciples.org/principles/index.php; the Kimberley Process, http://www.kimberleyprocess.com; Global Network Initiative, http://www.globalnetwork initiative.org/.

32. David Vogel, *The Market for Virtue: The Potential and Limits for Corporate Social Responsibility* (Washington, DC: Brookings Institution Press, 2006); Michael Porter and Mark Kramer, "The Big Idea: Creating Shared Value: How to Reinvent Capitalism—and Unleash a Wave of Innovation and Growth," *Harvard Business Review* (January–February 2011): 5.

33. Sosa v. Alvarez-Machain, 542 U.S. 692, 724, 729 (2004). Even though the ATS was adopted by the first Congress in 1789 for these three primary offenses

under the "law of nations," the US Supreme Court held in *Sosa* that "the door is still ajar [for judicial recognition of actionable international norms] subject to vigilant doorkeeping, and thus open to a narrow class of international norms today."

34. Kiobel v. Royal Dutch Petroleum, 569 U.S. ____ (2013).

CHAPTER SIX

An Emerging History of CSR
The Economic Trials at Nuremberg (1945–49)

Jonathan A. Bush

The doctrine of corporate social responsibility (CSR), that strange mixture of altruism and corporate communications, seems everywhere and ascendant. Sitting at the juncture of business and law, marketing and ethics, human rights and international relations, its proponents have identified CSR or urged its application across a broad range of regions, countries, and continents, industries and economic sectors, and social values including labor, consumer, environmental, health, and civil rights. To its more hopeful adherents, CSR is not only ameliorative and pragmatic but also directly linked with big goals like sustainability, social justice, and world peace.

Perhaps the best illustration of its doctrinal success is that CSR is no longer the exclusive province of mildly liberal business critics. The boardroom has appropriated CSR. Long gone is the day when shareholders sued a corporation for adopting CSR-infused policies, demanding there be market reasons to justify a business decision based on ethics more than profitability.[1] Instead, corporations tie CSR efforts to their core businesses. Entrepreneurs position start-ups to be green or inclusive or to engage in fair trade or reinvest in a local community, and consultants urge management to adopt policies that will both look good and serve the Good, a win-win for business.

One surprise in the torrent of literature, however, is that CSR is consistently portrayed as a doctrine largely without a past. The few books that allude at all to history point to a recent past, locating CSR in the first stirrings of the civil rights, consumer, and environmental movements, in responses to automobile failures, oil spills, DDT buildup, and segregated realtors. Some studies cite international campaigns against firms selling arms to the Pentagon during the Vietnam War or to Nigeria or Pakistan during their civil wars, generating pollution, displacing indigenous peoples, supplying shoddy products to the developing world, or bribing overseas officials. Almost all suggest that the origin of today's CSR lies in business responses to 1960s and 1970s exposés and protests, sometimes prompted first by church and university communities reconsidering their holdings.[2] Domestically the responses included adopting recycling programs, designing higher mileage cars or greener buildings, investing in inner cities, and implementing diversity programs; internationally, they included adopting codes of conduct like the Sullivan Principles for doing business in racist South Africa. Having presented these desiderata, CSR literature says little more about historical roots.

In principle there is no reason a vibrant doctrine focused on future business behavior should tarry with its own past. But making, growing, and exchanging what one has made or grown or had others make or grow are ancient activities, and non-market-maximizing or altruistic behavior is also very old. Surely it is worth exploring whether there might be something germane to CSR in this hoary past. Contrast the paucity of history with the way its doctrinal cousin, human rights, is usually presented as having a long past. There is every reason to think CSR has a past too.

As a first installment of that largely unwritten history, this chapter will survey CSR antecedents in one setting: the Nuremberg trials between 1945 and 1949, which included trials of some fifty businessmen and which are much discussed in legal writing about international business responsibility. The chapter in part examines how economic violations of the grossest kind, morally shocking but untested in law, were weighed at Nuremberg against norms that were asserted, developed, and used as the decisional basis for the first time in international law, and how those norms hardened from moral exhortation to legal rule. Yet in many ways Nuremberg's economic cases were failures, and the essay also asks how failure in the courtroom came to be a success afterward for law and for CSR.

The Novelty of Nuremberg, or The Case of the Missing CSR

Much has been written about the novelty of Nuremberg—new crimes, notions of international accountability, notions of fairness—but the trials were novel in another way as well, their emphasis on business wrongdoers and international standards for business. For those familiar with earlier examples, this may sound like a curious claim. But consider a few examples drawn from nineteenth-century Britain, which was beginning to have a business landscape that for the first time resembled today's, with companies operating around the world and with an engaged mass electorate, press readership, and consumer base with humanitarian sentiments. At first, one might sense familiar CSR norms. By the late eighteenth century there was already a parliamentary consensus to abolish the serf status of Scottish colliers; in 1792 there was a fast-growing movement to boycott slave-produced sugar; by the middle of the nineteenth century, many Britons saw their nation's funneling Indian opium into China as a specifically moral wrong; throughout the 1840s British tariffs differentiated between slave- and freely grown sugar; and Manchester workers in December 1862 disregarded the advice of their betters in the movement and sent an open letter to Abraham Lincoln saying they were willing to endure the closure of the cotton trade and of their workplaces so the North might win the Civil War.

Yet even in such high-profile examples, the focus was on not corporate behavior but government policies and personal moral qualities. Perhaps only with the 1908 discovery that the Cadbury Brothers, Quaker progressives, bought cocoa from Portuguese slave labor in Africa and ought to have known, was there a modern CSR campaign pointing to not only the evil of a trade but the obligations of those partaking. The novelty argument requires careful definition and fuller development, but for present purposes it suggests the context for Nuremberg. For many purposes there was no CSR until the twentieth century, the era that added to high Victorian conscience the tools of antitrust and democratic governance, instantaneous communications, the trauma of two world wars on the European mainland, and from Nuremberg, the notion of CSR above and beyond domestic legal duty.

CSR and Nuremberg through the Prism of US Courts

While Nuremberg is now a critical precedent and resource, it comes to contemporary CSR with two curious features. First, because the trials were criminal, the norms that they helped to implant did not emerge in the usual frontal way. The logic of CSR is ordinarily that a business-related evil is identified and then proponents, aggrieved but unable to rely on existing illegality, mobilize to encourage business to address the ill. In 1945 the massive evils, economic and otherwise, were finished, and the nation that had organized and encouraged them was conquered, and German business lay prostrate in law and reality. The point is obvious, but it underscores that Nuremberg economic norms were developed to justify trials and convictions of particular defendants rather than as part of an aspirational vocabulary to entice business to alter future behavior. Criminal law may be problematic terrain on which to explore the development of an emerging sensibility of business responsibility, but Nuremberg will hardly be the only time that CSR norms emerged from criminal trials or that trials influenced sensibility.

The second unusual feature is that Nuremberg enters CSR today not only through the front door, by scholars urging the relevance of landmark trials examining business wrongs, but also the back, through cases brought under the Alien Tort Statute (ATS),[3] an act from the first US Congress (1789) granting courts jurisdiction over civil actions by aliens for violations of international law. It is a familiar tale that the act, neglected for nearly two centuries, began its modern career with the celebrated *Filártiga* case (1980).[4] In the 1990s suits grew more numerous and courts more comfortable with them, and plaintiffs began to sue not only individuals but also corporations for violating the same international law.[5] The result has been a body of cases and briefs addressing modern business norms but drawn from the behavior and legal treatment of slave traders, pirates, merchants, and envoys in previous centuries. This body of learning almost became a down payment on the missing history of CSR, using ATS arguments of economic criminality to elicit historical business norms.

For many ATS litigants, a central part of this is the Nuremberg trials, meaning the four-power International Military Tribunal (IMT),[6] but even more five later trials, four brought against economic actors by the United States in Nuremberg (1947–49)[7] and one by France under an identical theory at Rastatt (1947–48).[8] The defendants were four dozen leaders of six German firms, Flick, I. G. Farben, Krupp, Roechling, Hermann Goering Works, and Dresdner Bank, and the acts—slave labor, plunder, prewar takeover of Jewish- and Czech-owned plants, unconsented human experimentation, manufacture of poison gas, participation in the illegal rearmament for aggressive war—were charged as crimes against humanity, war crimes, conspiracy, and crimes against peace. Why the interest by ATS litigants in Nuremberg? Perhaps it is because that Nuremberg is more recent and familiar than nineteenth-century mixed courts for slave traders, or that Nazi behavior became cultural shorthand for "the worst of the worst," or that Nuremberg courts wrote lengthy, easily located decisions, or that Nuremberg enjoys prestige among lawyers and a wider public and that its importance as a source of living law, as opposed to a final reckoning on Nazism, has grown with invocations by international and national courts engaged with law of war issues.

The Nuremberg precedents are also deeply relevant for contemporary CSR. The economic dimensions of the trials have been much discussed by ATS proponents and by business historians looking at German companies and using Nuremberg evidence along with documents made available partly because of the Swiss bank scandals. Given this, the discussion here will be content to offer five points: (1) that the Nuremberg program from first to last put an emphasis on economic malefactors; (2) that in so doing the trials asserted, often for the first time, a set of binding economic norms; (3) that while startlingly many of the economic defendants were acquitted, the norms and legal theories were rarely rejected and are available for later CSR proponents; (4) that Nuremberg was not only the best known but also almost the only forum in which Nazi behavior gave rise to economic norms, other jurisdictions having chosen not to bring cases; and (5) that the ancillary question raised in ATS litigation regarding the corporate status of an economic actor is an anachronism for Nuremberg, though one that must still concern prosecutors today. Beyond this, what the powerful but ambiguous Nuremberg precedents say for CSR must be for others to develop.

The Nuremberg Focus on Economic Crimes

The effort to prosecute German economic perpetrators began slowly.[9] None of the agencies, pressure groups, legal authors, or politicians who in 1941–42 first proposed war crimes trials spoke of trials for economic actors or large-scale economic offenses. A few might have recalled the last time there were calls for trials, in Versailles 1919, the US secretary of state and his legal aide, from the nation credited with the most progressive theories of war crimes liability, had warned that trials should reach uniformed troops for battle atrocities, not commanders, rarely civilians, and not new crimes far from the battlefield.[10] By 1943, the Justice and Treasury Departments and soon Congress were investigating I. G. Farben, but for other war crimes, espionage and blocking access to materiel, not for atrocities. Property crimes in war had long been punishable, as had enslavement, but these were also unhelpful precedents, addressing small larcenies, a corporal taking a farmer's crops without compensation, while the no-enslavement rule was aimed at one setting, Confederate officials in the Civil War threatening to enslave captured African American Union soldiers. By 1944, however, a handful of lawyers, most though not all Jewish and émigrés, most based in Washington or in New York but regularly visiting Washington, where forward thinking about trials was centered, had begun to write about the economic dimensions of Nazi rule, and that their ideas seem to have gained currency.

Enter Robert Jackson, the eloquent Supreme Court justice whom President Truman named in early May 1945 as proconsul for war crimes policy. Jackson's significance for the first Nuremberg trial between 1945 and 1946 has been widely discussed, but what matters for CSR is that he quickly committed to an ambitious trial program, perhaps influenced by his early hires, including Nuremberg innovator Murray Bernays. Jackson's first report to the president on June 6, 1945, was widely covered in the press and asserted jurisdiction over economic criminals. From his deputy, General William Donovan, head of the Office of Strategic Services (OSS), Jackson inherited investigators and planners, including some of the émigrés who had examined economic liability during the war. Others linked to economic theories, such as Raphael Lemkin, were not on staff but were consulted. In a clue to Jackson's thinking, he turned the economic case over to his closest colleague, assistant attorney general Francis Shea, who assembled a well-regarded group of lawyers, basing some at Farben headquarters in Frankfurt. Dossiers were assembled of hundreds of high-ranking businessmen who seemed to be strong candidates for trial, and Allied teams combed captured business headquarters and factories throughout Europe.

Summer 1945 to summer 1946 turned out to be the year of uncertainty for economic liability. Almost immediately there were difficulties; selecting a private-sector industrialist for the first trial, the four chief prosecutors indicted Gustav Krupp, head of the giant arms maker, but soon learned that he was ailing and that the judges would refuse to allow trial in absentia or a delay to include another defendant. Shortly before, Shea fell victim to Jackson's office politics, and with his resignation the economic case seemed rudderless. But the failure of the Krupp charges led the Allies to explore a possible second international trial for a half-dozen economic actors while the first trial had barely begun. Meanwhile, the large US staff gathered new evidence about Farben and other firms and personalities. When in early 1946 the system for identifying documents was changed, a series was created for economic evidence, ultimately growing to 15,681 items, over half of the items gathered for all cases.[11] General Telford Taylor, the New Deal lawyer leading the new program, recruited scores of lawyers with corporate litigation experience in private practice and government. Meanwhile in Japan in the winter of 1945/46, military governor General Douglas MacArthur's headquarters listed private citizens, including industrialists, as possible war crimes defendants, and the Australian delegation agreed, later circulating their own list.[12]

Any remaining hope for international trials soon ended, on both continents. The IMT judgment (September 30–October 1, 1946) contained a great deal of evidence of economic crimes—an inventory of IMT economic rulings prepared for later litigation ran to thousands of entries[13]— but with no single private defendant against whom that evidence could be offered and no high-level prosecutor presenting it, these parts of the judgment were fragmented. The judges interpreted IMT charter provisions on conspiracy and crimes against peace extremely narrowly as applied to public-sector defendants production czar Albert Speer and economics minister Hjalmar Schacht, meaning that critical theories would likely be useless in future economic cases. Shortly before, leaders in London and Washington, including Jackson, derailed a second international Nazi trial, while in Tokyo negotiators blocked the inclusion of Japanese industrialists. In both theaters, the JAG Corps of various Allied armed forces were well underway in what became large trial programs, but they used only their national versions of the traditional laws of war, which largely limited charges to atrocities by troops and commanders and comparable acts in concentration camps, and precluded almost all new Nuremberg-style offenses, like the liability of an industrialist for activities far from the front.

With other avenues closed, cases began in the one forum available: courts convened by single nations using international, Nuremberg-style law under Allied Control Council Law No. 10. With the British, despite the Labour government's skepticism of big business, spurning such cases and with no major industrialist so careless as to have been captured by the Soviets, the setting was again Nuremberg. US prosecutors filed their first economic case against leaders of Friedrich Flick's coal and steel empire on February 8, 1947. Cases against leaders of Farben (*U.S. v. Krauch*) and Krupp were filed on May 3 and August 16. Having been told by military governor General Lucius Clay that only two more cases would be allowed, Taylor consolidated planned cases against chiefs of the public Hermann Goering Works (HGW) and the Dresdner Bank into the Ministries case (*U.S. v. Weizsaecker*) filed on November 15. On November 25, 1947, the French filed a case in their zone using Nuremberg theory against Hermann Roechling, nephew Ernst, and three others. The total is almost fifty defendants, to which some add twenty-five SS, military, and government defendants who were charged in part for economic crimes, including Milch, who led Luftwaffe slave labor, Pohl and associates who ran the SS economic empire, and Puhl from the Reichsbank who trafficked in "victim gold." The scale of the task is shown by some numbers: for the entire US program, there were 1,700 staffers at peak, 10,000 interrogations, two hundred defense lawyers, hundreds of witnesses and tens of thousands of documents screened, and 1,200 days of court-days including large portions of the second-longest trial in US history. As Taylor put it, "the United States Government has made a heavy moral investment in [all] these trials." The significance for CSR is that the economic cases were a sustained effort to develop norms, reach acts, and punish actors using the law of war, the first cases ever, aside from a failed attempt twenty years earlier, to try the Roechlings.[14]

The Substance of Nuremberg's Economic Norms, and Their Primacy

If one reason for the CSR significance of Nuremberg is that economic actors were tried at all, others include the substance of the economic norms articulated there, their sheer number and richness, and the fact that most of them held businessmen to a different standard from that required by the law in effect at the time of the deeds. Consider first the substance of the norms, which can be surveyed from the indictments and judgments. Businessmen, these texts say in so many words, shalt not manufacture poison gas where they know or should know of its use for killing civilians (*Krauch*), shalt not organize involuntary human experimentation (*Krauch*), shalt not use slave labor (all cases), shalt not mistreat even permissibly recruited laborers, shalt not distinguish among POW laborers except as permitted by humanitarian treaties differentiating between officers and troops, and so on. These are colloquial renderings of just a few of the norms found in in the decisions, and legal activists have offered careful lists of the norms that pertain to individual crimes.[15] Yet the norms are more fine-grained and refined than a simplistic shalt-not formulation implies. Because defense counsel presented rebuttals to almost every prosecution claim and the judges responded to the more credible of those defenses, the judgments not only contain declaratory lists of shalt-not norms but also anticipate various scenarios and defenses. The *Krupp* court, for instance, not only articulated a no-plunder norm, it also refined that by explaining that it applied even in wartime, occupation, or national emergency, where no private rightsholder could be identified or was harmed, where the taking was under a supposed trusteeship, where no permanent claim to title was asserted, and so forth.[16] In short, the opinions offer a web of nuanced economic norms, exceptions, disallowed exceptions, and reasons.

Lawyers are accustomed to finding their rules in the four corners of a judge's published decision, but in this regard as in others Nuremberg may be said to be different. Prosecutors entered hundreds and for some defendants thousands of items of evidence, collected in thick "document books." They also submitted dozens of briefs addressing single charges and presenting the evidence and legal foundations for them. The more conscientious of the judges, as their extant papers show, went through these submissions with care. Given the volume of this material, little of it has been or will be published or known to today's lawyers, and for ordinary purposes they are perfectly safe in relying on the published judgments and evidentiary samples. The significance of this material, however, is that Nuremberg judges can be shown to have used it in their rulings.[17] If so—and further research is needed—the lists of a few dozen shalt-not norms drawn from published decisions should be length-

ened considerably by legal theories that were argued to the courts, usually unrebutted, and were incorporated or implied in the judgments. A
researcher might feel in at least two of the cases that the judges were
crying "uncle, enough, we believe you," and wrote decisions that contained enough facts and law to support the verdicts, but not everything
that they heard, accepted, and were incorporating as law. These prose-
cutorial submissions not expressly discussed in the judgments might, to
some, be like clichéd trees that fall in a forest with nobody to hear. But
if one is willing to go beyond the published extracts of the cases to see
what the parties discussed and judges knew and sometimes mentioned in
their opinions, one might find countless other violations and norms developed to judge them.[18]

The final significance of Nuremberg norms is that they were not only
numerous and specific, but that they also rested on the premise that
obeying domestic law is not enough. The starting point is that almost everything the Nazi industrialists had done was domestically legal. True,
there have been historical debates about administrators going beyond
whatever was provided in Nazi law and what that might say about how
the regime worked, and true also that to legal philosophers in the 1950s
there was an important difference between postwar trials where the acts
had been legal under Nazi law when committed and where they had
not.[19] But the "legality" distinction and the philosophers' debate, always
a bit otherworldly, have no relevance to the fifty industrialists whose defense was the reverse, that their acts had been legal, requiring them to
do what they did. In fact, there surely were instances where Flick bullied
a Jewish owner without legal basis, but he usually had authority or soon
secured it, in part because he or his allies held positions on agencies in
charge of planning, requisitioning, and allocating slaves, supplies, production, and properties for plunder. One illustration that defendants' argument of wartime business legality was maintained (and useful) is that
when sued for by camp survivors in German courts in the 1950s, some of
the same defendants' companies pleaded they had acted legally, on behalf of the state, and prevailed.[20]

Assuming the defendants' acts were legal when committed under domestic law, the prosecution's premise at Nuremberg had to be that the
defendants were subject to economic norms even though those were
not part of, went beyond, and in most cases contradicted domestic law.
A charge that Krupp violated a no-confiscations norm for property in
France and disputed Alsace-Lorraine even though his acts had been le-

gal in German law and blessed by Vichy, or violated a no-enslavement and no-murder of laborers norms in using and killing Hungarian Jewish girls even though he had German authority and Hungary had agreed,[21] had to rest on a theory of higher or natural law, human rights law, or something similar. The Nuremberg answer, in most accounts, was that international law—not old-fashioned international law that still immunized whatever governments did, but a new, human-rights-infused international law—both forbade what Nazi law allowed or required and also had primacy, or was non-derogable as might be said today.

This may be a perfect view of Nuremberg from anytime after 1980, from the age of human rights and in the vocabulary of *jus cogens* norms. But the view in 1947 looking back on 1942 was different. The international law on which Nuremberg prosecutors drew was at the time soft law. The sources supporting a no-enslavement norm were (1) frequent but hardly invariable customary practice, meaning that most occupiers had not enslaved civilian populations in recent European state-practice, backed by (2) consistent, strong, but unrealistic language of commentators, but (3) no prosecutions of violators. There were few treaties pertaining to large-scale economic crimes, none requiring trials, and no precedents for trials aside from the first *Roechling* case, vacated on technical grounds and not retried. This legal softness is one reason that prosecutors included charges of enslaving POWs, since that particular crime was addressed by clear treaty, and that Taylor's staff was happy to use British witnesses who had been slaves at Farben's Auschwitz facility.[22] For almost all the other victims and atrocities, though, prosecutors were using soft law, morally urgent law-in-the-making, crimes against humanity–type law rather than justifications from the older "law of war" tradition. Some Nuremberg charges might therefore have had a retroactivity problem—the point was extensively litigated—but to the extent the courts accepted the prosecution's claims, the courts were accepting, at least in extreme cases, a hierarchy in which soft law and moral norms had priority over vicious domestic law, a potent lesson for CSR.

But What about the Acquittals of Many Industrialists, and Do the Norms Still Matter?

The shadow hanging over this body of rules and norms is that alone among the Nuremberg trials, prosecutors lost many of the economic cases. Many industrialists were acquitted and legal theories dismissed or narrowed. In *Flick*, three of six defendants were acquitted of everything and the three others of many charges and given trivial sentences, in one case amounting to time served. In *Krauch*, all twenty-three defendants were acquitted of crimes against peace and ten of slave labor and plunder, and only a few defendants personally linked to Auschwitz were given "the heaviest of the very light sentences," with a half dozen others receiving eighteen-month to three-year terms. The normally equable Taylor was furious, writing that the *Flick* judges misapplied the defense of duress (which revealingly they called the "necessity defense") and that the majority in *Krauch* appeared to follow that error and paid no attention to the evidence. Even in *Krupp*, where ten of twelve defendants were given stiffer sentences, the charge of crimes against peace was dismissed before the case closed, and one judge offered unseemly sympathy to a convicted defendant. Some *Roechling* defendants were convicted of crimes against peace, but that was reversed and other sentences reduced. In *Weizsaecker* the judges adopted a rule that exculpated bankers of almost any crime, though they did issue stiff sentences for HGW defendants for slave labor.[23] A fair question from this is whether arguments that lost at Nuremberg have any weight for CSR.

The best answer is yes, for two reasons, legal and cultural respectively. The legal reason is found in the decisions themselves: almost no court rejected the substantive validity of an economic norm. One way to think of it is that there were four ways any Nuremberg court could use legal doctrine to acquit a defendant.[24] First, it could rule that the defendant was not guilty on the facts because he or she (two women were tried) was innocent or not shown guilty beyond a reasonable doubt,[25] an easier task where a norm had been narrowed.[26] Second, it could rule that a defendant had done the deed but had a good defense[27] or even that it was unlikely at law that persons in defendants' shoes could ever commit the crime.[28] Third, it could say that an indictment cited a crime but not one within the jurisdiction of international courts like Nuremberg established under Allied Control Council Law No 10, courts that were bound to follow the IMT.[29] Or, fourth, it could rule that the indictment did not correctly identify or rely on a crime under international law.

The significance for CSR is that even with many acquittals and dismissals, no court accepted the full-on formulation of argument four, that business actors were never bound by emerging international law embodying minimal norms of decent behavior where such norms were not yet part of domestic law.[30] Even more important, with only one possible exception in one count did a Nuremberg court ever hold that violating an alleged economic norm did not in fact constitute a crime. The exception, if it be, was in *Flick*, where the court held count 3, prewar aryanization (seizures for racial-religious reasons), seemed not to be an international wrong but also was outside of its jurisdiction because it occurred between 1936 and 1939, and that for one or the other of those reasons it failed.[31] Courts frequently reason in the alternative, but it makes for a muddy rule, which in this instance is often misstated as a decisive rule that race-based property seizures do not violate international law.[32] Defendants had pleaded that aryanization was legal under German law and a favor to Jews,[33] but even the *Flick* bench would not go that far. Overall, the courtroom losses do not equate to the irrelevance of Nuremberg because the norms prosecutors asserted were either accepted or at worst unchallenged, while the courts supported their adverse rulings on other grounds. Even charges that were rejected were almost never losses in principle, only in reality—small consolation to prosecutors and Holocaust victims but important for CSR.

The second, cultural reason that courtroom losses at Nuremberg do not negate the importance of the cases for CSR is that, paradoxically, having lost so much at the time, prosecutors have won in the court of history. Recall the long arc of the story. After many courtroom defeats in these cases, prosecutors and many others were dismayed that British, French, and American authorities established backdoor clemency processes that released almost all convicted Nazis in their custody, but their protests were soon forgotten.[34] The economic cases were among the first to be released, with US and French officials freeing their few convicted industrialists by 1951, most returning to industry in time to resume senior jobs as West Germany experienced its economic miracle. By the mid-1950s, the industrialists were safe. Nuremberg was repudiated in Germany and largely forgotten elsewhere. The economy was booming, and as a valued Cold War ally their country was largely immune to pressure, and shame. Their businesses had easily ducked Holocaust compensation liability in every judicial forum, with a few firms paying tiny sums ex gratia and the rest paying nothing. Messrs Flick and Krupp even spurned pleas from their powerful benefactor, former US high commissioner John J. McCloy for generosity.[35] Despite having brand names and a nationality that had been toxic in the West in 1945, the companies thrived. A few American Jews or Poles or lefties might shun Mercedes to "buy Detroit" but the losses were negligible, and young people soon came to love, and buy, the VW Beetle. The few lawsuits threatening to revive talk about Nazi business were easily swatted away, as were new suits by anti–Vietnam War activists that threatened bad publicity by alleging Dow Chemical's similarity with Farben.[36] Overall Germany had the good fortune that its exports leaned toward heavy machinery and components, immunizing most companies from visibility and consumer pushback. In short, neither moral suasion nor legal liability was available as a tool.

Contrast this with the new CSR-inflected world after 1990. The steady disclosure of revelations about Swiss banks forced that industry to the American negotiating table. Next German companies (and others) concluded agreements that, however inadequate, obliged firms to pay more than they dreamed. All this despite the fact that Germany—both its companies and the state—won every case brought in US courts, the center of the litigation. Call it the Swiss Bank Lesson, or the Revenge of the Nuremberg Economic Cases. This is not to say that all companies facing even grave allegations of human rights atrocities will (or should) settle. It is to say that the moral context for and perceptions of business has radically changed, becoming more receptive to human rights and CSR arguments. And in a complicated way, part of that change surely was the way that powerful German businessmen who beat the rap at Nuremberg and were not tried anywhere else were still widely identified (outside of West Germany) with monstrous wrongdoing. That is the relevance of even the unsuccessful Nuremberg claims; they injected business behavior into the courtroom, and through that into public memory, and ultimately back into the public arena, where they fueled a continuing and high-profile conversation about the legal and moral dimensions of business.

The Missing Alternative: Economic Trials Elsewhere and Their Relevance for CSR

Until now the question has been "why Nuremberg?" But perhaps it should be "why only Nuremberg?" In all four occupation zones of Germany, decisions were taken regarding businesses: which to close, freeze, seize, split, assign as reparations, purge, restore, or give to new managers. Many companies were also investigated for their crimes, or investigated themselves to prepare a more convincing exoneration. And there were thousands of Allied trials of persons who had committed retail-level atrocities against slave laborers in economic facilities. Yet neither the big-picture planning nor the small-scale trials led to moral reflection about the role of business as such. Decisions about the occupation reflected the Allies' different understandings of how best to demilitarize and de-nazify Germany, not how business should adopt any goals beyond rebuilding a shattered economy. As for the trials, in almost every instance they were no different from trials of SS guards for atrocities, meaning the economic context was incidental and the cases generated no law relevant to CSR.

The closest to a case implicating economic issues was *Tesch*, in 1946, a British trial of the sole owner of a firm distributing Zyklon B to Auschwitz and elsewhere, along with two aides, with one acquitted.[37] At first, it seems to illustrate both accountability for the gravest crime and affirmation of an economic norm. But as a military trial *Tesch* had summary procedure and a jury verdict, so the law is confined to the Judge Advocate's charge, available only in abstract. Like all British trials its basis was the Royal Warrant (1945),[38] covering wrongs to Allied personnel only, making the case less morally persuasive. *Tesch* is at best a hybrid, an economic case involving indirect use of an economic murder weapon, but a case eschewing universality and an ordinary atrocity case incidentally having economic dimensions. Nor was there discussion about ethics in the trials in liberated nations for economic collaboration. That crime is a textbook violation of CSR: that a virtuous corporation should avoid bad acts that are permitted or required by evil occupation law. But in Western Europe, the drive to punish industrialists who had collaborated or profited quickly dissipated.[39] In the East, there were trials, but the new Communist regimes used them to seize the property of those who had left the country, whether German expellees or Jewish survivors and refugees.[40] Throughout Europe there were no white-collar atrocity cases, and collaborator cases were tainted by politics and are best viewed as part of Cold War history and transitional legitimacy, not credible precedent.[41]

If there were to be significant economic trials, they would have had to be in West Germany. It was permitted to bring cases, its sovereignty largely restored in 1949. Documents and witnesses were there, survivors living in the Communist bloc would have been able to testify by affidavit, and officials who had loudly insisted that Nuremberg was flawed but that German law had adequate legal tools would have no cause to complain. Most importantly the targets were there, living openly. Thousands of firms had used slave laborers, from multinationals to small workshops and family farms. Scholars have painstakingly compiled lists of firms that ran camp facilities or rented slave labor, but just the bare outlines were known by 1946. No Allied prosecutor claimed that Farben et al. were the only guilty ones; the notion was that the Allies would start a process by trying leaders of companies they identified as the worst of the worst and that Germany would try others. Yet in sixty-five years it tried only one economic case, against Gerhard Peters, who testified in *Krauch* and worked with Tesch. Nuremberg prosecutors forwarded evidence on him to German colleagues in 1948. He was repeatedly tried, and in 1955, in his fifth retrial, had the case dismissed, the court saying that nobody should have to endure that.[42] Until the historical inquiries and financial settlements of the 1990s, that was the limit of real accountability for industrialists. Thus it was that with no economic trials elsewhere, the question is always Nuremberg.

Nuremberg and Corporate Entities

The final question is whether the trials are a precedent not only for social responsibility norms, but also for an unexpected issue relating to corporations.[43] Corporate status would have been jurisprudentially irrelevant to those who prepared Nuremberg, and may seem legalistic to those who work with social ethics in business today and think that moral goals apply regardless of a business's legal form. That changed around 2000, when ATS parties and judges began to suggest that the presence or not of corporate entities at Nuremberg could guide courts hearing claims against multinationals, and especially when the Supreme Court made entity status the focus of *Royal Dutch Shell v. Kiobel*.[44] As framed by proponents, the Nuremberg arguments for ATS liability were four: either (1) corporations were charged at the trials; or, if not, they were implicitly charged since (2) private parties were charged for business activities; (3) organizations were charged and businesses are one form of organization; and (4) corporations were the subject of other Allied actions akin to criminal trials, notably Farben, target of its own dissolution law, equivalent to a corporate "death penalty."

The arguments on both sides were thoroughly presented to a number of courts, including the Supreme Court, but in the end the better view seemed to be that no corporations were tried at Nuremberg, either directly, impliedly, or by analogy through an executive-type dissolution. The matter seemed settled. But before supporters or opponents of enterprise liability could make their respective decisions on how to discuss Nuremberg, it was realized that the issue was unexpectedly made more complex by new findings that postwar prosecutors had contemplated charging German business entities, debated legal theories in-house, and apparently declined to prosecute corporations for reasons of tactics and preferences, not because of any doctrinal bar. In fact, their memos make clear that prosecutors considered charging (i) natural persons, (ii) legal entities under German law like Flick or Farben, (iii) imputed entities such as the Ruhr iron and steel industry, using a conspiracy theory that almost prefigures American "RICO" defendants, and (iv) combinations of these types of defendants.[45]

Prosecutors knew but were unlikely to have worried that in charging a corporation, they might be innovating in either international or German law. On the contrary, they clearly felt that entity liability was one of a number of familiar ways that the law used to respond to the complex relationships between wrongdoers on the ground and others elsewhere who ordered, condoned, or arranged a wrong, and that doctrinal immunity drawn from a discredited German legal system ought not be binding. If there was nothing to preclude an entity charge, there was much in its favor. Many of the staff members were experienced in corporate cases from working in the Antitrust Division, the Securities and Exchange Commission, or other agencies or in private practice. Chief prosecutor Taylor had helped draft the Securities Exchange Act of 1934 and worked for a Senate subcommittee investigating shady railroad financing. He and his team had experience with both the tactics and advantages of corporate cases. Why no charges then? One reason was the December 1946 resignation of the gung-ho deputy who had pushed bold ideas for economic trials. Probably more important was the tactical consideration. While federal rules then and now allow charges against natural or legal persons or both, many prosecutors prefer charging individuals. They worry that in a case against both, the trier might convict only the corporation, swayed by a feeling that an individual was merely doing his job. Others fear the reverse, that a jury will convict only the individual thinking there must have been a tangible, jailable person behind the complexities. A case against a corporation alone risks acquittal of the entity now and of individuals later; a mixed case risks acquittal now of either or both.

Nowhere were the possibilities for mistaken or inconsistent verdicts more likely than at Nuremberg. Farben was the largest chemical company in the world, owned and controlled, as was German practice, not by widely dispersed shareholders but by other companies and banks. Prosecuting Farben as an entity risked making the loss fall in unpredictable places or charging the wrong entity. The prosecutors had vast documentation, but the likelihood of error was high with the complexity of the organizations and the incomplete state of the records due to war damage and corporate destruction of evidence.[46] New scholarship suggests, for instance, that responsibility for supplying gas to Auschwitz was not that of Farben as prosecutors charged, but rather of Degesch, a subsidiary of which Farben owned 42.5 percent and controlled board seats and the chair, and Tesch, the distributor who had worked for Farben and was executed by the British. Some suggest prosecutors erred in focusing on Farben and imply the court was right to acquit many defendants. On the contrary, none of it should matter; on these facts a prosecutor should get convictions against Degesch and Tesch as well as the Farben directors who by corporate law had responsibility.[47] Without intending to, the new histories support the prosecutors' hunch: why risk charging the wrong entity?

In fact, each of the corporate targets posed similar issues. The Flick Konzern was a recent conglomerate with hundreds of subsidiaries, some of them pretextual entities set up to control looted property. This was no decentralized assemblage of "silos"; one man and his inner circle controlled everything. Prosecutors in 1946 could spend years preparing a forensic accounting of the subsidiaries and trying to penetrate the pretextual companies—a problem that the Supreme Court had warned about as recently as 1943[48]—or they could charge exactly the right individuals. Krupp had changed its structure in 1943 from the A. G. form to a company owned solely by Alfried Krupp under a special law written to include only him, though the directors on a reconstituted advisory board were largely unchanged. Would that status change require different defendants, counsel, and separate trials for the pre- and post-1943 entities? As for HGW, it was government run, and the rule from the IMT was that even though organizations meant government rather than business entities, no new organizations could be charged after the initial case against six entities. All told, Nuremberg prosecutors charged only individuals for well-founded tactical reasons, just as a savvy white-collar prosecutor might today.

Returning to the present, for CSR purposes none of these debates should matter, except insofar as a future court might put weight on the corporate status distinction. For ATS purposes, the issue is comatose, losing vitality when the Supreme Court in 2012 redirected *Kiobel* from corporate status to extraterritorial jurisdiction. For the German companies at Nuremberg, the entity question turned out not to matter either. They were frozen and some of their leading figures held and then released, and they prospered, regaining properties of which they had been divested and coalescing into large units after being broken up. But even without that historical hindsight, the Nuremberg corporate entity question that seemed so urgent prior to *Kiobel* is anachronistic because of the context of 1947. Every argument ordinarily made in favor or against entity liability was irrelevant. Typically the argument in favor of entity liability is that because of its resources, size, and status the corporation did harm or magnified the harm of others distinct from and above what individual employees could do, and if not sanctioned might do more harm in future; in short, that the entity is too big or dangerous not to punish. Against liability is that innocent shareholders and employees will be affected by a corporate penalty, especially if the company is not just fined but closed and especially the newcomers, either employees or shareholders who came to the firm after the wrongdoing and could not have known of the potential liability but may bear the cost of their predecessors' malfeasance. At Nuremberg, none of this applied. There had been total war and surrender, production was halted, assets destroyed or frozen, supplies and labor unavailable, buyers and sellers gone, shareholders and everyone else wiped out, corporate value and legal rules in doubt. What prosecutor could weigh ordinary criteria, especially where future decisions would be determined politically? "Too big to fail" has no meaning for a company when an entire country has failed.

If Nuremberg offers no decisive precedent for entity liability, it may still have lessons for a changing culture of corporate liability and responsibility. For two generations, economists' views on the nature of the firm, agency theory, and decision making have trickled into the legal academy. But little of this penetrated or changed the practices of prosecutors. US prosecutors continued to charge corporations, either together with individuals (some states requiring an individual be charged along with a corporate defendant) or alone. Corporate prosecutions remained a familiar part of white-collar enforcement in antitrust, environmental, securities, government contracting, overseas bribery, and other areas of law. In the civil law, practice was similarly unchanged; German scholars still objected to corporate liability, less because of economic complexity than because a morally grounded criminal law was felt to require a guilty mind, which an inanimate corporate entity cannot have; what one wag said of economics in Germany, that it is treated as a branch of moral philosophy,[49] is more true of criminal law. Where the economists' nexus-of-contracts approach seemed to de-emphasize the formal corporate "body," the civil law scholars seemed convinced the corporation could not have a mind, at least one capable of criminal intent.

Outside of prosecutors' offices and the academy, though, things were changing rapidly around 1990. Activists brought corporate ATS cases, few but highly visible, basing claims on corporate international crimes. Internationally a growing number of conventions and agencies obliged corporations to do or refrain from certain acts. France and the Netherlands departed from their civil law tradition to create forms of corporate criminal liability. A few jurisdictions imposed criminal liability on the partnership, historically a status never seen as having legal personality.[50] On many fronts the current seemed to shift toward broadening liability. And famously, the US Supreme Court's cases on corporations' rights to political speech[51] and perhaps religious rights[52] seemed to underscore the possibility of correlative liabilities. Inevitably there were jurisdictional holdouts. Again the obvious example was Germany, which adhered to its doctrine that only natural persons could be tried, an objection that seems to have played a large part in negotiators' unwillingness to provide the ICC with jurisdiction over corporations.[53] But it is no small irony that another country has become identified in recent years with corporate immunity rather than liability—the United States, the home of corporate prosecutions.

At first this seems absurd. Every day seems to bring stories of criminal charges, pleas, and settlements requiring blue-chip companies to pay tens of millions of dollars in fines.[54] Yet the defendants are from pharmaceutical, agricultural, automotive, and other industrial sectors, not finance and banking. For that matter, few of the corporate cases even come to trial. They are settled instead by deferred prosecution agreements (DPAs) and nonprosecution agreements, recent tools that offer an accused company a way out from both a public trial and many consequences of a conviction. Explanations vary for the rise of the DPAs and administrative waivers. Perhaps they are an overreaction to the case against Arthur Andersen, the accounting firm driven into bankruptcy by charges later dismissed on appeal. Or DPAs are a rational choice because prosecutors and regulators are outgunned by big corporations, or they allow lucrative recoveries for the government while prosecutors move to easy-to-prove insider trading cases. Or perhaps, as one judge warned, prosecutors and regulators are hesitant to test certain doctrinal tools, too solicitous of the welfare of the banks, or too intent on restructuring the entity's future behavior without facing the painstaking difficulty of gathering evidence about the past.[55] Many of the reasons for the eclipse of entity prosecutions today resemble what officials in 1947 in their Berlin and Frankfurt headquarters likely said about Nuremberg: rein in these overzealous prosecutors, they don't realize how important the big companies are, we can fix the firms by trying a few individuals and overseeing new executives, and accountability for the past is only one of many interests to be served. Beyond that, Nuremberg is of little direct relevance.

Acknowledgments

For their generous help with this chapter and related explorations, I thank Gilad Bendheim, Donald Earl Childress III, David Eltis, Richard Grassby, Richard Helmholz, Elliott Horowitz, Richard Hoyle, William C. Jordan, Stephan H. Lindner, Gerald Lynch, Jürgen Matthäus, Henry Mayer, Douglas Morris, Daniel Richman, and Colm Tóibín. As always, mistakes are mine alone. Original spelling has been retained for all citations and quotations, including the variant spellings of Nuremberg. All law is stated as of June 1, 2014.

Notes

1. Dodge v. Ford Motor Co., 170 N.W. 668 (Mich. 1919).

2. Still one of the most thoughtful studies is John G. Simon, Charles W. Power, and Jon P. Gunnemann, *The Ethical Investor: Universities and Corporate Responsibility* (New Haven, CT: Yale University Press, 1972).

3. 28 U.S.C. § 1350, part the Judiciary Act, Ch. 20, § 9, 1 Stat. 73 (1789).

4. Filártiga v. Peña-Irala, 630 F.2d 876 (2d Cir. 1980).

5. Donald Earl Childress III, "The Alien Tort Statute, Federalism, and the Next Wave of International Law Litigation," *Georgetown Law Journal* 100 (2012): 709, 713 (citing 150 cases).

6. The official report, including indictment, full transcript, judgment, and samples of evidence, was published in the various official languages, the English version as *Trial of the Major War Criminals before the International Military Tribunal*, 42 vols. (Nuremberg, Germany: Allied Control Council, 1947–49), and in a complementary official US version, *Nazi Conspiracy and Aggression*, 8 vols. and 3 supplements (Washington, DC: Government Printing Office, 1946–48).

7. The official report, containing the indictment, judgment, and an inevitably much smaller sample of transcript and evidence for each of the twelve cases was published as *Trials of War Criminals before the Nuernberg Military Tribunals under Control Council Law No. 10*, 15 vols. (Washington, DC: Government Printing Office, 1949–1953) ("T.W.C.").

8. An English translation of the indictment and trial and appellate judgments is given in 14 T.W.C. 1061–1143.

9. Except where otherwise noted, the discussion in this and the following four paragraphs is drawn from Jonathan A. Bush, "The Prehistory of Corporations and Conspiracy in International Criminal Law: What Nuremberg Really Said," *Columbia Law Review* 109, no. 5 (2009): 1094, 1104–30.

10. Michael R. Marrus, ed., *The Nuremberg War Crimes Trial, 1945–46* (Boston: Bedford Books, 1997), 3–10 (majority and minority reports from the Versailles Commission on Responsibilities).

11. John Mendelsohn, *Trial by Document: The Use of Seized Records in the United States Proceedings at Nürnberg* (New York: Garland Publishing, 1988), 1, 5.

12. Gilad Bendheim, "The Nuremberg and Tokyo International Military Tribunals: A Comparative Analysis, 1944–1946" (M.Phil. diss., Cambridge University, June 2012), 69–71; "List of Major Japanese War Criminals Submitted by the Australian Government" (April–June 1946), [UK] The National Archives, CAB21/2292; John W. Dower, *Embracing Defeat: Japan in the Wake of World War II* (New York: W. W. Norton, 2000), 630.

13. Morris Abram, "Digest of 'The Economic Case' in the Record of Case I before the International Military Tribunal" (October 1, 1946), Prosecution memorandum, in US Holocaust Memorial Museum, Washington, DC, RG-06.005.02.*01.

14. See Telford Taylor, *Final Report to the Secretary of the Army on the Nuernberg War Crimes Trials under Control Council Law No. 10* (Washington, DC: Government Printing Office, 1949), 36, 43–45, 61, 100 (quotation), 184–202 esp. 186 n. 159 (Roechling), 296–344; Ernst Fraenkel, *Military Occupation and the Rule of Law: Occupational Government in the Rhineland, 1918–1923* (Lon-

don: Oxford University Press, 1944), 59–60 (Roechling); U.S. v. Flick, 6 T.W.C. 1028 (Roechling); U.S. v. Krupp, 9 T.W.C. 1341, 1344, 1429–31.

15. See James G. Stewart, *Corporate War Crimes: Prosecuting the Pillage of Natural Resources* (New York: Open Society Institute, n.d.), 96–108; Kevin Jon Heller, *The Nuremberg Military Tribunals and the Origins of International Criminal Law* (Oxford: Oxford University Press, 2011), 211–13, 217–24, 226–29, 247–49.

16. Krupp, 9 T.W.C. 1340–47; Weizsaecker, 14 T.W.C. 684–90.

17. This might apply more easily to cases where judges were persuaded by prosecution claims (*Krupp, Roechling,* and *Weizsaecker*) than where they were skeptical (*Flick, Krauch*), but the claim could be shown, in this author's opinion, for those latter cases as well. For examples of reasoning referring to or seeming to accept as proven facts and arguments that were introduced into court but that were not the subject of showcase charges in the indictment, see, e.g., Krupp, 9 T.W.C. 1361 (plunder), 1373–1435 (slave labor); Weizsaecker, 14 T.W.C. 681–94 (plunder).

18. This paragraph draws on research with papers from a number of Nuremberg judges, legal staff assigned to the Secretariat, and prosecutors. Judicial sifting and assessment of evidence not mentioned in the judgment is repeatedly shown, for instance, in the papers of William C. Christianson, judge in *Flick* and presiding judge in *Weizsaecker*. US Holocaust Memorial Museum, Washington, DC, 1998.A.0298 (hereafter Christianson Papers).

19. The issues of German legality are explored in Henry Friedlander, "Nazi Crimes and the German Law," in *Nazi Crimes and the Law,* ed. Nathan Stoltzfus and Henry Friedlander (Washington, DC: German Historical Institute, 2008), 15–33; and Henry Friedlander, "The Judiciary and Nazi Crimes in Postwar Germany," *Simon Wiesenthal Center Annual* 1 (1984): 27–44; the famed 1950s debate is found in H. L. A. Hart, "Positivism and the Separation of Law and Morals," *Harvard Law Review* 71, no. 4 (1958): 593–629; Lon L. Fuller, "Positivism and Fidelity to Law: A Reply to Professor Hart," *Harvard Law Review* 71, no. 4 (1958): 630–72.

20. Using a defense of domestic legality, but not superior orders or duress. Benjamin B. Ferencz, *Less Than Slaves: Jewish Forced Labor and the Quest for Compensation* (Bloomington: Indiana University Press, 2002), 56–57, 109, 177.

21. Krupp, 9 T.W.C. 1426–29, discussed in Ferencz, *Less Than Slaves,* 94–96, 99.

22. U.S. v. Krauch ("Farben"), 8 T.W.C. 603–25; "U.S. v. Krauch. Preliminary Memorandum Brief of the Prosecution. Part III: Slavery and Mass Murder" (December 13, 1947), 40–51, 97–101 (summarizing additional affidavits in Pros. Document Books 75, 78–79), in US Holocaust Memorial Museum; Krupp, 9 T.W.C. 1375–96.

23. Summaries of the trial results are widely available and are drawn here from Taylor, *Final Report*, 187–202, esp. 201 (quotation).

24. A fifth strategy, acquitting for extralegal reasons, because a defendant was personally virtuous as shown by testimonials from British or American friends or prominent churchmen or because he rescued individual Jews, can be seen in most defendants' document books and may have influenced some judges, see, e.g., Taylor, *Final Report*, at 189, but is beyond legal analysis. Sometimes it could backfire: Krupp testified that he built a hospital for his workers and that it was "a magnificent example" of his benevolence, which prosecutors countered by proving it was built with slave labor and did not treat Krupp's slaves. "U.S. v. Krupp: Closing Statement for the U.S.A." (June 24, 1948), 20–21, in Christianson Papers, box 15-1.

25. See Krauch, 8 T.W.C. 1153–72 (most of the slave labor charges and the poison gas and unconsented experimentation charges). Compare the experimentation acquittal with Peter Hayes, *Industry and Ideology: IG Farben in the Nazi Era* (Cambridge: Cambridge University Press, 1987), 370; Stephan H. Lindner, *Inside IG Farben: Hoechst during the Third Reich*, trans. Helen Schoop (Cambridge: Cambridge University Press, 2008), 307–36.

26. Compare Krauch, 8 T.W.C. 1134–35 and Flick, 6 T.W.C. 1203–04 (narrowing the definition of plunder) with Krupp, 9 T.W.C. 1345–46.

27. Especially easy where that legal defense had been misunderstood or inflated. Compare, e.g., Flick, 6 T.W.C. 1199–1202, and Krauch, 8 T.W.C. 1174–79 (the duress-necessity rulings), rejected in Krauch, 8 T.W.C. 1204 (Hebert, J., diss.), and Krupp, 9 T.W.C. 1435–48; and Bush, "Prehistory," 1218–20. See Hayes, *Industry and Ideology*, 366, 369–70.

28. See Weizsaecker, 14 T.W.C. 853 (banker liability); Krauch, 8 T.W.C. 1111–26, and Krupp, 9 T.W.C. 401, at 436–53 (Anderson, P. J., conc. in dismissal of counts 1 and 4, July 7, 1948) (crimes against peace).

29. See 15 T.W.C. 233–37 (rulings in three noneconomic cases regarding the charge of "conspiracy to commit war crimes and crimes against humanity"), discussed in Bush, "Prehistory," 1204–10; Weizsaecker, 14 T.W.C. 684–85 (surveying earlier Nuremberg decisions on prewar plunder).

30. See Flick, 6 T.W.C. 1026–30 (prosecutor rebuts claim of total immunity for private businessmen); Krauch, 8 T.W.C. 1136–37 (various tribunals reject the claim of immunity). The notion of private party immunity in international law was unwittingly recreated, curiously, by liberal judges in a series of ATS cases holding that nonstate actors are only liable for certain grave violations. See, e.g., Bigio v. Coca-Cola Co., 239 F.3d 440, at 448 (2d Cir. 2000) (discussing Tel-Oren, Kadic, the Restatement, and other familiar set-pieces), aff'd on other grounds and dismissed, 675 F.3d 1163 (2012). In time it may look as odd as Flick's claim.

31. Flick, 6 T.W.C. 1212–16, discussed in Taylor, *Final Report*, at 188–89; Bush, "Prehistory," 1185–86.

32. See Bigio, 239 F.3d at 448.

33. Flick, 6 T.W.C. 1139–44 (chief defense counsel arguing that aryanization was a favor to Jewish owners).

34. Clemency is discussed in Donald Bloxham, *Genocide on Trial* (Oxford: Oxford University Press, 2001), 162–72; Tom Bower, *Blind Eye to Murder: Britain, America, and the Purging of Nazi Germany—A Pledge Betrayed* (London: William Collins and Sons, 1981); Norbert Frei, *Adenauer's Germany and the Nazi Past*, trans. Joel Golb (New York: Columbia University Press, 2002); Peter Maguire, *Law and War: An American Story* (New York: Columbia University Press, 2000), 211–82. For protests by a prosecutor, see Telford Taylor, "The Nazis Go Free: Justice and Mercy or Misguided Expediency?" *Nation* 172, no. 8 (1951): 170–72.

35. Ferencz, *Less Than Slaves*, 56–57, 109, 177 (prevailing in court), and 78, 82–85, 166–69 (rebuffing McCloy).

36. Kelberine v. Societe Internationale, 363 F.2d 989 (D.C. Cir. 1966); Joseph Borkin, *The Crime and Punishment of I. G. Farben* (New York: Free Press, 1978), 206–22; George Wald, "Corporate Responsibility for War Crimes," *New York Review of Books* 15, no. 1 (1970).

37. Trial of Bruno Tesch and Two Others (The Zyklon B Case), (Brit. Milit. Ct., Hamburg, 1946), in 1 Law Reports of Trials of War Criminals 93–103 (1947). See Peter Hayes, *From Cooperation to Complicity: Degussa in the Third Reich* (Cambridge: Cambridge University Press, 2004), 277–88, 298.

38. Regulations for the Trial of War Criminals, A.O. 81/1945 (June 14, 1945), repr. in Taylor, *Final Report*, 254–55.

39. "Belgian Business Men Cleared of Aiding Foe," *New York Times*, April 18, 1947, p. 17; Martin Conway, "Justice in Postwar Belgium: Popular Passions and Political Realities," in *The Politics of Retribution of Europe: World War II and Its Aftermath*, ed. István Deák, Jan T. Gross, and Tony Judt (Princeton, NJ: Princeton University Press, 2000), 133, 140, 143–44, 146–47; Luc Huyse, "The Criminal Justice System as a Political Actor in Regime Transitions: The Case of Belgium, 1944–50," in Deák, Gross, and Judt, *The Politics of Retribution of Europe: World War II and Its Aftermath*, 157, 163, 166.

40. See Eduard Kubů and Jan Kuklík Jr., "Reluctant Restitution: The Restitution of Jewish Property in the Bohemian Lands after the Second World War," in *Robbery and Restitution: The Conflict over Jewish Property in Europe*, ed. Martin Dean, Constantin Goschler, and Philipp Ther (New York: Berghahn Books, 2007): 223, 226–34.

41. Henry Rousso, *The Vichy Syndrome: History and Memory in France since 1944* (Cambridge, MA: Harvard University Press, 1991), 20.

42. Hayes, *From Cooperation to Complicity*, 272–300; Bush, "Prehistory," 1233–34. For lists of German camps, participants, and types of work, see Martin Weinmann, ed., *Das nationalsozialistische Lagersystem (CCP)* (Frankfurt am Main: Zweitausendeins, 1990).

43. Unless noted, this and the next four paragraphs draw from an amicus brief to which the present author contributed. All views expressed here, however, are mine alone, no other participant in that brief having been consulted here. Brief Amicus Curiae of Nuremberg Historians and International Lawyers in Support of Neither Party (December 21, 2011), Kiobel v. Royal Dutch Petroleum Co. et al., no. 10-1491, available online on a variety of sites.

44. Changing that in Kiobel v. Royal Dutch Petroleum Co., 132A S.Ct. 1738 (March 5, 2012, order inviting reargument on jurisdiction rather than corporate status), 133 S.Ct. 1659 (2013).

45. Bush, "Prehistory," passim.

46. See, e.g., 15 T.W.C. 1014-39 (destruction in Farben); Krupp, 9 T.W.C. 1332.

47. Compare Peter Hayes, "The Degussa AG and the Holocaust," in *Lessons and Legacies: The Holocaust and Justice*, ed. Ronald Smelser (Evanston, IL: Northwestern University Press, 2002), 140, 163–66, and *Industry and Ideology*, 361–70; with "Preliminary Brief of the Prosecution. Part III," at 32–35, 54–55, 58–59.

48. United States v. Dotterweich, 320 U.S. 277, 279 (1943).

49. Charlemagne, "The Laws of Euro-Nomics," *The Economist*, April 12, 2014, p. 47. Perhaps it is no coincidence that Germany also clung to another metaphysically driven immunity notion, its doctrine that a sovereign government must be wholly immune from suit if it so wishes, a formulation seemingly out of step with human rights trends and with some other national definitions, but one that received the blessing of the International Court of Justice in a contentious case stemming from reparations for Nazi atrocities. Jurisdictional Immunities of the State (Germany v. Italy: Greece intervening), February 3, 2012, judgments cited at http://www.icj-cij.org/docket/index.php?p1=3&p2=3&case=143&p3=4.

50. English courts and a Canadian province extended criminal liability to partnerships, and the Scottish Law Commission studied partnerships that dissolve to avoid liability. Darcy L. MacPherson, "Criminal Liability of Partnerships: Constitutional and Practical Impediments," *Manitoba Law Journal* 33, no. 2 (2010): 329–90; Scottish Law Commission: Report on Criminal Liability of Partnerships (Scottish Law Commission No. 224, Cm 8238 SG/2011/246, December 2011), accessed at http://www.scotlawcom.gov.uk/news/partnerships -criminal-liability/; W. Stevenson & Sons (A Partnership) v. R., [2008] EWCA Crim 273.

51. Citizens United v. Federal Election Commission, 558 U.S. 310 (2010).

52. Conestoga Wood Specialties Corp. v. Burwell, docket no. 13–356 (argued March 25, 2014, pending as of June 1, 2014); Brief of Amici Curiae Historians and

Legal Scholars Supporting Neither Party , January 28, 2014, accessed at http://
www.americanbar.org/content/dam/aba/publications/supreme_court_preview/
briefs-v3/13–354-13–356_amcu_np_hls.authcheckdam.pdf, last visited May 1,
2014.

53. See Bush, "Prehistory," 1099–100.

54. See Jed S. Rakoff, "The Financial Crisis: Why Have No High-Level Executives Been Prosecuted?" *New York Review of Books*, January 9, 2014, pp. 4,
6, 8; Jesse Eisinger, "The Fall Guy," *New York Times Magazine*, April 30, 2014,
pp. 34–38, 48, 56, 62; Floyd Norris, "Banks Stay in Business as Felons," *New
York Times*, May 16, 2014, pp. B1–2.

55. Rakoff, "Financial Crisis," at 4 (discussing "willful blindness" or "conscious disregard" standard), 8 (discussing risks where prosecutors aim at an entity and get seduced).

CHAPTER SEVEN

The Impact of the War Crimes Tribunals on Corporate Liability for Atrocity Crimes under US Law

David Scheffer

In this chapter I examine US federal enforcement of the Alien Tort Statute,[1] focusing on federal court judgments that draw upon the statutes and jurisprudence of the international and hybrid war crimes tribunals.[2] The Supreme Court's judgment in *Kiobel v. Royal Dutch Petroleum Co.*[3] in 2013, while significant for Alien Tort Statute purposes in limiting the extraterritorial reach of the law, did not alter the fundamental reliance of the federal courts on tribunal jurisprudence. Federal courts remain respectful of, and cite tribunal jurisprudence and appear to take quite seriously, the Rome Statute of the International Criminal Court. There is much to learn from recent rulings in the United States because corporate responsibility for the commission of genocide, crimes against humanity, and serious war crimes is at the center of these cases, albeit for civil and not criminal remedies. Some day the existing personal jurisdiction of the International Criminal Court may well be invoked to reach corporate executives, just as the International Criminal Tribunal for Rwanda achieved that task in the *Media* case.[4] The time may also arrive when either the International Criminal Court or some other newly conceived tribunal holds corporations, as juridical persons, accountable with civil or criminal penalties for commission of or complicity in atrocity crimes.

Mitt Romney, the Republican presidential candidate in the United States in 2012, opined on an Iowa bale of hay during his campaign that "corporations are people."[5] He was aware that in 2010 the Supreme Court had ruled in *Citizens United v. Federal Election Commission* that corporations, for the purpose of the First Amendment free speech clause, are equal to human beings.[6] If that is the accepted wisdom, then such so-called people should be capable of committing atrocity crimes and be held responsible for them just as are natural persons.

The Alien Tort Statute is a 1789 law that constitutes one sentence: "The district courts shall have original jurisdiction of any civil action by an alien for a tort only, committed in violation of the law of nations or a treaty of the United States."[7] As the Supreme Court explained in *Sosa v. Alvarez-Machain*, its 2004 judgment concerning the Alien Tort Statute, "[T]he First Congress understood that the district courts would recognize private causes of action for certain torts in violation of the laws of nations. . . . Still, there are good reasons for a restrained conception of the discretion a federal court should exercise in considering a new cause of action of this kind. Accordingly, we think courts should require any claim based on the present-day law of nations to rest on a norm of international character accepted by the civilized world and defined with a specificity comparable to the features of the 18th-century paradigms we have recognized."[8] Those paradigms from the eighteenth century are three in number: offenses against ambassadors, violations of safe conduct, and individual actions arising out of prize captures and piracy.

The Alien Tort Statute is unique to the United States; no other nation has a law of comparable content. In fact, the law has been a remarkable extension of US jurisdiction to events and perpetrators overseas in order to uphold the most significant human rights norms of our times, and that is why it has proven so controversial both at home and abroad and why the Supreme Court reined in its extraterritorial reach in the *Kiobel* judgment. The law was necessary at the time, in the late eighteenth century, to demonstrate the new nation's commitment to international law and the protection of foreign diplomats and various interests on the high seas, in particular. But it was rarely enforced until 1980, with a pathbreaking case, *Filártiga v. Peña-Irala*, concerning a Paraguayan inspector general of police who kidnapped and tortured to death a seventeen-year-old Paraguayan boy.[9] He was sued in federal courts by the boy's sister, who won the case with monetary damages awarded to compensate for those acts of torture. Thereafter, a significant number of Alien Tort Statute cases were brought against individual violators of the law of nations. In the early 1990s, with the *Unocal* case concerning oil exploration in Burma,[10] corporations began to be targeted for civil damages under the Alien Tort Statute. So both natural persons, like the thuggish torturer, and multinational corporations, including the major oil companies and other extractive and manufacturing operations, became targets for civil actions in federal courts.

The results of these complaints have been mixed, with more actions against natural persons succeeding and far fewer surviving against corporations, although the latter often have been short-circuited on political question or other jurisdictional grounds, such as *forum non conveniens* or nonexhaustion of local remedies, or been settled prior to judgment to the benefit of the particular victims bringing the suit. With its *Kiobel* judgment, the Supreme Court has applied the presumption against extraterritoriality with respect to corporate defendants and thus further narrowed the instances where corporations may be held liable under the Alien Tort Statute. But the issue originally raised in the *Kiobel* case, namely, whether corporations are liable at all under the Alien Tort Statute, was not adjudicated by the Supreme Court. Indeed, for two decades, from 1990 to 2009, the federal courts never questioned the applicability of the Alien Tort Statute to corporations, as tortfeasors, and did not seriously undermine the most common form of corporate liability, complicity in the commission of the torts, with any challenge to the knowledge standard for aiding and abetting.

The federal courts have clarified that the reference to "torts" in the Alien Tort Statute includes commission of atrocity crimes, namely, genocide, crimes against humanity, and serious war crimes.[11] This is fundamental because the courts have turned to the war crimes tribunals to understand precisely what kind of torts, or that category of torts one can equate with atrocity crimes, actually fall within the subject matter jurisdiction of the Alien Tort Statute and thus unleash this powerful weapon for civil damages against corporations.

The Supreme Court, in *Sosa v. Alvarez-Machain*, explicitly noted, in describing the subject matter jurisdiction of the Alien Tort Statute, "that the door is still ajar subject to vigilant doorkeeping, and thus open to a narrow class of international norms today."[12] The court set the bar very high, and federal courts since 2004 have applied that high bar to legitimize only the most serious violations of international law, almost always being in the realm of egregious violations of human rights (such as torture) or the related field that is the subject matter jurisdiction of the war crimes tribunals, namely, the full spectrum of atrocity crimes.

In fact, it would be difficult to identify an atrocity crime—in which a corporation may be either complicit or a direct perpetrator—that is also free of Alien Tort Statute liability. Certainly, federal courts would not ponder too long the Alien Tort Statute's applicability to atrocity crimes. The statutes of the war crimes tribunals as well as their respective jurisprudence have established substantiality thresholds for charges of atrocity crimes.[13] This means that once a particular crime is charged and prosecuted before any one of the tribunals, it almost certainly will enter the realm of Alien Tort Statute liability. The International Criminal Court is a permanent court, and the determination of what level and character of criminal conduct falls within its jurisdiction will continue to evolve each year. A federal judge twenty years from now will have a rich body of jurisprudence, underpinned by law generated by the tribunals, to ascertain what does or does not constitute an atrocity crime. He or she will be able to use this knowledge to establish the parameters of Alien Tort Statute liability.

Thus when presented with an Alien Tort Statute claim, federal courts very often turn to the war crimes tribunals to understand whether the violation meets the high bar set by the tribunals for the crime itself. The federal courts also turn to the tribunals to understand how to determine the direct commission of the atrocity crime or whether the individual or corporation has aided and abetted in the commission of the atrocity crime.

Even though the tribunals only prosecute natural persons, that fact is irrelevant when the federal courts are trying to determine what constitutes a violation of international law that meets the eighteenth-century paradigms underpinning the Alien Tort Statute. If the violation constitutes an atrocity crime, then the federal courts will embrace it within the norms intended by the Alien Tort Statute. But with respect to aiding and abetting, some recent federal rulings—greatly contested now— have abandoned the jurisprudence of the International Criminal Tribunals for the former Yugoslavia and Rwanda ("Yugoslav Tribunal" and "Rwanda Tribunal") and seriously misinterpreted the Rome Statute of the International Criminal Court so as to undermine the "knowledge" standard for aiding and abetting. A highly controversial Yugoslav Tribunal Appeals Chamber judgment in 2012 applied a "specific direction" standard to aiding and abetting liability, only to be followed by a differently constituted panel of the Appeals Chamber that rendered a directly conflicting judgment in a different case in early 2014, leading the prosecutor to file a rare motion seeking review of the 2012 judgment. Through it all—the many federal judgments and the copious briefings that accompany federal cases of this nature—the statutes and jurisprudence of the Yugoslav and Rwanda Tribunals, the Special Court for Sierra Leone, the Extraordinary Chambers in the Courts of Cambodia, and International Criminal Court, as well as the Nuremberg Military Tribunal judgments, take center stage and indeed have become the primary sources of law for the federal courts.

Consider the debate in political, academic, and judicial circles in the United States about whether there should be any reference by federal judges in their opinions to international tribunal or foreign court judgments, and often even to customary international law that has not been internally codified yet as treaty law for the United States.[14] In fact, the federal courts are bursting at the seams with full-scale reliance upon the jurisprudence of the war crimes tribunals to determine the proper interpretation and enforcement of federal law. This paradox, of American courts fully embracing tribunal jurisprudence to determine the fate of claims under federal law while some political, academic, and judicial dialogue paints foreign and international rulings as somehow poisonous to the American system, becomes particularly stark when some senior conservative judges on the federal bench warmly invoke the Rome Statute of the International Criminal Court and then misinterpret it to establish both a narrow purpose standard for aiding and abetting and the denial of corporate liability under the Alien Tort Statute altogether.

The Rome Statute has not been ratified as treaty law of the United States, even though the United States signed the treaty on December 31, 2000. The world witnessed almost eight years of the George W. Bush administration trying to undermine the court. Would any right-thinking federal judge, particularly one of long-established conservative bearing, rely on the presumptively toxic Rome Statute for his or her reasoning on a federal statute such as the Alien Tort Statute? In fact they do, shamelessly.

This might best be described by relating my own journey in recent years through several Alien Tort Statute cases, and one Yugoslav Tribunal case itself infected with one of the federal rulings, in which I filed amicus curiae (friend of the court) briefs to help clarify some issues confronting the judges.

The story begins with *Presbyterian Church of Sudan v. Talisman Energy* in 2009.[15] This case concerned Alien Tort Statute claims by the

Presbyterian Church of Sudan and many non-Muslim Sudanese victims of human rights abuses who sued the Canadian oil company Talisman Energy in relation to its drilling operations in southern Sudan, now an independent nation. The plaintiffs alleged complicity by Talisman in genocide and ethnic cleansing, including massive civilian displacement; extrajudicial killing of civilians; torture; rape; and the burning down of villages, churches, and crops. While the issue of corporate liability per se did not yet arise in this case, the critical issue was the standard for aiding and abetting liability.

The Court of Appeals for the Second Circuit (which includes New York) relied upon a novel interpretation of Article 25(3)(c) of the Rome Statute of the International Criminal Court to conclude that customary international law requires that the aider and abettor essentially share the intent of the perpetrator of the atrocity crime. This would contrast with the aider and abettor being held to a knowledge standard, namely, possessing knowledge of or awareness of the perpetrator's commission of the atrocity crime and assisting or abetting such action, but not requiring the prosecutor to prove that the aider and abettor shares the perpetrator's specific intention.

The Second Circuit's interpretation rests upon the use of the word "purpose" in Article 25(3)(c), where this form of individual criminal liability under the Rome Statute is described as, "For the *purpose* of facilitating the commission of such a crime, aids, abets or otherwise assists in its commission or its attempted commission, including providing the means for its commission." The Second Circuit in *Talisman* reads "purpose" to reflect a requirement of "shared intent," and since, in its view, the Rome Statute reflects customary international law, it must mean that aiding and abetting liability requires demonstration of a shared intention with the perpetrator. Significantly, a knowledge standard for corporate aiding and abetting already had been confirmed by the US Court of Appeals for the Eleventh Circuit, by two district courts in the US Court of Appeals for the Ninth Circuit, and by several district courts in the Second Circuit, including the *Agent Orange Product Liability Litigation* in 2005 and the *South Africa Apartheid Litigation* in 2009.[16]

In the corporate realm, and in *Talisman*, it would be extremely difficult to prove corporate intent, shared with the government of the country of investment, to unleash government soldiers and militia to ethnically cleanse a swath of territory for oil exploration. One looks to aiding and abetting theories of liability, which are far more prevalent for corporate operations. The Second Circuit Court of Appeals knocked the legs out of corporate liability with this interpretation of the Rome Statute and then required US federal law to adhere to a significant misinterpretation of the Rome Statute. While the Second Circuit conveniently minimizes corporate liability for human rights violations, how odd it has been that some jurists would resort to the Rome Statute to make the case for corporate freedom from liability.

In my amicus brief, filed alongside the plaintiff-appellants' effort to seek an en banc ruling from the Second Circuit, I argued that the Rome Statute was never intended, in its entirety, to reflect customary international law.[17] Articles 5, 6, 7, and 8 of the Rome Statute indeed were negotiated to record customary international law regarding the substantive crimes. If one applies the *Sosa* standard to the Rome Statute, one can confidently identify the international crimes defined therein as representing the types of crimes that have universal character and are of a magnitude that falls within the jurisdictional scope of the Alien Tort Statute. But that sharp focus on customary international law for subject matter jurisdiction was never the aim of the negotiations regarding many other provisions of the Rome Statute. While some of these other articles, including within general principles of law, could be viewed as expressions of customary international law, Article 25(3)(c) is not one of them.

That provision was negotiated not to codify customary international law but to resolve the competing views of common law and civil law experts on what both camps could live with as an agreed bargain on individual criminal responsibility. I do not recall a single discussion prior to or during the Rome negotiations where the text of Article 25(3)(c) on aiding and abetting as a mode of participation was being settled as a matter of customary international law.

In earlier drafts, negotiators stumbled repeatedly over what eventually was consolidated in Article 30 of the Rome Statute regarding the required mental element for all of the atrocity crimes. For the longest time we could not agree, between common law delegations and civil law delegations, precisely how the mens rea language would be resolved. The Preparatory Committee draft in 1998, which was the initial working draft in Rome, reflected this continued indecision in the aiding and abetting language of what would become Article 25(3)(c): "[W]ith [intent] [knowledge] to facilitate the commission of such a crime, aids, abets or otherwise assists."[18]

It was only after negotiators reached Rome in the summer of 1998 that they finally arrived at compromise language. We knew that Article 30 of the Rome Statute, which deals with the required mental element, was our agreed formula on how both intent and knowledge would be described and applied as the mental element for all of the crimes. Article 30(2)(b) had long been settled and easily captured the mens rea requirement for aiding and abetting, namely, "[i]n relation to a consequence, that person means to cause that consequence or is aware that it will occur in the ordinary course of events." In the negotiations, we did not relegate aiding and abetting only to the first prong of "means to cause that consequence" or to the second prong of "is aware that it will occur in the ordinary course of events." Of course, it is within the second prong of awareness or knowledge that aiding and abetting traditionally occurs and is validated under Yugoslav Tribunal and Rwanda Tribunal jurisprudence.[19]

Even if one were to argue successfully that the Rome Statute requires specific intent for an aider or abettor, that would be a highly peculiar feature of the Rome Statute. There is no evidence to seriously suggest that it represents international customary law. Since the judges of the International Criminal Court have not ruled on this issue yet, there is no guidance from them on how to interpret the Rome Statute. I argued in my amicus curiae brief that the inquiry into what constitutes customary international law for aiding and abetting should be conducted elsewhere, namely, in the jurisprudence of the international and hybrid criminal tribunals and in scholarly textbooks of recent date, almost all of which confirm a knowledge standard for aiding or abetting. My footnotes in the *Talisman* amicus brief and subsequent amicus briefs in other cases and my coauthored article on this issue in the *Berkeley Journal of International Law* are replete with citations to tribunal jurisprudence upholding the knowledge standard.

Furthermore, the Appeals Chamber of the Special Court for Sierra Leone directly addressed the Article 25(3)(c) standard in the Rome Statute in its 2013 judgment convicting Charles Taylor of aiding and abetting atrocity crimes in Sierra Leone.[20] The Appeals Chamber found that the "Rome Statute has no bearing on the *mens rea* elements of aiding and abetting liability under customary international law. . . . [T]he Appeals Chamber reaffirms that knowledge is a culpable *mens rea* standard for aiding and abetting liability under Article 6(1) of the Statute [of the Special Court for Sierra Leone] and customary international law."[21] It also concluded, "The final responsibility to interpret the Rome Statute rests with the ICC Appeals Chamber. . . . Until it has made its views known, speculative exercises do not assist in the identification of the law, and established customary international law, as consistently articulated and applied in the jurisprudence of international criminal tribunals from the Second World War to today, must bear more weight than suppositions as to what Article 25(3)(c) does or does not mean."[22]

Talisman Energy, having avoided liability under the high bar for aiding and abetting set by the Second Circuit, once again prevailed when the Second Circuit denied the application for a rehearing en banc. In a last-ditch effort, the Sudanese victims filed a petition for writ of certiorari before the Supreme Court. I filed a new amicus curiae brief at the Supreme Court in support of that petition.[23] The Supreme Court denied the petition, without comment, in October 2010.[24] Thus the Second Circuit's novel interpretation of aiding and abetting liability, relying heavily on a misinterpretation of the Rome Statute and casting aside years of the war crimes tribunals' jurisprudence, still stands as federal law in the Second Circuit.

The *Talisman* judgment was quickly followed by *Kiobel v. Royal Dutch Petroleum*, again in the Second Circuit.[25] This Alien Tort Statute case involved Nigerian residents who accused Royal Dutch Petroleum Company and Shell Transport and Trading Company, acting through a Nigerian subsidiary, of aiding and abetting the Nigerian government in committing human rights violations, including killings, torture, and forced exile, among other crimes. The plaintiffs alleged that Royal Dutch Shell aided these violations by providing transportation to Nigerian forces, allowing their property to be used as staging grounds for attacks, and providing food and compensation to soldiers. The Second Circuit invoked the new *Talisman* intent standard for aiding and abetting to dismiss the claims against Royal Dutch Shell. But the Court of Appeals in *Kiobel* went much further, ruling for the first time in American jurisprudence, and in defiance of two decades of Alien Tort Statute litigation against multinational corporations, that there is no corporate liability under the Alien Tort Statute. The judges' source of law for this remarkable ruling was none other than the Rome Statute.

Two of the three judges on the Second Circuit Court of Appeals panel concluded that because the Rome Statute excluded juridical persons from criminal prosecution for atrocity crimes before the International Criminal Court, then the negotiators must have concluded that corporate liability of any character for such crimes must not exist under international law. The Circuit Court drew from its misinterpretation of footnote 20 of *Sosa v. Alvarez-Machain*, the requirement that corporate liability be a "specific, universal, and obligatory" legal norm in order to hold Royal Dutch Petroleum or any other corporation liable under the Alien Tort Statute. Footnote 20 of *Sosa* reads: "The Supreme Court instructed the lower courts to consider when ruling on ATS claims 'whether international law extends the scope of liability for a violation of a given norm to the perpetrator being sued, if the defendant is a private actor such as a corporation or an individual.'"[26]

By misconstruing footnote 20, the Second Circuit required that the character of the tortfeasor must be firmly established as a matter of international law in order to attract liability. The circuit court misinterpreted the drafting history of the Rome Statute as revealing that the global community lacks a "consensus among States concerning corporate liability for violations of customary international law." The two appeals court judges relied heavily on the Rome Statute to argue for the lack of corporate liability under international law, and thus they shielded multinational corporations even from civil liability. But they did so by utterly misinterpreting Supreme Court precedent (the *Sosa* decision) and then misinterpreting what negotiators were examining in Rome when corporations were excluded from the personal jurisdiction of the International Criminal Court.[27]

Judge Leval, the third judge, thoroughly rebutted the views of Judges Jacobs and Cabranes on corporate liability and found ample authority, while applying commonsense reading to both US and international law, to solidly lock in corporate liability under the Alien Tort Statute. The *Kiobel* judgment was appealed to the Supreme Court in a petition for writ of certiorari; I filed an amicus curiae brief at the Supreme Court explaining what happened to corporate liability in the Rome Statute talks. I wrote in that brief,

While it may be true that some countries allow certain civil penalties to arise within domestic criminal actions, *Sosa*, 542 U.S. at 762, the negotiators at Rome could not agree either on criminal liability for corporations or the punishment for "convicting" a corporation, including the formula for imposing civil penalties alongside mandatory criminal penalties. As a result, we decided to retain our narrow focus on criminal liability of individuals only—under a statute designed to create an international criminal court—and left civil damages for natural and juridical persons out of the discussion and the court's jurisdiction. To read the failure to agreed on and resulting omission of *criminal* liability for juridical persons under the Rome Statute as an *"express rejection . . .* of a norm of corporate liability in the context of human rights violations," *Kiobel,* 621 F.3d at 139 (emphasis in original), is incorrect. To then posit that one can infer, under *Sosa,* that lack of criminal liability in the Rome Statute should dictate a lack of *civil* liability for juridical persons under the Alien Tort statute is both a misunderstanding of the negotiations at Rome and an illogical reading of *Sosa.*[28]

Relying upon the Second Circuit's reasoning in *Kiobel,* the Fourth Circuit Court of Appeals applied the purpose standard for aiding and abetting in its judgment in *Aziz v. Alcolac, Inc.,* a case seeking to enforce the Alien Tort Statute.[29] Thus only the Second and Fourth Circuit Courts of Appeal have embraced the purpose, or intent, standard for aiding and abetting under the Alien Tort Statute.

The Supreme Court agreed to consider *Kiobel* and did so during two sessions of oral arguments, the first on February 28, 2012, and the reargument on October 1, 2012.[30] Because the Supreme Court never reached either the corporate liability or aiding and abetting issues in its judgment, rendered on April 17, 2013, there remains a circuit split in the US federal courts on the aiding and abetting liability standard and on corporate liability for atrocity crimes, as they are framed under the Alien Tort Statute. In the Seventh Circuit, a district court in Indianapolis held in *Flomo v. Firestone Natural Rubber* (a child labor case in Firestone rubber plantations in Liberia) that the *Kiobel* ruling in the Second Circuit was persuasive enough on corporate liability to scuttle the plaintiffs' case in the Seventh Circuit.[31] That case went on appeal to the Court of Appeals for the Seventh Circuit, sitting in Chicago, and I sat behind plaintiffs' counsel during the hearing in early June 2011.

The oral arguments were remarkable. There sat perhaps the three most conservative judges on the Seventh Circuit, led by one of the most famous conservative Court of Appeals judges in America, Judge Richard Posner. Posner crucified Firestone's counsel on the issue of corporate liability. At one point he exclaimed to the appellate litigator, who seemed not to appreciate the importance of Nuremberg or any international law since then and who argued that the Second Circuit's judgment in *Kiobel* absolved Firestone of all responsibility, "Well, you lost me!" The Seventh Circuit Appeals judgment completely upheld corporate liability under the Alien Tort Statute.[32] But the judges dismissed the case

against Firestone because, in their view, the plaintiffs had not substantiated that the child labor charges rose to the standard of violations of international law required by *Sosa*—in other words, they were not shown
to be atrocity crimes or even human rights violations of indisputable
character under customary international law—and thus they fell outside
the subject matter jurisdiction of the Alien Tort Statute. Nonetheless,
this was a victory for corporate liability under the Alien Tort Statute.

Meanwhile, the US District Court for the Central District of California followed the Second Circuit's ruling in *Kiobel* on both the aiding and abetting and corporate liability standards when it dismissed the
case of *John Doe I, II, and II v. Nestle USA*, which concerns Malian
child slaves who were allegedly trafficked from Mali to Côte d'Ivoire and
forced to work twelve- to fourteen-hour days with no pay, little food or
sleep, and frequent beatings—all to meet the labor demands of Nestle,
Archer Daniels Midland Company, and Cargill Cocoa.[33] The US Court
of Appeals for the Ninth Circuit, sitting en banc, reversed and vacated
the district court's dismissal on September 4, 2014.[34] (In 2010, I filed an
amicus curiae brief challenging the district court's findings on both aiding and abetting and corporate liability.[35]) The Court of Appeals rejected the defendants' argument that corporations could never be sued
under the Alien Tort Statute and, reaffirming its earlier ruling in *Sarei
v. Rio Tinto*,[36] held that "a court should look to international law and determine whether corporations are subject to the norms underlying that
claim."[37] The Court of Appeals described corporate liability under the
Alien Tort Statute as being guided by three principles: "First the analysis proceeds norm-by-norm; there is no categorical rule of corporate
immunity or liability. Second, corporate liability under an ATS claim
does not depend on the existence of international precedent enforcing
legal norms against corporations. Third, norms that are 'universal and
absolute,' or applicable to 'all actors,' can provide the basis for an ATS
claim against a corporation. To determine whether a norm is universal, we consider, among other things, whether it is 'limited to states' and
whether its application depends on the identity of the perpetrator. We
conclude that the prohibition against slavery is universal and may be asserted against the corporate defendants in this case."[38]

Regarding corporate liability for aiding and abetting, the Court of Appeals affirmed the substantiality test for such assistance but "declined to
decide whether the assistance must also be specifically directed towards
the commission of the crime." The Court of Appeals then "remanded to

the district court with instructions to allow the plaintiffs to amend their complaint in light of recent decisions of international criminal tribunals addressing the 'specific direction' requirement."[39] That case thus remained pending for further adjudication at the time of this writing. We will examine shortly the "recent decisions of international criminal tribunals" that proved so influential with the federal judges of the Ninth Circuit Court of Appeals by the summer of 2014.

Another significant development occurred in the DC Circuit Court of Appeals in the case of *John Doe VIII et al. v. Exxon Mobil Corporation, et al.*, a complaint under the Alien Tort Statute by fifteen Indonesian villagers from the Aceh territory alleging that Exxon's security forces committed murder, torture, sexual assault, battery and false imprisonment, and various common law torts.[40] They alleged that Exxon took actions both in the United States and at its facility in the Aceh province that resulted in their injuries. In a judgment handed down on July 8, 2011, the Court of Appeals rejected the entire *Kiobel* analysis on aiding and abetting and on corporate liability, citing my *Talisman* brief before the Supreme Court and in five instances citing my coauthored *Berkeley Journal of International Law* article of early 2011, all to clarify that the Rome Statute simply does not mean what the two Second Circuit appeals judges interpreted it to mean.[41]

The DC Circuit Court of Appeals also looked to war crimes tribunal jurisprudence to confirm the knowledge standard for aiding and abetting liability. The Court of Appeals held: "The court therefore looks to customary international law to determine the standard for assessing aiding and abetting liability, much as we did in addressing availability of aiding and abetting liability itself. Important sources are the international tribunals, mandated by their charter to apply only customary international law. Two such tribunals, the International Criminal Tribunals for the Former Yugoslavia and Rwanda, are considered authoritative sources of customary international law [*Hamdan, Abagninin, Ford v. Garcia*]. They have declared the knowledge standard suffices under customary international law."[42] The majority reversed the lower court's dismissal of the Alien Tort Statute claims and remanded the combined cases to the district court. The lengthy majority opinion is a definitive treatment of both the aiding and abetting and corporate liability issues.

Thus, the Seventh, Ninth, Eleventh, and DC Circuit Courts of Appeal have confirmed corporate liability under the Alien Tort Statute, and the Eleventh and DC Circuit Courts of Appeal have confirmed the knowledge standard for aiding and abetting, while the Ninth Circuit has left that issue open for further review. The Second Circuit is the outlier by denying corporate liability and joins with the Fourth Circuit in requiring a specific intent standard for aiding and abetting. In the future, the Supreme Court may be asked to resolve the circuit split within the federal circuits. If and when the Supreme Court is so tasked, the briefing will be dense with tribunal jurisprudence and interpretative analysis of the Rome Statute. One can expect the Supreme Court, if the opportunity arises, to rely on the war crimes tribunals and the Rome Statute for guidance. Of course, there may emerge a different perspective from some of the justices on whether the court should look to international sources of this character to interpret the Alien Tort Statute, but the most interesting element of the end game in federal jurisprudence doubtless will be federal judges' reliance on tribunal jurisprudence and statutory interpretation to confirm the character of federal law. Who would have predicted such reliance in the early 1990s, when the Alien Tort Statute began to be enforced against corporations and when the tribunal-building era began?

The Appeals Chamber of the Yugoslav Tribunal still could influence the end game for the Alien Tort Statute. To begin with, there was a long-standing appeal before the Appeals Chamber by former General Dragoljub Ojdanić, sentenced to fifteen years' imprisonment for crimes against humanity against Kosovo Albanians.[43] He amended his appeal on the heels of the *Talisman* ruling to argue that the mens rea requirement of aiding and abetting as established under customary international law had been defined properly by the *Talisman* judgment of the Second Circuit Court of Appeals to require the Yugoslav Tribunal to abandon its long-standing knowledge standard and embrace the intent standard, which probably would have been more difficult for the prosecutor to prove.[44] I filed an amicus curiae brief with the Appeals Chamber, which accepted it, challenging resort to *Talisman* and urging the Appeals Chamber to stay the course with the knowledge standard on aiding and abetting.[45] However, on January 25, 2013, Ojdanić fully accepted the judgment of the Trial Chamber, withdrew his appeal, and agreed to serve out his sentence.[46] So ultimately the Appeals Chamber did not address the issue in *Ojdanić*.

But shortly thereafter, on February 13, 2013, the Appeals Chamber of the Yugoslav Tribunal shattered the consensus on the *actus reus* standard for aiding and abetting that had long held firm in that court and in other international tribunals. In *Prosecutor v. Perišić*, a split panel (4–1) of the Appeals Chamber judges reversed the Trial Chamber judgment that had found Momčilo Perišić, the chief of general staff of the Yugoslav Army and thus its most senior officer, guilty of aiding and abetting assistance to the Army of Republika Srpska and the Army of the Serbian Krajina by making a substantial contribution to the commission of crimes in Sarajevo and Srebrenica between 1993 and 1995, by knowing that his assistance aided in the commission of the charged crimes, and by being aware of the general nature of the crimes.[47] The Appeals Chamber required a higher threshold for conviction, ruling that "specific direction" is an element of aiding and abetting liability and that no conviction for aiding and abetting a crime may be entered if specific direction has not been proved beyond reasonable doubt. The majority held that the element of specific direction points to establishing a culpable link between assistance provided by the accused and the crimes of the principal perpetrators, and that had not been proven with respect to Perišić.[48] The Appeals Chamber acknowledged "that specific direction may involve considerations that are closely related to questions of mens rea."[49] It is indeed difficult to imagine an aider and abettor specifically directing the commission of a crime without also having the specific intent to join the primary perpetrator in committing that crime, thus vitiating any knowledge standard for aiding and abetting. The Appeals Chamber acquitted Perišić.

Relying on the Appeals Chamber ruling, a Trial Chamber of the Yugoslav Tribunal shortly thereafter, in another split decision (2–1), acquitted Jovica Stanišić and Franko Simatović of aiding and abetting in the ethnic cleansing of Croats and Muslims in Croatia and Bosnia-Herzegovina.[50] The Trial Chamber found that the accused's assistance was not specifically directed toward commission of the crimes of murder, deportation, forcible transfer, or persecution but allowed for the reasonable conclusion that the assistance was specifically directed toward establishing and maintaining Serb control over these areas. The majority in *Stanišić and Simatović* was unable to conclude, under the specific direction standard, that the assistance rendered in fact aided and abetted the charged crimes. "Proof of specific direction in such circumstances requires evidence establishing a direct link between the aid provided by an accused and the relevant crimes committed by principal perpetrators."[51]

Dissenting Judge Michèle Picard found the *Perišić* jurisprudence on aiding and abetting "overly restrictive" and yet also determined "that the 'specific direction' requirement can be inferred from the Accused's actions."[52] She concluded, "The Accused in this case knowingly funded and armed criminals, and even trained them in illegal warfare (human shields) so that they could commit the crimes which the Accused knew (majority: *must have known*) these men would ultimately commit. If we cannot find that the Accused aided and abetted those crimes, I would say we have come to a dark place in international law indeed. It is a place, in the words spoken by the Honorable Judge Robert H. Jackson in 1949, where 'law has terrors only for little men and takes note only of little wrongs.'"[53]

Not surprisingly, the tide soon began to turn back to the substantiality and knowledge standards for aiding and abetting. On September 26, 2013, the Appeals Chamber of the Special Court for Sierra Leone upheld the Trial Chamber conviction of former Liberian president Charles Taylor on charges of aiding and abetting rebel forces against the civilian population of Sierra Leone over five years of civil war.[54] The Appeals Chamber applied the knowledge standard to its aiding and abetting analysis, as had the Trial Chamber, in upholding the conviction of Charles Taylor.[55] The judges explicitly rejected the "specific direction" standard set by the Yugoslav Tribunal Appeals Chamber in the *Perišić* judgment, finding that it lacked a "clear, detailed analysis supporting the conclusion that 'specific direction' *is* an element of aiding and abetting under customary international law."[56]

In conclusion, the Appeals Chamber of the Special Court for Sierra Leone rejected the *Perišić* criteria for aiding and abetting liability and upheld the overwhelming jurisprudence of the Yugoslav Tribunal and other tribunals confirming that (a) "the *actus reus* of aiding and abetting liability under Article 6(1) of the Statute [of the Special Court for Sierra Leone] and customary international law is that an accused's acts and conduct of assistance, encouragement and/or moral support had a substantial effect on the commission of the crimes charged for which he is to be held responsible,"[57] and (b) "[t]he Appeals Chamber's review of the post–Second World War jurisprudence and subsequent case law demonstrates that under customary international law, an accused's knowledge of the consequence of his acts or conduct—that is, an accused's knowing participation in the crimes—is a culpable *mens rea* standard for individual criminal liability. In light of the foregoing, the Appeals Chamber reaffirms that knowledge is a culpable *mens rea* standard for aiding and abetting liability under Article 6(1) of the Statute and customary international law."[58] The Appeals Chamber failed to find any evidence "of state practice indicating a change in customary international law from the existing parameters of personal culpability for aiding and abetting the commission of serious violations of international humanitarian law."[59]

Then, on January 23, 2014, in *Prosecutor v. Šainović et al.*, a different panel of Yugoslav Tribunal Appeals Chamber judges from that constituted for the *Perišić* case rejected (4–1) the "specific direction" element for aiding and abetting under customary international law and restored the knowledge standard:

> [A]s correctly stated in the *Furundžija* Trial Judgement and confirmed by the *Blaškić* Appeal Judgement, under customary international law, the *actus reus* of aiding and abetting "consists of practical assistance, encouragement, or moral support which has a substantial effect on the perpetration of the crime." The required *mens rea* is "the knowledge that these acts assist the commission of the offense." The Appeals Chamber reaffirms the position taken by the *Blaškić* Appeal Judgement in this regard.
>
> Accordingly, the Appeals Chamber confirms that the *Mrkšić and Šlijivančanin* and *Lukić and Lukić* Appeal Judgements stated the prevailing law in holding that "'specific direction' is not an essential ingredient of the *actus reus* of aiding and abetting," accurately reflecting customary international law and the legal standard that has been constantly and consistently applied in determining aiding and abetting liability. Consequently, the Appeals Chamber, Judge Tuzmukhamedov dissenting, unequivocally rejects the approach adopted in the *Perišić* Appeal Judgement as it is in direct and material conflict with the prevailing jurisprudence on the *actus reus* of aiding and abetting liability and with customary international law in this regard.[60]

The prosecutor of the Yugoslav Tribunal filed a motion before the Appeals Chamber on February 3, 2014, requesting reconsideration of its acquittal of Perišić for aiding and abetting charged crimes. The prosecutor wrote, "Reconsideration is justified in light of the Appeals Chamber's recent holding in the *Šainović* Appeal Judgement that the *Perišić* Appeals Chamber erred in law by requiring, for the first and only time, proof of specific direction as an element of aiding and abetting contrary to the Tribunal's consistent jurisprudence and customary international law."[61] Not surprisingly, the same panel of the Appeals Chamber that had ruled in the *Perišić* case denied the prosecutor's motion, ruling that it had no power to reconsider final judgments and emphasizing the importance of certainty and finality of judgments.[62] The Appeals Chamber once again will deliberate on the issue of specific direction in aiding and abetting liability during the appeal by the prosecutor in *Stanišić & Simatović*.

One should not be surprised if federal courts seize upon these developments in the Yugoslav Tribunal and the Special Court for Sierra Leone when adjudicating future cases, particularly under the Alien Tort Statute, concerning individuals and corporations where the claim rests with aiding and abetting atrocity crimes. When combined with a proper reading of the Rome Statute and the preponderance of tribunal jurisprudence upholding the substantiality and knowledge standards, federal courts (including perhaps some day the Supreme Court) should find the Second and Fourth Circuits' criteria for aiding and abetting seriously flawed, either for individuals or corporations.

Nonetheless, the Supreme Court's judgment in *Kiobel*, which narrows the reach of the Alien Tort Statute over corporations because of the court's application of the presumption against extraterritoriality, accords prominence to the Second Circuit's invitation in its own ruling in that case to give more serious consideration to civil actions against corporate officers and their often considerable personal assets for such individuals' critical roles in guiding corporate conduct leading to atrocity crimes and other human rights abuses. As the Second Circuit appeals court wrote, "We note only that nothing in this opinion limits or forecloses suits under the ATS against the individual perpetrators of violations of customary international law—including the employees, managers, officers, and directors of a corporation—as well as anyone who purposefully aids and abets a violation of customary international law."[63] While bringing a civil action against a corporation is perhaps easier than against a chief executive of that company, in terms of discovery and remedies, the Second Circuit opened the door wide for the legal academy to strategize ways in which to hold corporate executives accountable with civil remedies before federal courts. So this story is by no means over in the United States, either for corporate liability or executive officer liability.

The former prosecutor of the International Criminal Court, Luis Moreno-Ocampo, created a firestorm in 2004 when he told reporters during an International Bar Association meeting in San Francisco that corporate officials who participate in atrocity crimes may be subject to prosecution by the court.[64] The American business community pounced on him, as did federal judge Michael Chertoff (later to become secretary of Homeland Security under President George W. Bush) who criticized what he considered the dangerous overreach of the International Criminal Court.[65] But the reality of corporate operations that may be connected to the commission of atrocity crimes will not fade away; corporate executives doubtless will be exposed to inquiries and possible investigations.

When the crime of aggression is activated for the International Criminal Court, perhaps as early as 2017,[66] such codification of the individual's criminality could have profound impact on corporate officers in terms of criminal prosecution. It also could expose corporations engaged in war-related enterprises, such as arms manufacturing and military contracting, to Alien Tort Statute liability. A ruling by the International Criminal Court invoking its jurisdiction over the crime of aggression could be interpreted by a federal court as establishing the basis for Alien Tort Statute liability over an atrocity crime, as similar rulings by the war crimes tribunals since 1995 have deeply influenced the range of torts, or atrocity crimes, that fall within the violations of the law of nations established by the Alien Tort Statute.

It would be surprising if federal courts ceased drawing upon the jurisprudence of the international war crimes tribunals to interpret and enforce the Alien Tort Statute. Despite the Supreme Court's restraint on the enforceability of that law in 2013, one can expect a good number of Alien Tort Statute cases in the future.[67] Federal judges will continue to seek informed guidance about the character of the atrocity crimes at stake, the nature of participation in illegal conduct by an individual or corporation, and whether corporations and their executives can be held accountable. International criminal justice has generated and will continue to offer sophisticated perspectives for such challenges ahead.

Notes

1. 28 U.S.C. §1350 (2010).

2. An earlier version of this chapter appeared in David Scheffer, "*Tribunal Influence in Recent U.S. Jurisprudence on Corporate Liability for Atrocity Crimes*," in *Proceedings of the Fifth International Humanitarian Law Dialogs*, ed. *David M. Crane and Elizabeth Anderson (Washington, DC: American Soci-*

ety of International Law, 2012), 47–75. The international and hybrid war crimes tribunals include the International Criminal Court, the International Criminal Tribunals for the former Yugoslavia and Rwanda, the Special Court for Sierra Leone, the Extraordinary Chambers in the Courts of Cambodia, and the Special Tribunal for Lebanon.

3. 133 S.Ct. 1659 (2013).

4. International Criminal Tribunal for Rwanda, "Judgement," Prosecutor v. Nahimana, Barayagwiza and Ngeze (November 28, 2007).

5. Ashley Parker, "'Corporations Are People,' Romney Tells Iowa Hecklers Angry over His Tax Policy," *New York Times*, August 12, 2011, A16, http://www.nytimes.com/2011/08/12/us/politics/12romney.html?scp=1&sq=Romney%20corporations%20as%20people&st=cse.

6. 558 U.S. 50 (2010).

7. 28 U.S.C. §1350 (2010).

8. Sosa v. Alvarez-Machain, 542 U.S. 692, 724–25 (2004).

9. Filártiga v. Peña-Irala, 630 F.2d 876 (2nd Cir. 1980).

10. Doe I v. Unocal Corp, 395 F.3d 932 (9th Cir. 2002).

11. See David Scheffer, *All the Missing Souls: A Personal History of the War Crimes Tribunals* (Princeton, NJ: Princeton University Press, 2012), 428–37.

12. Sosa v. Alvarez-Machain, 542 U.S. 692, 729 (2004).

13. See David Scheffer, "Genocide and Atrocity Crimes," *Genocide Studies and Prevention* 1 (2006): 229, 238–44.

14. See, e.g., David Scheffer, "Introductory Note to Military Commissions Act of 2006," *International Legal Materials* 45 (2006): 1241–42, 1275; Awad v. Ziriax, 2010 U.S. Dist. LEXIS 119660 (W.D. Okla. 2010) (finding that proposed "Save Our State" constitutional amendment violated the Establishment Clause of the US Constitution and granting a preliminary injunction to prevent certification of the referendum results), aff'd, 670 F.3d 1111 (10th Cir. 2012); Penny M. Venetis, "The Unconstitutionality of Oklahoma's SQ 755 and Other Provisions Like It That Bar State Courts from Considering International Law," *Cleveland State Law Review* 59 (2011): 189–217.

15. The Presbyterian Church of Sudan et al. v. Talisman Energy, Inc., 582 F.3d 244 (2nd Cir. 2009).

16. See David Scheffer and Caroline Kaeb, "The Five Levels of CSR Compliance: The Resiliency of Corporate Liability under the Alien Tort Statute and the Case for a Counterattack Strategy in Compliance Theory," *Berkeley Journal of International Law* 29 (2011): 334, 345–46.

17. "Brief of David J. Scheffer, Director of the Center for International Human Rights, as Amicus Curiae in Support of the Petitioner and Rehearing En Banc," The Presbyterian Church of Sudan, et al., v. Talisman Energy, Inc., No. 07-0016-cv (2d Cir. 2009): 2–3.

18. "United Nations Diplomatic Conference of Plenipotentiaries on the Es-

tablishment of an International Criminal Court, Rome 15 June–17 July 1998, Official Records, Volume III," U.N. Doc. A/CONF.183/13 (Vol. III) (2002), 31.

19. See Antonio Cassese, *International Criminal Law*, 2nd ed. (New York: Oxford University Press, 2008), 211, 214–18; International Criminal Tribunal for the former Yugoslavia, Prosecutor v. Furundzija, "Judgement" (December 10, 1998), paras. 236–45; "Brief for International Law Scholars William Aceves et al. as Amici Curiae Supporting Petitioners," The Presbyterian Church of Sudan v. Talisman Energy, Inc., 2010 U.S. LEXIS 7652 (2d Cir. April 30, 2010) (No. 09-1262), 12–15.

20. Special Court for Sierra Leone, "Judgment," Prosecutor v. Taylor, SCSL-03–01-A, September 26, 2013, paras. 435–36, 447–51 (Appeals Chamber).

21. Ibid., paras. 435, 437.

22. Ibid., para. 451

23. "Brief of David J. Scheffer, Director of the Center for International Human Rights, as Amicus Curiae in Support of the Issuance of a Writ of Certiorari," Presbyterian Church of Sudan, et al., v. Talisman Energy, Inc., No. 09-1262 (2d Cir. 2010), 9–11.

24. Presbyterian Church of Sudan v. Talisman Energy, Inc., 582 F.3d 244 (2d Cir. 2009), *cert. denied*, 131 S.Ct. 79 (2010).

25. Kiobel v. Royal Dutch Petroleum Co., 621 F.3d 111 (2d Cir. 2010).

26. Sosa v. Alvarez-Machain, 542 U.S. 692, 732 n.20 (2004).

27. See David Scheffer and Caroline Kaeb, "The Five Levels of CSR Compliance," 334, 359–65.

28. "Brief of Ambassador David J. Scheffer, Northwestern University School of Law, as Amicus Curiae in Support of the Issuance of a Writ of Certiorari," Kiobel v. Royal Dutch Petroleum, No. 10-1491 (2d Cir. 2011), 8–9.

29. Aziz v. Alcolac, Inc., 658 F.3d 388, 398 (4th Cir. 2011).

30. The Supreme Court granted the petition for writ of certiorari and held oral arguments on February 28, 2012. I filed an amicus curiae brief focusing on the corporate liability issue. See "Brief of Ambassador David J. Scheffer, Northwestern University School of Law, as Amicus Curiae in Support of the Petitioners," Kiobel v. Royal Dutch Petroleum, No. 10-1491 (2d Cir. 2011). The Supreme Court thereafter requested reargument on additional issues, and that reargument was heard October 1, 2012. I filed an amicus curiae brief for this second hearing focusing on corporate liability and on aiding and abetting issues. See "Supplemental Brief of Ambassador David J. Scheffer, Northwestern University School of Law, as Amicus Curiae in Support of the Petitioners," Kiobel v. Royal Dutch Petroleum, No. 10-491 (2d Cir. 2012).

31. Flomo v. Firestone Natural Rubber Co, 744 F.Supp.2d 810 (S.D. Ind. 2010).

32. Flomo v. Firestone Rubber, 643 F.3d 1013 (7th Cir. 2011).

33. Doe I v. Nestle, S.A., 748 F.Supp.2d 1057 (C.D. Cal. 2010).

34. Doe I v. Nestle, S.A., No. 10-56739, slip op. and order reversing and vacating district court's dismissal (9th Cir. Sept. 4, 2014) ("Nestle").

35. "Brief of David J. Scheffer as Amicus Curiae in Support of Appellants and Reversal," Doe I v. Nestle USA, Inc., No. 10–56739 (9th Cir. 2011).

36. 671 F.3d 736, 748 (9th Cir. 2011).

37. Nestle, supra note 34, at 2.

38. Ibid., 17–18 (footnotes omitted).

39. Ibid., 3. See also "Amicus Curiae Brief of David J. Scheffer in support of Appellants' Opposition to Petition for Rehearing and Rehearing En Banc," Doe I v. Nestle USA, Inc., No. 10-56739 (9th Cir. 2014).

40. Doe v. Exxon Mobil Corp., 654 F.3d 11 (D.C. Cir. 2011).

41. Ibid., footnotes 24, 25, 35, 38, 43.

42. Doe v. Exxon Mobil Corp., 654 F.3d 11, 33 (D.C. Cir. 2011).

43. International Criminal Tribunal for the former Yugoslavia, "Judgement," The Prosecutor v. Nikola Šainović, Dragoljub Ojdanić, Nebojša Pavković, Vladimir Lazarević, Sreten Lukić (February 26, 2009).

44. International Criminal Tribunal for the former Yugoslavia, "General Ojdanić's Motion to Amend His Amended Notice of Appeal," The Prosecutor v. Nikola Šainović, Dragoljub Ojdanić, Nebojša Pavković, Vladimir Lazarević, Sreten Lukić Sainovic, Case No. IT-05-87A (July 29, 2009).

45. International Criminal Tribunal for the former Yugoslavia, "Amicus Brief on Behalf of David J. Scheffer, Director of the Center for International Human Rights, Northwestern University School of Law," The Prosecutor v. Nikola Šainović, Dragoljub Ojdanić, Nebojša Pavković, Vladimir Lazarević, Sreten Lukić Sainovic, Case No. IT-05-87-A (July 29, 2010).

46. Marija Ristic, "Yugoslav General Admits War Crimes," *Balkan Transitional Justice*, January 28, 2013, http://www.balkaninsight.com/en/article/yugoslav-army-general-admits-kosovo-crimes.

47. International Criminal Tribunal for the former Yugoslavia, "Judgement," Prosecutor v. Momčilo Perišić, Appeals Chamber (February 28, 2013) ("*Perišić*").

48. Ibid.

49. Ibid.

50. International Criminal Tribunal for the former Yugoslavia, "Judgement," Prosecutor v. Jovica Stanišić and Franko Simatović (May 30, 2013).

51. Ibid.

52. Ibid.

53. Ibid.

54. Special Court for Sierra Leone, "Judgment," Prosecutor v. Taylor, SCSL-03-01-A, September 26, 2013 (Appeals Chamber).

55. Ibid., para. 438.

56. Ibid., para. 477.

57. Ibid., para. 482.

58. Ibid., para. 483.

59. Ibid., para. 484.

60. International Criminal Tribunal for the former Yugoslavia, "Judgement," Prosecutor v. Nikola Šainović, Nebojša Pavković, Vladimir Lazarević and Sreten Lukić (January 23, 2014), paras. 1649–50. See also International Criminal Tribunal for the former Yugoslavia, "Judgement," Prosecutor v. Vujadin Popović (January 30, 2015), paras. 1732, 1758.

61. International Criminal Tribunal for the former Yugoslavia, "Motion for Reconsideration," Prosecutor v. Momćilo Perišić (February 3, 2014), 1.

62. International Criminal Tribunal for the former Yugoslavia, "Decision on Motion for Reconsideration," Prosecutor v. Momćilo Perišić (March 20, 2014), http://www.icty.org/x/cases/perisic/acdec/en/140320.pdf.

63. Kiobel v. Royal Dutch Petroleum Co., 621 F.3d 111, 122 (2d Cir. 2010).

64. James Podgers, "Corporations in Line of Fire: International Prosecutor Says Corporate Officials Could Face War Crimes Charges," *ABA Journal*, January 2, 2004, http://www.abajournal.com/magazine/article/corporations_in_line _of_fire/.

65. Michael Chertoff, "Justice Denied: The International Criminal Court Is Even Worse Than Its Critics Have Said," *Weekly Standard* 9, April 12, 2004, http://www.weeklystandard.com/author/michael-chertoff.

66. See David Scheffer, "The Crime of Aggression," in *Beyond Kampala: Next Steps for U.S. Principled Engagement with the International Criminal Court*, ed. Rachel Gore, ASIL Discussion Paper 87 (2010), 87–107; David Scheffer, "States Parties Approve New Crimes for International Criminal Court," *ASIL Insight* 14, no. 16 (June 22, 2010), http://www.asil.org/insights/volume/14/ issue/16/states-parties-approve-new-crimes-international-criminal-court; David Scheffer, "The Complex Crime of Aggression under the Rome Statute," *Leiden Journal of International Law* 23 (2010): 897–904.

67. Oona Hathaway, *Kiobel Commentary: The Door Remains Open to "Foreign Squared" Cases*, SCOTUSBlog, April 18, 2013, 4:37 pm, http://www .scotusblog.com/2013/04/kiobel-commentary-the-door-remains-open-to-foreign -squared-cases/.

CHAPTER EIGHT

Sanction and Socialize

Military Command Responsibility and Corporate Accountability for Atrocities

Scott A. Gilmore

For decades, the corporate social responsibility (CSR) movement has faced a dilemma: should corporate obligations to respect human rights be binding law or voluntary principles? The problem is more pointed when it comes to international crimes: genocide, war crimes, and crimes against humanity. Is industry self-regulation a proper response to mass atrocity? If not, how should law and public policy intervene? Once confined to scholarly journals, the debate is playing out in the courtroom. In 2004, Ronen Shamir posited that dueling strategies of CSR were being litigated into existence: lawsuits filed by human rights advocates sought to translate CSR norms into enforceable law, while corporate defendants and lobbyists sought to resist CSR's legalization.[1] A decade later, this struggle has crystallized into two competing—and often mutually exclusive—visions of corporate responsibility.[2] One rests on the power of penalties to rein in corporate abuses. The other rests on the power of socialization to induce businesses to internalize best practices and aspire to good corporate citizenship. One invokes a penal code, the other an honor code.

This chapter seeks to escape this binary. CSR must embrace the penal code of legal sanctions and the honor code of socialization if it is to achieve a well-incentivized regime for corporate responsibility. And it can draw on a powerful model: the international laws of war. Mitigating the human rights impact of war and business are similar projects. Both seek to graft humanitarian concerns onto hierarchical organizations whose core missions seem indifferent—or opposed—to protecting human rights. A corporation exists to make profits, an army to wage war. Even so, international law has developed a powerful legal regime for setting humanitarian limits on armed conflict: the doctrine of command responsibility. This regime fuses external policing with self-regulation, sanctions with socialization. It has a preventive component that instills humanitarian concerns through training and oversight. But it also has a punitive component: commanders can be prosecuted if they knew, or should have known, that their subordinates were committing crimes and they failed to make reasonable efforts to prevent the abuses or punish the perpetrators.

For the laws of war, these regimes of sanction and socialization are complementary and mutually reinforcing. In contrast, the CSR project has yet to achieve this symmetry. Although CSR has promoted industry self-regulation, it has not realized any meaningful sanctions for corporate abuses. Further, no international court has ever prosecuted a business entity, despite revelations of corporate complicity in atrocity crimes. Since Nuremberg, only a handful of corporate officers have stood in the dock of international justice.

If corporate accountability has been a blind spot for global criminal justice, it has fared little better in domestic courts. In a series of three decisions, the US Supreme Court gutted the decades-long effort to hold multinationals civilly liable under the Alien Tort Statute for atrocities committed around the world.[3] Prosecution has been a nonstarter. The United States has never prosecuted a corporation or its officers for a human rights crime. In Europe, new opportunities—and obstacles—have emerged for prosecuting extraterritorial corporate abuses. Meanwhile, across the global South the disparity of power and resources between multinationals and local regulators has created an accountability gap.

Faced with this gap, the CSR movement should redouble its efforts to establish binding legal obligations rather than retreat into voluntary self-regulation, not least because industries most likely to violate human rights—the extraction, arms, and private military sectors—are also the least susceptible to volunteer CSR initiatives. This chapter argues that in these high-risk sectors, the CSR movement should look to the laws of war. The command responsibility doctrine offers a regulatory model that leverages sanctions to induce businesses to adopt cultures of compliance. CSR advocates should press courts, prosecutors, and legislators to apply the command responsibility doctrine to the corporate chain of command. In companies, as in armies, the lines of control—between managers and employees, entities and officers, and parents and subsidiaries—should define the lines of liability.

Companies of War and Business: Historical, Structural, and Transnational Ties

War was a business affair long before President Eisenhower warned against the rise of the military-industrial complex. There is a long though little studied history of business in war. It is no accident that the word *company* shares military and commercial connotations: the modern corporation and the modern military share a common nucleus. The private mercenary armies of the Thirty Years' War were some of Europe's first joint stock firms, while global mercantile companies, like the English East India Company, fielded their own armies. To this day, corporations and militaries share structural features. And it is often their transactions that give rise to the most devastating business impacts on human rights. This section examines these ties, laying a foundation for the models of regulation explored below.

Common Origins: Mercenary and Mercantile Companies

Today, one tends to think of the military as an arm of the state. But for centuries in premodern Europe, the greatest weapon of prince and king was not the sword but the contract. War was a private enterprise. Large-scale mercenarism flourished in fourteenth- and fifteenth-century Europe. Indeed, as Janice E. Thomson notes, military contractors—the free companies and *condottieri*—dominated not just warfare but also the economy, establishing one of Europe's first free markets.[4] By the Thirty Years' War in the seventeenth century, the private army of Count Albrecht von Wallenstein had become "the biggest and best organized private enterprise seen in Europe before the twentieth century."[5]

These private armies sowed the seeds of modern business and military entities. Wallenstein's army took a recognizable business form: its officers were investors, receiving stock in exchange for fielding men and equipment.[6] Wallenstein also pioneered military organization, creating a general staff system, payroll, and specialized officers for training, logistics, and justice.[7] Even firms that were not in the business of war had fighting forces. The mercantile companies of the seventeenth and eighteenth centuries—prototypes of the modern multinational corporation—maintained armies and navies and put territory under armed occupation.[8] In 1661, the English East India Company received a royal charter to make war.[9] By 1757, the company had established English rule in India: a corporation conquering a country.[10]

Despite these shared origins, the modern military and corporation took divergent paths. After the Peace of Westphalia in 1648, nation-states gradually monopolized organized violence, integrating militaries into government.[11] The corporation, in contrast, saw a reverse trend. It came to be viewed less as a public body—a creature of law and sovereign charter—and more as a private association of individuals—a creature of contract.[12]

Common Structures: Hierarchy and Extraterritoriality

Today, despite the obvious differences, there remain structural similarities between the two institutions, especially the globe-spanning multinationals that are distant cousins of the East India Company. Both are hierarchical organizations: militaries have their rank and regiments, corporations their shareholders, directors, and officers. And both are constituted for a narrow mission: an army's raison d'être is warfare, a corporation's profit. Both are subject to internal and external controls. A corporation has its charter, bylaws, and codes of conduct. But corporations are also policed by government regulators—and influenced by shareholders, consumers, and other stakeholders. Similarly, militaries have their codes of military justice and their courts martial. Yet their members are normally subject to civilian authority and, for war crimes, to civilian prosecutors in domestic and international courts.

Finally, militaries and multinationals are often extraterritorial entities. They can operate across borders, legal jurisdictions, and polities. This liminal nature can tempt both institutions to leave ethical norms behind when they enter foreign battlefields or foreign markets. Conduct unthinkable at home can be rationalized when "doing business in a tough neighborhood." At the same time, home states seeking to avoid diplomatic friction can be reluctant to police misconduct committed abroad.[13] Thus the transnational nature of both institutions can create serious governance gaps.

Common Problems: The Risks of Business in Conflict

It is in these gaps that transactions between militaries and corporations often give rise to serious human rights violations. Consider three examples: the pillage of natural resources in conflict zones, the arms trade, and private military contracting. From Colombia to the Congo, the illegal exploitation of natural resources has become a primary means of financing twenty-first-century conflict.[14] As James G. Stewart notes, international and domestic courts can prosecute corporate actors for the war crime of pillage.[15] Yet there has been no meaningful legal accountability since German industrialists were put on trial after World War II. The arms trade is another intersection; private sales of weaponry to armed groups or repressive regimes have enabled massive civilian casualties.[16] Although a tribunal at Nuremberg established that the German makers of Zyklon B could be prosecuted for the mass killings they enabled, that precedent has rarely been followed; few arms dealers have been tried for abetting atrocities.[17]

Finally, mercenarism has returned. The use of private military and security contractors by national governments and the United Nations has exploded in the past two decades; estimates of annual revenue for the private military industry range from $20 to $100 billion.[18] Yet accountability has not followed military contractors onto the battlefield. Although bound by the laws of war, in practice, contractors often elude enforcement. In the United States, a lack of political will has barred prosecutions or limited them to low-ranking culprits. Meanwhile, efforts to hold contractors civilly liable for war crimes have been derailed by sovereign immunity, state secrets, and other avoidance doctrines.[19] Given these links between business and warfare, and the structural parallels between corporations and militaries, the next sections explore how these entities are regulated on either side of the transaction.

Humanizing War: Military Responsibility for Atrocities

Over centuries, international law has developed a powerful legal regime for imposing humanitarian limits on armed conflict. War has always been highly regulated; from Sun Tzu's *The Art of War* to Roman custom, codes of conduct and rules of engagement have ancient origins.[20] These customary norms later crystallized into written law with the emer-

gence of international humanitarian law (IHL) in the nineteenth century. Since the first Geneva Convention was adopted in 1864, rules for
the protection of civilians, the wounded, and cultural objects in warfare
have been propagated by civil society, embraced by military leaders, and
enforced by tribunals.[21] IHL's emergence as a regulatory force has many
lessons for the corporate responsibility movement. But one key concern
is how IHL is structured as a "regime," to borrow a term from international relations theory; that is, a set of rules, expectations, and inducements that shape social behavior.[22]

IHL fuses two regimes. It joins external policing with self-regulation,
sanctions with socialization. Central to both regimes is the notion of
command responsibility. Commanders are vested with the duty to instill
and oversee a corporate culture of compliance with humanitarian law.
And they face criminal sanctions if they fail to prevent or punish abuses
committed by their subordinates.[23] Embedded in this concept are two
very different mechanisms of social influence—what Ryan Goodman
and Derek Jinks call coercion and acculturation. Coercion relies on
sanctions and rewards to influence an actor's behavior "not by reorient-
ing their preferences, but by changing the cost-benefit calculations."[24]

Acculturation, in turn, is a process by which an actor is influenced
to emulate practices and internalize norms through social and cognitive pressures to conform.[25] Drawing on research in social psychology,
Goodman and Jinks argue that individuals and organizations often mirror the behavioral patterns of a given reference group, be it a community
of neighbors or an assembly of states, as they seek membership, esteem,
and legitimacy. IHL features coercion and acculturation in complementary and mutually reinforcing ways. First, it has a preventive component
that seeks to acculturate humanitarian concerns through training, best
practices, and oversight. As the US Supreme Court observed in 1946,
"the law of war presupposes that its violation is to be avoided through
the control of the operations of war by commanders."[26]

Commanders have the task of maintaining order in the ranks, training subordinates, and inculcating a law-abiding culture. Creating this corporate culture, with its positive images of the "honorable warrior" and its
pressure to conform to those ideals, is key to maintaining an effective—
and lawful—fighting force.[27] These group identity mechanisms are crys-
talline examples of acculturation. But acculturation works both ways.
Militaries can foster cultures of compliance *or* cultures of deviance. In hi-

erarchical units, acting under stress, a leader who dehumanizes an enemy, disregards civilians, or tolerates lawlessness can habituate subordinates to war crimes. The pressure to conform to this deviant group identity can be enormous. So material inducements to resist that pressure are critical.

IHL has developed these inducements by crafting negative and positive incentives for maintaining a culture of compliance. The first inducement is the doctrine of "responsible command." Under international law, the legal right to wage war is premised on the command of a "person responsible for his subordinates."[28] An effective chain of command is the key to the kingdom; with it come the benefits of lawful belligerent status—the right to kill combatants and prisoner of war status.

Beyond this positive incentive, IHL has developed a powerful negative sanction: the doctrine of command responsibility. This legal doctrine makes military and civilian leaders liable for the unlawful acts of their subordinates. It subjects superiors to criminal or civil penalties if they knew, or should have known, that their subordinates were committing abuses, and they failed to take all necessary and reasonable measures to prevent those abuses or punish the perpetrators.[29] The Nuremberg and Tokyo tribunals relied on this doctrine to convict senior Nazi and Japanese leaders.[30] Years later, the International Criminal Tribunals for Yugoslavia and Rwanda used the doctrine to prosecute leaders who were far removed from the killing fields.[31]

Command responsibility is best understood as a tool of regulation, rather than a mere retributive device. It does not simply mete out just deserts to bad actors. Indeed, it holds commanders liable even if they did not personally participate in the crime.[32] Rather, it punishes superiors for failing to socialize their ranks into a corporate culture of respecting humanitarian norms. This makes for a distinct model of deterrence: command responsibility aims to dissuade the commission of war crimes, not just by altering the cost-benefit calculus of individual actors but also by expressing a social preference for one corporate culture over another. It calls one military culture honorable, the other shameful.

Command responsibility also aims to achieve a degree of self-regulation; in the chaos of distant battlefields, commanders are best positioned to monitor and remedy misconduct. So militaries maintain their own separate body of criminal law and procedure for internal discipline. When these internal systems fail, external regulators step in. Historically, war crimes have been prosecuted by civilian prosecutors—or by the courts martial of foreign powers. Members of the Axis high command, for example, were tried by Allied military commissions.

These regimes of sanction and socialization, self-regulation and external enforcement reinforce one another. The threat of individual punishment incentivizes leaders to adopt cultures of ethical compliance, while those cultures in turn prevent future violations. They are also tailored to institutional features, adapting chains of command to humanitarian ends. Finally, they promote internal systems of discipline and monitoring so that when a military unit enters a foreign battlefield, it does not abandon the rule of law. Are these regimes often honored in the breach? No doubt. But their impact can be measured by the slowly growing number of war crimes prosecutions and the universality of their acceptance; there are more parties to the Geneva Conventions than members of the United Nations.[33]

Humanizing Business: Corporate Social Responsibility without Sanctions?

CSR has achieved none of this symmetry. It offers a voluntary acculturation regime, but few meaningful sanctions. CSR initiatives have proliferated, including "soft law" tools as diverse as voluntary codes of conduct, ethics committees, ombudsmen, and hiring procedures to screen for human rights standards. Indeed, these tools of acculturation have come to be synonymous with the CSR project. But CSR has little regulatory bite. Unlike IHL, it lacks legal sanctions to incentivize and ensure compliance with these initiatives. And by focusing on voluntarism, CSR has minimized—and perhaps delegitimized—government enforcement of public values on private industry.

As John Ruggie acknowledges, the rise of voluntary CSR initiatives was driven largely by the potential threat of legal liability.[34] But this threat rings hollow as prosecutors fail to charge corporate human rights abuses, courts curtail victims' rights to bring civil actions, and legislators do little to shore up the enforcement gap. As the threat of liability wanes, so goes its power to compel compliance. James Stewart sums up the anemia of corporate accountability in international criminal justice: "there is perfect impunity for international crimes perpetrated by corporate actors and their agents, broken momentarily after WWII and in one or two sporadic instances in the past decade."[35]

The Lack of Legal Accountability

Today, no international criminal tribunal has jurisdiction over corporate entities. And in the sixty years since Nuremberg, only a handful of corporate officers have ever stood in the dock for atrocity crimes. In theory, international criminal law applies to corporations and their agents, just as it applies to military actors. But in practice, no prosecution has ever had the transformative effect on corporate governance that the Nuremberg trials had on military governance. As a result, the international law of corporate accountability is still embryonic. Legal doctrines for imputing criminal blame to corporate entities, or tracing lines of individual liability through the corporate command structure, remain woefully undeveloped.

Domestic efforts have fared little better. The United States has never prosecuted a corporate actor under its torture, war crimes, or genocide statutes. Instead, victims and advocates have turned to civil litigation. For decades, a vital tool in the arsenal of corporate responsibility has been the Alien Tort Statute (ATS), a two-hundred-year-old law that gives foreign nationals the right to sue in US court for violations of international law. Since Burmese victims of brutal forced labor first brought an ATS suit against the California oil company Unocal in 1996, the threat of ATS liability has been a driver for CSR. The ATS promised to put the "risk" in human rights risk management; massive money judgments and the public relations costs of trial could be powerful incentives for companies to police themselves to prevent abuses. However, in a troika of decisions handed down between 2012 and 2014, the US Supreme Court dealt a blow to the ATS enterprise. First, in *Kiobel v. Royal Dutch Petroleum Co.*, a case concerning the alleged complicity of Shell Oil in Nigerian military abuses, the court severely restricted the circumstances in which the ATS could apply to abuses committed overseas.[36] Only ATS claims that sufficiently "touch and concern" the United States can now proceed.

Yet no one seems to know precisely what the court meant by "touch and concern"—the standard has no basis in ATS jurisprudence, international law, or principles of federal jurisdiction. Instead, it works as a cipher, inviting trial courts to summarily dismiss ATS claims involving foreign atrocities rather than struggle through the court's sphinx-like opinion. So far many, though not all, trial courts have accepted that invitation.

Second, in *Mohamad v. Palestinian Authority*, the court ruled that the Torture Victim Protection Act only imposes liability on individuals, not on legal entities such as corporations.[37] Finally, in *Daimler AG v. Bauman*, the court dismissed an ATS suit brought by Argentine plaintiffs against a German parent company, alleging that its Argentine subsidiary had collaborated with the Pinochet regime during the "Dirty War." The court ruled that the presence of a US subsidiary is not enough to subject a foreign parent company to the jurisdiction of American courts.[38]

The upshot is that businesses that are complicit in war crimes, genocide, or torture around the globe might now find a legal safe harbor in the United States. Certainly, they may choose to respect human rights around the world, but the courts of the United States will not force them to do so. Could other countries fill the gap *Kiobel* left? Possibly. Several criminal cases have been filed in European jurisdictions accusing companies of complicity in human rights crimes committed abroad.[39] But none has reached judgment, and several EU states, notably Spain, have limited their courts' jurisdiction over international crimes.[40] Meanwhile, across the global South the power disparity between multinationals and many host states still precludes effective policing. In a recent study, Amnesty International concluded that all too often global corporations exercise undue influence on local regulators, leveraging developing countries' dependency on foreign investment and expertise.[41]

The Limits of Self-Regulation

The threat of ATS-type liability is withering away, leaving behind it a question: Can CSR still be effective without sanctions? After all, there are other drivers of CSR. Market-based pressures from consumers and investors can incentivize companies to implement the CSR tool kit. And governments have various "soft law" tools to encourage CSR compliance, while stopping short of criminal or civil penalties. Transparency measures, such as securities disclosure rules, are just one example of policies that promote CSR. However, the sectors that have the worst impact on human rights are often the least susceptible to market pressures. Consider the arms trade. How credible a driver is consumer choice? A government or rebel force embroiled in a dirty war is unlikely to ask its suppliers to exercise human rights due diligence. Nor is investor pressure or securities regulation effective when many arms dealers operate through closely held companies. By the same token, investor or consumer pressure often has limited influence on military contractors. Since few of these firms are publicly traded, securities regulations would have limited impact. And government consumers have strong incentives not to scrutinize contractors too closely; state actors may be tempted to outsource dirty work to contractors, creating a layer of plausible deniability and moral compartmentalization.

In the United States, the taxpaying public has had limited success in placing ethical checks on private security firms.[42] The lack of prosecutions against senior executives, and the dismissal of ATS suits under *Kiobel*, has kept evidence of contractor crimes out of court.[43] Yet it is precisely this sort of public accounting that would enable taxpayers to make informed decisions about government contracts. Absent a sanctions regime, market pressure can become market failure. Even the great extractive multinationals, which *are* publicly traded and *do* sell to the general public, are often insulated from market-based drivers of CSR. The extractives market—from rare earth metals to diamonds—tends to rely on "juniors," closely held companies that are often created specifically for high-risk commercial speculation in conflict zones.[44] These transnational layers of corporate structure make it difficult to address complicity in war crimes through investor or consumer awareness.

In these high-risk sectors, market-based incentives can only go so far. How then should the CSR movement respond to the accountability gap *Kiobel* left? Voluntarism and philanthropy are not enough. Acculturation regimes may suffice to regulate certain sectors against social or environmental harms, where corporate behavior is more easily influenced by market pressure. But the zone of transaction between businesses and fighting forces—a zone that produces the worst human rights violations—demands a different approach. The hybrid regime that regulates militaries on one side of a deal should apply to companies on the other side. Corporate social responsibility should embrace corporate command responsibility.

Corporate Command Responsibility

Given the military model, one can conceptualize a corporate responsibility regime that fuses sanctions and socialization. Like military responsibility, corporate accountability should start at the top of the chain of command. Organizational theorists have long recognized that leaders within a decision-making hierarchy shape the normative expectations and behaviors of an organization's members. For "decision theorists" such as Richard Scott, it is the systems of "control, management, [and] supervision . . . in formal organizations" that establish corporate culture.[45]

Top executives can drive corporate responsibility by socializing the work environment to value respect for human rights and to hold up ethical actors as models for esteem and emulation. They can establish formal policies and mechanisms to direct managers and employees to identify and avert human rights risks.[46] Critically, they can establish an independent compliance unit, allowing employees to "report misconduct up a chain of command that is separate from the operational employee management chain."[47] They can do all this—if the right incentives are in place.

These methods to promote cultures of compliance all have echoes in the military. Particularly since the Vietnam War, the United States military has developed a robust program of training troops in the laws of war, pairing judge advocates with operational commanders, and developing independent mechanisms for reporting misconduct. Nevertheless, such measures are not always successful. Abu Ghraibs still occur. But as Laura Dickinson argues, the abuses at Abu Ghraib and other recent breakdowns in the rule of law were largely a product of *civilian* defense authorities undermining the judge advocate system.[48] That some of the most vocal criticisms of the Bush administration's detainee policy came from uniformed personnel is testament to the military's efforts to instill respect for humanitarian norms. Those efforts are premised on powerful incentives: the reward of "responsible command" and the sanction of "command responsibility."

Both of these regulatory models can apply to corporations, and with powerful effect. First, just as "responsible command" is the key to the kingdom of lawful belligerent status, responsible corporate governance should be the key to the kingdom of business legitimacy. The CSR movement should press public and private regulators to reward companies for maintaining corporate cultures of human rights compliance—especially in the crucial sectors of extractives, arms, and security contracting. Stock exchange listing, export permits, government contracts, and licenses should be conditioned on compliance. Businesses must demonstrate a system for training and monitoring employees—and subsidiaries—to prevent gross human rights abuses and for reporting international crimes to the proper authorities.[49] These positive rewards would incentivize companies to make the mechanisms of CSR an integral part of their corporate culture.

Second, the command responsibility doctrine should be used to enforce self-regulation. This doctrine should be applied to all rungs of the corporate hierarchy—employees to officers, officers to entities, subsidiaries to parents. This would reinforce cultures of compliance and weed out cultures of deviance. The CSR movement should press international and national prosecutors to charge senior corporate officers—and if necessary the entities themselves—for human rights offenses under a command responsibility theory.

Corporate command responsibility is not such a strange concept. After all, customary international law and the Rome Statute of the International Criminal Court already recognize that the doctrine of command responsibility applies to *civilian* leaders.[50] Control, not status, is the touchstone of command responsibility. What triggers the legal duty is a superior's ability to exercise effective control over subordinates—that is, the power to issue orders, demand compliance, and punish disobedience.[51] With such control comes the responsibility to foster, formalize, and monitor a culture of compliance.[52] And since this authority can arise in a variety of institutions, the doctrine is portable from military to business organizations, so long as they are hierarchical in form.

International law therefore imposes a duty on business leaders to take reasonable and necessary measures to prevent and punish their subordinates' participation in international crimes. They can discharge this duty by maintaining systems of training, monitoring, and compliance and by punishing perpetrators and referring them to the competent authorities for prosecution. But law is only as good as its enforcement. To date, there have been few applications of command responsibility in the corporate setting. In the *Roechling* case, a Nuremberg military tribunal convicted a German ironworks executive for failing to prevent or punish the brutalization of forced laborers by factory police.[53] Decades later, the UN Tribunal for Rwanda convicted the director of a tea factory and the senior management of a radio station for failing to prevent or punish their employees' genocidal or persecutory acts.[54]

Despite these precedents, some national courts and prosecutors have been reluctant to apply the doctrine to business leaders. In *Giraldo v. Drummond*, an ATS case accusing an Alabama mining company of complicity in Colombian paramilitary violence, a district court held that command responsibility only applies to military leaders or civilian defense authorities—not to private business executives.[55] And although federal white-collar criminal law has long imputed criminal responsibility up the chain of command under the "responsible corporate officer" doctrine, that theory of liability has been limited to regulatory public welfare infractions, not to violent felonies.[56] The CSR movement should seek to reverse this trend and press for judges and prosecutors to recognize that command responsibility applies to business as well as military superiors.

More radically, CSR advocates should press to extend command responsibility from flesh-and-blood executives to the corporation itself. A key conceptual problem in corporate criminal theory is how the law should assign blame to a company for the acts of its human agents. As the British jurist Baron Edward Thurlow remarked, "Corporations have neither bodies to be punished, nor souls to be condemned; they therefore do as they like."[57] Nonetheless, corporations have long been recognized as legal persons with rights and duties and capable of suing and being sued. They can also be prosecuted. In Anglo-American and Continental law, corporate criminal liability has emerged as a pragmatic response to the limits of private, civil lawsuits to police corporate excess.[58]

Yet corporate criminal liability remains controversial; jurists struggle with how to assign blame to a legal fiction. Without a guilty mind, can an entity be morally blameworthy? Or does "the guilty mind of the directors or managers . . . render the company itself guilty?"[59] One way to assign blame is through the principle of agency. More than a century ago, the US Supreme Court situated corporate guilt in the tort notion of *respondeat superior*, a form of strict liability in which a corporation may be held vicariously liable as a principal for the crimes of its agents, so long as the agents acted within the scope of their employment and to the benefit the company.[60] Yet strict liability focuses on wrongful individual conduct, not on deviant corporate culture. Hence, it blunts the penal law's power to voice moral censure and define what good corporate citizenship looks like.

The principle of control offers a more promising path to corporate guilt, since it recognizes the power of organizational culture to foster or deter criminality. Corporations act through a chain of command, a set of superior-subordinate relationships between officers and employees, parents and subsidiaries. Lines of culpability should follow these lines of control. If executives fail to prevent abuses by operationalizing a culture of compliance, and fail to report the perpetrators to the competent authorities, then blame can be imputed up the chain of command to those leaders—and to the legal entity itself. Similarly, if a parent company has the practical ability to control the actions of a subsidiary or contractual partner, it should have a duty of care to monitor compliance and discipline abuses.[61]

In the end, command responsibility offers a strong regulatory incentive: corporations and executives can avoid liability by taking all reasonable measures to prevent and punish abuses. In other words, due diligence and prompt reporting of misconduct would be a defense to liability. Thus command responsibility—in its civil or criminal, individual or corporate applications—can do more than punish deviants. It can shape institutional cultures. Command responsibility offers CSR a means to fuse sanction and socialization. Ultimately, it might resolve CSR's core dilemma: the penal code can reinforce the honor code.

Notes

1. Ronen Shamir, "Between Self-Regulation and the Alien Tort Claims Act: On the Contested Concept of Corporate Social Responsibility," *Law and Society Review* 38 (2004): 636, 650–51.

2. Compare Christian Aid, *Behind the Mask: The Real Face of Corporate Social Responsibility*, 2–6, 15, http:// www.globalpolicy.org/socecon/tncs/2004/ 0121mask.pdf (favoring legal sanctions) with Jeremy Moon and David Vogel, "Corporate Social Responsibility, Government, and Civil Society," in *The Oxford Handbook of Corporate Social Responsibility*, ed. Andrew Crane et al. (Oxford: Oxford University Press, 2008), 312 (favoring "soft law" and industry self-regulation).

3. 28 U.S.C. § 1350.

4. Janice E. Thomson, *Mercenaries, Pirates, and Sovereigns: State-Building and Extraterritorial Violence in Early Modern Europe* (Princeton, NJ: Princeton University Press, 1996), 10.

5. V. G. Kiernan, "Foreign Mercenaries and Absolute Monarchy," in *Crisis in Europe, 1560–1660*, ed. Trevor Aston (Abingdon: Routledge, 2011), 132.

6. P. W. Singer, "The Ultimate Military Entrepreneur," *Military History Quarterly* (Spring 2003): 9.

7. Ibid., 6.

8. Thomson, *Mercenaries, Pirates, and Sovereigns*, 35.

9. Ibid.

10. Ibid., 40.

11. Ibid., 10–15.

12. Phillip I. Blumberg, *The Multinational Challenge to Corporation Law: The Search for a New Corporate Personality* (Oxford: Oxford University Press, 1993), 25–28.

13. Kiobel v. Royal Dutch Petroleum Co., 133 S. Ct. 1659 (2013).

14. Philippe Le Billon, *Wars of Plunder: Conflicts, Profits, and the Politics of Resources* (Oxford: Oxford University Press, 2013).

15. James G. Stewart, "A Pragmatic Critique of Corporate Criminal Theory: Lessons from the Extremity," *New Criminal Law Review* 16 (2013): 265.

16. Ibid., 265–66.

17. Trial of Bruno Tesch and Two Others (The Zyklon B Case), British Military Court, Hamburg, 1 *Law Report of Trials of War Criminals*, 93 (March 8, 1946). See also Prosecutor v. Van Anraat, Netherlands, LJN: BA6734, Gerechtshofs-Gravenhage, 2200050906-2 (May 9, 2007) (charging Dutch businessman with complicity in war crimes for selling chemical weapons to Saddam Hussein).

18. Laura A. Dickinson, *Outsourcing War and Peace* (New Haven, CT: Yale University Press, 2011), 4.

19. See Mohamed v. Jeppesen Dataplan, Inc., 614 F.3d 1070, 1087–88 (9th Cir. 2010); Saleh v. Titan Corp., 580 F.3d 1, 9 (D.C. Cir. 2009).

20. See Michael A. Newton and Casey Kuhlman, "Why Criminal Culpability Should Follow the Critical Path: Reframing the Theory of 'Effective Control,'" *Netherlands Yearbook of International Law* 40 (2009): 6.

21. Martha Finnemore, "Rules of War and Wars of Rules: The International Red Cross and the Restraint of State Violence," in *Constructing World Culture: International Governmental Organizations since 1875*, ed. John Boli and George M. Thomas (Stanford, CA: Stanford University Press, 1999), 149–65.

22. See Stephen D. Krasner, "Structural Causes and Regime Consequences: Regimes as Intervening Variables," in *International Regimes*, ed. Stephen D. Krasner (Ithaca, NY: Cornell University Press, 1983), 1.

23. Newton and Kuhlman, "Why Criminal Culpability Should Follow the Critical Path."

24. Ryan Goodman and Derek Jinks, *Socializing States: Promoting Human Rights through International Law* (Oxford: Oxford University Press, 2013), 23.

25. Ibid., 25–27.

26. In re Yamashita, 327 U.S. 1, 15 (1946).

27. See Newton and Kuhlman, "Why Criminal Culpability Should Follow the Critical Path," 59–61; Guénaël Mettraux, *The Law of Command Responsibility* (Oxford: Oxford University Press, 2009), 53–55.

28. Convention (IV) respecting the Laws and Customs of War on Land and its annex: Regulations concerning the Laws and Customs of War on Land, Annex IV, Art. 1. The Hague, October 18, 1907.

29. Command responsibility has been codified in modern treaties, including Articles 86 and 87 of Protocol I to the Geneva Conventions of August 12, 1949 (1977), and Article 28 of the Rome Statute of the International Criminal Court, UN Doc. A/CONF 183/9, 2187 UNTS 90 (1998).

30. In re Yamashita, 327 U.S. 1, 15 (1946).

31. Prosecutor v. Delalić, Trial Judgment, Case No. IT-96-21-T (ICTY November 16, 1998); Prosecutor v. Nahimana, Case No. ICTR 99-52-A, Appeal Judgment (ICTR November 28, 2007).

32. See Mirjan R. Damaska, "The Shadow Side of Command Responsibility," *American Journal of Comparative Law* 49 (2001): 468.

33. Finnemore, "Rules of War and Wars of Rules," 150.

34. John Ruggie, "Kiobel and Corporate Social Responsibility: An Issues Brief," September 4, 2012, http://www.hks.harvard.edu/m-rcbg/CSRI/KIOBEL _AND_CORPORATE_SOCIAL_RESPONSIBILITY.pdf.

35. Stewart, "A Pragmatic Critique of Corporate Criminal Theory," 298.

36. Kiobel, 133 S. Ct. at 1669.

37. Mohamad v. Palestinian Authority, 132 S. Ct. 1702, 1708 (2012).

38. Daimler AG v. Bauman, 134 S. Ct. 746, 761–62 (2014).

39. See "French firm Amesys probed over 'complicity in torture,'" France24 .com, last modified May 22, 2012, http://www.france24.com/en/20120522-libya -france-gaddafi-amesys-war-crimes-technology-firm-court-justice/.

40. Jim Yardley, "Spain Seeks to Curb Law Allowing Judges to Pursue Cases Globally," *New York Times*, February 11, 2014, A7.

41. Amnesty International, *Injustice Incorporated: Advancing the Right to Remedy for Corporate Abuses of Human Rights* (London: Amnesty International, 2014), 183–92.

42. Dickinson, *Outsourcing War and Peace*, 54–59 (noting that contractors in Iraq were accused of more unjustified uses of force than regular units, but investigated less frequently).

43. See Al Shimari v. CACI Int'l, Inc., 951 F. Supp. 2d 857, 865 (E.D. Va. 2013) (holding that the ATS did not apply to torture allegedly committed at Abu Ghraib prison by employees of a Virginia-based government contractor).

44. Stewart, "A Pragmatic Critique of Corporate Criminal Theory," 272.

45. W. Richard Scott, "Symbols and Organizations: From Barnard to the Institutionalists," in *Organization Theory: From Chester Barnard to the Present and Beyond*, ed. Oliver E. Williamson (Oxford: Oxford University Press, 1995), 38–39.

46. Diane L. Swanson, "Top Managers as Drivers for Corporate Social Responsibility," in Crane et al., *The Oxford Handbook of Corporate Social Responsibility*, 232–33.

47. Dickinson, *Outsourcing War and Peace*, 149.

48. Ibid., 157.

49. See Wolfgang Schulz and Thorsten Held, *Regulated Self-Regulation as a Form of Modern Government: An Analysis of Case Studies from Media and Telecommunications La*w (Eastleigh, UK: John Libbey, 2004), 62–64.

50. Mettraux, *The Law of Command Responsibility*, 102–10; Rome Statute, Art. 28(b) (establishing separate command responsibility regime for nonmilitary superiors).

51. Mettraux, *The Law of Command Responsibility*, 156.

52. Ibid., 38.

53. Government Commissioner v. Roechling, Superior Military Government Court of French Occupation Zone in Germany (June 30, 1948), Law Reports, Vol. XIV, Appendix B, p. 1075, para. 1092 (1950).

54. Prosecutor v. Nahimana, Case No. ICTR 99–52-A, Appeal Judgment, para. 785 (November 28, 2007) (holding media executives liable for employees' incitement of genocide and persecution); Prosecutor v. Musema, Case No. ICTR-96-13-T, Trial Judgment, paras. 864–78, January 27, 2000 (holding that a tea factory manager had effective control and command responsibility over employees who participated in genocide).

55. Giraldo v. Drummond Company, Inc., No. 2:09-CV-1041 at 8 (N.D. Ala. July 25, 2013).

56. Timothy Wu and Yong-Sung Kang, "Criminal Liability for the Actions of Subordinates—the Doctrine of Command Responsibility and Its Analogues in United States Law," *Harvard International Law Journal* 38 (1997): 279.

57. Quoted in *Literary Extracts* 1, ed. John Poynder (London: John Hatchard and Son, 1844), 268.

58. Stewart, "A Pragmatic Critique of Corporate Criminal Theory," 262.

59. H. L. Bolton (Engineering) Co. Ltd. v. T. J. Graham & Sons Ltd. [1957] 1 QB 159, 172 (U.K.).

60. New York Central and Hudson River Railroad v. United States, 212 U.S. 481 (1909).

61. See OECD, Guidelines on Multinational Enterprises, Ch. II, para. 9 (2011) (stating that compliance programs should extend to subsidiaries).

CHAPTER NINE

Law, Morality, and Rational Choice

Incentives for CSR Compliance

Caroline Kaeb

Introduction

So far, almost all lawsuits holding corporations accountable for human rights violations have been brought in US courts under the Alien Tort Statute (ATS).[1] However, recent developments in ATS litigation before US courts have significantly weakened the role of the ATS as a primary venue of enforcement of corporate social responsibility norms.[2] Thus the US Supreme Court in its 2013 decision in *Kiobel v. Royal Dutch Petroleum* has significantly constrained the extraterritorial reach of the ATS over violations of international law overseas on the part of multinational corporations.[3] In addition, the Second Circuit Court of Appeal in its 2009 judgment in *The Presbyterian Church of Sudan v. Talisman*[4] has created uncertainty with regard to the mens rea requirements for aiding and abetting liability under the ATS that resulted in a circuit court split that still persists after the Supreme Court's decision in *Kiobel*.[5]

These most recent developments should be understood as an opportunity that provides momentum for careful consideration of different remedies (judicial and nonjudicial) in a CSR context. The changed realities in a US context have set the stage for examining the wider picture with regard to CSR enforcement, especially regarding the role of intrinsic motivation. After "hyperfocus" on the ATS as the main vehicle to hold companies accountable for human rights violations relating to their overseas operations,[6] the time is ripe to consider the breadth of method-ologies across different disciplines to identify ways to induce compliance effectively.

This chapter aims to encourage a qualified perspective on the con-ventional wisdom that hard law liability rules and enforcement are the most effective way to influence corporate behavior. Recent efforts for an international treaty on business and human rights[7] further amplify the need to examine the role of intrinsic motivation (and endogenous mea-sures of CSR implementation) in relation to external incentives induced by law and legal enforcement. The discussion of CSR in the economics literature has focused heavily on endogenous compliance mechanisms as a solution. However, this understanding is highly under-accounted-for in legal scholarship.

The approaches to CSR implementation have been multifold; they feature a broad spectrum of hard law and soft law approaches to CSR across different industries, legal systems, and economic markets. On one side of the spectrum are hard law methodologies in the form of, most prominently, civil litigation under the ATS and, more recently, treaty codification efforts on issues of business and human rights, as well as the promulgation of section 1502 on conflict minerals under the Dodd-Frank Act.[8] In Europe, legal systems provide for criminal liability of corporations for involvement in international crimes overseas.[9] On the other end of the spectrum, there has always been a solid movement sur-rounding voluntary multistakeholder initiatives and self-regulatory stan-dard setting; some of these efforts have been considered highly effec-tive in inducing compliance, such as the Kimberley Certification Process on conflict diamonds,[10] which has been celebrated as a success story,[11] and most recently, the European Accord on Fire and Building Safety in Bangladesh.[12]

The role of enforcement has been described by Amartya Sen from a game-theoretical perspective as a situation where all players "would be both better off with a mutual non-confession contract, but it would be in the interest of each to break it unless there is enforcement. Rousseau's much-researched-on statement on the necessity of being 'forced to be free' seems to be shockingly relevant. But in the absence of enforcement, they are both worse off despite strictly 'rational' behavior."[13]

Although this is the common premise of the compliance dilemma, controversy remains over what the most effective basis for enforcement would be from a behavioral incentives perspective: rationality, morality, or external intervention? This chapter draws upon the behavioral economics and psychology scholarship dealing with the relationship between intrinsic and extrinsic motivations. Here I join Lynn Stout when she posits that "largely missing from all this talk about 'incentives' and accountability is any serious discussion of the possibility that we might encourage or discourage particular behaviors by appealing not to selfishness, but instead to the force of conscience."[14] In light of this untapped power of conscience in a compliance setting, I will argue that law (as an external incentive) is but one driver for CSR compliance that can be effectively complemented by intrinsic motivation in the form of morality. Thus this chapter proposes a hybrid framework of hard law and voluntary standards as an expressive function of social norms and a sense of morality.[15] How these different incentives, especially law and morality, affect one another and how this understanding should inform a behavioral science approach to corporate regulation reaches beyond the scope of this chapter, but it is nonetheless important to bear in mind for future research.

CSR and the Law

Traditionally, CSR norms have been considered to be voluntary, not externally enforceable by the legal system, and left to the realm of corporate self-regulation.[16] However, the policy debate has been rather ambiguous over the right approach to ensure that global business is conducted in a socially responsible and sustainable manner.[17] Even within the European Union's own institutional structure there is no consensus on the question of regulation or self-regulation of CSR. Thus the European Commission promotes a strictly voluntary approach to CSR,[18] whereas the European Parliament champions a mixed approach that also entails regulation and adjudication of issues related to the CSR agenda.[19]

The Limits of Fiduciary Duties

First, the scope of a corporation's social responsibility needs to be understood within the limits of corporate law. While CSR constitutes a function of social norms benefiting the interests of a company's broader stakeholder base, corporate law has traditionally centered on protecting interests of shareholders as the owners of the corporation.[20] Under standard economic and corporate law theory, corporate managers are under a fiduciary duty to further shareholder—and not public—interests. This can put corporate managers and officers who pursue public interest objectives in their decision making at odds with their fiduciary duties as prescribed under the law. This delineation of fiduciary duties is in line with Milton Friedman's position that businesses have no responsibilities other than profit maximization.[21]

Einer Elhauge has examined the question of whether corporate managers have the discretion to "sacrifice profits in the public interest" or whether such an operational decision would constitute a violation of management's fiduciary duty toward its shareholders and therefore open management up to shareholder litigation in the form of derivative actions.[22] The answer first depends on whether or not a social norm is also enshrined in a legal norm. Under well-established law, managers have a fiduciary duty not to violate the law in pursuit of profit maximization.[23] If, however, a particular conduct is not illegal but is still considered socially irresponsible, the situation is less clear.[24] A commonly raised objection against corporate decision making in the social interest is that profit sacrificing to further a public interest goal imposes a "tax" on dissenting shareholders.[25] This concern does not take into account, however, that managerial discretion is necessary (even in a system of strict shareholder primacy) since "economic efficiencies that come from delegating the management of a business to someone other than shareholders . . . cannot be achieved without creating such discretion."[26] For agency costs to be at an optimal level in economic terms, a tradeoff between the costs of monitoring and of allowing managerial discretion is indispensable.[27] This understanding of corporate law allows management to exercise discretion to pursue public interest goals that promote the long-term profitability of a firm even if it might be profit minimizing in the short run.[28]

Ultimately, the decisive factor is how management's fiduciary duty to act "in the interest of the corporation" is being construed in light of the respective legal culture and case law. The approaches vary among legal systems around the world. Traditionally, common law countries have favored a shareholder-focused approach and thus have construed fiduciary duties narrowly to extend merely to shareholders and their interests, whereas civil law jurisdictions in Europe and Asia have embraced stakeholder-centric governance structures.[29] However, even in common law systems the focus is slowly shifting toward stakeholder inclusion. Thus, the United Kingdom amended its Companies Act in 2006 to expand directors' fiduciary duties to include the duty "to promote the success of the company for the benefit if its members as a whole, and in doing so have regard (amongst other matters) to . . . the interests of the company's employees, the need to foster the company's business relationships with suppliers, customers, and others, [and] the impact of the company's operations on the community and the environment."[30]

Also, in the United States, thirty states have adopted constituency statutes that allow managers to take nonshareholder interests into account, including the interest of employees, customers, suppliers, and society as a whole.[31] Even the Delaware court system has affirmed by case law that managers are permitted to reject a takeover bid because of "the impact on 'constituencies' other than shareholders (i.e., creditors, customers, employees, and perhaps even the community generally)."[32] Supporters of a traditional profit-maximization duty have often interpreted this statutory and case law narrowly so as to permit "managers making donations, being ethical, and considering nonshareholder interests only to the extent that doing so maximizes profits in the long run,"[33] whereas others have argued that it also allows stakeholder-sensitive operational decisions such as "declining to make profitable sales that would adversely affect national foreign policy, [or] keeping an unprofitable plant open to allow employees to transition to new work."[34]

The Conflation of Soft Law and Hard Law

Despite the often-perceived dichotomy between a hard law and soft law methodology in the realm of CSR, the line is more blurred than it might seem at first. The effect of voluntary standards, as the result of an endogenous process, can be legalized in various ways. Thus contract law can be used to include social standards in supplier and employment contracts, and thus make those standards legally enforceable. Also, regulatory agencies have often referred to voluntary company and industry codes as mandatory reporting requirements under their institutional structure.[35] Eventually, a public endorsement of voluntary standards can give rise to claims of misrepresentation or misleading conduct in the courts of law.[36] Even where these legal vehicles are not available, corporate codes of conduct and other sources of soft law can have a normative effect and eventually lead to the creation of new legal standards in the field. Underlying this reasoning is the premise that state behavior can be shaped by the social environment in which those states are embedded.[37] Thus legal standards can be induced by social behavior, rather than merely stirring behavior in a regulatory function.[38]

Incentive Models for Corporate Compliance: The Compliance Problem

Corporate compliance with the social contract[39] poses two independent choice problems that have to be overcome. One must distinguish between the entry into the agreement and the compliance with the norms under the agreement.[40] Entering into an agreement, such as the social contract, is a case of ex ante rational bargaining that requires the impartial rationality in the form of the acceptance by all players recognizing mutual benefits under the agreement. Compliance, on the other hand, is a case of ex post personal rationality decision to violate or comply with the agreement contingent upon the predicted behavior of the other players.[41] While the choice required when entering into an agreement focuses on joint benefits and fair distribution thereof, the choice required at the compliance level is based upon personal incentives to violate or comply with the norm agreed upon.[42]

From a game-theoretical perspective, unlike entering into an agreement, which constitutes a cooperative game, compliance follows the rules of a noncooperative game.[43] The rationale is an underlying conflict between individual rationality and social optimality.[44] The compliance problem presents itself as a classical "prisoner's dilemma." Therefore, even though it would be in the best interest of all parties (and thus in the collective interest) if they all complied, each player is even better off if he defects (in pursuit of his individual self-interest). This noncooperative behavior produces suboptimal results.[45]

In a CSR context, since the only equilibrium point is noncompliance, the Rousseauian "social contract" cannot be complied with. Rather, the underlying Hobbesian "state of nature" would need to be changed by agreeing on a mode of mutually cooperative behavior instead of self-interested noncooperative interaction between the players in the game. Obviously, such a cooperative agreement is not consistent with individual egotistic incentives to act. Therefore, additional features must be added to the game in order to change the "state of nature" so as not to generate a "prisoner's dilemma."[46] Scholars in the field have suggested several different attempts in order to change the preferences in a way that not only includes egotistic self-interest but also reconciles the discrepancy between individual and societal interest.

Incentive Models for Corporate Compliance: Solutions to the Compliance Problem

Trust

An increasing body of economic scholarship has elucidated the significance of trust as an incentive and motivational driver in economic interactions. Trust has widely been recognized to be a key determinant for economic performance. Kenneth Arrow has argued that a lack of trust and moral values can create serious market inefficiencies.[47] This hypothesis has been supported by cross-country empirical evidence, which found that there is a positive correlation between higher trust levels and higher economic performance.[48] Trust, for example, can foster cooperation among actors and thus create market efficiencies.[49]

There can be many determinants of trust, including "sociality." Avner Ben-Ner and Louis Putterman have demonstrated the critical role of "sociality" trust determinant (experimentally supported in trust games) and have suggested an "extended preference" model beyond "simply payoff maximization."[50] The underlying reasoning is that "while the company itself is not a human being with an evolved social nature, its managers . . . employees, customers, and even the politicians who determine relevant regulations and their constituents, are."[51] Thus in order for a company to operate successfully in a world of individuals, it will have to show a "human face" to its customers, employees, and its other constituents.[52] Only then will a company be relatable in a way that creates trust on the part of those individuals.[53]

Conventions

Focusing instead on a company's intrinsic motivation to comply with social norms, the conventionalist school of thought has offered a different solution to the compliance problem.[54] David Hume described a convention as a "general sense of common interest; which sense all members of society express to one another, and which induces them to regulate their conduct by certain rules."[55] However, conventional theory is only of limited use to solve the compliance problem since it overstates the significance of repeated models.[56]

Rational Choice and Moral Dispositions

In another effort to reconcile rationality and morality in the compliance game, some scholars have suggested revising rationality to include the rational choice of psychological dispositions to comply with a social norm.[57] The self-proclaimed goal of this moral theory is the "generation of moral constraints as rational."[58] However, this approach also proves problematic since it reduces a moral disposition to comply with a norm of cooperation to a question of rationality. This framing of moral dispositions as a matter of rational choice produces inherent contradictions.[59] Lorenzo Sacconi, Marco Faillo, and Stefania Ottone illustrate where a strictly rational choice approach to morality falls short and how morality should be introduced differently into the compliance game in order to yield optimal outcomes:

> What seems mistaken in this approach, however, is not the idea of analyzing moral dispositions but the idea that undertaking moral dispositions may be a matter of practical reasoning and sophisticated instrumental decision calculus, whereas it could be a matter of developing a moral sentiment (the "desire" to be just) endowed with some motivational force on its own, and capable of generating additional motivational drives to act that can be introduced into the players' preference systems—under proper conditions to be defined.[60]

Amartya Sen has also pointed to the conceptual shortfalls of framing morality as a rational choice, as morality "would seem to require a judgment among preferences whereas rationality would not."[61] This makes both concepts incompatible by nature. Sen therefore suggests changing the focus of choice analysis to capturing morality "in form of choice between preference patterns rather than between actions."[62] The following compliance model under a social contract paradigm delivers on this very premise.

A "Sense of Justice" under a "Contractarian" Compliance Model

The "contractarian" compliance approach offers a different solution to the compliance problem drawing upon John Rawls's "sense of justice"[63] as the basis for an intrinsic incentive structure.[64] As Sacconi, Faillo, and Ottone have illustrated, Rawls's theory "was long overlooked by economists and game theorists because it is at odds with the methodologies of rational choice";[65] rather, it assumes a moral sentiment as a sociopsychological result, which, independent from rational choice, induces just and fair behavior. But it is exactly this sociopsychological approach to moral sentiments that makes Rawls's theory so uniquely suited to capture the role and functioning of CSR in modern-day society. It seems to align more with reality to assume CSR compliance as a product of a higher moral sentiment than as a matter of rational choice considering that, at least under a traditional model of the firm, a firm's self-interest is shareholder value maximization and not societal interests. The idea of Rawls's theory "is that motives to act are now enriched with a *new motivation* able to overcome the counteracting tendency to injustice" in terms of defecting in a "prisoner's dilemma"–like situation.[66]

This compliance model links the notion of moral sentiment to a social contract paradigm. The contractarian model describes the "sense of justice" as a psychological equilibrium based on conformist preferences, thus providing a means of endogenous social contract compliance.[67] Accordingly, economic agents are not only incentivized by consequentialist, that is, egoistic, but also by conformist preferences in terms of intrinsic motivation to act in accordance with an agreed-upon principle contingent on reciprocal beliefs and actions of the other agents.[68] The findings show that agents are not only incentivized by material payoffs but also by psychological payoffs.[69] Psychological payoffs are introduced to the preference system of the firm (and its stakeholders) by virtue of the *rational choice* of a social contract agreement and the subsequent development of a *moral sentiment*.

The "contractarian" compliance model offers a solution to the compliance problem that is not at odds with rational choice theory but still accounts for the sociopsychological reality of CSR. It is also in line with the increasingly prominent understanding of the nature of the corporation as a nexus of contracts.[70] Behavioral economic studies have also added intrinsic motivation (in the form of psychological payoffs) to the

preference system in order to explain the relationship between motivation and behavior beyond the mere "price effect."[71] For example, Bruno
Frey has shown that even when *monetary* incentives in the form of fines
or awards are involved, behavioral preferences are influenced by *psychological* payoffs as well.[72]

"A Fine Is a Price": The Risk of Commoditizing Social Norms

Whatever theory one considers the basis for compliance incentives, all
the abovementioned schools of thought provide an important common
insight that ought to be introduced in the legal debate—namely, that law
(as an external incentive) is only *one* driver for CSR compliance that can
be effectively complemented by morality, whether in the form of conventions, rational choice, psychological preferences, or an overarching
"sense of justice."

The effect of (endogenous) incentives on behavior has been subject to
long-standing scholarship in psychological, legal, and recently also economic studies. Even though the literature diverges on some caveats and
specifications of the theory, the following deterrence hypothesis is accepted across the different disciplines: the introduction of a penalty reduces the behavior.[73] Legal and psychological scholarship have been defining the specific conditions under which the deterrence theory holds,
arguing that a punishment is most effective if it is severe, certain, and
instantly follows the behavior.[74] Behavioral psychology can inform our
thinking about corporate compliance with CSR norms and provide important lessons for the way we can stir corporate behavior through effective regulatory design.

A much-cited case study in behavioral psychology has shown that
the standard prediction under the deterrence theory, as a cornerstone
of psychology and the understanding of law deterrence, does not always hold.[75] The study looked at the effect of fines on the frequency with
which parents arrive late to pick up their children from day care centers and yielded the following results, which refute the predictions under
conventional theory. The introduction of a fine in fact resulted in a significant *increase* in the number of parents arriving late at a rate that was
higher than when there was no fine imposed. Even after the fine was removed, the level of late-coming parents remained at the same high level.

It is critical to note, however, that the monetary fine that was imposed was low but not insignificant.[76] The study shows that the deterrence effect could hold if the fine introduced was very large and thus a severe punishment, as predicted by law and psychology theory.

From this field study, Uri Gneezy and Aldo Rustichini conclude that the introduction of a fine changes how we perceive our environment and our obligations therein or, put in economic terms, how we perceive the game and the equilibrium.[77] The reason is that a fine is usually introduced into an incomplete contract that does not specify the consequences of misbehavior. Introducing a monetary fine, even though it makes the actual consequence of misbehaving worse, provides information and removes uncertainty about the punishment. It is precisely this uncertainty about what might happen if one misbehaves that restrained the actors. Thus the process of information gathering and learning diminishes psychological regulators. After the fine was introduced, parents tested the reaction of the day care center and learned that the fine imposed was in fact the worst consequence that would occur.[78]

Multinational corporations are confronted with many legal uncertainties in a global regulatory system with diverging legal standards across their different operational markets.[79] While it is desirable for business and society alike to aim to codify relevant legal standards more coherently, we should pay closer attention to how this objective ought to be achieved. Critically, behavioral psychology teaches us that monetary fines (in the form of civil damages or criminal penalties) might come at a cost and might have limited ability to effectively spur corporate behavior toward better compliance. A formulation of concrete normative prescriptions about how sanctions ought to be structured and how regulations ought to be designed under these premises requires a more indepth treatment that goes beyond the scope of this chapter.

Typical legal standards and social norms pertaining to the social responsibility of corporations across different legal systems and cultures frequently induces such uncertainty in the system that Gneezy and Rustichini have identified as effectively compelling corporate behavior. A codification of a minimum standard—like that promoted by the recent efforts for an international treaty on business and human rights—can therefore result in deference to a required baseline (provided that the probability and the severity of punishment is high enough) but might at the same time compromise aspirational commitments beyond that minimum standard. This might offset psychological regulators and encourage a culture of box checking within corporations' risk metrics rather than higher levels of compliance.

Still, reputational risks can be considered the greatest factor of uncertainty for global brands. The reputational damage that could ensue from allegations of human rights abuses overseas or complicity therein could be significant. Even though empirical evidence shows that a connection between socially responsible business and profitability is "at best . . . inconclusive,"[80] reputational costs and benefits have increasingly become part of corporations' calculus in the form of their risk management as well as their branding and marketing efforts.[81] Within Gneezy and Rustichini's framework, the uncertainty about the reputational hit and associated costs a company could incur, through investor and consumer pressure respectively, is an "unspecified and uncertain but possibly more serious consequence"[82] than concrete fines imposed under hard law mechanisms.

It is clear that deterrence theory does not hold at an equilibrium point considering the experiences and learning that the imposition of monetary fines provides. That is not to say, however, that a mandatory minimum standard, especially with regard to human rights responsibilities, should not be codified. Nevertheless, this chapter cautions against all "quick fixes" and argues in favor of a complementary approach that draws upon external and internal motivating factors in the realm of corporate social responsibility compliance with an eye toward the lessons of behavioral studies.

Aside from filling information gaps, the imposition of a (low yet significant) fine has been shown to change the perception of the wrongful act and can consequently lead to a shift in social norms, which increases misbehavior and persists even if the fine is removed again. By imposing a monetary fine, the relationship between parties shifts from a nonmarket to a market orientation since the fine puts a price on wrongdoing, and thus commoditizes it.[83] A social relationship thus becomes a market exchange.

Consequently, if firms consider CSR to be a nonmarket aspect, then firms could perceive the environment and society in which they operate as the constituent that granted them the generous privilege to do business and of which they ought not to take advantage. Under this paradigm, firms would more likely strive to "do the right thing" and not do harm by exercising due diligence. However, if by means of fines, damages, or settlement awards a price is put on human rights, then firms could perceive violations as mere costs and collateral damage of conducting global business that can be compensated for if and as much as necessary. Imposing a monetary fine could prevent guilt or shame from emerging in this context, since buying a commodity or paying a cost is a neutral act.[84]

While this translation of behavioral studies into a CSR scenario might appear overstated, the findings of this study have proven valid and have been confirmed by the burgeoning literature at the intersection of psychology and economics.[85] Moreover, the hypothesis of commoditizing nonmarket activities through legal liability awards also provides valuable lessons to the legal debate about social norms and the law.[86] Some might argue that a case study on a day care center and tardy parents is very different from human rights abuses in the context of global business activities. It is acknowledged that in substance the two scenarios might be different. But as shown above, they share common traits that allow similar conclusions with regard to the effect of monetary punishment on behavior. Gneezy and Rustichini themselves declare their findings applicable to both private and *social* contracts.[87] The increasing literature on behavioral economics has supported their findings in varied settings, such as legal rules enforcement and taxation.[88]

Conclusion

Sometimes more order can be achieved not only with law but also by relying on intrinsic motivation. This is an important point to introduce into the discussions about corporate human rights litigation and CSR in general. Granted, legal liability can be an effective, and sometimes indispensable, tool to ensure corporate compliance. However, to optimize compliance performance we need to start thinking critically and constructively about how to leverage both legal and nonlegal incentives to affect corporate compliance behavior in the most effective and impactful way, with a willingness to learn from other legal systems and without fear of uncovering counterintuitive and perhaps undesired results pertaining to existing corporate regulation. Behavioral science can provide important insights for designing effective regulation since it provides insights into the effects that law can have on psychological regulators. The US government has recognized this and has adopted a behavioral approach to regulatory design following in the footsteps of previous experiences in the United Kingdom that have spearheaded this methodology through the "Test, Learn, Adapt" framework.[89] It is time to introduce this thinking into the debate about CSR compliance.

Notes

1. The ATS, passed by the first Congress in 1789, confers on district courts "original jurisdiction of any civil action by an alien for a tort only committed in violation of the law of nations or a treaty of the United States." 28 U.S.C. § 1350. See Beth Stephens, "Judicial Deference and the Unreasonable Views of the Bush Administration," *Brooklyn Journal of International Law* 33 (2008): 773–814; see also Jan Wouters and Leen Chanet, "Corporate Human Rights Responsibility: A European Perspective," *Northwestern Journal of International Human Rights* 6 (2008): 262.

2. This paper applies the understanding of corporate social responsibility as spearheaded by the United Nations Global Compact office. Therefore, corporate social responsibility includes issues of human rights, labor, environment, and anticorruption.

3. Kiobel v. Royal Dutch Petroleum, 569 U.S. ____ (2013).

4. The Second Circuit Court of Appeals in *Talisman* established a "purpose" criterion for aiding and abetting liability under the ATS. The Presbyterian Church of Sudan v. Talisman Energy, Inc., 582 F.3d 244 (2d Cir. 2009). This has raised the bar from a mere "knowledge" standard, as previously endorsed by the United States Court of Appeals for the Eleventh Circuit (see among others, Romero v. Drummond Co., 552 F.3d 1303 (11th Cir. 2008); Aldana v. Del Monte Fresh Produce, N.A., Inc., 416 F.3d 1242 (11th Cir. 2005)) and by several district courts in the Second Circuit (see among others, Almog v. Arab Bank, PLC, 471 F. Supp. 2d 257, 288–94 (E.D.N.Y. 2007); in re Agent Orange Prod. Liab. Litig., 373 F. Supp. 2d 7, 91 (E.D.N.Y. 2005)) to a mens rea standard that requires that the aider and abettor shares intent to commit the crime.

5. There exists a decided circuit split on the mens rea standard for aiding and abetting as well as on corporate liability under the ATS, which persists after the Supreme Court's decision in Kiobel v. Royal Dutch Petroleum. Currently, the Court of Appeals of the Seventh Circuit (Flomo v. Firestone Nat. Rubber Co., LLC, 643 F.3d 1013 (7th Cir. 2011)), of the Eleventh Circuit (Sinaltrainal v. Coca-Cola Co., 578 F.3d 1252 (11th Cir. 2009)), and the DC Circuit (Doe VIII v. Exxon Mobile Corp., No. 09-7125, 2011 WL 2652384 (D.C. Cir. July 8, 2011)) endorse corporate liability under the ATS. Moreover, the Eleventh and DC Circuit Court of Appeals endorse a knowledge standard for aiding and abetting un-

der the ATS. The Second Circuit Court of Appeals is the outlier on both issues. Judgment on both issues is still pending before the Ninth Circuit Court of Appeals: Doe 1 v. Nestle, S.A., 748 F. Supp. 2d 1057 (C.D. Cal. 2010).

6. See Beth Stephens, "Translating Filártiga: A Comparative and International Law Analysis of Domestic Remedies for International Human Rights Violations," *Yale Journal of International Law* 27 (2002): 1–58.

7. John Ruggie, "A UN Business and Human Rights Treaty Update," *Harvard Kennedy School* (May 1, 2014).

8. Dodd–Frank Wall Street Reform and Consumer Protection Act (Pub.L. 111-203, H.R. 4173) (December 2, 2009).

9. See Robert Thompson, Anita Ramasastry, and Mark Taylor, "Translating Unocal: The Expanding Web of Liability for Business Entities Implicated in International Crimes," *George Washington International Law Review* 40 (2009): 841–902; Beth Stephens, "Corporate Liability: Enforcing Human Rights through Domestic Litigation," *Hastings Journal of International and Comparative Law* 24 (2001): 408–9.

10. The Kimberley Process (KP), at http://www.kimberleyprocess.com/.

11. "Protect, Respect, and Remedy: A Framework for Business and Human Rights, Report of the Special Representative of the Secretary-General on the Issue of Human Rights and Transnational Corporations and Other Business Enterprises," A/HRC/8/5 (2008), 6.

12. Caroline Kaeb, "Executive Perspective: A View from Europe on Corporate Accountability," *Thompson Reuters*, March 3, 2014, http://sustainability .thomsonreuters.com/2014/03/03/executive-perspective-view-europe-corporate -accountability/.

13. Amartya Sen, "Choice, Orderings, and Morality," in *Practical Reason*, ed. Stephan Körner (Oxford: Blackwell, 1974), 66.

14. Lynn Stout, *Cultivating Conscience: How Good Laws Make Good People* (Princeton, NJ: Princeton University Press, 2010), 5.

15. Wouters and Chanet have also argued for a hybrid of a voluntary and regulatory approach to CSR. See Jan Wouters and Leen Chanet, "Corporate Human Rights Responsibility: A European Perspective," *Northwestern Journal of International Human Rights* 6 (2008): 265–66.

16. See Lorenzo Sacconi, "Corporate Social Responsibility (CSR) as a Model of 'Extended' Corporate Governance: An Explanation Based on the Economic Theories of Social Contract, Reputation, and Reciprocal Conformism," in *Reframing Self-Regulation in European Private Law*, ed. Fabrizio Cafaggi (Alphen aan den Rijn, Netherlands: Kluwer Law International, 2006): 289–343.

17. For a critical perspective on a stakeholder-centric approach to corporate governance, see Michael Jensen, "Value Maximization, Stakeholder Theory, and the Corporate Objective Function," *Business Ethics Quarterly* 12 (2002): 235–56.

18. Commission Green Paper (EC) COM (2001) 366 final on Promoting a European Framework for Corporate Social Responsibility, 8 (July 18, 2001).

19. Parliament Resolution (EC) of April 1999 on EU Standards for European Enterprises Operating in Developing Countries: Towards a European Code of Conduct, 1999 O.J. (C 104/180), Recital F (stressing that "voluntary and binding approaches to corporate Regulation are not mutually exclusive").

20. See Dodge v. Ford Motor Co., 170 N.W. 668 (Mich. 1919).

21. Milton Friedman, *Capitalism and Freedom* (Chicago: University of Chicago Press, 1962), 133.

22. Einer Elhauge, "Sacrificing Corporate Profits in the Public Interest," *New York University Law Review* 80 (2005): 733–869.

23. Kent Greenfield, "Ultra Vires Lives! A Stakeholder Analysis of Corporate Illegality (With Notes on How Corporate Law Could Reinforce International Law Norms)," *Virginia Law Review* 87 (2001): 1316–18; Miller v. AT&T Co., 507 F.2d 759, 762–63 (3d Cir. 1974).

24. Elhauge, "Sacrificing Corporate Profits in the Public Interest," 761.

25. Stephen M. Brainbridge, *Corporation Law and Economics* (St. Paul, MN: Foundation Press, 2002), 421–22.

26. Elhauge, "Sacrificing Corporate Profits in the Public Interest," 776.

27. Michael Jensen and William Meckling, "Theory of the Firm: Managerial Behavior, Agency Costs, and Ownership Structure," *Journal of Financial Economics* 3 (1976): 305.

28. See Elhauge, "Sacrificing Corporate Profits in the Public Interest," 780; see also Margaret Blair and Lynn Stout, "A Team Production Theory of Corporate Law," *Virginia Law Review* 85 (1999): 275, 285.

29. Michael Kerr, Richard Janda, and Chip Pitts, eds., *Corporate Social Responsibility: A Legal Analysis* (Ontario: LexisNexis, 2009), 113–14, 162.

30. U.K. Companies Act 2006, Art. 172 (1).

31. Jonathan D. Springer, "Corporate Constituency Statutes: Hollow Hopes and False Fears," *Annual Survey of American Law* 85 (1999): 95.

32. Unocal Corp. v. Mesa Petroleum Co., 493 A.2d 946, 955 (Del. 1985).

33. See Elhauge, "Sacrificing Corporate Profits in the Public Interest," 766 (internal citation omitted).

34. Elhauge, "Sacrificing Corporate Profits in the Public Interest," 764.

35. David Kinley and Junko Tadaki, "From Talk to Walk: The Emergence of Human Rights Responsibilities for Corporations at International Law," *Virginia Journal of International Law* 44 (2004): 957.

36. See the case against Nike as an example of such a claim arguing that Nike's public statement about good labor conditions in its Asian factories violates California consumer protection laws. Nike, Inc. v. Kasky, 123 S.Ct. 2554, 2555 (2003) (Stevens, J., concurring).

37. See Anne-Marie Slaughter, "A Liberal Theory of International Law," *American Society of International Law Proceedings* 94 (2000): 240.

38. Jennifer Johnson, "Public-Private-Public Convergence: How the Private Actor Can Shape Public International Labor Standards," *Brooklyn Journal of International Law* 24 (1998): 347–48.

39. Jean-Jacques Rousseau, *On the Social Contract* (Indianapolis: Hackett, 1988).

40. David Gauthier, *Morals by Agreement* (Oxford: Oxford University Press, 1986): 116–18; Sen, "Choice, Orderings, and Morality," 66.

41. Sen, "Choice, Orderings and Morality," 66.

42. Gauthier, *Morals by Agreement*, 116–18.

43. See ibid.

44. Ibid.

45. See Sen, "Choice, Orderings, and Morality," 56–57.

46. Lorenzo Sacconi, Marco Faillo, and Stefania Ottone "Contractarian Compliance and the 'Sense of Justice': A Behavioral Conformity Model and Its Experimental Support," *Analyse and Kritik* 1 (2011): 275–76.

47. Kenneth Arrow, *The Limits of Organization* (New York: Norton, 1974).

48. See Robert Putnam, Robert Leonardi, and Raffaella Nanetti, *Making Democracy Work: Civil Traditions in Modern Italy* (Princeton, NJ: Princeton University Press, 1993); see also Stephen Knack and Philip Keefer, "Does Social Capital Have an Economic Payoff? A Cross-Country Investigation," *Quarterly Journal of Economics* 112 (1997): 1251–88.

49. Gianluca Grimalda and Luigi Mittone, "Generalized Trust: An Experimental Perspective," in *Social Capital, Corporate Social Responsibility, Economic Behaviour and Performance*, ed. Lorenzo Sacconi and Giacomo Degli Antoni (New York: Palgrave Macmillan, 2011), 260, 278.

50. Avner Ben-Ner and Louis Putterman, "Trusting, Trustworthiness, and CSR: Some Experiments and Implications," in *Corporate Social Responsibility and Corporate Governance: The Contribution of Economic Theories and Related Disciplines*, ed. Lorenzo Sacconi et al. (New York: Palgrave Macmillan, 2011), 410, 413.

51. Ibid.

52. See Caroline Kaeb, "Putting the 'Corporate' Back into Corporate Personhood: A Comparative Legal Analysis," *Northwestern Journal of International Law and Business* 35 (2015) (arguing that the interests of a corporation's human constituents, primarily its shareholders and—depending on the respective legal system—its other stakeholders should inform the understanding of the nature of the corporation and the doctrine of corporate personhood).

53. See ibid., 428.

54. See, e.g., David Lewis, *Convention: A Philosophical Study* (Cambridge,

MA: Harvard University Press, 1969); Masahiko Aoki, *Toward a Comparative Institutional Analysis* (Cambridge, MA: MIT Press, 2001) (exploring the mechanism of evolution of different organizational conventions).

55. David Hume, *A Treatise of Human Nature* (1740; Oxford: Oxford University Press, 2000), 490.

56. Sacconi, Faillo, and Ottone, "Contractarian Compliance and the 'Sense of Justice': A Behavioral Conformity Model and Its Experimental Support," 278.

57. See David Gauthier. "Economic Man and the Rational Reasoner," in *From Political Economy to Economics—and Back?*, ed. James Nichols Jr. and Colin Wright (San Francisco: ICS Press, 1990), 105–31; see also Edward McClennen, "Rationality Constitutions and the Ethics of Rule," *Constitutional Political Economy* 4 (1993): 94–118.

58. Gauthier, *Morals by Agreement*, 7.

59. See e.g., Kenneth Binmore, *Game Theory and the Social Contract*, vol. 1, *Playing Fair* (Cambridge, MA: MIT Press, 1994).

60. Sacconi, Faillo, and Ottone, "Contractarian Compliance and the 'Sense of Justice': A Behavioral Conformity Model and Its Experimental Support," 284.

61. Sen, "Choice, Orderings, and Morality," 55.

62. Ibid., 59.

63. John Rawls, *A Theory of Justice* (Cambridge, MA: Belknap Press of Harvard University Press, 1971). According to John Rawls, the "sense of justice" is evolving from an ex ante agreement (under a "veil of ignorance") on principles of justice and is then providing its own endogenous support of the stability of just institutions in a well-ordered society.

64. Sacconi, Faillo, and Ottone, "Contractarian Compliance and the 'Sense of Justice': A Behavioral Conformity Model and Its Experimental Support," 286, 291.

65. Ibid., 284.

66. Ibid., 287.

67. Ibid., 285.

68. Ibid., 292–93.

69. See Giacomo Degli Antoni and Lorenzo Sacconi, "Modeling Cognitive Social Capital and Corporate Social Responsibility as Preconditions for Sustainable Networks of Relations," in Sacconi and Antoni, *Social Capital, Corporate Social Responsibility, Economic Behaviour and Performance*, 161, 165.

70. Henry Butler, "The Contractual Theory of the Corporation," *George Mason University Law Review* 11 (1989): 99.

71. The "price effect" states that as the price increases, supply increases and demand falls.

72. Iris Bohnet, Bruno Frey, and Steffen Huck, "More Order with Less Law: On Contract Enforcement, Trust, and Crowding," *American Political Science Review* 95 (2001): 131–44.

73. Uri Gneezy and Aldo Rustichini, "A Fine Is a Price," *Journal of Legal Studies* 29 (2000): 3.

74. See Jeremy Bentham, *An Introduction to the Principles of Morals and Legislation* (Oxford: Clarendon Press, 1789); Gary Becker, "Crime and Punishment: An Economic Approach," *Journal of Political Economy* 76 (1968): 169–217; Isaac Ehrlich, "Crime, Punishment, and the Market for Offenses," *Journal Economic Perspectives* 10 (1996): 43–67; William Estes, "An Experimental Study of Punishment," *Psychological Monographs* 57 (1944): 1–40.

75. Gneezy and Rustichini, "A Fine Is a Price," 1–17.

76. The day care fee for each child per month is NIS 1400 (New Israeli Shekel); the penalty fee in the study is NIS 10 for a delay of 10 minutes or more. Ibid., 4–5.

77. Ibid., 3, 15–16.

78. Ibid., 10–11.

79. See Caroline Kaeb and David Scheffer, "The Paradox of Kiobel in Europe," *American Journal of International Law* 107 (2013): 852. Even within one legal system, like for example the United States, the liability standards for violations of CSR norms, especially human rights, are far from clear. The ATS is rather vague in its prescribed scope, and even after the recent Supreme Court judgment in *Kiobel v. Royal Dutch Petroleum* many questions still remain unclear, such as the exact extent of its extraterritorial use and the mens rea standard for corporate aiding and abetting.

80. David Vogel, *The Market for Virtue: The Potential and Limits for Corporate Social Responsibility* (Washington, DC: Brookings Institution Press, 2006), 29.

81. See Kerr, Janda, and Pitts, *Corporate Social Responsibility: A Legal Analysis*, 45–46.

82. Gneezy and Rustichini, "A Fine Is a Price," 10.

83. Ibid., 14–15.

84. Ibid, 14.

85. Several scholars have explored the relationship between intrinsic and extrinsic motivation and found that under specific conditions there is a tradeoff between the two. Lepper and Greene have been referring to this phenomenon as "hidden costs of rewards." Mark Lepper and David Greene, *The Hidden Costs of Rewards: New Perspectives on the Psychology of Human Motivation* (Hillsdale, NJ: L. Erlbaum Associates, 1978). Deci has described the same phenomenon as "the corruption effect of extrinsic motivation," and Bruno Frey has framed it as a "crowding out effect." Edward Deci, *Intrinsic Motivation* (Dordrecht: Plenum, 1975); Bruno Frey, *Not Just for the Money: An Economic Theory of Personal Motivation* (Cheltenham-Brookfield: Edward Elgar, 1997).

86. For the role of social norms with regard to the law and legal compliance, see Cass Sunstein, "Social Norms and Roles," *Columbia Law Review* 96 (1996): 903–68.

87. Gneezy and Rustichini, "A Fine Is a Price," 1.

88. Bohnet, Frey, and Huck, "More Order with Less Law: On Contract Enforcement, Trust, and Crowding," 131–44; Benno Torgler, "Tax Morale and Direct Democracy," *European Journal of Political Economy* 21 (2005): 525–31; Lars Feld and Bruno Frey, "Trust Breeds Trust: How Taxpayers Are Treated," *Economics of Governance* 3 (2002): 87–99.

89. Richard Thaler, "Watching Behavior before Writing," *New York Times*, July 7, 2012, http://www.nytimes.com/2012/07/08/business/behavioral-science -can-help-guide-policy-economic-view.html?pagewanted=all&_r=0.

CHAPTER TEN

Multistakeholder Initiative Anatomy

*Understanding Institutional Design
and Development*

Amelia Evans

Introduction

A decade ago, if a business announced it was joining a multistakeholder initiative, the response would likely have been little more than blank stares and confusion: *a multi-what?* Today, the term *multistakeholder initiative* (MSI) has mainstreamed into corporate social responsibility (CSR) practice, and the issue of whether to join an MSI is now a core consideration of civil society engagement strategies and government policy. MSIs, which bring together stakeholders concerned about the negative impacts of an industry on particular communities, rose to prominence as a tool capable of bridging the governance gap that exists in regulating the human rights or environmental impacts of transnational corporations.[1] They have now been embraced by most major global industries, setting standards and establishing frameworks to tackle a myriad of issues that formal domestic and international legal regimes have left unaddressed. The status of MSIs as mechanisms for preventing and remedying human rights abuses by private actors was further cemented by their inclusion in the *Guiding Principles on Business and Human Rights*, approved by United Nations Human Rights Council in 2011.[2]

Despite the rapid growth of MSIs, their conceptual and theoretical consensus as institutions remains weak.[3] There is not even agreement on the name to be used for this phenomenon of different stakeholders—governments, civil society, business, or affected communities—working collaboratively to address the externalities of private actors, with "MSI" being perhaps the most popular, but by no means the only, label used.[4] The dearth of material on institutional aspects of MSIs may in part be because many commentators and MSI members are quick to emphasize the uniqueness of the specific MSI under consideration, noting the particularities of the industry to which that MSI applies, the underlying human rights issue it seeks to address, or the geographic region to which it applies: how can one view an initiative established to monitor labor standards in factories as having any bearing on a scheme devoted to protecting freedom of expression on the Internet? While each individual MSI undoubtedly operates within its own context and raises specific and unique issues, the author's discussions with individuals from government, industry, and civil society involved in, or concerned by, MSIs has demonstrated that there are broad commonalities in the formation process, structure, implementation, and membership patterns of an MSI.

Understanding these commonalties allows for the development of a framework for analyzing whether MSIs are effective instruments for addressing the adverse impacts of industry. It also allows those involved in—or concerned by—an MSI to better understand how to craft the most robust initiatives. This chapter takes a necessary first step toward those goals by outlining the common development, design, and implementation features of those MSIs that set standards to address the negative externalities of transnational business.[5] It draws out practical lessons to ensure that they are more consciously and carefully designed to achieve societal change. These lessons range from overcoming roadblocks in the negotiation of an initiative, through to being cognizant of the consequences of establishing voluntary standards that are inconsistent with international law. Importantly, the chapter also critically considers the best measures and proxies of "success" of an MSI, where assessing the impact of the MSI on the ground is not feasible. For example, it highlights the pitfalls of exclusively focusing on the number of companies participating in an MSI as an indicator of impact, while offering the counterintuitive view that MSIs that publicly acknowledge noncompliance with their standards may in fact be demonstrating their capacity to effect change.

Harnessing the Impetus for the MSI

Before understanding how MSIs form, it is first important to interrogate why they form. As with other forms of CSR, establishing an MSI requires changing the motivations of companies to break from the status quo and agree to abide by voluntary standards.[6] From an economic perspective this implicitly requires increasing the cost of companies "not acting."[7] For most MSIs, this cost or motivation is triggered by a period of high-profile confrontation, where a global crisis or agenda-setting process successfully pressured businesses into subscribing to a collaborative form of voluntary regulation. In other words, the MSI was created as a direct result of a degree of "prior conflict between government, business, and civil society."[8] Direct action by affected communities may also spur change. For example, one of the first MSIs was formed following high-profile campaigning by 326 NGOs and dam-affected communities that began in 1994 and highlighted the social and environmental costs of constructing dams.[9] After three years of sustained pressure, dam builders, financiers, and related parties agreed that the World Bank should hear the concerns of civil society through a multistakeholder workshop on the issue.[10] The result was the formation of the World Commission on Dams in 1997, which created a framework for the funding and building of dams that includes weighing societal considerations.[11] Many other first-generation MSIs developed in the 1990s involved such confrontational beginnings. These include the Fair Labor Association, which was created following widespread campaigning of the apparel industry's use of sweatshop labor in the early 1990s; the Voluntary Principles on Security and Human Rights, which was formed following sustained lobbying by NGOs against oil companies that were particularly enraged by the execution of Ken Saro Wiwa in 1995;[12] and the Kimberley Process, whose formation process began in 1999 following a targeted NGO campaign on blood diamonds.[13]

However, MSIs do not have to begin with conflict.[14] Indeed, it seems that some more recent MSIs are being formed as a result of proactive mutual agreement among stakeholders that a particular issue is not on the global agenda, but should be. These initiatives tend to be the result of a concerted effort of one or more stakeholders to frame an issue and resolve it through engagement and noncoercive approaches. An example is the Global Reporting Initiative (GRI), an MSI that provides standardized reporting guidelines for companies disclosing their environmental, social, and governance performance.[15] The concept was the brainchild of Robert Massie and Allen White, who ran an environmental NGO, Ceres.[16] They recognized the joint societal and commercial benefits of standardizing the environmental impact reports that companies had begun to release and hosted a two-year project to assess the feasibility of establishing common disclosure guidelines.[17] To maximize future participation and increase the likelihood of establishing a universally accepted form of reporting, the feasibility project was open to anyone, and it was agreed that it would be consensus-based model that, if successful, would lead to the creation of an MSI. Many companies saw the benefits of being involved in the early development and adoption of standardized reporting and agreed to pilot the system, leading to the subsequent establishment of GRI.

However, conflict and cooperation are not binary states. Corporate human rights and environmental issues have experienced a general increase in attention following the confrontational agenda setting by civil society, particularly during the antiglobalization campaigns of the 1990s. On this basis, it is arguable that all MSIs—including non-issue-specific MSIs such as the United Nations Global Compact—are the result of that increased pressure. Similarly, it may be that within an MSI, some companies were motivated to join through confrontation, while others effectively joined of their own accord, perhaps seeing a competitive advantage to forming that MSI. Nonetheless, it is possible to distinguish between MSIs that are created following *direct* confrontation between constituent stakeholders and those that may arise simply out of a climate where conscientious corporate behavior is increasingly valued.

It is unclear whether, and to what extent, direct confrontation affects the development, design, or impact of an MSI. It may be that qualitative features of an MSI, such as the levels of trust and closeness among stakeholders, are higher in an MSI formed without confrontation. These qualitative features of stakeholder relationships are crucial to an MSI, as one of the key differences between traditional legal standards and standards made through voluntary initiatives is the degree of separation between the rule makers and enforcers, and those who lobby for the rules or to whom the rules apply.[18] In a traditional legal system those actors are separate.[19] By comparison, voluntary initiatives are characterized by the participation of both those who will be regulated and those who seek the regulation, not only in the development of that regulation but also by holding decision-making positions that inherently relate to their own behavior. As a result, intangible features such as the stakeholders' preexisting relationships and ability to work together have a significant effect on whether stakeholders can reach agreement on developing and running a robust and effective MSI. Equally however, it may be that an MSI precipitated by confrontation causes such reputational harm and shareholder backlash that a company is more deeply driven to make meaningful change and cooperate with other stakeholders to prevent history from repeating.

While further research is needed in this area to determine the differences, if any, that the presence of a conflict or confrontation has on the end results of an MSI, it is critical that the initial motivation or enthusiasm for creating an initiative is harnessed at the outset to ensure that a robust MSI with strong incentivizing and accountability structures is created. One of the inherent risks of MSIs is that where civil society, government, or community groups cease applying pressure or confrontation on companies or an industry, and focus on working cooperatively with companies to improve their societal impacts (as is inherent in an MSI), the external forces driving a company to change their behavior may cease, leading to a diminished motivation to change. There is significant value in the shared learning and dialogue that is inherent in MSIs, especially as these may lead to changing deeper structural change in the company regarding outlooks on human rights and environmental responsibilities.[20] However, the risk—and concern of many skeptics—is that an MSI does no more than facilitate such dialogue, without any certainty that those conversations translate to change on the ground.

Even in the case of "cooperatively formed" MSIs, it is difficult to accurately determine whether companies who choose to form an MSI are genuinely motivated to improving their societal impacts[21] or whether they are potentially joining the initiative with more nefarious intentions, such as to use it as a mask to avoid more stringent government regulation or to lessen NGO antagonism. As a result, structures should be agreed upon that guarantee the initiative will be capable of sustaining change even if that original motivation or enthusiasm for change itself dissipates (or was never there).[22] Unless the initiative has strong foundations at the outset that provide assurances as to the integrity of its eventual design, it may be better for noncompany stakeholders seeking societal improvement to continue down alternate paths, such as campaigning or pressing for legislative change, rather than to establish an initiative whose ability to improve human rights or environmental impacts is contingent upon goodwill or an unspecified number of future dialogues.

Development of the MSI

Once stakeholders accept that there is a need for an MSI, the process of developing the conceptual idea into a constituted framework begins.[23] While the development process tends to vary markedly from initiative to initiative, an analysis of these processes reveals two general insights. First, that there are several structural components to MSIs, which indicate different levels of development. These include setting standards or norms of behavior, establishing internal governance systems, instigating accountability mechanisms, and building procedures for ongoing review and development. Second, that MSIs that are started without a clear roadmap on how to build all these features at the outset often struggle to develop them, particularly those related to accountability.

Generally, an MSI begins with a group of stakeholders working together to agree on the specific scope of the MSI in terms of the issues, industry, and geographic regions it will address.[24] The events that led to the instigation of the MSI will generally have already provided some shape for its scope. Thus, high-profile NGO-led campaigns to expose sweatshops and poor labor conditions broadly spurred negotiations about how to address labor rights within apparel companies, leading to the development of a plethora of MSIs focusing on this issue (for example, the Fair Labor Association and the Worker Rights Consortium in the United States, and the Fair Wear Foundation in Europe and Ethical Trading Initiative in the United Kingdom).[25] NGO campaigns about the role that diamonds played in funding civil conflict in Africa prompted the international discussions that led to the Kimberley Process focusing exclusively on diamonds produced by "rebel movements or their allies to finance conflict aimed at undermining legitimate governments."[26] This resulted in the initiative being hamstrung when faced with allegations that diamonds were being certified by the Kimberley Process that had resulted from killings and widespread violence by the Zimbabwean military in the Marange region, issues that fell outside its mandate.[27] By comparison, those formed without direct confrontation, such as GRI, the United Nations Global Compact, and even the Fair Trade Labeling

Organization, have generally led to much broader initiatives in terms of the issues and industries they seek to address.

Formalistically, the scope of an MSI is definable by reference to its stated mission or purpose statement. In practice, however, it is the standards that an MSI develops for targeted actors to follow that truly indicate its scope or mandate. An MSI might purport to address the social and environmental impacts from an industry, but if it only sets standards relating to environment, that should be deemed its true scope. In this way, the standards are really the "core" of the MSI, establishing what substantive changes or expectations are placed on targeted actors. Indeed, MSIs can simply consist of a set of standards and intentionally develop no further, existing simply as a charter of promises or code of conduct for members.[28]

Unfortunately, too many MSIs express their standards in weak language, lacking specificity of the exact obligations placed on targeted actors. Obligatoriness provides an indispensable form of credibility for MSIs, on the basis that while they are voluntary to join, upon joining a member is expected to abide by certain standards. Also, basing the standard on international law is critical to providing a legitimate basis for the standards by using norms that have global acceptance.[29] Many MSIs are established with standards that are significantly less onerous than international legal norms.

The possible upside to forming initiatives with weak standards, such as those that are not mandatory or based on international law, is that it increases the likelihood of companies agreeing to participate, as the costs of joining are low owing to the smaller behavior change that is expected from members. The presumed rationale is that it is better to have companies "in not out" and that over time there will be "change from within" the MSI.[30] However, unless a weak but popular MSI does in fact become more rigorous or demonstrate widespread industry change, there is a risk that the MSI may instead do little more than consume value resources of civil society and contribute to an appearance of market-wide change, while dampening other efforts to improve the societal footprint of industry.[31]

Testing the Functionality of the MSI

Once the MSI is implemented, the matter of how smoothly it functions can provide considerable insight into the incentives and motivations of targeted actors to change, as well as the strength of the mechanisms developed. This is often the best proxy for the more difficult assessment of whether an MSI is causing behavioral change in the industry and improving outcomes for affected communities.

At the most basic level of functionality, the question is whether an MSI is discharging the responsibilities it has set for itself. For example, the Kimberley Process mandated that it should be "subject to periodic review," with the first review to occur within three years of its launch.[32] While the first review did occur in 2006, a little over three years after the launch in November 2002, there has been no subsequent review in the years following, and many of its recommendations have not been addressed.[33] Other MSI-level obligations include conducting annual meetings, releasing an annual report on the MSI's achievements, or collecting membership fees. If an MSI is unable to meet the functional obligations it places on itself or all its participants, this raises questions about its effectiveness and the willingness of its members to achieve change.

The second level is that of targeted actors discharging the obligations specifically placed on them. Again the Kimberley Process, which requires member countries to provide annual reports on their implementation efforts by March 31 in the following year, is a helpful example.[34] The obligation to report is described by the United Nations General Assembly (UNGA) as Kimberley Process's "main comprehensive and regular source of information,"[35] yet a review of the Kimberley Process's website four months after the reports were due for 2011 shows only 44 percent of listed participants have submitted an annual report.[36] Unsurprisingly, a recent UNGA resolution called upon participants "to submit consistent and substantive annual reports in order to conform to this requirement."[37] Where companies are not meeting their obligations even at face value, this demonstrates a basic struggle exists for those members to truly alter their behavior.

This is not to be confused with an assumption that to be functional an MSI must demonstrate that its members are always in compliance with an MSI's standards. While MSIs are formed on the basis that they may be able to reduce or eliminate a significant societal problem caused by industry, it is unrealistic to expect that this could occur instantly. Transforming ingrained industry practices or views on social responsibility relies not only on making paper-based changes to systems, but also on altering deeper institutional factors that take considerable time to change, such as cultural adjustment or development of internal expertise. Bearing this in mind, exposing high levels of noncompliance or revealing significant instances of noncompliance are likely to be positive signs that the MSI has developed standards that are directed at real and prevalent issues, and that there are sufficiently robust, transparent, and accountable procedures in place to detect instances where companies are not meeting those standards. For example, over a one-year period when the Ethical Trading Initiative (ETI)[38] was first implemented, it recorded that members increased the level of monitoring from 20 percent of their supply base to 67 percent. Concomitant to this was an increase in the instances of noncompliance found in suppliers, from 11 percent in the first year to a doubling of 23 percent the following year. The ETI celebrated this discovery, noting that this was likely to be evidence that "unacceptable working conditions are a reality."[39] ETI concluded that what was important was to see a decline in the number of unacceptable working conditions over time. This seems sensible: initial high levels of reporting may be indicative that the initiative has effective monitoring systems, and, assuming these systems remain effective, the hope is that over time the initiative causes deep behavioral change that leads to improved protection and promotion of environmental and human rights. This would then translate to a decline in instances of noncompliance over time. To the contrary, it may be more suspicious if an MSI rarely, or never, reports incidents of noncompliance, as this suggests either that the MSI does not have sturdy monitoring systems or lacks basic levels of transparency to disclose noncompliance.

Analyzing the Participation of Stakeholders and Composition of Membership

A lot of emphasis tends to be placed on the increase in the number, or overall market share, of companies (or governments) that have signed up to an initiative. When new companies or governments join, press releases are issued triumphantly. The underlying rationale is presumably that the larger the membership base of governments or companies, the wider the application of the MSI, and thus the greater the impact of the initiative. However, this assessment is far too simplistic to be a reliable indicator of impact or success on its own. In addition to understanding the structural features of an MSI, an assessment of the composition of an MSI's membership is critical.

The underlying rationale behind MSIs is that the transnational problems global MSIs address are complex, requiring a vast range of resources, capacities, and knowledge to sufficiently address them, and that no one stakeholder has the necessary mix of skills, resources, and experience to do so.[40] By pooling the different capacities and areas of knowledge of a variety of stakeholders, there is a greater understanding of the problem and how it may best be addressed. Inclusion of stakeholders is also necessary because an MSI, and the standards it sets, does not have the inherent authority or legitimacy of a traditional law-making body. Thus in order for the MSI to create a perception that it is "desirable, proper, or appropriate,"[41] respected MSIs have focused on including a range of stakeholders during their formation, as well as their implementation, on the basis that people involved in the process will then accept and support the initiative.[42] This helps to create an initiative that reflects the differing needs and expectations of the constituent stakeholders while increasing the likelihood of sustaining support for the initiative in the long term. As a result, inclusiveness is seen as central to giving an MSI its authority, legitimacy, and respect.

Indeed, without involvement from multiple stakeholder groups, a multistakeholder initiative would, by definition, cease to exist. A failure to identify and include key stakeholders "could endanger the entire negotiation process"[43] of an initiative, and some dialogues have collapsed completely as a result of the exclusion of a core stakeholder group.[44] Even if the result is less extreme than total collapse, low levels of involvement from core stakeholder groups can be highly damaging. For example, the United Nations Global Compact (UNGC) was first devised with a disproportionately larger contingent of businesses than civil society actors, and all the civil society actors were internationally focused, with no local actors.[45] This led to distrust by some stakeholders at the outset, who campaigned publicly against the UNGC. In response, the UNGC made concerted efforts to open itself up to membership from a greater and more diverse array of civil society actors, but not before several scathing reports were released by civil society organizations.[46]

Identifying and including stakeholders is a challenging task. The classical definition of a stakeholder is "any group or individual who can affect or is affected by the achievement of the organization's objective."[47] This definition has been accused of being so broad as to leave the "field of possible stakeholders unambiguously open to include virtually anyone."[48] Taken to its extreme, a highly inclusive MSI could have an almost endless number of stakeholders involved. Indeed, a growing number of MSIs are now making the entire constitutional process open to any interested party.[49] When large numbers of stakeholders wish to participate there are inevitable challenges regarding how to manage such a group. In particular, questions arise on how best to address power imbalances among stakeholder groups and provide adequate representation for stakeholders, without frustrating the ability to make decisions in a timely and effective manner.[50]

These difficulties should not be used as an excuse to exclude stakeholders from the formation process, but embraced as one of the core characteristics and benefits of MSIs that needs to be appropriately managed. If an MSI is unable to grapple with working with a wide group of players with differing interests at the outset, it is unlikely to be able to survive through to implementation with sufficient support and legitimacy from the relevant stakeholder groups. There have been some very creative responses to incorporating large and varied stakeholder groups during the constitutional process.[51]

MSIs have generally identified and included high-profile global stakeholders, such as governments, large corporations, and international civil society organizations.[52] However, they have not been as inclusive of less powerful or visible actors, such as locally and nationally based organizations, communities affected by the MSI, and stakeholders from the global South.[53] Despite the fact that many MSIs are set up with a core purpose of improving the living conditions of specific local communities, these communities—and the vulnerable populations within them— have been noticeably absent in the design and implementation of MSIs. Indeed, the United Nations Commission on Sustainable Development's database of MSIs, which contains over 350 registered MSIs,[54] recorded that less than 1 percent had members from local community groups, such as farmers, workers and trade unions, indigenous people, women, youth, or children. Civil society is not a sufficient substitution for the involvement of these communities and groups.[55]

MSIs also exert significant influence in the global South, through shaping normative concepts and through their establishment of regulatory schemes that have impact in the South.[56] However, the evidence demonstrates significant underrepresentation of southern actors throughout the phases of MSIs. The extent of northern influence in some MSIs is so dramatic that it has led to certain MSIs being perceived by some as protectionist measures that impose nontariff barriers for southern producers trying to enter the global market or as vehicles for driving the northern agenda into the South by "extend[ing] capitalist domination abroad." The exclusion of the South undermines the very notion of whether MSIs are truly a form of "global" governance.[57]

Another overlooked aspect of participation is not just those who have been excluded by way of a lack of invitation or facilitation to participate, but also those that have actively refused to participate in an MSI. This may include those actors who quit an MSI, or those who were invited to join an MSI and declined. It is perhaps inevitable that an MSI will experience internal conflict given the markedly different agendas and experiences of stakeholders. Consequently, it is common for specific stakeholders to walk out of discussions when the MSI is under formation. For example, Amnesty International and World Organization for Human Rights USA participated in the formation of the Global Network Initiative (GNI), but left because it was "not strong enough" to address human rights concerns, citing ambiguous standards in particular.[58] Others NGOs remained, but this nonetheless suggests that the final design for GNI was not as strong as some NGOs had hoped. Analyzing those stakeholders who actively choose not to commit to an MSI, whether it is companies, civil society, communities, or governments, may therefore provide considerable insight into the potential of the MSI itself.

The decision to quit an operational MSI may be even more indicative. For noncompany actors it generally can be read as a statement that while the MSI had developed terms the actor believed could lead to change, or had the potential to develop such terms, those terms are now irreparably ineffective or unable to be met. This is evident by the walk out of Global Witness from Kimberley Process in 2011, a founding member of the initiative, on the basis that after nine years of operation, the scheme's "main flaws and loopholes have not been fixed."[59] Where it is targeted actors that are leaving, the reverse may be true: that the terms of the MSI are significantly more difficult to meet than anticipated. This suggests that the MSI is placing obligations on targeted actors that require significant change, but which are too costly for the company to voluntarily undertake.

Conclusion

The failure to identify and critique MSI features and developmental processes over the last decade has mystified MSIs and left them poorly understood at an individual and an institutional level. This has made it difficult for all actors, whether grassroots human rights activists or policy makers, to determine whether a particular MSI is capable of improving the impacts of industry or whether it is a hand brake on effecting change. For those involved in MSIs, there has also been little practical advice generated for establishing MSIs or improving the effectiveness of existing ones. Finally, and most importantly, it has made it difficult to resolve the critical question of whether MSIs are capable of being effective human rights and environmental instruments.

However, a deeper institutional assessment of MSIs demonstrates that there are common features to MSIs, regardless of the unique context or issue that drives their operation. By appreciating how factors such as accountability mechanisms or involvement of local stakeholders affect the internal dynamics of an initiative as well as its capacity to effect change, it is hoped that stakeholders will be able to make more effective initiatives, while critics will have analytical tools available to provide more insightful critiques. Further exploration of the institutional design of MSIs is encouraged. The greater awareness of their design, the closer we are to having a framework for resolving the critical question of whether, and if so how, MSIs can be designed and implemented to effectively address the human rights and environmental conditions of affected communities.

Notes

1. Shepard Forman and Derk Segaar, "New Coalitions for Global Governance: The Changing Dynamics of Multilateralism," *Global Governance: A Review of Multilateralism and International Organizations* 12, no. 2 (2006): 205–25.

2. John Ruggie, *Guiding Principles on Business and Human Rights: Implementing the United Nations "Protect, Respect, and Remedy" Framework*, U.N. Doc. A/HRC/17/31, 21 March 2011, Principles 23 and 30.

3. Klaus Dingwerth, "North-South Parity in Global Governance: The Affirmative Procedures of the Forest Stewardship Council," *Global Governance: A Review of Multilateralism and International Organizations* 14, no. 1 (2008): 53, 54.

4. Terms that have been used to describe this phenomenon, with varying degrees of specificity, include "multistakeholder partnerships," "multistakeholder networks," "global action networks," "private standard initiatives," "societal learning and change initiatives," "global public policy networks," "non-

state market-drive governance systems," "trisectoral networks," "multilateral transnational governance schemes," "private transnational governance," "public private partnerships," and "civil regulation." The term "multistakeholder initiative" appears to have been first used prior to the United Nations Conference on Environment and Development (the Rio Summit) in 1992. Lucy Koechlin and Richard Calland, "Standard Setting at the Cutting Edge: An Evidence-Based Typology for Multi-Stakeholder Initiatives," in *Non-State Actors as Standard-Setters*, ed. Anne Peters et al. (Cambridge: Cambridge University Press, 2009), 84, 85.

5. While the chapter is primarily concerned with global multistakeholder initiatives (MSIs) that address issues caused, or contributed to, by transnational businesses—particularly human rights or environmental impacts—by setting standards for members to follow, the framework and arguments set out in the chapter will apply at a general level to MSIs that seek to regulate any form of business behavior, whether global or nonglobal, standards-based, or otherwise. For ease of discussion the chapter refers to companies as the targeted actors of an MSI, however the analysis applies equally to MSIs where governments are the targeted actors, for example, the Kimberley Process and Extractive Industry Transparency Initiative.

6. See generally, Ruth V. Aguilera, Deborah E. Rupp, Cynthia A. Williams, and Jyoti Ganapathi, "Putting the S Back in Corporate Social Responsibility: A Multilevel Theory of Social Change in Organizations," *Academy of Management Review* 32, no. 3 (2007): 836–63.

7. See S. Bernstein and B. Cashore, "Can Non-State Global Governance Be Legitimate? An Analytical Framework," *Regulation and Governance* 1, no. 4 (2007): 347, 356.

8. Jem Bendell, "In Whose Name? The Accountability of Corporate Social Responsibility," *Development in Practice* 15, no. 3–4 (2005): 362, 363. The role of ethical campaigns and their impact on MSI formation is discussed generally in Alex Hughes, Neil Wrigley, and Martin Buttle, "Global Production Networks, Ethical Campaigning, and the Embeddedness of Responsible Governance," *Journal of Economic Geography* 8, no. 3 (2008): 345–67; Tim Connor, "Time to Scale Up Cooperation? Trade Unions, NGOs, and the International Antisweatshop Movement," *Development in Practice* 14, no. 1–2 (2004): 61–70; Peter Asmus, Hank Cauley, and Katharine Maroney, "Turning Conflict into Cooperation," *Stanford Social Innovation Review* (2006): 52–61.

9. These organizations had united to sign the Manibeli Declaration, which directly called for the World Bank to impose a moratorium on funding for dams until certain conditions had been met, including an independent review of the societal cost of dam building. Patrick McCully "The Use of a Trilateral Network: An Activist's Perspective on the Formation of the World Commission on Dams," *American University Law Review* 16, no. 6 (2001): 1453, 1456.

10. Jennifer M. Brinkerhoff, "Global Public Policy, Partnership, and the World Commission on Dams," *Public Administration Review* 62, no. 3 (2002): 324, 327.

11. World Commission on Dams, *Dams and Development: A New Framework for Decision-Making*, Report of the World Commission on Dams (World Commission on Dams, November 2000).

12. Michael E. Conroy, *Branded! How the "Certification Revolution" Is Transforming Global Corporations* (Gabriola, BC: New Society Publishers, 2007), 62–63; Bennett Freeman, Maria B. Pica, and Christopher N. Camponovo, "A New Approach to Corporate Responsibility: The Voluntary Principles on Security and Human Rights," *Hastings International and Comparative Law Review* 24 (2000–2001): 423, 426–27.

13. Ingrid J. Tamm, *Diamonds in Peace and War: Severing the Conflict-Diamond Connection* (Cambridge, MA: Report for World Peace Foundation, 03, 2002).

14. Steve Waddell, *Societal Learning and Change* (Austin, TX: Greenleaf Publishing, 2005), 18.

15. Global Reporting Initiative *What Is GRI?*, http://www.globalreporting .org/AboutGRI/WhatIsGRI/.

16. Ceres was formed in 1989 and is a network of investors, NGOs, labor unions, and other organizations that works with US companies to address environmental sustainability issues. Until 2000 it was known as CERES, the Coalition for Environmentally Responsible Economies.

17. Halina Szejnwald Brown, Martin de Jong, and Teodorina Lessidrenska, "The Rise of Global Reporting Initiative (GRI) as a Case of Institutional Entrepreneurship," *Environmental Politics* 18, no. 2 (2009): 182, 190; Global Reporting Initiative History, http://www.globalreporting.org/AboutGRI/WhatIsGRI/ History.

18. On the distinctions between voluntary initiatives and public law generally, see Kernaghan Webb and Andrew Morrison, "The Law and Voluntary Codes: Examining the 'Tangled Web,'" in *Voluntary Codes: Private Governance, the Public Interest, and Innovation*, ed. Kernaghan Webb (School of Public Policy and Administration, Carleton University, 2004), 125–52.

19. This is not to deny that governments often spend significant resources to consult with constituents and those interested in and affected by proposed laws, and that governments are frequently lobbied by those with an interest in the law. Nonetheless, the parties are separate legal entities.

20. Volker Rittberger, *Global Governance: From "Exclusive" Executive Multilateralism to Inclusive, Multipartite Institutions* (International Studies Association, March 27, 2008).

21. In the case of MSIs that are prompted by direct confrontation, it can generally be concluded that the industry, or least some member companies, would

likely not have subscribed to the MSI "but for" that pressure. The question then arises: if that pressure is lifted, will the motivation to change remain? Even for companies who join an MSI without any direct prompting or confrontation, and with strong, genuine intentions of adhering to human rights or environmental standards, this proactive spirit may change over time. The perceived competitive advantage of participating may diminish, the costs or benefits of joining the MSI may have been miscalculated, or the management and culture of the company or administration may simply change.

22. Stakeholders have expressed differing views on whether that agreement should be simply high-level commitment for development or a more detailed decision on the mechanism.

23. There has been no detailed examination of the conditions in which stakeholders choose to establish an MSI as a form of CSR to address the impacts of transnational business, as opposed to businesses developing an industry code or other stakeholders pressing for legislation, has not been closely examined. However, understanding when and why MSIs are preferred—and how this has changed over the last decade as MSI popularity has grown—is an important factor in analyzing and understanding their impact.

24. Some MSIs may be spearheaded by one stakeholder, such as the WWF which has convened two MSIs: WWF, *Certification and Roundtables: Do They Work?* (2010), 9.

25. See Dara O'Rourke, "Market Movements: Nongovernmental Organization Strategies to Influence Global Production and Consumption," *Journal of Industrial Ecology* 9, no. 1–2 (2005): 115, 122.

26. Kimberley Process, *Kimberley Process Certification Scheme* (2002), 12.

27. See Global Witness, "Kimberley Process Lets Zimbabwe off the Hook (Again)," press release, November 2, 2011.

28. Examples include the Aquaculture Dialogue or the Access to Basic Services for All initiative.

29. Barbara Lang, "Experiences with Voluntary Standards Initiatives and Related Multi-Stakeholder Dialogues," GTZ publication (2008), available at http://www.gtz.de/en/themen/uebergreifende-themen/sozial-oekostandards/16064.htm, accessed February 25, 2011.

30. This analysis also applies to other aspects of MSI design aside from standards. See Ian Smillie, "Natural Resources: Diamonds and Human Security," in *Globalization and Security: Social and Cultural Aspects*, ed. G. Honor Fagan et al. (Santa Barbara, CA: ABC-CLIO, 2009), 239, 245, which describes the development of the Kimberley Process and how NGOs decided to "accept a weak agreement and work later to strengthen it from the inside."

31. See, for example, David Humphreys, "From Corporate Social Responsibility to the Democratic Regulation of Transnational Corporations," *Interna-*

tional Journal of Environmental, Cultural, Social, and Economic Sustainability 5, no. 4 (2009): 207, 210.

32. Kimberley Process, *Kimberley Process Certification Scheme* (2002), 11.

33. See Ad Hoc Working Group on the Review of the Kimberley Process Certification Scheme, *The Kimberley Process Certification Scheme Third Year Review* (2006). While an ad-hoc committee was formed in November 2011 and mandated "with coordinating the periodic review of the KPCS," a further review has not yet been conducted. Kimberley Process, *Ad-Hoc Committee Administrative Decision on the Periodic Review of the KPCS* (2011), 1.

34. Kimberley Process Administrative Decision: KPCS Peer Review System (2007), 1.

35. United Nations General Assembly, *The Role of Diamonds in Fuelling Conflict* (January 11, 2012) A/66/L.34 at para. 11.

36. Based on those participant countries without a 2011 Annual Report listed at Kimberley Process, *Participants*, http://www.kimberleyprocess.com/web/kimberley-process/kp-participants, last accessed July 25, 2012. The statistic excludes Russia and Sierra Leone, whose reports are not made public, and therefore from whom it is impossible to verify if a report has been filed.

37. United Nations General Assembly, *The Role of Diamonds in Fuelling Conflict* (January 11, 2012) A/66/L.34 at para. 11.

38. The Ethical Trading Initiative (ETI) is an MSI that seeks to improve labor standards in the general consumer goods market.

39. Mike Blowfield, "ETI: A Multi-Stakeholder Approach," in *Corporate Responsibility and Labour Rights: Codes of Conduct in the Global Economy*, ed. Rhys Jenkins et al. (London: Earthscan, 2002), 184, 188.

40. Volker Rittberger, *Global Governance: From "Exclusive" Executive Multilateralism to Inclusive, Multipartite Institutions* 9 (International Studies Association, March 27, 2008).

41. M. C. Suchman, "Managing Legitimacy: Strategic and Institutional Approaches," *Academy of Management Review* 20, no. 3 (1995): 571, 574.

42. Nancy Vallejo and Pierre Hauselmann, Multi-Stakeholder Governance: A Brief Guide, Pully, Switzerland, February 6, http://assets.panda.org/downloads/finalpiconsultingpaperenglish.pdf.

43. Jan Martin Witte, Wolfgang H. Reinicke, and Thorsten Benner, "Beyond Multilateralism: Global Public Policy Networks," *International Politics and Society* 2 (2000): 176, 181.

44. This occurred during the failed attempt by the OECD to create an MSI framework to govern international investment flows in 1995. Although negotiations began with a high level of consensus, the process included some nonstate stakeholder groups yet specifically excluded NGOs. The collective alienation led to high profile campaigning and to pressure being placed on states not to partic-

ipate in the process. Many consider this exclusion to have been the sole cause of the collapse of the discussions. Mickael Wigell, *Multi-Stakeholder Cooperation in Global Governance* 9 (Ministry for Foreign Affairs of Finland, Working Paper No. 58, 2008).

45. Tariq Banuri and Erika Spanger-Siegfried, "The Global Compact and the Human Economy," *Journal of Human Development* 2, no. 1 (2001): 7–17.

46. Indeed, the UNGC now has more than six times as many local NGOs as global NGOs: United Nations Global Compact, *Participants and Stakeholders: Civil Society Organizations,* http://www.unglobalcompact.org/Participants AndStakeholders/civil_society.html.

47. R. Edward Freeman, *Strategic Management: A Stakeholder Approach* (Cambridge: Cambridge University Press, 1984).

48. Ronald K. Mitchell, Bradley R. Agle, and Donna J. Wood, "Toward a Theory of Stakeholder Identification and Salience: Defining the Principle of Who and What Really Counts," *Academy of Management Review* 22, no. 4 (1997): 853, 856.

49. See, for example, the Global Reporting Initiative and Aquaculture Dialogue.

50. The issues surrounding the tradeoff between inclusiveness, and thus legitimacy, and efficient decision making are discussed in Thorsten Göbel, *Too Many Cooks Spoil the Broth? The Influence of Inclusiveness on Effectiveness* (Offene Tagung der Sektion Internationale Politik der Deutschen Vereinigung für Politische Wissenschaft, July, 13–14, 2007).

51. An extreme example is the Aquaculture Dialogues, which is currently working with more than two thousand aquacultural farmers, retailers, NGOs, scientists, and other industry stakeholders worldwide to develop standards for responsible aquaculture. The MSI is open to anyone who wishes to participate, and where underrepresentation of certain groups of stakeholders based on geography, scale, and expertise is recognized, active solicitation of involvement from such stakeholders is sought. The standard-setting process is split into eight standards development groups, based on species-type. Within each group, stakeholders are classed into subgroups, based on the skills of the stakeholder and her desired level of participation and commitment. These groups range from external stakeholders, who are not expected to attend meetings but are free to provide written input and comments, through to full dialogue stakeholder groups, technical working groups, and advisory groups. Aquaculture Dialogues, *Process Guidance Document* 4 (September 29, 2008). Although the quality of these finalized standards has not yet been critically examined, the process appears to have been efficient (with four of the eight groups having completed their development in less than five years).

52. Witte, Reinicke, and Benner, "Beyond Multilateralism: Global Public Policy Networks."

53. Frank Biermann, Man-san Chan, Aysem Mert, and Philipp Pattberg, "Multi-Stakeholder Partnerships for Sustainable Development: Does the Promise Hold?" Paper presented at the 2007 Amsterdam Conference on the Human Dimensions of Global Environmental Change, Vrje Universiteit Amsterdam, the Netherlands, 2007.

54. The United Nations Commission on Sustainable Development (CSD) database is a voluntary records of MSIs, to which governments are a members, that contribute to the implementation of Agenda 21, the Programme for the Further Implementation of Agenda 21 and the Johannesburg Plan of Implementation United Nations Commission on Sustainable Development, Partnerships for Sustainable Development Database, http://webapps01.un.org/dsd/partnerships/public/welcome.do.

55. Peter Utting, "Regulating Business via Multistakeholder Initiatives: A Preliminary Assessment," in *Voluntary Approaches to Corporate Responsibility: Readings and a Resource Guide*, ed. United Nations Research Institute for Social Development, UN Non-Governmental Liaison Service (NGLS), and UNRISD, Geneva, Switzerland, May 2002.

56. See Klaus Dingwerth, "Private Transnational Governance and the Developing World: A Comparative Perspective," *International Studies Quarterly* 52 no. 3 (2008): 607–34.

57. For more discussion on the global North bias in global governance generally, see Henk Overbeek, Klaus Dingwerth, Philipp Pattberg, and Daniel Compagnon, "Forum: Global Governance: Decline or Maturation of an Academic Concept?" *International Studies Review* 12 (2010): 696.

58. Bobbie Johnson, "Amnesty Criticises Global Network Initiative for Online Freedom of Speech," *The Guardian*, October 30, 2008.

59. Global Witness, "Global Witness Leaves Kimberley Process, Calls for Diamond Trade to Be Held Accountable," press release, December 5, 2011.

CHAPTER ELEVEN

The Virtue of Voluntarism

*Human Rights, Corporate Responsibility,
and UN Global Compact*

Ursula Wynhoven
Yousuf Aftab

Introduction

Corporate responsibility[1] (CR) is evolving as human rights are increasingly taking center stage in shaping stakeholder expectations of business. Respect and support for human rights have long been key tenets of CR—as demonstrated by their place in the UN Global Compact's ten principles of corporate sustainability.[2] More recently, however, the UN's "protect, respect and remedy" framework, as elaborated in the *Guiding Principles on Business and Human Rights*[3] (*Guiding Principles*), has provided additional specific and practical guidance on how companies of all types, sizes, and locations should operationalize respect for human rights. The *Guiding Principles*' framework is now widely accepted as the benchmark for business respect for human rights.[4]

The *Guiding Principles* are significant because they establish a language and framework to define business responsibility for human rights complementary to, but also distinct from, state duties for human rights:

> The responsibility to respect human rights is a global standard of expected conduct for all business enterprises wherever they operate. It exists independently of States' abilities and/or willingness to fulfill their own human rights obligations, and does not diminish those obligations. And it exists over

and above compliance with national laws and regulations protecting human rights.[5]

This quotation furnishes two essential principles of a new CR framework and language for human rights. First, business bears responsibility for respecting[6] human rights. This in itself marks a significant departure from the traditional state-centric focus of the human rights movement. Second, the responsibility is independent of state obligations for human rights. Business's responsibility, at least morally, transcends any national limitations in passage or enforcement of human rights law.

The *Guiding Principles* add clarity and structure to the scope of business responsibility for human rights. By placing emphasis on the minimum expected of business, they refocus CR in important ways, encouraging a reordering of priorities. Nevertheless, the challenge for companies is practical implementation of the *Guiding Principles* and especially the corporate responsibility to respect human rights. The challenge for stakeholders includes holding companies accountable when rights are not respected. The two challenges are intricately interwoven, as CR aspires to practicality for business and impact and accountability for society.

This chapter is about how voluntarism and voluntary initiatives can contribute to meeting both challenges as a complement not substitute for the law. The discussion will be anchored by the example of the UN Global Compact, the world's largest voluntary corporate sustainability initiative. Drawing on the UN Global Compact's experience, we identify and elaborate on the contributions that voluntary initiatives can make to CR,[7] specifically for human rights.

While a consideration of voluntary initiatives necessarily brushes against the limits of law, a dichotomy between law and voluntarism is false. To draw on economic terms, voluntarism and law are not locked in a zero-sum game where the advance of one is inevitably to the detriment of the other. There is nothing in the discussion of voluntarism's virtues that is inherently opposed to law. Rather, we take as a given that the ideal end is defined by responsible business behavior—respect for human rights—and assess how voluntarism can facilitate the end. We urge the reader not to take anything in this chapter to suggest that law is inimical to, or even less-than-desirable for, the pursuit of CR.

To the contrary, this chapter's approach is consistent with Amartya Sen's discussion of the limits of law in the pursuit of human rights:

> The point is not so much whether the legislative route can make the social ethics of human rights more effective. It certainly can do this in many cases. The point, rather, is that there are other routes as well, which too help to make the ethics of human rights more influential and effective.[8]

In the pursuit of CR for human rights, voluntary initiatives are the kinds of "other routes" that can help make the pursuit more sustainable and effective. First, their voluntariness itself facilitates embedding of respect for human rights in the corporate culture so that it gains autonomous force independently of the law. Second, voluntary initiatives provide practical guidance for businesses to determine how best to respect human rights. Third, voluntary initiatives are able to reach contexts that law cannot. This chapter will first consider the virtues of voluntarism before examining the specific example of the UN Global Compact.

What We Mean by "Voluntary Initiatives" and "Voluntarism"

Voluntary initiatives, as we use the term in this chapter, are programs that promote corporate self-regulation to the end of CR and are either led by business or have significant business involvement. They can involve just one or many stakeholders and may or may not include civil society or government. The range of such initiatives is vast. But they have three defining features: participation in them is voluntary, they each address one or more dimensions of CR, and they all afford some measure of dialogue to advance their focus area. By participating in a voluntary initiative, companies publicly commit themselves to a set of shared standards and principles of responsible behavior.

Voluntary initiatives have long played a prominent role in the CR sphere. A complete taxonomy is not possible here, but some of the more prominent initiatives are the UN Global Compact, the Kimberley Process,[9] the Voluntary Principles on Security and Human Rights,[10] and the Global Network Initiative;[11] there are many others.[12]

Voluntarism is the spirit animating voluntary initiatives. It represents corporate commitment to better citizenship. The best voluntary initiatives harness this commitment by building a space for diverse stakeholders to develop innovative solutions to the challenge of integrating sustainable corporate practices. They create a culture of transparency and accountability to ensure that businesses meet, and ideally exceed, their responsibilities.

The Virtues of Voluntarism

Understanding the virtues of voluntarism depends on placing the CR discussion in the proper context. We must identify the end being pursued. If the pursuit is merely bolstering the existing, state-centric, human rights regime, the tools will be found in that tool kit—of greater regulation and better enforcement. But if the end is better corporate behavior, the tools may have to be different, they may need to be more diffuse, less blunt, and more malleable to reshape corporate ends sustainably. We need a "smart mix of measures—national and international, mandatory and voluntary—to foster business respect for human rights."[13]

Voluntarism can help business and society approximate the ideal end by drawing on the power of the market to embed CR in business decision making. Specifically, voluntarism provides three types of benefits: (1) it reshapes business drivers, (2) it supports learning and flexibility of implementation approach, and (3) it reaches realms that the law cannot. Each of these will be discussed in more detail below.

Voluntarism Reshapes Business Drivers

The voluntarism in CR movement is built on the belief that it is possible to reform business ambition endogenously—that the profit motive, at least as currently understood, need not be business's sole reason for acting. Or if it is, that too can be harnessed to reshape business action so that the market creates the incentives needed to encourage business to pursue responsible behavior, particularly in the realm of human rights. This idea is embedded in the concept of business's "enlightened self-interest," which the UN Global Compact has recognized as a key driver of CR since its inception.[14]

Milton Friedman wrote in *Capitalism and Freedom* that the proponents of the social responsibility of business are beholden to "a fundamental misconception of the character and nature of a free economy. In such an economy, there is only one social responsibility of business—to use its resources and engage in activities designed to increase profits so long as it stays within the rules of the game, which is to say, engages in open and free competition without deception or fraud."[15] This view has long influenced the discussion of CR in the fields of economics. It informs the "shareholder approach" to CR, under which the only way to encourage corporate respect for human rights is to change the rules of the game.[16]

The debate regarding how best to ensure corporate respect for human rights is still largely framed by Friedman's perspective. Those who suggest that regulation alone is the answer implicitly embrace the idea that business is no more than a profit-making institution, restrained in this pursuit only by minimal "rules of the game." From this starting point, the focus is on changing the law to tame business's implicit and inescapable ends. But the basis of the movement to encourage voluntarism is different: it is to redefine corporate ends—to redefine "profits"—to incorporate nonmonetary social benefits, including respect for human rights.[17]

To many observers, responsible corporate behavior is simply the result of business recognizing that CR is necessary to protect and advance its financial bottom line.[18] As David Vogel notes: "in the final analysis, CSR is sustainable only if virtue pays off . . . companies will engage in CSR only to the extent that it makes business sense for them to do so."[19] But if CR is only undertaken for profit maximization, there is little need for a theory; companies will happen across it in any event as they pursue profits.[20]

The belief underpinning the pursuit of voluntarism is that, even if Friedman was right, his conclusion is limited by a dated and flat conception of "profit." The definitions of "business sense" and "financial profit" are not necessarily congruent. To the extent they once were effectively synonymous, that does not mean they always will be. Rather, business as an institution can embrace nonmonetary ends as part of its decision-making calculus—and it can do so independently of rules mandating such a change. Just as the pursuit of profit need not be legislated, so the pursuit of responsible behavior can become an endogenous business concern that walks hand in hand with the pursuit of monetary gain. The only question is how.

History is rife with examples of our evolving expectations of social institutions, and their evolving expectations of themselves. The evolution of the modern western state may be the best example. The Hobbesian state's only concerns were security and the assurance of wealth. The compact to create the state, as Hobbes imagined, was therefore to create a "mortal God" with ultimate sovereignty over all citizens.[21] The emergence of republican ideals over the next two centuries reshaped the responsibility of the state, so that its raison d'être shifted from simply providing security to protecting certain fundamental rights. The Lockean social contract accorded all individuals natural rights derived from natural law and posited that government's purpose was to protect these rights.[22] This tradition inspired the English Bill of Rights of 1689 and the American and French revolutions of the late eighteenth century.

The change in dominant philosophy regarding the state's role was fundamental to effect practical societal changes. It marked an essential reconceiving of the state's role as an institution in society that radically altered society's expectations and future interactions with the state. Of course, the radical change was neither instantaneous nor perfect. Vast swathes of the population remained disenfranchised. But the paradigm shift that brought individual rights to the fore of the state's responsibility allowed for a revised interaction between society and the state—one that was critical to the diffusion of rights and the march toward a steady enfranchisement of the entire population over the last two centuries.

Voluntarism's chief role is in instilling—in business as much as in society—the conceptual changes necessary to make business responsible. The state evolved as a social institution, with an increase in the scope of relevant stakeholders and responsibilities owed to them, under pressure applied by changing societal ideals. A similar pressure can reshape society's expectations of business. Business has already demonstrated a capacity to integrate social concerns in its pursuit of profit. Over the last two decades, for example, Nike and myriad other US clothing and apparel manufacturers have implemented mechanisms to monitor labor conditions at supplier factories in developing countries; Ikea has provided support to families in India to keep children out of the labor force; Starbucks has committed to selling only fair trade coffee; Shell has adopted policies to address human rights and environmental abuses in developing countries; PepsiCo has withdrawn investments from Myanmar due to human rights concerns.[23] While also a reaction to pressure from civil society, these voluntary actions in turn became baselines of business conduct against which other businesses are judged by society. They facilitate and further propel the evolution of business.

As long as we conceive of business as being a static institution with static character, we deny it the opportunity to aspire and evolve in ways that it has already showed it can. Support for voluntarism in the pursuit of CR is built on the ambition that "business sense" (or "profits") can be redefined in the same manner as the role of state was redefined. Voluntarism facilitates this redefinition by affording business the opportunity to embrace CR of its own free will and thereby engage with a broader array of stakeholders than its shareholders alone. Business's willing incorporation of responsibility for human rights can allow it to fashion for itself an end beyond mere financial remuneration, with a definition of profit that captures social ends.

At a fundamental level, of course, business will remain financially responsible to its owners. But owners (and consumers) consistently demonstrate the capacity for ethical evolution. These ethical shifts influence their interactions with business, which in turn shape the ends of business through the market. A number of studies have found that, in addition to profit, companies are often motivated to act responsibly in pursuit of moral or ethical beliefs.[24] And the growth of socially responsible investment funds demonstrates that owners and potential owners often value a broader understanding of performance than monetary profits alone.[25]

Michael Porter and Mark Kramer have noted that a key flaw uniting the current approaches to CR is the positioning of responsible behavior as a "cost" or a "constraint" rather than an "opportunity."[26] The danger in such a conception is that it encourages "cosmetic" responses to CR issues.[27] At its best, voluntarism allows businesses to, in the words of Porter and Kramer, "analyze their prospects for social responsibility using the same frameworks that guide their core business choices" and thus to treat CR as "a source of opportunity, innovation, and competitive advantage."[28]

Companies must, of course, comply with the law, whether or not it can be enforced. But voluntary initiatives have the unique potential to become corporate drivers. They can lead companies to strive to be better than the law requires and move beyond lowest-common-denominator standards or rules. Involvement in voluntary initiatives can inspire stakeholders' ambition and imagination, and can embed the quest for responsible behavior in the corporate culture. In this way, voluntary initiatives can ensure that if enforceable regulation is passed, it does not simply become a ceiling, but remains a floor.

Below are four specific ways in which voluntarism helps shape responsible corporate behavior endogenously:

(1) *Voluntarism can foster competition among organizations to be better corporate citizens*: Transparent and accountable, the best voluntary initiatives cast light on companies' true commitment to CR. Voluntary initiatives can thus draw on the corporate pursuit of competitive advantage to encourage innovation in search of the best sustainable practices. Evidence of this trend can already be found in the market as companies increasingly seek to differentiate themselves by marketing their CR activities.[29] Recent observations by private and public actors support this evidence.[30]

(2) *By shaping internal corporate drivers, voluntary initiatives can help bridge regulatory gaps*: The strength of voluntarism is that it can become self-sustaining. Voluntary initiatives can help bridge the void while regulation is being developed and raise the bar when regulation is either insufficient or improperly enforced. One notable example is Caring for Climate, a joint program of the UN Global Compact and the UN Environment Programme, which offers an interface for business and governments at the global level with the aim of (i) driving the development of pragmatic business solutions that transcend national interests (and law) and (ii) responding to the global nature of the issue at stake.[31]

(3) *Voluntary initiatives provide a forum for companies to inspire their employees*: More than ever before, the most qualified people are pursuing employment opportunities at companies whose principles align with their own. Recruits are willing to sacrifice income to work for companies with better reputations for CR and ethics.[32] Voluntary initiatives give companies the ability to differentiate themselves by demonstrating that CR is more than an obligation—it is an aspiration.

(4) *Voluntary initiatives help companies build brand equity*: The public increasingly demands corporate commitment to human rights, labor rights, environmental standards, and anticorruption measures. Voluntary initiatives encourage companies to pay heed to public demands by showcasing their commitment to CR in a way that mere legal compliance could never accomplish. The effect of CR initiatives on consumer goodwill is well documented.[33]

Voluntarism Supports Learning and Flexibility of Implementation

One of the repeatedly noted gaps in the CR sphere is the absence of implementation guidance.[34] Voluntarism provides a manner and venue to address this gap. As John Dewey noted about individuals' ability to reform themselves, "habits must intervene between wish and execution."[35]

Voluntary initiatives have the capacity to help business develop such habits. Dewey presented the example of a man learning to stand upright to illustrate the importance of practical implementation of an idea in order to perfect it:

> If we could form a correct idea without a correct habit, then possibly we could carry it out irrespective of habit. But a wish gets definite form only in connection with an idea, and an idea gets shape and consistency only when it has a habit back of it. Only when a man can already perform an act of standing straight does he know what it is like to have a right posture and only then can he summon the idea required for proper execution.[36]

Voluntarism can help shape business's understanding of CR by reshaping corporate ends through practice. Voluntary initiatives can create the practical foundation to explore and implement sustainable corporate practices. This learning and practical experience can, in turn, inform the development of effective regulation. Moreover, regulation may specify the required outcome but not how it is to be achieved. Voluntary initiatives can provide the opportunity for businesses and other stakeholders to come together to work out the best practices to achieve the required result.

Below are four examples of how voluntarism promotes adaptability and tailored CR measures:

(1) *Voluntary initiatives can facilitate the emergence of stakeholder consensus*: Legitimacy is critical to effective CR. Voluntary initiatives can inspire collaboration between stakeholders and business. In doing so, voluntary initiatives can help create new norms, building consensus that CR ought to be a mainstream business concern. For instance, the investors participating in the Principles for Responsible Investment, a voluntary investor initiative in partnership with the UNEP Finance Initiative and the UN Global Compact, used that initiative to develop a mandatory sustainability reporting policy that they then urged governments to adopt.[37] UN Global Compact has also managed to attract hundreds of commitments from CEOs of companies in different sectors around the world for its principles on climate, water, and women's empowerment.[38]

(2) *Voluntary initiatives provide flexibility to develop well-tailored responsible practices*: Sustainable corporate practices should be developed and implemented with sensitivity to the needs of different communities and stake-

holders. There is no one-size-fits-all approach. As Porter and Kramer note: "The same manufacturing operation will have very different social consequences in China than in the United States."[39] Responsible corporate practices must cater to different countries' and regions' governance institutions, history, business culture, and geography. Voluntary initiatives are invaluable in this regard: they can offer stakeholders a forum in which to apprehend locale-specific responses to unique challenges. Indeed, this is a key function of the Global Compact Local Networks—clusters of Global Compact participants who come together to advance the UN Global Compact and its principles within a particular geographic context. Among other things, they help anchor the UN Global Compact within different national, cultural, and language contexts.

(3) *Voluntary initiatives can limit the risks and costs of CR*: Effective CR programs require investment of time and resources. Voluntary initiatives can lower these costs by bringing together stakeholders from business and civil society to cooperate in developing shared standards and common understanding of best practices for implementation. This cross-spectrum cooperation can help stakeholders to identify, prevent, and mitigate business risks while implementing approaches that cater to the interests of many different stakeholders. One area of fruitful collaboration is sustainable supply chain management, where the costs of identifying and addressing risks can be very high. As a result, many businesses have joined voluntary initiatives to improve their efficiency and effectiveness in managing such risks.[40]

(4) *Voluntary initiatives can provide a forum for cross-spectrum stakeholder collaboration*: Developing effective CR standards depends on learning from past actions and adapting to changing circumstances. There are no definitive answers. Voluntary initiatives spur the learning process by providing a space for diverse stakeholders—from business to civil society—to discuss issues and collaborate in resolving them. Regulation, in contrast, almost never incorporates this "partnership" dimension. UN Global Compact constantly sees the value in such collaboration and has consequently focused on developing multistakeholder working groups, including on human rights.

Voluntarism Reaches Realms That Law Cannot

The unique issues that arise with business responsibility for human rights are all the more reason for the virtues of voluntarism. Voluntarism can perform functions the law cannot. Law offers, although does not always deliver, the virtue of enforceability. A breached law accords the state the right to exercise the prerogatives of the legitimate monopoly of violence. But law is not a panacea for all. In particular, as Amartya Sen has noted, understanding human rights solely through a legal lens may be "foundationally mistaken."[41]

There are at least four limitations in law's ability to ensure that companies respect and support human rights. First, law often sets itself up in opposition to the free will—its enforceability defines it, undermining the substance it carries by virtue of its form. Second, law is inherently fixed, limited in jurisdictional scope and predictable. If not, it is arguably not law at all. But these virtues facilitate the pursuit of evasive measures by those who have been set up in opposition to it. Third, law is fundamentally reactive. It addresses transgressions of the past while attempting to envision wrongs of the future, but always with the limited scope that history offers. Fourth, as Sen notes, it would be difficult to accept that the only relevant human rights are the ones protected by legislation.[42] That is, the pursuit of human rights has been and should remain forward-looking; it is necessarily grounded in ideals that to some extent are reflected in, but also that transcend, the law. Thus even the corporate responsibility to respect human rights is not wholly a legal responsibility; nor does it exist in a "law free zone."[43]

The question for proponents of CR, then, is how to address the law's weaknesses. In short, how can we bolster law? And how, in particular, can we bolster the deficiencies of law in the context of business and human rights? In a world of perfect laws perfectly enforced, there might be no need for business to bear a specific, defined responsibility for human rights—compliance with law would be sufficient to attain that end. But the push for CR is largely a product of the drive to help perfect the law. In the words of John Ruggie, CR for human rights suggests that stakeholders and business be willing to look "beyond compliance."[44]

The human rights responsibility of business under the *Guiding Principles* is, on its face, vast: "Business enterprises should respect human rights. This means that they should avoid infringing on the human rights of others and should address human rights impacts with which they are involved."[45] Whereas the state obligation for human rights flows from a deemed control over a particular territory and a monopoly on the legitimate use of violence, the obligation borne by business is qualitatively different because it has neither deemed control nor the state's role as arbiter of justice.

Defining the scope of this responsibility, and its mandates in particular circumstances, is a herculean task that may never be fully accomplished by law or jurisprudence. In the first place, there is great divergence regarding the interpretation of even the most fundamental rights. For example, the Indian Supreme Court understands the right to life far more expansively than the American Supreme Court; the conception of freedom of religion in France and Turkey permits far more limitations on religious practice than in Canada or the United Kingdom; freedom of speech is arguably more circumscribed in the European Union than in the United States; and the socioeconomic rights recognized in South Africa and India receive a far chillier reception in North America. Against this backdrop, the business context adds the complicating nuance of causation to apprehend a private actor's liability for any particular human rights violation. Businesses "should avoid infringing on the human rights of others and should address adverse human rights impacts with which they are involved."[46] The scope of "involvement" extends to human rights impacts (1) that are "caused" or "contributed to" by the business and (2) those that are "directly linked to their operations, products or services by their business relationships, even if they have not contributed to those impacts."[47] The scope of actions and omissions caught by this responsibility will take much time to define.

Voluntarism offers the only manner of approximating the desired end of business respect for human rights while law crystallizes. Given the nature of the enterprise, however, voluntarism will always be necessary to ensure that business is aspiring to adopt the spirit of the obligation in good faith even if law is passed. As the law develops to solidify the meaning of such inchoate concepts as "directly linked to," it is incumbent on business to do its very best to develop or contribute to the development of meaningful guidance. Otherwise, it is human rights that suffer.

Case Study: The Contribution of the UN Global Compact as a Voluntary Corporate Sustainability Initiative

Launched in mid-2000, the UN Global Compact has for over a decade been the world's largest CR initiative, with over twelve thousand business and civil society signatories in more than 145 countries and approximately one hundred Local Networks at the country level around the world. Participating companies voluntarily commit to align their business strategies and operations with ten universally accepted principles, derived from UN Conventions and Declarations, in the areas of human rights, labor, the environment, and anticorruption, as well as to take additional voluntary actions in support of UN goals, such as the Millennium Development Goals. The initiative's mandate comes from the UN General Assembly: to advance United Nations values and responsible business practices within the United Nations system and among the global business community.[48]

The overall mission of the Global Compact is to contribute to bringing about more sustainable and inclusive global markets through advancing the practice of corporate sustainability globally. Global Compact defines corporate sustainability as a company's delivery of long-term value in financial, social, environmental, and ethical terms.[49] The social dimension of corporate sustainability encompasses business "respect" and "support" for human rights and international labor standards. It includes both preventing and addressing harm to human rights linked to their business ("respect") and encourages additional voluntary action in support of realizing human rights ("support").[50] Such voluntary action can be in the form of core business approaches, such as inclusive business models or innovation in product and service design and delivery, strategic social investment/philanthropy, public policy engagement/advocacy, or partnerships or other forms of collective action. Corporate participants are required to communicate their progress in implementing the principles to their own stakeholders on an annual basis, and, to make such communications more transparent, they are required to also share them through the UN Global Compact website.

The UN General Assembly has called the Global Compact "an innovative public-private partnership"[51] and recognized the "positive contribution of the Global Compact and its ten principles in the promotion of responsible business practices."[52] Survey results support the General Assembly's conclusion that the Global Compact makes a positive contribution to CR. The first extensive survey of Global Compact participants was conducted by McKinsey & Company in 2004 as part of the review that they conducted of the initiative's first four years of operations. The independently prepared report, "Assessing the Global Compact's Impact," was based on extensive data analysis, interviews, and surveys conducted with a range of stakeholders, including Global Compact participants as well as outside observers and detractors. Their overall assessment was that the Global Compact has had "noticeable, incremental impact on companies, the UN, governments and other civil society actors. A solid participant base and the power of the idea of high-level UN engagement with the private sector have largely driven these successes to date."[53]

While also revealing opportunities for improvement, their survey found that 67 percent of survey respondents said that they had changed their corporate policies in relation to human rights, labor, and environmental principles since joining the Global Compact, and 40 percent attributed the Global Compact as a significant driver of these changes.[54] Their survey also found that approximately 67 percent of survey respondents from developing countries said that they had joined the Global Compact to become more familiar with CR issues, thus helping to embed them in the agenda in those countries.[55] One of the conclusions of the McKinsey Report was that the "symbolism of the Global Compact's creation and its established brand" are surprisingly influential.[56] It also noted that "corporate citizenship champions within companies have leveraged their leaders' commitments to the Global Compact as a wedge to push their corporate citizenship agendas."[57]

Research conducted more recently confirms such trends. It supports the conclusion that the Global Compact is having a significant impact on improving the overall level of CR of its corporate participants. For the past six years, the initiative has worked with the Wharton School of the University of Pennsylvania to conduct an annual implementation survey to gauge the initiative's impact and track participant performance. The Global Compact Implementation Survey assesses how—and to what extent—participating companies are implementing policies and taking action on the ten principles and in support of broader UN goals and issues. The results of the most recent survey are published in the 2013 Global Compact Sustainability Report.[58] In 2013, 1,712 companies from 112 countries responded to the Global Compact Implementation Survey on which the report is based—making it the world's largest annual study conducted on CR policies and practices by business globally. In the survey, Global Compact participants are asked a range of questions about their current level of sustainability performance, what their needs are from the Global Compact, and the Global Compact's impact on their sustainability strategy and actions.

Key findings from the most recent survey included that companies committed to the UN Global Compact are moving from good intentions to significant actions. However, while progress is being made, there is a long journey ahead for companies to fully embed responsible practices across their organizations and supply chain. Companies are making commitments, defining goals, and setting policies at high rates, but still have much work to do to on the action steps. For example, 65 percent of respondents develop sustainability policies at the CEO level, while only 35 percent currently train managers to integrate sustainability into strategies and operations. Moreover, while small and large companies are committing to the UN Global Compact in equal numbers, large companies are significantly more likely to move beyond commitment to action across all issue areas. Supplier sustainability ranks as the top barrier for large companies in their advancement to the next level of sustainability performance. While a majority of companies have established sustainability expectations for their suppliers, they are challenged to track compliance and help suppliers reach goals. And the survey found that 70 percent of Global Compact companies are advancing broad UN goals and issues by aligning their core business strategy, tying social investment to core competencies, advocating the need for action, and implementing partnership projects.[59]

The survey conducted in 2012 also looked at the top reasons why companies engage in the UN Global Compact and found that they were: to increase trust in their company, integration of sustainability issues, the universal nature of the UN Global Compact principles, and the opportunity to network with other organizations.[60] It also showed that more than 90 percent of participants considered that their participation in the Global Compact has had a positive impact on the quality of their CR policies and practices.[61] Thirty-eight percent of companies stated that participation in the Global Compact has either significantly helped or was essential to advancing their CR policies and practices. Eighty-one percent of companies indicated at least moderate impact on their CR performance from engaging in the Global Compact.

These results are consistent with findings of an OECD study in 2001, which analyzed a large variety of CR initiatives and concluded, already at that time, that the proliferation of CR initiatives was a key trend and a global phenomenon.[62] The study looked at the potential benefits for businesses and society of such initiatives, noting as some of the benefits: improved legal compliance, management of litigation risks, brand and reputation enhancement, smoother stakeholder relations, and increased employee morale.[63] The main benefit for society observed was concrete improvement in business practices.[64] The study drew on the OECD experience that compliance with behavioral norms does not result solely from monitoring and threats of punishment and focused on two intangible assets that they considered play an important role in achieving greater compliance with those norms: consensus and management expertise.[65] The study pointed to "growing recognition that a critical mass of understanding, agreement and consent underpins any effective system for controlling business behavior."[66] A brief review was provided of some literature on the limits of law enforcement alone to ensure compliance and the value of supplementing law with other approaches that build consensus around social norms and promote voluntary compliance.[67] A key conclusion of the report was that voluntary initiatives were already making progress in helping to accumulate these assets—consensus and expertise—on a global scale, although much more remains to be done.[68]

The value of a smart mix of voluntary and regulatory instruments in propelling CR forward is underscored by a study conducted for the UN Global Compact by Accenture in 2013. It examined more than one thousand CEOs' attitudes toward the trajectory for corporate sustainability. It revealed that more than two-thirds of chief executives believe that business is not doing enough to address global sustainability challenges. While showing that CEOs are strongly committed to embedding sustainability throughout their organizations, the vast majority are now calling for action to incentivize and reward sustainability leaders in order to accelerate progress. The study demonstrates broadening awareness on the part of global business of the opportunities presented by sustainability. Seventy-eight percent of the surveyed CEOs see sustainability as a route to growth and innovation, and 79 percent believe that it will lead to competitive advantage in their industry. Nevertheless, CEOs see the economic climate and a range of competing priorities creating obstacles to embedding sustainability at scale within their companies. While 84 percent believe that business should lead the way in addressing sustainability challenges, they point to a number of barriers: lack of financial resources making it difficult to embed sustainability into core business; the failure to make the link between sustainability and business value; lack of interest on the part of consumers (even though 82 percent of CEOs think this is critical to harnessing sustainability as a transformative force in the economy); and insufficient investor interest (while

52 percent of respondents saw investor interest as an incentive for them to advance sustainability practices, only 12 percent saw investor pressure as a leading motivator). Sixty-nine percent believed that investor interest will be increasingly important in guiding their approach. In addition, 83 percent of respondents thought more efforts by governments to provide the enabling environment for corporate sustainability will be integral to the private sector's ability to advance sustainability. As well as pointing to the role of regulation (55 percent), respondents highlighted government subsidies and incentives (43 percent) and taxation (31 percent) as important policy tools. The results underscore that there are important opportunities for consumers and investors as well as policy makers to play their role in creating demand for higher performance on CR, but also that business has a key role to play in creating sustainable products and services at prices that people can afford and impressing investors not just by saving costs, but also by generating business value.[69] These are functions that regulation alone is ill suited to mandate.

Some research conducted with AccountAbility in 2013 elaborated on the kinds of benefits that business can derive from making voluntary corporate sustainability commitments that can help the business to improve its corporate sustainability performance regardless of the stage they are at in their corporate sustainability journey.[70] It highlighted the following as flowing from making a voluntary corporate sustainability commitment, such as joining the UN Global Compact: building internal and external credibility, improving risk management processes and systems, enhancing brand reputation, identifying new business opportunities, developing innovative practices and policies, and attracting and retaining talent.[71] Regulation alone does not deliver such benefits.

For those with a maturing CR strategy, the research identified the business value that could flow from scaling up engagement around a voluntary corporate sustainability commitment such as adopting performance management systems that increase organizational efficiency, engaging in more constructive dialogue with all stakeholders, improving reporting processes and external accountability, and enhancing human capital through education and training.[72] And for those that are fairly advanced in their implementation of voluntary CR commitments, the study highlighted the following benefits for more deeper engagement: setting new industry standards and aspirations, promoting shared values and collective benefits, improving business performance through the creation of new business practices and systems of governance, and engaging in policy development to advance sustainability commitment adoption.[73] Reinforcing the case made in this article, such benefits derive from voluntary engagement and not from regulation alone. For such reasons, the UN Global Compact continues to advocate for the smart mix of voluntary and regulatory approaches, of carrots and sticks, of incentives and disincentives, and a role for all stakeholders, including but not limited to governments, in scaling up corporate sustainability.

Conclusion

The business and human rights movement is at a watershed moment. The UN Human Rights Council's formal endorsement of the *Guiding Principles* in June 2011 marked a critical level of acceptance for business responsibility for human rights. Accepting this principle offers a remarkable opportunity. On the one hand, proponents of CR could focus their attention exclusively on restraining the market by advocating the passage of laws forcing business to respect human rights. On the other, the CR movement could seek to reshape the way business is done altogether, by drawing on changing social ideals and ethics to influence the ends business pursues endogenously as a complement not substitute for other approaches.

Voluntarism has significant virtues in this regard. Rather than setting up CR for human rights as a constraint on the pursuit of profit, voluntarism draws on the power of the market to redefine what companies expect of themselves. The growing recognition that business is a social institution—by society, government, and business itself—offers proponents of CR the opportunity to seize on business's internal motivators to recast the natural ends of business. Business, for its part, is increasingly appreciating that voluntarism in the field of human rights offers clear business benefits. As one executive of a multinational recently explained:

> We do not just need a social license to operate, we need a social license to operate and *grow*. With our growth plans, it is not enough to be merely tolerated. An important element of our future business success and achieving our ambitious business goals will depend on our operations being welcome in the communities and societies where we operate.[74]

Notes

This chapter is adapted from Ursula Wynhoven and Yousuf Aftab, "Why We Volunteer: Corporate Responsibility, Human Rights, and the UN Global Compact," *In-House Defense Quarterly*, Winter 2013, 44–70.

1. Over time, the Global Compact has used a variety of terms to describe its main focus area: *corporate citizenship*, *corporate responsibility*, and more recently *corporate sustainability*.

2. "Ten Principles," UN Global Compact, accessed April 1, 2014, http://www .unglobalcompact.org/aboutthegc/thetenprinciples/.

3. "Guiding Principles on Business and Human Rights: Implementing the United Nations 'Protect, Respect and Remedy' Framework," [Guiding Principles] Office of the High Commissioner for Human Rights, accessed April 12, 2014, http://www.ohchr.org/Documents/Publications/GuidingPrinciplesBusiness HR_EN.pdf.

4. The *Guiding Principles* were unanimously endorsed by the UN Human Rights Council and have been incorporated in the "OECD Guidelines for Multinational Enterprises," Organisation for Economic Co-operation and Development, last accessed April 12, 2014, http://www.oecd.org/daf/inv/mne/48004323 .pdf; and the IFC Performance Standard guidance materials, which emphasize that Performance Standard 1, concerning Assessment and Management of Environmental and Social Risks and Impacts, "reflects the 'respect' and 'remedy' aspects of [the *Guiding Principles*]," "Guidance Note 1: Assessment and Management of Environmental and Social Risks and Impacts," International Finance Corporation, accessed April 16, 2014, http://www.ifc.org/wps/wcm/connect/ b29a4600498009cfa7fcf7336b93d75f/Updated_GN1-2012.pdf?MOD=AJPERES.

5. *Guiding Principles*, Commentary to Art. II.A.11.

6. This chapter draws on the concept of "respect" as it is used in the *Guiding Principles*, incorporating the responsibility to avoid "causing or contributing to adverse human rights impacts" and the responsibility to "seek to prevent or mitigate adverse human rights impacts that are directly linked to their operations." (Guiding Principles, Art. II.A.13.)

7. Consistently with the UN Global Compact's preferred terminology, we will use the terms *corporate responsibility* and *corporate sustainability* rather than *corporate social responsibility*.

8. Amartya Sen, "Human Rights and the Limits of Law," *Cardozo Law Review* 27, no. 6 (2006): 2919.

9. "Kimberley Process," accessed April 16, 2014, http://www.kimberley process .com.

10. "Voluntary Principles on Security and Human Rights," accessed April 16, 2014, http://www.voluntaryprinciples.org.

11. "Global Network Initiative," accessed April 16, 2014, http://www.global networkinitiative.org.

12. In 2005, the USCIB compiled a compendium of the major corporate responsibility initiatives grouped by type of originating organization (government or intergovernmental, private sector, NGO). They selected twenty-five. "Compendium of Corporate Responsibility Initiatives," USCIB, accessed April 16, 2014, http://www.uscib.org/index.asp?DocumentID=2602.

13. Report of the Special Representative of the Secretary-General on the issue of human rights and transnational corporations and other business enterprises, John Ruggie, Guiding Principles on Business and Human Rights: Implementing the United Nations "Protect, Respect and Remedy" Framework, A/HRC/17/31, p. 8.

14. See, e.g., Georg Kell, "Dilemmas in Competitiveness, Community, and Citizenship Business and Human Rights Seminar—Toward Universal Business Principles," remarks presented at the London School of Economics and Political Science, London, United Kingdom, May 22, 2001, accessed April 16, 2014, http://www.unglobalcompact.org/NewsAndEvents/speeches_and_statements/london_school_of_economics.html.

15. Milton Friedman, *Capitalism and Freedom* (Chicago: Chicago University Press, 1962), 133.

16. Marcel van Marrewijk, "A Typology of Institutional Frameworks Supporting Corporate Sustainability," accessed April 16, 2014, http://www.vanmarrewijk.nl/pdf/Typology%200f%20institutional%20frameworks%20supporting%20CS.2.pdf.

17. A related shift entails seeing business's role as doing well by doing good (CR), rather than doing well in order to do good (philanthropy alone). Friedman seemed to be particularly opposed to the latter.

18. See, e.g., David A. Waldman, Donald S. Siegel, and Mansour Javidan, "CEO Transformational Leadership and Corporate Social Responsibility," *Rensselaer Working Papers in Economics* 0415 (2004), accessed April 16, 2014, http://www.economics.rpi.edu/workingpapers/rpi0415.pdf; Herman Aguinis and Ante Glavas, "What We Know and Don't Know about Corporate Social Responsibility: A Review and Research Agenda," *Journal of Management* 38, no. 4 (2012): 932–68.

19. Waldman, Siegel, and Javidan, "CEO Transformational Leadership and Corporate Social Responsibility," 3–4.

20. But are all business decisions rational? See, e.g., D. Ariely, "The End of Rational Economics," *Harvard Business Review*, July 2009, http://hbr.org/2009/07/the-end-of-rational-economics/ar/1.

21. Leo Strauss, "The Spirit of Hobbes's Political Philosophy," in *Hobbes Studies*, ed. K. C. Brown (Oxford: Basil Blackwell, 1965), 12–13.

22. Paul Gordon Lauren, "A Human Rights Lens on U.S. History: Human

Rights at Home and Human Rights Abroad," in *Bringing Human Rights Home: A History of Human Rights in the United States*, ed. Cynthia Soohoo, Catherine Albisa, and Martha F. Davis (Philadelphia: University of Pennsylvania Press, 2009), 9.

23. David Vogel, *The Market for Virtue: The Potential and Limits of Corporate Social Responsibility* (Washington, DC: Brookings Institution Press, 2006), 2.

24. Pratima Bansal and Kendall Roth, "Why Companies Go Green: A Model of Ecological Responsiveness," *Academy of Management Journal* 43 (2000): 717–36; Ruth V. Aguilera, Deborah E. Rupp, Cynthia A. Williams, and Jyoti Ganapathi, "Putting the S Back in Corporate Social Responsibility: A Multilevel Theory of Social Change in Organizations," *Academy of Management Review* 32 (2007): 836–63; James H. Davis, F. David Schoorman, and Lex Donaldson, "Toward a Stewardship Theory of Management," *Academy of Management Review* 22 (1997): 20–47.

25. "Report on Sustainable and Responsible Investing Trends in the United States 2012," The Forum for Sustainable and Responsible Investment, accessed April 15, 2014, 5, http://www.ussif.org/files/Publications/12_Trends_Exec _Summary.pdf: "For example, the Principles for Responsible Investment has more than 1,000 signatory firms—with assets over $30 trillion—estimated to represent 20 percent of the total value of global capital markets. These signatories include not only the pioneers of sustainable and responsible investing but also more conventional investment firms that are beginning to develop SRI divisions or to analyze how portfolio companies' environmental, social and corporate governance (ESG) policies affect their financial returns. Today, there is no longer any 'typical kind of firm' engaged in SRI."

26. Michael E. Porter and Mark R. Kramer, "Strategy and Society: The Link between Competitive Advantage and Corporate Social Responsibility," *Harvard Business Review* (2006), accessed April 16, 2014, http://efnorthamerica .com/documents/events/ccc2008/Mark-Kramer-Keynote/Strategy-Society.PDF.

27. Ibid.

28. Ibid.

29. Adam Lindgreen and Valerie Swaen, "Corporate Social Responsibility," *International Journal of Management Reviews* 12 (2010): 1–7.

30. See http://www.unglobalcompact.org/NewsAndEvents/news_archives/ 2008_01_25.html; see also Norwegian Ministry of Foreign Affairs, Report No. 10 to the Storting (2008–2009), "Corporate Social Responsibility in a Global Economy," accessed April 16, 2014, http://www.regjeringen.no/pages/2203320/ PDFS/STM200820090010000EN_PDFS.pdf.

31. Ibid.

32. Deborah E. Rupp, Jyoti Ganapathi, Ruth V. Aguilera, and Cynthia A. Williams, "Employee Reactions to Corporate Social Responsibility: An Orga-

nizational Justice Framework," *Journal of Organizational Behavior* 27 (2006): 537–43; Sean Valentine and Gary Fleischman, "Ethics Programs, Perceived Corporate Social Responsibility, and Job Satisfaction," *Journal of Business Ethics* 77 (2008): 159–72.

33. Steven Brammer, Andrew Millington, and Bruce Rayton, "The Contribution of Corporate Social Responsibility to Organizational Commitment," *International Journal of Human Resource Management* 18 (2007): 1701–19; Isabelle Maignan and David A. Ralston, "Corporate Social Responsibility in Europe and the U.S.: Insights from Businesses' Self-Presentations," *Journal of International Business Studies* 33 (2002): 497–514.

34. See, for instance, Lindgreen and Swaen, "Corporate Social Responsibility," 1–7.

35. John Dewey, *Human Nature and Conduct: An Introduction to Social Psychology* (New York: Cosimo, 2007), 30.

36. Ibid.

37. "PRI Supports Corporate Sustainability Reporting Coalition," Principles for Responsible Investment, accessed April 16, 2014, http://www.unpri.org/press/pri-supports-corporate-sustainability-reporting-coalition.

38. See "Climate Change," UN Global Compact, http://www.unglobalcompact.org/Issues/Environment/Climate_Change/, www.ceowatermandate.org and www.weprinciples.org.

39. Porter and Kramer, "Strategy and Society," 4.

40. Many of these initiatives are highlighted in the Global Compact/CSE Europe supply chain resource portal: http://supply-chain.unglobalcompact.org.

41. Sen, "Human Rights and the Limits of Law," at 2914.

42. Ibid., 2915.

43. See, for example, John F. Sherman III, The UN Guiding Principles for the Corporate Legal Advisor: Corporate Governance, Risk Management, and Professional Responsibility, April 4, 2012.

44. John Ruggie, "Business and Human Rights: The Evolving International Agenda," Corporate Social Responsibility Initiative, Working Paper No. 31 (Cambridge, MA: John F. Kennedy School of Government, Harvard University).

45. *Guiding Principles*, Art. II.A.11.

46. Ibid., Art. A.II.11.

47. Ibid., Art. A.II.13.

48. United Nations General Assembly Resolution A/RES/66/223, Preamble, accessed April 16, 2014, http://www.unglobalcompact.org/docs/about_the_gc/government_support/FINAL_A_RES_66_223.pdf.

49. See, e.g., UN Global Compact, Global Corporate Sustainability Report 2013, http://www.unglobalcompact.org/docs/about_the_gc/Global_Corporate_Sustainability_Report2013.pdf, accessed August 17, 2014.

50. UN Global Compact and OHCHR, UN Guiding Principles on Busi-

ness and Human Rights: Relationship to UN Global Compact commitments, at http://www.unglobalcompact.org/docs/issues_doc/human_rights/Resources/GPs_GC%20note.pdf.

51. United Nations General Assembly Resolution A/RES/64/223, Art. 13.

52. Ibid., Art. 14.

53. McKinsey & Company, "Assessing the Global Compact's Impact," UN Global Compact, accessed May 11, 2004, http://www.unglobalcompact.org/NewsAndEvents/news_archives/2004_06_09.html.

54. Ibid.

55. Ibid.

56. Ibid., 13.

57. Ibid.

58. UN Global Compact "Global Compact Sustainability Report 2013," accessed April 17, 2014, http://www.unglobalcompact.org/AboutTheGC/global_corporate_sustainability_report.html.

59. Ibid.

60. "Annual Review of Business Policies and Actions to Advance Sustainability," 2011 Global Compact Implementation Survey, 2012, accessed April 16, 2014, http://www.unglobalcompact.org/docs/news_events/8.1/2011_Global_Compact_Implementation_Survey.pdf.

61. Ibid.

62. "Corporate Responsibility: Private Initiatives and Public Goals," OECD (2001), accessed April 16, 2014, 9, http://www.oecd.org/industry/inv/corporate responsibility/35315900.pdf.

63. Ibid., 10.

64. Ibid.

65. Ibid., 12.

66. Ibid., 16.

67. Ibid., 15–16.

68. Ibid.

69. The UN Global Compact-Accenture CEO Study on Sustainability 2013: Architects of a Better World, http://www.accenture.com/Microsites/ungc-ceo-study/Pages/home.aspx?c=mc_prposts_10000048&n=otc_1013, accessed April 17, 2014.

70. AccountAbility and UN Global Compact, Growing into Your Sustainability Commitments: A Roadmap for Impact and Value Creation, accessed April 17, 2014, http://unglobalcompact.org/docs/publications/AA_UNGC_Report.pdf.

71. Ibid.

72. Ibid.

73. Ibid.

74. Dan Bena, Pepsico, as told to Ursula Wynhoven.

PART III

Africa as CSR Laboratory

Twenty-First-Century Corporate
Strategy and State Building

Charlotte Walker-Said

The doctrine of economic rights in their late twentieth-century expression is a core component of Africa's monetary policies as well
as its central political claim. "Economic rights" have origins in early
twentieth-century liberalism articulated by Western leaders, jurists, and
scholars. In 1932, Franklin Roosevelt called for a framing of economic
and social guarantees as rights, stating, "Private economic power is, to
enlarge an old phrase, a public trust as well." Roosevelt later developed
the philosophical foundations of economic rights in his Four Freedoms,
particularly the "freedom from want." After Czech jurist Karel Vasak
positioned economic rights as part of a "second generation" of human
rights that would outline the responsibilities of governments in the postwar period, economic rights were delineated in Chapter IX of the UN
Charter and the Universal Declaration of Human Rights (UDHR) as
well as the 1966 International Covenant on Economic, Social and Cultural Rights (CESCR).

With the rise of transnational economic linkages during the 1970s,
the world's leaders expressed the need for employment and social security to provide the economic context within which other human rights
could be achieved. W. Arthur Lewis, a founder of development economics and the architect of Ghana's postindependence economy, was shaped

by postwar concerns for economic progress and pioneered early development programs that were structured around rights that would lead to human betterment. Pursuant to this, "the right to development" was coined
by the Senegalese jurist Kéba M'baye in 1972, and in 1981, the right to
development was written into the African Charter on Human and Peoples' Rights and passed as a United Nations charter in 1986. During the
1970s and 1980s, development rights consciousness pushed itself to the
forefront of the human rights agenda in Africa, as postcolonial nation-
states and regions of communist revolution were often unsuccessful in
translating utopian visions into lived realities for political and economic
justice. In these new transnational declarations, the African citizen was
entitled not only to legal security and civic and political participation
but also to economic security and social well-being. However, during the
late 1970s and 1980s, citizenries across the continent faced currency de-
valuations, oil shocks, and national debt crises, which plunged a great
majority into penury and consequently shook the political foundations
of states. The remedy presented during the late 1980s was a cleared path
for the shift in idealizations of the state in Africa as the guarantor of liberty and capacity toward the private sector as the emancipator of unfree
markets, unfree labor, and unfree populations.

Theories on the human rights obligations of international monetary cooperation, global economic development, and poverty reduction, and their dependence on agents of capital, still appear to be moving
the world toward a new "utopia" of supranational governance and away
from the nation-state framework. Currently, economic development is
controlled as much (or more) by agents of capital as by nation-states, and
while states can instigate or support development processes, agents outside of the state often determine growth parameters and returns on investment. The state's unmooring as the fundamental source of human
rights guarantees partially reflects the state's own support for the doctrine of economic rights as a means to secure development. Throughout
Africa, states have procured aid and foreign direct investment by employing the rhetoric of global economic justice. Those African governments excluded from the decision-making processes of international financial institutions have been left to appeal to humanitarian concerns
for poverty. However, despite the power and influence of markets, the
state in Africa remains deeply relevant and often a primary determinant
regarding the returns on development investment, despite evidence for
the growing strength of substate actors, as Will Reno, Charlotte Walker-

Said, Lauren Coyle, and Richard Joseph, Kelly Spence, and Abimbola Agboluaje illustrate here.

The authors of this section engage directly with the history of the decades-long struggle against poverty and dispossession on the African continent and the contemporary tensions between international human rights regimes, economic rights mandates, local development agendas, and the transformation of the nation-state in Africa. These scholars examine abstract concepts such as market forces and rights theories as well as concrete agents like civil society leaders, rebel groups, government ministers, and corporate CEOs—offering compelling evidence that discourses can stimulate practices and compel action. Each chapter presented here illustrates a particular agency's, government's, or entity's pragmatic engagement with a corporation or corporations' CSR agenda and the consequences of such engagement.

While private enterprises and industries can dominate the economic and the political space of nations, and can thus influence political and economic outcomes for citizens, these corporate agents are being forced to contend with an increasing variety of competitors in the economic and political spheres. For instance, as Coyle as well as Joseph, Spence, and Agboluaje discuss, NGOs have forged subnational, transnational alliances to increase financial ties and knowledge sharing and coordinate political protest. Reno's work draws connections between international criminal enterprises and domestic militant factions—demonstrating that economic integration can benefit those who operate above and below the nation-state. Advanced communications, monetary flow, transportation, and deregulation have created unprecedented opportunities for a greater variety of actors who not only compete with the state but also compete in and with the market for power and profit. Walker-Said demonstrates that market-oriented multilateral institutions and investment-hungry nation-states have created a blended ideology—sustainability—that champions human, state, and corporate rights concomitantly in order to protect economic and political stability and to guarantee better outcomes for most.

The African experience with rights agendas and CSR governance reveals that humanitarian ideals and transnational governmental programs are powerful forms of agency and legitimization. As these chapters reveal, they can be forces for mass principled engagement and mobilization, but they can also posit challenging agendas that are then co-opted by institutions that are far from human-centered.

CHAPTER TWELVE

CSR and Corporate Engagement with Parties to Armed Conflicts

William Reno

The efforts of international organizations and others to sanction corporations that do business with armed groups in ongoing conflicts follow the logic of doctrines, such as the Responsibility to Protect, that empower the international community to intervene to shield civilians from serious harm when their own government is unable or unwilling to do so.[1] These efforts to sanction such corporations also reflect the development of more targeted and effective international sanctions schemes from the late 1990s. The first section of this chapter examines how historical precedent, particularly the prosecution of corporate actors for war crimes before the Nuremberg tribunal after the Second World War, shapes the evolution of recent efforts to define the limits of legitimate corporate action in armed conflicts and how to prosecute corporations that operate outside these bounds.

Ultimately, this effort to define CSR in armed conflicts in terms of sanctions and prosecutions has political impacts—intended and unintended—that affect the courses of these conflicts and the resources and interests of a broad array of armed actors. The second section of this chapter focuses on these political effects. In particular, it traces how parties to armed conflicts learn to manipulate for their own interests the nascent efforts to prosecute corporations for war crimes. These efforts to prosecute corporations, like other international efforts to sanction actors in armed conflicts, tend to favor actors that represent sovereign states. This outcome reflects how evolving global norms concerning CSR

in conflict zones and armed conflict more generally reflect structural bi-
ases that favor sovereign interlocutors that are built into the contemporary international system. This is a paradoxical development, given that
these norms are predicated on a willingness to infringe on customary
sovereign prerogatives that include protection against outside interference. Of greater practical importance is how sovereign actors that are
generally regarded as having weak internal capabilities and relatively little influence in global society learn to use evolving CSR norms, including sanctions against corporations, to bolster their domestic and international political positions.

The third section of this chapter investigates an emerging broader political effect of this application of CSR in conflict zones that is related to
the empowerment of sovereign actors—the contrary tendency of evolving global norms to hinder the fortunes of rebel groups. While this is
often the intended impact, particularly of CSR in war zones, this section examines how rebels and civilian populations perceive these actions. Some may perceive that prosecutions of corporations that do business with rebels will weaken armed actors that are systematic violators
of human rights; others may view this as an obstacle to the right to rebel
against a tyrannical government and a powerful conservative force that
favors incumbent sovereign power.

Precedent

It is no surprise that armed groups engage in commerce in wartime. Most
armed groups at some point need to seek out commercial contacts to buy
weapons, particularly if they lack the capacity to capture weapons from
their enemies. Bolshevik revolutionaries in the 1900s robbed banks to finance arms purchases and revolutionary activities, for example. Prior to
the First World War, one of their number, Maxim Litvinov, traveled in
Europe with these ill-gotten resources, posing as a businessman to buy
guns and ammunition from arms dealers.[2] After their seizure of power
in 1917, the Soviet Union's new leaders invited foreign firms to negotiate
for concessions to exploit oil and other mineral resources in areas they
controlled even though many governments still considered the Bolshe-
viks to be rebels and had not recognized their government.[3]

Armed groups often use coercion to influence or appropriate commercial activities in territories they control. This activity can include the

theft of property during wartime that is then sold to raise income. Scholars link this commerce, particularly in portable natural resources, to violent behavior that violates the rights of civilians because it provides incentives to armed groups to compete with one another to exploit these rent-seeking opportunities. This in turn favors more violent first movers at the expense of those that take time to build more durable relations with civilians that have benefits for both.[4] Armed groups that receive incomes from sales of logs, minerals, and other assets that they capture and sell to foreign corporations essentially loot other people's property to increase their capacities to buy weapons and to get more resources to attract new members. These armed groups attract a more self-interested membership that focuses on looting that involves the use of physical violence against civilians to sustain these armed groups.[5]

Reaching further back in history, one might have regarded the Soviet offers of concessions after 1917 to foreign firms to have constituted theft of property during wartime on the basis of the nonrecognition of the Soviet government as the legitimate sovereign authority of that country. But the US government tolerated the activities of American firms in Russia provided they understood that this activity was at their own risk, even though the US government had recently assisted anti-Bolshevik forces in a civil war and refused to extend diplomatic recognition to the Soviet government.[6] This decision recognized the de facto control that the Soviet government exercised over territory and their responsibility to administer it. This appropriation of property and assignment of concessions to private foreign investors was not seen as constituting pillage under The Hague Convention of 1907, which forbade the pillage of properties in the course of combat and the exploitation of civilians in occupied areas.[7]

In essence, under this standard rebels or the invading army of another country were regarded as a sort of government once they controlled territory and communities, regardless of their diplomatic or political standing in international society. This allowed them to dispose of properties in the course of running an administration for the benefit of the population, even if other governments did not formally recognize their sovereign right to do so. The responsibility to administer has remained a key element of international humanitarian law (IHL). As we will see below, judgments about whether combatants measure up to this standard follow a global political logic that has shifted in recent decades, with considerable consequences for definitions of CSR in conflicts and the prosecution of wayward firms.

The theft of properties in the course of armed conflicts is defined as pillage in IHL, provided that there is some element of private or personal use or gain involved. Article 4(2) (g) of the Additional Protocol II of 1977 to the Geneva Conventions reiterates the prohibition of acts of pillage in wartime.[8] The International Committee of the Red Cross notes that prohibitions against pillage constitute a norm in IHL, given its definition as a war crime in the Report of the Commission on Responsibility that followed the First World War and especially in the Charter of the International Military Tribunal (Nuremberg Tribunal) after the Second World War.[9] The prohibition of pillage was reaffirmed in the Geneva Conventions of 1949 after the Nuremberg Tribunal prosecuted corporate actors that participated in the extraction of resources from Nazi-occupied territories during World War II.[10] Pillage appears as a war crime in the protocols of the International Criminal Tribunal for Rwanda and the Special Court for Sierra Leone. States codify it in their laws, that is, the US War Crimes Act, which simply cross-references relevant treaties. Prosecutions for pillage were enforced in the International Criminal Tribunal for the Former Yugoslavia and in cases brought before the International Criminal Court.[11]

This stress on the private nature of gain in prosecutions of the war crime of pillage reinforces an important distinction in whether uses of violence to appropriate material resources was for personal aggrandizement or to support a local administration. As has long been the case, it is not explicitly prohibited for armed forces of a state or a rebel group to seize private property in the course of conflict. But the view after the Second World War and particularly after the Cold War has been that the personal interests of individual combatants play a large role in driving the actions of many armed groups. This view accords with the idea that recent and contemporary conflicts are more likely than conflicts in the past to look more like a mutual criminal enterprise. More recent conflicts are seen as often organized around identity politics that is constructed through war rather than a Clausewitzean geopolitical or ideological contest of wills. They are financed though predatory private enterprise rather than through taxing or mobilizing populations. This view of the changing nature of conflict identifies shifts in global economic structures toward greater decentralization and deregulation that create conditions in which persistent violence rather than winning in an old sense serves combatants' political and economic interests.[12]

Economists' analyses that explore individuals' incentives to fight have been particularly disposed to frame conflicts as involving motives for private gain. Some of these analyses have become influential in shaping intellectual and policy discussions about the nature of contemporary wars.[13] Other scholars, such as Mary Kaldor, have noted the influences of the forces of globalization behind new kinds of wars that "involve a blurring of distinctions between war (usually for political motives)[,] organized crime (violence undertaken by privately organized groups for private purposes, usually financial gain)[,] and large-scale violations of human rights (violence undertaken by states or politically organized groups against individuals)."[14]

The addition of the assumption that armed group coalitions contains criminal elements marked a further divergence from widely held perceptions about the ideological nature of rebel groups in previous decades such as in the course of rebellions against colonial rule and apartheid. Regardless of whether these earlier rebels appropriated properties in the course of conflicts, much of the international community regarded these armed groups as legitimate political actors, governing liberated zones free of colonial or apartheid state control to show what the sovereign state would look like once the rebels overthrew the government. This alternative post–Second World War legacy privileges the political aims of rebels, mostly centered in agendas of self-determination, over possible criminal behavior and corporate collusion in that political project. For example, Katanga's secession from Congo from 1961 to 1963 occurred with support from several Belgian corporations involved in mining copper, gold, and uranium in that region. Katanga never received recognition by another state, including Belgium, yet corporate commercial engagement with these rebels passed with little consequence for the firms involved. Like foreign investors who pursued offers of concessions from the Soviet government in the early 1920s, this engagement was at their own risk; perhaps undesirable for encouraging separatists and involving mercenaries, but this situation was not framed in terms of commercial activities of armed groups promoting human rights abuses.[15]

In any event, anticolonial and antiapartheid rebels enjoyed access to internationally legitimate sources of material support that lessened the need to seek partnerships with corporations to exploit resources in areas they controlled. The Organization of African Unity, for example, created a Liberation Committee in 1963 to decide which rebel groups should be recognized as the legitimate representatives of colonized peoples. If visits to areas under rebel control convinced Liberation Committee members that a rebel group was serious about the pursuit of its political goals, the committee's approval was supposed to signal to foreigners which rebel group was the most genuine and effective at promoting the desired political agenda. State backers such as the Soviet Union, European countries, especially in Scandinavia, and others often backed rebel groups with material support, even if they did not always follow Liberation Committee recommendations. The UN system also certified rebel groups. The Palestinian Liberation Organization (PLO) and the Southwest Africa People's Organization (SWAPO), for example, received observer status in the UN General Assembly by the 1970s as quasi-governmental organizations in recognition of the wide acceptance of the legitimacy of their political projects.

Contemporary ideas about the essentially criminal nature of many rebellions (and the legitimacy of state efforts to defeat them) de-link the appropriation of resources from the political aims of rebel groups. In essence, forcible appropriation of property is tolerated under international law if it occurs in the course of a rebel group's pursuit of what are determined to be legitimate aims. If rebels are regarded simply as a collection of armed individuals who fight for personal gain, appropriations of resources, including in collusion with foreign corporations, would be more likely to be seen to constitute a war crime. Journalist Robert Kaplan conflated war and crime more generally in his influential 1994 essay about conflicts in West Africa as "the symbol of worldwide demographics, environmental, and societal stress, in which criminal activity emerges as the real 'strategic' danger" as the breakdown of governments unleashed armed predators to terrorize these societies.[16]

This shift in views of rebel groups away from considerations of armed groups' political programs or complaints is reflected in the appearance in the 1990s of inquiries into the role of commerce in natural resources in fueling conflicts in Africa. These reports reinforced new ideas about the motivations of combatants in politically unstable countries with weak governments and the essential criminal nature of those who were involved in commercial transactions that sustained fighting. Initially interested in "naming and shaming" actors involved in conflicts, the UN Security Council passed Resolution 1173 in 1998 to apply sanctions against the diamond mining operations of Angola's UNITA rebel group after the breakdown of a peace agreement.[17] UNITA fought on, so in 1999 the UN Security Council gave Canadian diplomat Robert Fowler and a panel of expert investigators the authority to investigate how sanctions were violated. In their report released in March 2000, the experts revealed how UNITA used ties to businessmen and companies to sell or trade several billion dollars in diamonds to acquire weapons.[18]

The advent of the Kimberley Process certification scheme to stop the trade in "conflict diamonds" in 2003 was designed to give teeth to international sanctions against trade in resources that sustained combatants who engaged in violations of IHL. Although this approach highlighted activities of governments as well as rebels that violated IHL, the conventions of diplomacy ensured that states were treated as the principal interlocutors. Offending states can be sanctioned for allowing diamonds from conflict zones to be traded, but armed groups that fight state forces lack a mechanism to make appeals that they are legitimate combatants and that trade in diamonds is a necessary element of their strategies. The strong bias toward state authority appears in the UN's definition of conflict diamonds as "diamonds that originate from areas controlled by forces or factions opposed to legitimate and internationally recognized governments, and are used to fund military action in opposition to those governments, or in contravention of the decisions of the Security Council."[19]

This sanctions regime geared toward limiting the resources available to combatants has created a framework to identify and target the transactions of key individuals in armed groups and their corporate partners. For the first time since the Second World War, corporations came under sustained critical examination for activities associated with pillage and became the focus of specific sanctions. This development required the suspension of the idea that their armed group partners pursued legitimate goals or really any collective political goals at all, and discounted the earlier argument that rebels could forcibly appropriate resources if these were used to support the administration of civilian communities. This approach was not interested in whether rebels in the 1990s and after set up local administrations—as some indeed did[20]—and whether these appropriated resources were used to that end.

Intended and Unintended Consequences

At first glance, international sanctions in the context of the doctrine of the Responsibility to Protect seem to undermine the positions of the governments of sovereign states to operate as they please in warfare.

These limitations on sovereign prerogatives are real. Sanctions since 2000 against governments involved in conflicts such as in Sudan, Côte d'Ivoire, Libya, Guinea-Bissau, Congo, and the Central African Republic have chipped away at the notion that sovereignty shields governments from external scrutiny when they conduct counterinsurgency operations. Corporate investors have been put on notice that a new standard of enforcement of CSR is at hand. These developments to signal that targeting actors for sanctions, and by extension that actors who violate sanctions can be identified, cast the shadow of prosecution for war crimes over commercial actors who become involved with violators of IHL.

Governments of sovereign states, however, enjoy practical advantages in international society when confronted with rebel groups. States benefit from accredited diplomatic staffs and membership in international organizations that they can use to manage their ongoing relations with the outside world, even if they have to engage governments and organizations that are critical of their domestic politics. Governments also find that they can target and manipulate the strategic concerns of their state interlocutors. For example, it is not controversial in international society for a government to recruit a stronger state to shield it from sanctions. Thus Sudan's government became adept at manipulating the anxieties of US officials who are concerned about cooperation on counterterrorism issues, maintaining Sudanese oil production, or who fear that pressuring Sudan's government could produce greater instability in a vulnerable region rather than the desired change of behavior. Other states that are targets of sanctions generally have a greater capacity than most rebel groups to exploit clashing interests within foreign states. For example, sanctions against Angola's government risked complicating commercial ties to US oil companies that operated there. The threat to exercise the sovereign prerogative to bar a corporation's entry into these markets raises fears among US officials about the impact on the US economy of Angolan ire, forcing those officials to weigh whether they care more about the defense of human rights or about the impact of even minor disruptions in energy supplies on the attitudes of voters.

It is much harder for rebel groups to develop extensive official contacts with governments, much less manipulate the interests of officials abroad. This difference in the relative capacities of states versus rebels became particularly pronounced after the demise of the institutionalized pathways for the inclusion of rebel groups into the international system as the Cold War came to an end. Contemporary separatist rebels, for example, cannot attract the intensity of international material or political support that was available to rebels who fought against colonial occupation and apartheid. There is no equivalent for twenty-first-century separatist rebels of the UN General Assembly's Resolution 1514 of 1960 that proclaimed "the necessity of bringing to a speedy and unconditional end colonialism in all its forms and manifestations"[21] that was often taken to endorse anticolonial rebellions when colonial rulers delayed their exit.

This diplomatic marginalization of rebel groups, coupled with assumptions about the criminal nature of rebels' objectives and motives, exposes those who conduct commerce with them to considerable risk. Heightened risk in turn influences what kinds of firms would be likely to do business with such rebels. Clandestine businesses may discount threats of prosecution since they already operate outside the law and have developed ways to conceal their operations. These firms include specialists in sanctions-busting and traders in illicit commodities. But even these enterprising businesses draw attention from states and international organizations for supporting rebels who are fighting against established states and political interests, as seen in the willingness of states to prosecute noted business associates of rebel leaders for war crimes.

In an illustration of this changing international environment for rebels and corporations, some small firms in the early 1990s answered appeals from Charles Taylor's National Patriotic Front of Liberia (NPFL) to take over logging concessions in areas the NPFL controlled. This kind of commercial engagement would have attracted little attention in the years immediately before, and was not widely noted even then. In any event, a lot of these businessmen assumed that the NPFL would soon prevail militarily and become the recognized government of Liberia, and only the most rugged among operators remained once it became clear that the conflict would be protected.[22] A decade later, specific logging firms and their officers that did business in this conflict zone featured in the reports of the UN panels of experts.[23]

These firms attracted increased scrutiny from foreign observers as traffickers in pillaged resources, as the human rights abuses of the NPFL became more widely known. Corporate partners received more attention in 2003 when Charles Taylor was indicted before the ad hoc tribunal, the Special Court for Sierra Leone, "to obtain access to the mineral wealth of Sierra Leone" in association with a "joint criminal enterprise" to help another rebel group take political power in Sierra

Leone.[24] Although by that time Taylor was the leader of a globally recognized sovereign state, international attention focused on him for his
support of rebels in neighboring countries. This was a sign of how the
new activism surrounding conflict resources was shaping how conflict
itself was interpreted.

This growing shadow of exposure and prosecution also appeared in
Congo's conflict that began in 1996. Several mining companies signed
concession agreements with the Alliance des Forces Démocratiques
pour la Libération du Congo-Zaïre (AFDL) soon after the rebel group
began to take control over territory in the eastern part of the country.
But by the late 1990s, even the ascension of the rebel group to the seat
of power in the capital did not protect these firms from scrutiny for their
roles in supplying financial resources to what was then a rebel group in
return for access to minerals. These accusations associated corporations
with acts of pillage and were featured in the reports of UN panels of experts that referred to the "illegal exploitation" of resources in the course
of this conflict.[25]

Most of the individuals connected to the conflict in Congo who
have been indicted before the International Criminal Court (ICC) are
charged with leading or assisting armed groups that committed human rights violations.[26] Specific firms are cited for "assistance to illegal
armed groups," mostly as providers of transport or commercial services
to raise revenues from the sales of looted minerals. ICC indictments for
pillage in Congo and in other countries such as Uganda are directed
against individuals while also recognizing the close linkage between the
exploitation of natural resources, the revenues this produces, and the
perpetration of human rights abuses in the course of conflict. Thus corporations seeking resources in these conflict zones find that they are increasingly hemmed in by experts' reports, sanctions committees, certification schemes (such as the Kimberley Process for diamonds), and their
own growing need to conduct due diligence before engaging in business with these armed groups. The NGO Global Witness targets this last
imperative, with warnings to corporations of even indirectly receiving
goods from armed groups that engage in pillage and that commit human
rights abuses.[27]

In sum, the criminalization of warfare against established state authority brought greater official and public attention to the problem of
pillage through more intensive scrutiny of corporate collusion with rebel
groups. Thus while many government acquisitions of resources during

conflicts are also scrutinized for violations of IHL, virtually any rebel acquisition of resources can be seen as pillage, and any corporation that does business with rebels will risk liability for collusion in this pillage. This shift in international approaches toward states and rebel groups that are in conflict has increased the risks to corporations that do business with armed groups. Even though state actors can be indicted for pillage and war crimes, recent events have shown that rebel groups appear to attract greater scrutiny and to have fewer resources for protecting corporate partners from risks associated with the international community's growing awareness of the links between the exploitation of natural resources, conflict and human rights violations.

Charges of criminal behavior against corporate associates are more likely if the rebel group is viewed as a criminal enterprise rather than a political group that is fighting for legitimate objectives. The standing of sovereign governments in the courts of foreign countries reinforces this divergence. For example, firms doing business with rebels risk lawsuits in their home countries that allege that these dealings constitute contract violations. These governments pursue their rebel challengers on the basis of the claim that concession agreements for the exploitation of minerals and other resources require corporations to pay taxes and royalties to the legally constituted government of the country. This is because in most countries the state—as recognized in international diplomacy—has sovereignty over natural resources, a situation that contributes to the inequality between the treatment of states and rebel groups in international law.[28] If a corporation finds that it has to come to agreements with armed groups that actually control the territory of the concession, even if the corporation faces extortion with threat to damage or confiscate corporate assets, the government can claim that it is the victim of theft of resources.[29] While not falling under the rubric of pillage under international law, the legal standing of governments that is denied to rebel groups highlights the ascendancy of sovereign governments over rebel groups in international society.

Thus a central irony of increased scrutiny and prosecutions for pillage, and especially the shadow of future prosecutions of corporations that these measures cast, is that developments that are intended to chip away at the shield of sovereignty to assert a uniform and heightened standard of observance for IHL inadvertently strengthen the hands of state actors against rebels. Rebels that seek commercial partners to raise revenues for what is an inherently violent enterprise may find that commercial partners will become harder to find and that the quality of those who are willing to do business will decline. In turn, this process may reinforce the loss of legitimacy of armed rebellion against governments, particularly if the rebels continue to lack the degree of support from powerful countries and international organizations for their objectives that many of their Cold War–era counterparts enjoyed.

CSR and the Right of Rebellion

The prosecution of pillage under IHL has evolved from individuals and corporations that were associated with the Nazi state after the Second World War to a contemporary approach that targets individuals associated with rebel groups and some state officials for pillage and other war crimes. When prosecution has involved state officials, these have been individuals who violated United Nations sanctions and who played key roles in perpetrating these crimes. Prosecutions of heads of state include Charles Taylor of Liberia and Laurent Gbagbo of Côte d'Ivoire. Although significant in their own right, these prosecutions affected only leaders who committed serious crimes and, perhaps more important, who were unable to secure protection and political support from a more powerful state. These two heads of state also came to be seen among many foreign actors as impediments to conflict resolution and were targets of multiple UN Security Council resolutions. These are very important, but also exceptional cases of the withdrawal of sovereign immunity of suspected war criminals.

The lesson that might be learned from the experience of prosecutions of state actors is that avoiding prosecution requires that one's government not fall into the categories of weak and friendless. This has implications for corporations that would do business with alleged war criminals. The failure of the ICC to secure the arrest of Sudan's president, Omar al-Bashir, on counts of war crimes and crimes against humanity after issuing a warrant for his arrest in 2009 illustrates these principles. In 2011 he was received in Beijing to discuss the exploitation of his country's oil reserves and prospects for Chinese investments, and since then he has visited a number of other states. Sovereignty when backed with a real capacity to engage in reciprocal relations with other states still serves as a shield against unwelcome external interference, including in commercial activities. It is unlikely that corporations that engage in commerce with these officials will face prosecutions either, since at present it is harder to argue that a state can steal its own resources than it is to argue that rebels steal resources. Misrule and corruption are regrettable and may be crimes in various legal systems, but they are hardly isolated problems.

Concerns about pillage thus focus on those that do business with rebels and other armed groups. This is reflected in the fact that the bulk of sanctions and prosecutions for war crimes have targeted rebels and other nonstate actors. While actions against such individuals may be justified on many grounds, the broader issue concerns whether the aggregate of these actions, coupled with a global shift toward a narrative that equates rebellion with criminality, effectively outlaws rebellion. This narrative in turn may shape the degree of legitimacy that observers across various circumstances and contexts accord to this evolving global norm.

The uprisings associated with the "Arab Spring" from early 2011 appear to belie this assessment. Rebels in these Middle Eastern countries seemed to secure some support from American officials who viewed their causes in line with US support for democratic values in other countries.[30] The relationship of US government officials to prodemocracy activists who sparked rebellions resembled elements of the old Cold War relationships with anticommunist "freedom fighters" but without promises of weapons or other extensive covert support. Armed rebels in Kosovo, Sudan, Iraq, Libya, and Afghanistan have received US support since the end of the Cold War. In these cases, they opposed governments that were at odds with the United States over key issues. In a further break with global norms, two of these rebel groups, the Kosovo Liberation Army and the Sudan People's Liberation Army, succeeded with US support to fulfill their separatist aims to create their own internationally recognized states.

These instances of extensive state support for rebel groups tend to be ad hoc, and presumably corporations that did business with them would have less fear of sanction or prosecution. It is far more typical for rebels to find that they have little access to international society beyond occasional clandestine support from neighboring country governments that try to use them as proxies in regional politics. Otherwise, the bulk of these groups either risk being labeled as terrorists if they operate in countries that are of strategic importance and friendly to a powerful hegemonic state, or as criminal organizations if they fight for state power in very poor and unstable countries. State officials exploit this isolation from international society. Officials in Uganda discovered that they could call upon the ICC to investigate the crimes of the Lord's Resistance Army to further marginalize their enemies. When the ICC began to investigate the Ugandan government for possible criminal behavior, this process stalled. At the same time Uganda played a major role in a US-supported multinational peacekeeping force in Somalia, and US trainers were developing extensive programs with the Ugandan military.[31] While this is a particularly clear case of strategic uses of sovereign prerogatives to fend off international law, for most governments that face rebellions this marginalization of rebels already is extensive.

The international marginalization of rebels may facilitate the future prosecution of their corporate partners for war crimes, and as noted above, this already has resulted in campaigns to link CSR more generally to abstention from doing business in conflict zones. The dilemma is that this development risks undermining the legitimacy of IHL among people and communities that believe that particular rebels fight for laudable goals. Often these can include parochial goals, such as protection of an ethnic community from a corrupt and violent government in the capital, a bid to acquire what communities regard as just compensation for local resources, and separatist aspirations. These rebels may attack civilians and loot private properties. Such crimes may have been committed in the past when narratives of conflict focused more on political aims, which, rather than excusing them, illustrates that such rebellions simultaneously can contain these elements of legitimacy and criminality.

The right to rebel clashes with the realities of abuses that accompany a state's loss of the monopoly over coercion and the weak discipline that rebel commanders often exercise over recruits. Behavior of this sort, which often included systematic serious abuses of human rights, appeared even in the "virtuous" struggles against colonial rule and apartheid in the latter half of the twentieth century.[32] But this sort of behavior attracted less attention alongside the narratives of an international system that certified rebel groups as "legitimate" representatives of a community and a struggle. As noted above, this certification required conformity to standards of behavior that included control over a territory, the administration of civilians, and discipline and commitment of the rebel group to the original cause, which may have had the effect of encouraging armed group leaders to minimize (or at least hide) violations of human rights. One can imagine a contemporary process of accreditation or at least partial access to international forums that would include scrutiny for adherence to IHL.

Recognition of rebel groups would extend to them some of the prerogatives of sovereignty in an attempt to stress socialization rather than coercion to abide by other global norms. This would raise the associated issue of whether these rebels would be permitted to seek corporate partners to exploit resources in the aid of their causes. CSR under such circumstances would be a very tricky proposition, subject to international decisions that particular rebel groups are more acceptable than others, and that international engagement with them will change their behavior.

Historical instances of partial recognition of rebels often occurred alongside limitations placed upon the sovereignty of their state foes. In 1971, for example, the International Court of Justice ruled that South Africa's government lacked the legal right to grant title to Namibia's natural resources, even though South Africa had occupied and administered that territory for more than half a century.[33] Two years later, SWAPO received observer status in the UN General Assembly (as had the PLO), and the United Nations Fund for Namibia supported the training of administrators at the UN Institute for Namibia in Zambia. Foreign governments openly sided with groups like SWAPO in the pursuit of an end to colonial rule and apartheid.[34]

A contemporary version of rebel recognition would have to incorporate some notion of CSR that is compatible with corporate engagement with rebels. The key element of a departure from contemporary ideas of CSR of this sort would require relaxing the assumptions that most rebellions are criminal enterprises and that corporate engagement with rebel groups is tantamount to a war crime.

One can foresee pitfalls in the systematic partial recognition of rebel groups and its impact on CSR in conflict zones. As during the Cold War, it is not clear who would have the authority to choose which rebel groups received recognition and which were excluded from it. The Cold War saw many split decisions, with the United States and its allies recognizing one rebel group and the Soviet Union and its allies recognizing another. This situation led to prolonged stalemates in places like Angola and Mozambique in the 1970s and 1980s, where contending rebel groups received supplies and diplomatic support from opposite sides of the Cold War divide. Partial recognition of this sort arguably prolonged these conflicts, with adverse impact on civilians.

Recognition of rebels would require a consensus among members of the international community of the appropriateness of the rebellion's goals. This was closer to the situation in the early 1960s when the United States, the Soviet Union, and many other governments supported the right of people in colonial possessions to exercise a right to self-determination. Like slavery in the nineteenth century, within a generation or two the concept of colonial rule lost its wide acceptance to become anathema to most of international society. It is difficult to envision what kind of an agenda would attract widespread support now. Contemporary rebels articulate goals as diverse as regional separatism, the construction of a universal religious community in the place of states, and rejection of the economic and cultural influences of globalization, for example. It is unlikely that utopian ideas or ethnic chauvinism would receive widespread international support. But citizens' movements to overthrow dictators who have established records of systematic violations of basic human rights might attract broad support. The challenge then would be to define the limits of tolerated behavior among rebels and the role of CSR in that endeavor. Here too, the states they fight would have to be situated on the geostrategic margins, as we saw above in the rare international prosecutions of sovereign state officials.

In any event, these ideas are worth pondering. Prosecution of corporations for pillage and other war crimes in current circumstances otherwise risks entrenching a status quo that frustrates the aspirations of communities. It risks conveying to people who live in the poorest and most oppressive parts of the world that prosecutions for war crimes, including pillage, are reserved for the weak, especially those who lack powerful friends. Although it is not necessarily the intention to do so, the contemporary international posture toward rebellion—integrally linked to efforts to prosecute war crimes—also may be unsustainable. As the Congress of Vienna of 1815 showed when trying to stuff the genie of nationalism back into the bottle of peaceful order, aspirations for self-determination simply reemerged later with increased vigor. Self-determination has been one of the most significant driving forces of politics for the past two centuries. During that time it has become more, not less, powerful. This is the reality that CSR and the broader issue of how rebels are treated in the context of prosecutions for war crimes need to be taken into account.

Notes

1. International Commission on Intervention and State Sovereignty, *The Responsibility to Protect: Report of the International Commission on Intervention and State Sovereignty* (Ottawa: International Development Research Centre, 2001).

2. Hugh Phillips, "From a Bolshevik to a British Subject: The Early Years of Maksim Litvinov," *Slavic Review* 48, no. 3 (1989): 388–98.

3. Philip Gillette, "American Capital in the Contest for Soviet Oil, 1920–23," *Soviet Studies* 24, no. 4 (1973): 477–90.

4. Philippe Le Billon, *Wars of Plunder: Conflicts, Profits, and the Politics of Resources* (New York: Columbia University Press, 2012); Michael Ross, "What Do We Know about Natural Resources and Civil Wars?" *Journal of Peace Research* 41, no. 3 (2004): 337–56.

5. Jeremy Weinstein, *Inside Rebellion: The Politics of Insurgent Violence* (New York: Cambridge University Press, 2007), 47–49.

6. Antony Sutton, *Western Technology and Soviet Economic Development, 1917 to 1930* (Stanford, CA: Hoover Institution on War, Revolution and Peace, 1968), 295–99.

7. The Hague Convention of 1907, Articles 47–56, http://www.icrc.org/ihl.nsf/full/195, accessed September 24, 2014.

8. International Committee for the Red Cross, Protocol Additional to the Geneva Conventions of 12 August 1949, and relating to the Protection of Victims of Non-International Armed Conflicts (Protocol II), June 8, 1977, http://www.icrc.org/ihl.nsf/full/475?opendocument, accessed September 24, 2014.

9. International Committee for the Red Cross, Customary IHL, Rule 52, Pillage, http://www.icrc.org/customary-ihl/eng/docs/v1_rul_rule52, accessed September 24, 2014.

10. International Committee for the Red Cross, Geneva Convention Relative to the Protection of Civilian Persons in Time of War of 12 August 1949, Art. 16 & 33, http://www.icrc.org/eng/resources/documents/publication/p0173.htm, accessed September 24, 2014.

11. Larissa Van den Herik and Daniella Dam-de Jong, "Revitalizing the Antique War Crime of Pillage: The Potential and Pitfalls of Using International Criminal Law to Address Illegal Resource Extraction during Armed Conflict," *Criminal Law Forum* 15 (2011): 266–71.

12. David Keen, *Useful Enemies: When Waging Wars Is More Important than Winning Them* (New Haven, CT: Yale University Press, 2012); Mary Kaldor, "In Defence of New Wars," *Stability* 2, no. 1 (2013): 1–16.

13. Paul Collier, "Rebellion as a Quasi-Criminal Activity," *Journal of Conflict Resolution* 44, no. 6 (2000): 839–53.

14. Mary Kaldor, *New and Old Wars: Organized Violence in a Global Era* (Palo Alto, CA: Stanford University Press, 2006), 2.

15. Lawrence Devlin, *Chief of Station, Congo: A Memoir of 1960–1967* (New York: PublicAffairs, 2008); John Kent, *America, the UN, and Decolonization: Cold War Conflict in the Congo* (New York: Routledge, 2011).

16. Robert Kaplan, "The Coming Anarchy," *Atlantic Monthly*, February 1994, 45.

17. United Nations Security Council, Resolution 1173 (1998) Adopted by the Security Council at its 3891st meeting, on 12 June 1998, S/RES/1173 (1998), http://www.refworld.org/docid/3b00f21018.html, accessed September 24, 2014.

18. United Nations Security Council, *Report of the Panel of Experts on Violations of Security Council Sanctions against UNITA*, March 10, 2000, http://www.un.org/News/dh/latest/angolareport_eng.htm, accessed September 24, 2014.

19. United Nations General Assembly, Conflict Diamonds: Sanctions and War, http://web.archive.org/web/20121023004513/http://www.un.org/peace/africa/Diamond.html, accessed September 24, 2014.

20. Ana Arjona, "Social Order in Civil War" (PhD diss., Yale University, 2010).

21. United Nations General Assembly, Resolution 1514 of 1960, http://daccess-dds-ny.un.org/doc/RESOLUTION/GEN/NR0/152/88/IMG/NR015288.pdf?OpenElement, accessed April 19, 2014.

22. Observations of the author in the course of field research in the region.

23. United Nations Security Council, *Report of the Panel of Experts Pursuant to Security Council Resolution 1343 (2001), paragraph 19, concerning Liberia*, 26 Oct 2001, 70–75, http://www.un.org/Docs/sc/committees/Liberia2/1015e.pdf, accessed September 24, 2014.

24. The Special Court for Sierra Leone, The Prosecutor against Charles Ghankay Taylor, Indictment, 7 March 2003, 4–5, http://www.sc-sl.org/scsl/Indictments/SCSL-03-01-PT%20Taylor%20Indictment.pdf, accessed April 19, 2014.

25. United Nations Security Council, *Report of the Panel of Experts on the Illegal Exploitation of Natural Resources and Other Forms of Wealth in the Democratic Republic of Congo*, 12 April 2001, http://www.un.org/News/dh/latest/drcongo.htm, accessed September 24, 2014.

26. United Nations Security Council, *List of Individuals and Entities Subject to the Measures Imposed by Paragraphs 13 and 15 of Security Council Resolution 1596 (2005), as Renewed by Paragraph 3 of Resolution 1952 (2010)*, 28 Nov 2011, http://www.un.org/sc/committees/1533/pdf/1533_list.pdf, accessed September 24, 2014.

27. Global Witness, *Do No Harm: A Guide for Companies Sourcing from the DRC* (London: Global Witness, 2010), available at http://www.globalwitness.org/

sites/default/files/pdfs/do_no_harm_global_witness.pdf. See also International Alert, http://www.redflags.info/.

28. Nico Schrijver, *Sovereignty over Natural Resources: Balancing Rights and Duties* (New York: Cambridge University Press, 1997), 57–70.

29. National Patriotic Reconstruction Assembly Government, "Memorandum of Understanding," Gbarnga [Liberia], January 17, 192; Interim Government of National Unity, Bureau of Concessions, "Memorandum," Monrovia, March 31, 1993. Both documents concerned Firestone's operations in rebel-held territory.

30. For example, Margaret Scobey, [Wikileaks cable] "Activist on His US Visit and Regime Change in Egypt," December 30, 2008, http://wikileaksupdates .blogspot.com/2011/01/april-6-activist-on-his-us-visit-and.html, accessed September 24, 2014.

31. Craig Whitlock, "U.S. Trains African Soldiers for Somali Mission," *Washington Post*, May 13, 2012, accessed September 24, 2014, http://www .washingtonpost.com/world/national-security/us-trains-african-soldiers-for -somalia-mission/2012/05/13/gIQAJhsPNU_story.html.

32. Stathis Kalyvas, "'New' and 'Old' Civil Wars: A Valid Distinction?" *World Politics* 54, no. 1 (2001): 99–118. A good example of such behavior among "good" rebels appeared in the struggle against the white minority regime in Rhodesia (Zimbabwe), noted in Norma Kriger, *Zimbabwe's Guerrilla War: Peasant Voices* (New York: Cambridge University Press, 1992).

33. International Court of Justice, Legal Consequences for States of the Continued Presence of South Africa in Namibia (South West Africa) notwithstanding Security Council Resolution 276 (1970), http://www.icj-cij.org/docket/?sum =296&code=nam&p1=3&p2=4&case=53&k=a7&p3=5, accessed September 24, 2014.

34. For example, Tor Sellström, *Sweden and National Liberation in Southern Africa: Solidarity and Assistance, 1970–1994* (Uppsala: Nordiska Afrikainstituteten, 2002).

CHAPTER THIRTEEN

Corporate and State Sustainability in Africa

The Politics of Stability in the Postrevolutionary Age

Charlotte Walker-Said

Introduction

This chapter analyzes the corporate social responsibility agenda of sustainability as a movement that is maturing into one of the prevailing credos of human rights as well as development economics and global finance. Today the ethics, policy programs, and science of sustainability are coalescing within corporate strategies to maximize long-term growth and state agendas for managing national economies, national landscapes, and their citizenries. The United Nations, along with the World Bank, the OECD, and the IMF, consider sustainability frameworks to be critical components of economic development agendas, which currently operate as these organizations' primary vehicle for the fulfillment of human rights.[1] As sustainable development is posited as a human right and a global necessity, environmental, industrial, and human management approaches are assessed according to specific criteria that must meet approved sustainability doctrines.[2] A growing body of research also points to the long-term materiality of sustainability on investment outcomes. Sustainable corporate policy is thus coinstructed via the world's financial organizations and markets, multilateral institutions, and national governments, whose leaders believe in the humanistic concerns and promises of dependable outcomes contained in sustainability doctrines.

As a result of the participatory nature of sustainable development strategies, economic leaders are increasingly dependent on networks and are moving away from centralized, rule-making authorities. Networks, therefore, are critical in implementing Anne-Marie Slaughter's vision of the "transgovernmental order": a global rule of law without centralized global institutions.[3] As part of this order, sustainability is not just a struggle over practices but also over the locus of authority of governance, as well as an assessment of corporations' and governments' obligations to support the rule of law, freely compete, manage resources efficiently, and relieve suffering.[4] Furthermore, sustainability takes a unique and, some might argue, radical approach to human rights, which relies on building consensus regarding the balance between business obligations, government stability, resource availability, and the obligation to prevent humanitarian emergencies.

In this chapter I argue that while the global sustainability movement has roots in economic and environmental philosophies, many of its applied strategies are firmly political and contribute to an emerging manifestation of human rights as an indicator of political reliability. Sustainability champions science and industrialization as well as consistent governance. Corporations adhering to sustainability mandates tend to favor decentralized governance through cooperative agents as the most effective tools in the quest to maintain a steady state of economic growth, respond to the threat of resource exhaustion, and preserve or rescue the livelihoods and futures of local populations.[5] Today, sustainability doctrines—managed by agents of global governance as well as national economies—advocate for social trust of government, scientific institutions, corporations, and global markets and obtain consent from individuals and communities on the ground in a number of ways.

This chapter examines the sustainability platforms that have become part of national plans for economic development in South Africa and Cameroon and argues that sustainability regimes in Africa forward explicitly statist agendas that also depend on market mechanisms and competition between corporate agents to balance the extractive and hegemonic strategies of state institutions. It also demonstrates that global capitalism has energetically embraced sustainability as a critical measure of robust long-term financial outcomes and that it has progressively twinned its goals with that of nation-states. Lastly, this chapter claims that human rights and global governance institutions' commitment to issues like corporate transparency, responsible investment, and environmental and social guardianship indicates their belief that world politics have moved beyond revolution and counterrevolution. Currently, the ultimate struggle of human rights is not for justice, equality, or the rights of man and citizen, but rather for a durable future.

The cases of South Africa and Cameroon demonstrate that corporate social responsibility (as a critical driver of sustainability) can be used as a check on government corruption, state inconstancy, malfeasance, human rights abuse, and ecological destruction—threats that illustrate the fundamentally polyvalent inadequacies of neoliberal governments in Africa.[6] Evidence also reveals, however, that CSR sustainability doctrines prevent or inhibit abuses through economic and financial mechanisms and not through political empowerment or emancipation. Corporate respect for human rights is motivated by the protection of corporate interest rather than through philosophical commitments to ethics, but nonetheless, it is clear that corruption and malfeasance are costly for both companies and societies. The ability of corporations to reduce corruption and locate the market value of avoiding or remedying other moral wrongs is considered a key component of corporate "resiliency"—a pillar of sustainability.[7] Corporate resiliency and sustainability are calibrated using a body of empirical research that aims to quantify the political situation, environmental capacity, human need, and industrial productivity in the region in which the corporation is active.[8]

South Africa's and Cameroon's sustainability agendas are influenced by local as well as transnational development ideologies to guarantee increasing production and profit as well as stability of outcomes and political constancy. These countries' political leaders believe stability to be a precondition for the fulfillment of economic rights and the expansion of human capabilities. As such, they build on theories that forward that the quest for the achievement of full human rights for humanity should not endanger the stability that is a precondition for protecting human rights.[9] State leaders such as South Africa's Rejoice Mabudafhasi, the deputy minister of water and environmental affairs; Cameroon's Pierre Hele, minister for the environment and the protection of nature; and global governance leaders such as Kofi Annan frequently espouse theoretical links between economic rights, sustainability, and development—constructing an authoritative dictum that sustainability will guarantee progress and guard against scarcity and volatility.[10] These and other Af-

rican leaders are also expanding their participation in "protection partnerships" in the realm of national security.[11]

As a prevailing form of CSR and international human rights coordination, sustainability has few ideological links with the political and civil
rights articulations of the post–World War II era. Postwar human rights
achievements sought to entrench equality and nondiscrimination into
law and state policy, with guarantees in a judicial apparatus and constitutional decree.[12] During the 1950s, Cameroon's radical Union of the Populations of Cameroon (UPC) party and a collection of other political organs demanded self-determination and political parity with the French
government managing the empire.[13] In the 1970s and 1980s, South Africa was the site of one of the most powerful and difficult struggles for
human rights in the form of political and social inclusion: the antiapartheid struggle. Today, these nations' movements for sustainability make
no declarations to safeguard the personal liberties or social entitlements
that were delineated in the UDHR, nor do they fulfill their own national
postcolonial demands for democratic participation. These governments
designate the current era as one in which the struggle for democracy and
social justice has passed (and therefore must have prevailed) and the human rights mandate that remains to be fulfilled is the integration of the
local economy into the global.[14]

Corporations operating in Africa have communicated their support
of human rights and sustainability, and in doing so, have signaled to their
investors their ability to manage long-term global economic interests as
well as assume the mantle of global governance. Goldman Sachs has
stated, "Companies that are considered leaders in ESG [environmen-
tal, social, and governance] policies are also leading the pack in stock
performance by an average of 25%."[15] Other financial institutions have
made pronouncements such as: "There is increasing evidence showing
that superior performance in managing climate risk is a useful proxy for
superior, more strategic corporate management, and therefore for superior financial value and shareholder value-creation."[16] In the hopes of realizing greater cooperation between the worlds of finance and industry
on sustainability concerns, the United Nations has launched the UN Environment Programme Finance Initiative to partner with banks, insur-
ers, and fund managers to understand the impacts of environmental and
social considerations on the financial performance of corporations.[17]

Sustainability indicators are rapidly becoming not only financial performance indicators but also indicators of human rights performance.

The most prevalent standard for corporate sustainability has been outlined by the international nonprofit, the Global Reporting Initiative (GRI), which seeks to make sustainability reporting as systematic as financial reporting for corporations. The GRI converges human rights performance indicators with general sustainability metrics, associating practices regarding nondiscrimination, freedom of association, child labor, indigenous rights, and forced and compulsory labor with environmental resource conservation, climate change preparedness, waste management, corruption risk mediation, and other impacts and assessments. In promoting sustainability as a critical assessment of corporate performance equivalent to other current standards such as return on equity, the GRI has recently succeeded in joining the New York Stock Exchange (NYSE) as well as seven other stock exchanges in the United Nations' Sustainable Stock Exchanges (SSE) initiative. The SSE, coorganized by the UN Global Compact, brings together investors, regulators, and companies to make environmental, social, and governance issues more prominent in considerations of corporate performance, and, by extension, market performance.[18] As sustainability's relevance as a metric grows within capital markets, it signals the expression of a new social compact, which is an implicit agreement between industries, nation-states, and market overseers to limit a broad variety of social and environmental threats to the stability that safeguards growth.

Sustainability mandates continue to take new forms within CSR and economic expansion in Africa, and this chapter examines African regulatory frameworks for economic growth, which have embedded sustainability principles in mandatory and commonplace policies, regulations, and reports. Africa has been a staging ground, or "laboratory," for myriad forms of progressive politics, ecological preservation endeavors, and experimental economic policies throughout its history.[19] Thus Cameroon's and South Africa's experiences present major specificities linked to their histories that are relevant to analyzing the human rights implications of sustainability.

Sustainability and Market Politics in Late Twentieth-Century Africa

A Google Ngram of the term *sustainability* reveals its origins as a common reference point in the early 1980s, after which its usage increased

every year.[20] At the 1972 Stockholm Conference on the Human Environment and the 1980 World Conservation Strategy of the International
Union for the Conservation of Nature and Natural Resources (IUCN),
"sustainability" was proposed as a core environmental value that championed preservation and conservation as well as resource use equilibrium.[21] This ethos found itself in conflict, however, with rapidly circulating agendas for "sustainable development" championed by the United
Nations, the World Bank, and the World Commission on Environment
and Development, which promoted economic growth and the integration of the natural sciences and technical assessments of environmental
utility into corporate strategy and national policies.[22] At the 1992 United
Nations Conference on Environment and Development, Swiss industrial
magnate Stephan Schmidheiny founded the World Business Council for
Sustainable Development, which candidly declared itself to promote the
interests of business in global policy development on the issue of environmental resource use and economic growth.[23]

After calls for increased awareness of sustainable development thinking in the late 1980s, the following decade witnessed corporate leaders
enthusiastically embracing sustainability initiatives. Corporations translated "sustainability" into the business language of "the triple bottom
line" (social, environmental, and financial), which formed the core of
some of the earliest CSR platforms that were broadcast to shareholders,
clients, and investors.[24] Catchy slogans, including "3P: people, planet,
profits" and "win-win-win business strategies," circulated in business literature and shareholder reports, including Shell's first *Shell Report* on
the social and environmental impacts of its business.[25] By the late 1990s,
the business world and its investors were intensively funding sustainability science and integrating its findings into long-term corporate growth
strategies.[26]

Many of the world's governments have also keenly adopted sustainability principles. South Africa is arguably one of the world's most en-
thusiastic devotees of "sustainable development" logics. In 2002, the
World Summit on Sustainable Development was held in Johannesburg
and emphasized the need for a more coherent institutional framework
of international environmental governance, with better coordination
and monitoring. Soon afterward, South African Supreme Court judge
Mervyn King—with the full support of the government—published the
King II Report, urging the adoption of new standards for corporate reporting that stipulated the inclusion of an "environmental report" for

all companies listed on the Johannesburg Stock Exchange (JSE).[27] In 2009, the JSE introduced new listing requirements based on the subsequent King III Report, which stipulated that the environmental report become integrated into the general report on corporate performance. A new standard, termed the "integrated report," which documented sustainability in human rights, environmental impact, social engagement, and future strategic orientations, "mainstreamed" the theme of sustainability into corporate governance.[28] The draft Code for Responsible Investing by Institutional Investors in South Africa (CRISA) states that institutional investors should incorporate environmental, social, and governance considerations into their investment analysis and activities, and this includes an assessment of a company's integrated report.[29] In adopting corporate reporting and investment measures specifically aimed at quantifying and analyzing each corporations' assessments of sustainability, South Africa established itself early in the twenty-first century as a nation firmly in control of managing economic development through markets that championed sustainability policies, which South African leaders claimed would help achieve "the correct balance between conformance with governance principles and performance in an entrepreneurial market economy."[30]

While market economy logics are ascendant in the global South, sustainability frameworks demonstrate that the market is also highly vulnerable. Investors and corporate leaders are antagonistic toward shifting factors, deficiencies, major events, and other intangibles. This vulnerability has the potential to put the market and its corporate agents in a *reactive* mode, rather than a positive, interactive mode of communication and negotiation.[31] In other words, while critics of market-oriented policies (neoliberal agendas) decry that such laws place economic concerns above social and environmental rights and therefore become rights-denying mandates, it is becoming apparent that social and environmental rights violations, and particularly labor distrust and ecological depletion, are *threats* to economic growth, political and social peace, and perceptible measures of progress that are rewarded by the market. What the market economy and the nation-state in Africa and around the world are currently striving for is absoluteness: control over outcomes and factors that influence the integration of markets. This means that human rights are and will continue to be salient features of national and international law but will act as sentries of political harmony and cooperative economic reciprocity, not as codes that ground and motivate political mobilizations.

Mervyn King, now chairman of the Global Reporting Initiative, predicts the integration of human rights and sustainability measurements into standard financial reporting on a global level.[32] King argues that human rights "crises," biodiversity threats, and "ecological overshoot" indicate that the corporation will not survive. If corporations cannot be trusted to thrive, then the markets cannot support them. Markets demand "holistic representations" of growth, which includes information on the human and environmental condition in the field of operation. All this is essential, states King, for "mitigating risks."[33] Jane Diplock, of the Singapore Exchange Limited, echoes this, stating: "Capitalism needs financial stability and sustainability to succeed. Integrated reporting will underpin them both, leading to a more resilient global economy."[34] The world's stock markets, including European Union markets and the New York Stock Exchange, similarly attest to the value of statements and measures of sustainability, and its greatest current champion is the Financial Stability Board, an international body that monitors and makes recommendations about the global financial system.[35] Throughout the world, predictability, resiliency, and stability are now the critical end goals of corporate and financial agents operating across the developed and developing worlds—binding the logics of market economics with current political understandings of human rights. As Thomas Piketty has observed: "Regardless of what measure is used, the world clearly seems to have entered a phase in which rich and poor countries are converging."[36]

Sustainability and the State

In 1973, Sir Hersch Lauterpacht argued that the dominant trend of the last half of the twentieth century was one in which human rights would force the sovereign state to yield to the "sovereignty of humankind."[37] Jean and John Comaroff perceive the dominant trend at the turn of the twenty-first century to be "millennial capitalism"—a force that wills the sovereign state to yield to the "sovereignty of the free market."[38] However, deeper analysis reveals that the sovereign state—like the free market—remains a robust agent within capitalist development and deploys human rights as an instrument of management and control, rather than yielding to its creeds. In the new transgovernmental order, argues Slaughter, the state does not disappear but rather disaggregates into distinct components. Corporate social responsibility approaches depend on this feature, as specific government agencies network with corporations to more effectively solve national problems.[39]

Sustainability policies have demonstrated they can strengthen the state in Africa as African governments are forced to coordinate with an ever-growing community of international experts and must respond to demands for audits, reports, and compliant policies. Cameroon's creation and expansion of the Ministry of Forests and Fauna (MINFOF) (an extension of the earlier Ministry of Environment and Forests [MINEF]), was a direct corollary of the 1994 Forest Regime Law, which was, itself, part of the World Bank's Structural Adjustment Credit II and III programs (CAS II and III).[40] Along with the Ministry of Environment and the Protection of Nature (MINEP) (another government agency that was extended as part of CAS programs), MINFOF hired and trained thousands of local employees to survey, map, and monitor environmental resources in Cameroon. Policies and mandates to use, contract, extract, and develop Cameroon's natural resources greatly accelerated during the post-1994 period, when CAS policies began to be fully implemented. As part of the expansion of access to natural resources, Cameroon's government and its employees fully cooperated with the World Bank financially and accepted the technical expertise and coordinated training of Global Witness, Resource Extraction Monitoring, Global Forest Watch, the World Wildlife Fund, the Wildlife Conservation Society, and the Union Mondiale pour la Nature.

While structural adjustment in Africa during the 1980s and 1990s typically included a variety of measures to deeply reduce state services and minimize state bureaucracies in the name of curtailing public expenses, structural adjustment also initiated new bureaucratic apparatuses, which were launched to implement World Bank and IMF policies. Sustainability platforms in Cameroon strengthened the ability of state agencies to interface with their corporate and nongovernmental organization partners and to better understand the economic potential of the nation's landscape. Sustainable development policies in Cameroon also insured that industry agents, investors, and government leaders could effectively articulate their environmental needs, although it did not necessarily do the same for all national citizens.[41] Nevertheless, through the government's initiatives, sustainability achieved a particular moral authority in making claims to prevent resource exhaustion, depletion, catastrophe, and collapse and cultivated a wide array of supportive constituencies on the ground

The experience of South Africa also refutes the characterization of the post-1980 period in Africa as the retreat of the state. After apartheid, the South African state enthusiastically embraced the economic agenda of the Washington Consensus and deftly managed market transitions, deregulation, and privatization, and, in many cases, used neoliberal agendas to strengthen their control over constituencies and consolidate power blocs.[42] Furthermore, along with many other African countries, South Africa's government articulated strong support for the doctrine of economic rights as a means to secure development funding and foreign direct investment.[43] Many of these nations' commitments to justice in the form of civil and political rights was flimsy at best, but their calls for the recognition of economic rights via corporate investment and emergency aid contributed to the global consensus on the policies of how to best promote human well-being. South Africa's privatization program has surprisingly not limited the state in the sphere of economic development. Rather, corporate sustainable development projects have operated alongside state politics and have legitimized the power of the government and its elite.[44] Paradoxically, CSR and sustainability regimes articulate human rights in the language of victims and the dispossessed, but their results demonstrate that these forms of governance empower institutions rather than individuals and do not redress the claims of individual South Africans.

In Cameroon, the government's embrace of the sustainability mandates that accompanied market-oriented policies largely paralleled economic crises. Cameroon's first crisis emerged in 1985 with the decline in the value of primary agricultural exports. By 1999, Cameroon's gross domestic product was at 63 percent of its 1986 level.[45] In this period of economic regression, the steady rise of world timber prices coincided with global financial institutions' imperatives to generate revenue in order to restore the economic growth of previous decades. Thus Cameroon's forest sector emerged as a leading engine of prosperity during the 1990s. The materialization of large-scale commercial timber operations in densely forested regions not only generated critical export revenue but also aided in the development of rural infrastructure, engaged Cameroon in negotiations with international corporate concessions, and created or expanded the roles of the Cameroonian government in the regulation and monitoring of natural resource extraction. There are roughly 150 timber firms presently active in Cameroon and numerous government sectors and programs responsible for overseeing forestry activities.[46]

However, notwithstanding streamlined and facilitated interactions between government and corporate agents in Cameroon, environmental theft and corporate malfeasance increased during the early 1990s. A 2002 study commissioned by the United Kingdom's Department for International Development (DFID) estimated the loss of revenue due to illegal logging in Cameroon over a period of five years at 75 million euros in tax revenue annually for a total estimated loss of between 400 and 600 million euros.[47] After DFID's report, Cameroon's government and the international community decided to eliminate clientelist structures that allowed corporate agents to make extralegal deals with government agencies.[48] After 2003, "sustainable development" policies in Cameroon transitioned from a purely economic growth-oriented strategy involving the use of natural resources into one that fully incorporated political anticorruption measures.

These anticorruption/corporate resiliency measures demanded that Cameroon transition to awarding long-term forest contracts using a market-based forest concession allocation system in which concessions, once awarded on a discretionary, short-term basis known as *ventes de coupe* (VC), became auction based and open to public competition. Under the auction system, concessions transitioned to longer-term access grants, known as *unité forestière d'aménagement* (UFA), which typically endured for a three-year temporary concession, renewable for a fifteen-year rotation (contingent upon the completion of a sustainable forest management plan). As sustainability studies revealed that long-term plans tended to reduce corruption and clientelism by reducing the renewal of contracts based on personal relationships and ensuring the firm's implementation of more ecologically sound forest replacement and forest management policies, the new competitive auction-based concessions sought to grant a long contract to firms while simultaneously eliminating the cultivation of personal relationships between government administrators and groups or individuals at corporations.[49]

Sustainability regimes challenge predictions that capitalism works only toward deregulation, undermining the nation-state, depriving it of capital flow, and denying it advantages of long-term planned investment.[50] The harmonization of financial, corporate, juridical, and administrative aims has allowed many African states to accrue power and manage politics in a form that disallows violence, constrains environmental exploitation, and limits corruption because they threaten economic growth. As sustainability builds concern for the political and economic status of nations, the state is more likely to respect human rights as part of its obligation to fulfill capitalist objectives.

Twenty-First-Century Sustainability and the Economic Transformation of South Africa

There is a need to understand "sustainability" and "sustainable development" as a new civilizing mission in Africa with renovated ethics aimed at education and the transmission of a new consciousness about the corporation and the citizen's place in the natural, industrial, and political landscape. South Africa has, since the end of apartheid, intermingled its discourses on sovereignty, nation building, sustainability, and development. Legislation such as the 1998 National Environmental Management Act (which stipulated that economic development must be "socially, environmentally, and economically sustainable") privatized state forests, which was supported by the United Nations as "in the interests of sustainability" and defended the policy as one that would lead to "increased investment in the sector, improved management, and better social conditions."[51] Subsequently, the 2002 adoption of corporate reporting standards for sustainability spurred numerous other national sustainability initiatives, including sustainable management of its national parks and reserves, and perhaps most importantly, the National Strategy for Sustainable Development and Action Plan, signed in 2011.[52]

Former political prisoners and exiles with links to the ANC assumed leadership positions within these sustainability and economic expansion initiatives, occupied seats in directors' boards, and/or received financing from the state to acquire equity in new and existing companies. Established conglomerates backed new business ventures by those with political power in return for influence with the ruling party.[53] As M. Anne Pitcher describes, even party organs, like the ANC Youth League, and civic organizations joined the corporate community following the end of apartheid. Along with platforms for privatization, the National Empowerment Fund, the Industrial Development Corporation, and the Development Bank of Southern Africa all forwarded sustainability agendas in the mid- to late 1990s that would guarantee long-term stability of economic growth and resource utility. Since the diffuse benefits of sustainability strategies take a long time to emerge, the government of South Africa coordinated so that the state would remain sufficiently insulated from pressures in order to carry out sustainability reforms by creating autonomous technocratic change teams who acted free from political interference.[54]

In the decades since the fall of the apartheid regime, South African activists and labor organizations, along with multilateral institutions such as the World Commission on Environment and Development, have considered economic development and land reform essential components of democratization in South Africa.[55] ANC discussions about the sustainability of economic development have centered on restitution, redistribution, and land tenure reform. In this way, sustainability has profoundly been about *political* sustainability. "Sustainable governance"— although never articulated—was the underlying motive that undergirded much of the postapartheid economic transformation.[56] The endurance of a stable government would guard against the violence and instability that ended in revolution, damaged the South African economy, and isolated the nation from the world during the 1980s.[57] Conservation scientists and activists became allies in South African sustainable development movements and employed the rhetoric of security in advocating its utility, claiming that conservation efforts "stabilize populations," and "diminish competition over deteriorating resources."[58] However, conservation and sustainability have often been forcefully imposed without regard to real social justice or equality. Stabilization has been championed and scaffolded using the menace of depletion, while "sustainable development" projects have imposed increasing constraints on choice, access, and opportunity for those without capital, property rights, or political voice.

Concluding Thoughts

Sustainability is, above all, a risk assessment as well as a powerful new mode of stabilization. Mass poverty is a risk. Corruption is a risk. Environmental destruction and social unrest are risks. These considerable risks factor increasingly into human rights and capitalist agendas that focus on peace, constancy, and long-term development. In addition, framings of conservation and stewardship transcend human and environmental limits and define a morality that emphasizes corporations and governments as critical agents of economic and social transformation. As both a humanitarian and survivalist tactic, sustainability ultimately neutralizes demands for more radical political transformations—which, admittedly, may or may not advance human rights further. Revolutions and political instability, however, have historically been linked to the ultimate advancement of political freedoms and representative democracy. In the current era, however, these goals are sidelined in favor of economic measures of improved human well-being. Some argue that over time, increases in wealth allow just forms of government to emerge. Stephen Hopgood has suggested that a growing economy with a consistently expanding middle class can create an environment where human rights may thrive as aspirational Western norms.[59] His reasoning builds on Mancur Olson's observation that middle-class advocates played a disproportionate role in organized political action as a result of their surplus time and money.

Sustainability regimes at work today in Africa and throughout the world seek not to counteract disenfranchisement but rather to build a structure of guarantees. As a system of economic, environmental, and political governance, sustainability has the capacity to elevate some human rights standards and improve general social well-being. However, as an ethos it reflects Gil Anidjar's claim that human rights—with its focus on the sufferer—believes that the world is not what must be made through political action but what must rather be survived.[60] In the end, sustainability and our current political understanding of human rights are not only mandates for stability, they are also strategies for survivability. In many of its practices, sustainable development focuses on creating the necessary conditions for majority human endurance, rather than holistic flourishing, while simultaneously guaranteeing returns on investment, political constancy, and market expansion.

Notes

1. Angus Maddison, *The World Economy: A Millennial Perspective* (Paris: OECD, 2001); Jeffrey Sachs, *The End of Poverty: How We Can Make It Happen in Our Lifetime* (London: Penguin, 2005). For a critique of the international

development community's lack of respect for civil and social rights in favor of development measures, see William Easterly, *The Tyranny of Experts: Economists, Dictators, and the Forgotten Rights of the Poor* (Washington, DC: Basic Books, 2014).

2. United Nations, *Millennium Declaration*, UN Doc.A/RES/55/2, September 18, 2000; William F. Felice, *The Global New Deal: Economic and Social Human Rights in World Politics* (Lanham, MD: Rowman and Littlefield, 2010); Thomas Pogge, *World Poverty and Human Rights* (Malden, MA: Polity, 2002); United Nations Non-Governmental Liaison Service, "Human Rights Approaches to Sustainable Development," *NGLS Roundup*, United Nations Publications Issue 90, May 2012; Arjun Sengupta, "The Right to Development," in *Human Rights in the World Community*, ed. Richard Pierre Claude and Burns H. Weston (Philadelphia: University of Pennsylvania Press, 2006), 249–61.

3. Anne-Marie Slaughter, *A New World Order* (Princeton, NJ: Princeton University Press, 2005).

4. For examples of this, see "Chevron Launches Partnership to Reduce HIV Transmissions in Africa," *Philanthropy News Digest*, July 20, 2012; "We Built a School in Gulu Worth USD 100,000 for Internally Displaced Children," Standard Chartered Bank Sustainability and Corporate Social Responsibility Platform, http://www.standardchartered.com/ug/sustainability/en/; "Cargill Wins Prestigious Platinum Indonesian CSR Award," Cargill press release, Jakarta, Indonesia, December 16, 2011.

5. See Jürgen Runge and James Shikwati, *Geological Resources and Good Governance in Sub-Saharan Africa: Holistic Approaches to Transparency and Sustainable Development in the Extractive Sector* (Boca Raton, FL: CRC Press, 2011); Andres Liebenthal, Roland Michelitsch, and Ethel Tarazona, *Extractive Industries and Sustainable Development: An Evaluation of the World Bank Group's Experience* (Washington, DC: World Bank Publications, 2005).

6. James Ferguson, "The Uses of Neoliberalism," *Antipode* 41 (January 1, 2010): 166–84.

7. Toby J. Bishop and Frank E. Hydoski, *Corporate Resiliency: Managing the Growing Risk of Fraud and Corruption* (Hoboken, NJ: Wiley, 2009).

8. Robert W. Kates, "What Kind of Science Is Sustainability Science?" *Proceedings of the National Academy of Sciences of the United States of America* 108, no. 49 (2011): 19449–50; Luis M. A. Bettencourt and Jasleen Kuar, "Evolution and Structure of Sustainability Science," *Proceedings of the National Academy of Sciences of the United States of America* 108, no. 49 (2011): 19540–45.

9. Michael Ignatieff, *Human Rights as Politics and Idolatry* (Princeton, NJ: Princeton University Press, 2001), 29.

10. "Accolades for South Africa as Deputy Minister of Water and Environmental Affairs Bows for Sustainability Leadership Award," Department of Environmental Affairs of the Republic of South Africa, June 21, 2012, http://www

.environment.gov.za; Giuseppe Topa et al., *Forêts tropicales humides du Camer-oun: Une décennie de réformes* (Washington, DC: La Banque Mondiale, 2010), 174. See also Statements of Kofi Annan, first chairman of the Alliance for a Green Revolution in Africa at the launch of the Alliance for a Green Revolution in Africa (AGRA) during the World Economic Forum session on "Investing in Growth: A Green Revolution in Africa," Cape Town, South Africa, June 14, 2007, available at http://www.agra-alliance.org/about/pr061407-speech.html.

11. These transnational forms of authority enable African states to manage political crises and guarantee stable social institutions. Adam Branch, "Neither Liberal nor Peaceful? Practices of 'Global Justice' by the ICC," in *A Liberal Peace? The Problems and Practices of Peacebuilding*, ed. Susanna Campbell, David Chandler, and Meera Sabaratnam (London: Zed Books, 2011), 121–37.

12. Elizabeth Borgwardt, *A New Deal for the World: America's Vision for Human Rights* (Cambridge, MA: Belknap Press of Harvard University Press, 2005).

13. Meredith Terretta, *Nation of Outlaws, State of Violence: Nationalism, Grassfields Tradition, and State-Building in Cameroon* (Athens: Ohio University Press, 2014); Richard A. Joseph, *Radical Nationalism in Cameroon: Social Origins of the U.P.C. Rebellion* (Oxford: Oxford University Press, 1977).

14. Here I am grateful to the work of Robert Meister in his analysis of how societies reach a consensus that evil is past. Robert Meister, *After Evil: A Politics of Human Rights* (New York: Columbia University Press, 2011).

15. Goldman Sachs, Goldman Sachs Global Investment Research, "Overview: Introducing GS SUSTAIN," July 2, 2007.

16. Innovest Strategic Value Advisers, "Carbon Beta and Equity Performance: An Empirical Analysis: Moving from Disclosure to Performance," October 2007.

17. United Nations Environment Programme Finance Initiative, *Sustainability Metrics: Translation and Impact on Property Investment and Management*, UNEP FI Property Working Group report (United Nations, May 2014).

18. "GRI stakeholder, NYSE Euronext, strengthens its commitment to corporate transparency," *Global Reporting Initiative*, August 22, 2013, https://www.globalreporting.org/information/news-and-press-center/Pages/GRI-stakeholder-NYSE-Euronext-strengthens-its-commitment-to-corporate-transparency.aspx.

19. Helen Tilley, *Africa as a Living Laboratory: Empire, Development, and the Problem of Scientific Knowledge, 1870–1950* (Chicago: University of Chicago Press, 2011); Frederick Cooper and Ann Laura Stoler, *Tensions of Empire: Colonial Cultures in a Bourgeois World* (Berkeley: University of California Press, 1997); Gwendolyn Wright, *The Politics of Design in French Colonial Urbanism* (Chicago: University of Chicago Press, 1991).

20. Google Books Ngram Viewer, "sustainability."

21. International Union for Conservation of Nature and Natural Resources, *World Conservation Strategy: Living Resource Conservation for Sustainable Development*, IUCN, 1980, data.iucn.org/dbtw-wpd/edocs/WCS-004.pdf.

22. Andres Edwards and David Orr, *The Sustainability Revolution: Portrait of a Paradigm Shift* (Gabriola, BC: New Society Publishers, 2005).

23. Stephan Schmidheiny, *Changing Course: A Global Business Perspective on Development and the Environment* (Cambridge, MA: MIT Press, 1992).

24. John Elkington, "Enter the Triple Bottom Line," in *The Triple Bottom Line: Does It All Add Up?*, ed. Adrian Henriques and Julie Richardson (London: Earthscan Publications, 2004), 1–16.

25. Shell.com, Annual Reports and Publications, http://reports.shell.com/sustainability-report/2011/.

26. Sandra A. Waddock and Samuel B. Graves, "The Corporate Social Performance—Financial Performance Link," *Strategic Management Journal* 18, no. 4 (1997): 303–19; World Business Council for Sustainable Development, *Environmental Performance and Shareholder Value* (Geneva: WBCSD Publications, 1997); World Business Council for Sustainable Development, *The Business Case for Sustainable Development* (Geneva: WBCSD Publications, 2001); David Wheeler and Maria Sillanpaa, *The Stakeholder Corporation: A Blueprint for Maximising Shareholder Value* (London: Pitman, 1997).

27. Integrated Reporting Committee of South Africa (IRC), "Framework for Integrated Reporting and the Integrated Report," Discussion Paper January 25, 2011, www.sustainabilitysa.org.

28. Anthony Hopwood, Jeffery Unerman, and Jessica Fries, *Accounting for Sustainability: Practical Insights* (London: Earthscan, 2010); Robert Eccles, Michael P. Krzus, and Don Tapscott, *One Report: Integrated Reporting for a Sustainable Strategy* (Hoboken, NJ: Wiley, 2010).

29. Integrated Reporting Committee of South Africa (IRC), "Framework for Integrated Reporting and the Integrated Report," Discussion Paper January 25, 2011, www.sustainabilitysa.org.

30. As of 2011, a KPMG international survey revealed that 95 percent of the 250 largest companies in the world now report on their "sustainability" measures and initiatives. Cliffe Dekker Attorneys, *King Report on Corporate Governance for South Africa 2002*, www.cliffedekker.com.

31. Mervyn King, "Sustainability: The Moral and Economic Imperative of the 21st Century," Radio Today Podcast, March 9, 2010, http://www.mervynking.co.za/news/archives/2010_archives.htm.

32. Mervyn King, "Mervyn King, Chairman, Global Reporting Initiative (GRI) on accountability with AngloGold Ashanti," AngloGold Ashanti Annual Report 2010 Podcast, http://www.anglogoldashanti.co.za/subwebs/informationfor investors/reports10/podcasts.htm.

33. Mervyn King, AngloGold Ashanti Annual Report 2010 Podcast.

34. Jane Diplock, International Integrated Reporting Council website, http://www.theiirc.org/; see also Jane Diplock, "Sustainable Capitalism: The Future of Finance and the Future of the Planet," International Integrated Reporting Council Symposium, Tokyo, Japan, October 31, 2012.

35. Andreas Dombret and Otto Lucius, *Stability of the Financial System: Illusion or Feasible Concept?* (Cheltenham, UK: Edward Elgar Publishing, 2013).

36. Thomas Piketty, *Capital in the Twenty-First Century* (Cambridge, MA: Harvard University Press, 2014), 67.

37. Hersch Lauterpacht, *International Law and Human Rights* (New York: Garland, 1973), 47.

38. Jean Comaroff and John L. Comaroff, *Millennial Capitalism and the Culture of Neoliberalism* (Durham, NC: Duke University Press, 2001), 28–29.

39. Slaughter, *A New World Order*, 131–62.

40. Topa et al., *Forêts tropicales humides du Cameroun*.

41. M. Rodwan Abouharb and David Cingranelli, *Human Rights and Structural Adjustment* (Cambridge: Cambridge University Press, 2007).

42. M. Anne Pitcher, *Party Politics and Economic Reform in Africa's Democracies* (Cambridge: Cambridge University Press, 2012), 180–90. Frederick Cooper also claims that global economic pressures to downsize governments and privatize economies do less to create a market system in which individuals enter into transactions, and rather increase the importance of personal networks and strengthen the role of politics. See Frederick Cooper, "Networks, Moral Discourse, and History," in *Intervention and Transnationalism in Africa: Global-Local Networks of Power*, ed. Thomas M. Callaghy, Ronald Kassimir, and Robert Latham (Cambridge: Cambridge University Press, 2001), 23–46. For evidence of this in the case of Russia, see Bernard Black and Anna Tarassova, "Institutional Reform in Transition: A Case Study of Russia," *Supreme Court Economic Review* 10 (2003): 211–78; Markku Lonkila, "Post-Soviet Russia: A Society of Networks?," in *Russia: More Different Than Most?*, ed. Markku Kangaspuro (Helsinki: Kikimora Publications, 2001), 99–112.

43. Daniel Whelan emphasizes this in his argument regarding human rights indivisibility and economic justice for the global South. See Daniel J. Whelan, *Indivisible Human Rights: A History* (Philadelphia: University of Pennsylvania Press, 2010), chapter 8.

44. Saskia Sassen, *Territory, Authority, Rights: From Medieval to Global Assemblages* (Princeton, NJ: Princeton University Press, 2006); David Forsyth, *Human Rights in International Relations* (Cambridge: Cambridge University Press, 2000).

45. "Ten Years of Forest Reform in Cameroon," World Bank Report No. PID9198, Forest and Environment Sector Development Program (PSFE), Central Africa, June 2005, 8.

46. Jim Beck, Otodo Kede, Frederic Medjo, Susan Minnemeyer, Roger Ngoufo,

Lawrence Ayenika Nsoyuni, and Maria Jacoba Van de Pol, *Interactive Forestry Atlas of Cameroon* (World Resources Institute, Global Forest Watch, 2006). Available at http://www.globalforestwatch.org/english/centralafrica/index.htm.

47. P. Auzel, T. Fomété, J. Odi, and J.-C. Owada, *Evolution de l'exploitation des forêts du Cameroun: Production nationale, exploitation illégale, perspectives*, Présentation réunion DFID, MINEF, Banque Mondiale et FMI, Yaoundé 2003.

48. "Africa's Rainforests Depend on Cutting Out Corruption," February 5, 2005, Greenpeace International, http://www.greenpeace.org/international/press/releases/africa-s-rainforest-depend-on/.

49. "Ten Years of Forest Reform in Cameroon," 11–12.

50. Daniel Yergin and Joseph Stanislaw, *The Commanding Heights: The Battle for the World Economy* (New York: Free Press, 2002); Comaroff and Comaroff, *Millennial Capitalism and the Culture of Neoliberalism*.

51. Francesca Romano and Dominique Debb, Forestry Department, Food and Agriculture Office of the United Nations, "Understanding Forest Tenure in Africa: Opportunities and Challenges for Forest Tenure Diversification," www.fao.org.

52. Department of Environmental Affairs of the Republic of South Africa, *National Strategy for Sustainable Development and Action Plan (NSSD1), 2011–2014*, approved by Cabinet on November 23, 2011, Johannesburg.

53. Pitcher, *Party Politics and Economic Reform in Africa's Democracies*, 195.

54. Ibid.

55. Robin Attfield, Johan Hattingh, and Manamela Matshabaphala, "Sustainable Development, Sustainable Livelihoods, and Land Reform in South Africa: A Conceptual and Ethical Inquiry," *Third World Quarterly* 25, no. 2 (2004): 405–21.

56. See Richard Wilson, *The Politics of Truth and Reconciliation in South Africa: Legitimizing the Post-Apartheid State* (Cambridge: Cambridge University Press, 2001) for further discussion on how the postapartheid South African government instrumentalized human rights and development policies to serve its own interest in guaranteeing the durability of the new government.

57. It is critical to mention, however, that such instability was essential for the revolutionary transformation that brought about justice and a multiracial democracy.

58. Saleem H. Ali and Julia Marton-LeFevre, *Peace Parks: Conservation and Conflict Resolution* (Cambridge, MA: MIT Press, 2007); Ken Conca, *Environmental Peacemaking* (Baltimore: Johns Hopkins University Press, 2002).

59. Stephen Hopgood, *The Endtimes of Human Rights* (Ithaca, NY: Cornell University Press, 2013), 173.

60. Gil Anidjar, "The Meaning of Life," *Critical Inquiry* 37, no. 4 (2011): 697–723.

CHAPTER FOURTEEN

Tender Is the Mine

*Law, Shadow Rule, and the
Public Gaze in Ghana*

Lauren Coyle

In early 2011 transnational mining giant AngloGold Ashanti (AGA) received the ignominious "Public Eye Award," by which international civil society organizations formally christened it the "most irresponsible company in the world" for the previous year. This was on account of protracted environmental and social conflicts arising from the company's operations in Obuasi, a legendary mining center in the Ashanti Region of Ghana that is home to Africa's third-largest gold mine. AGA officials found the timing particularly ill-starred, as AGA "won out" over fellow nominee British Petroleum (BP) in the same year as BP's notorious and heavily publicized oil spill in the Gulf.

The Berne Declaration and Greenpeace annually organize the Public Eye Awards ceremony in Davos as a "critical counterpoint to the World Economic Forum." They confer the award with the express aim of inciting public ire and a stream of reputational consequences, possibly including socially responsible divestment or other forms of what has come to be known as "shareholder activism." In the wake of the award, rumors of possible divestment abounded, threatening the profile of AGA, the world's third-largest gold producer. The Public Eye Award organizers also seek to embolden NGO campaigns and social movements in their campaigns against various corporate depredations, even where the legal systems of the corporations' host countries or those of transnational jurisdictions have failed to address—or even acknowledge—certain forms of conflict, destruction, violence, or injury.

The official website for the awards declares, "The Public Eye Awards aim to contribute to the overarching goal of social and ecological justice and demonstrate the necessity of effective and legally binding measures on a national and international level. Corporations need to be held accountable for their irresponsible business practices in their home state—no matter where these wrong-doings occur."[1]

The website also details the spirit of the revelations and repercussions the awards facilitate:

> Whether exploitative working conditions, environmental sins, intentional disinformation, or other disregards of corporate social responsibility [. . .] the most evil offenses appear on the short list [. . .] And those firms placed in the pillory will feel the heat: our renowned naming and shaming awards shine an international spotlight on corporate scandals and thereby help focused NGO campaigns succeed.

By what means did AGA—otherwise figuring itself a champion of socially responsible operations, an oft-celebrated public benefactor, a venerable engine of development across the global South—come to assume this ignoble global status?

In nominating AGA for this "award," the Ghana-based mining advocacy NGO, Wacam, drew upon clamorous grassroots land and human rights mobilization, environmental studies, and various campaigns from over a decade of organizing in Obuasi and other mining towns across Ghana. Prominent transnational donors have heavily funded most of the campaigns. Principal among them have been Ibis and Oxfam-America. Wacam members argued that AGA's surface mining destroyed vital farmlands and streams with little or no compensation. They also documented instances in which the company had used torturing tactics in interrogating or apprehending alleged illegal miners on its concession. Likewise, Wacam advocates established that AGA, in the past, had released guard dogs on such suspects—at least in the days before AngloGold's 2004 merger with its corporate predecessor in Obuasi, Ashanti Goldfields.

As one of the early Obuasi-based stalwarts, a district assemblyman of one community that had lost all traditional farmlands to the mine, put the matter:

We had lost our farms, crops, trees, and streams—many of them sacred—
everything. We were farmers before. We lost our lives and were not paid ad-
equately at all. And our chief sold us out. When the mine wouldn't mind us,
wouldn't take us seriously or listen to our demands, I decided to go to the international media. BBC from the UK, they were here. And then I would go
speak at conferences. And sometimes, I would speak to investors. I would
tell them straightaway that this is blood money [Twi: *mogya sika*]. A lot of
people have been sacrificed for this gold, so that it has come in such great
amounts. Many of us—and our ways of life—have been sacrificed, so that the
mine could become so rich.

The assemblyman did not mean this as mere metaphor. Obuasi rests
within Akan territory. In Akan cosmology, gold (*sika*) itself is a spirit, an
aspect of Nyame, the ultimate creator god.[2] The spirit of the gold must
be propitiated and sufficiently "charmed" before it will even appear for
the taking, through sacrifices and other rituals performed through local priests and priestesses (*akomfo*). Thus many believe that the mine
has spilled much blood to have been able to "win" and "possess" such a
great deal of the sacred ore. The sacrifices can be "effective" ones—as in
the case of the ruination of a people's farms, trees, lives, and livelihoods,
with all of the ensuing poverty, suffering, death, and social disruption.
Or they can be direct, involving the "natural" slaughtering of an animal
with local priests or priestesses for charming the gold, securing the permission of the local principal earth deity (named Bona), and pacifying
other local spirits who may interfere with mining in the territory.[3]
  The mine responded to the initial news of the Public Eye Award by
swiftly assembling a counterpoint press conference, in which the Obuasi
member of parliament (MP) addressed a collection local chiefs, assem-
blypersons, and "concerned citizens of Obuasi" to denounce what he
proclaimed to be Wacam's unjust tarnishing of AGA's image with the
award. Local journalists then aired the story in the national papers. Wacam members countered with a rebuttal, also circulated in the national
media, in which they upbraided the Obuasi MP for his callous ignorance
of some of the most severe issues that beset his own constituents. The rebuttal enumerated some of the more spectacular instances of alleged violence and dispossession without adequate compensation.[4] Informally,
local advocates also bemoaned the theatricality of the event. It was obvious, they said, that the mine had staged the whole event, paying the

MP and the attendees in an early effort to mitigate or undo the damage that the "award" brought. Further, several participants had suggested as much.

What was the truth of the allegations that Wacam's nomination leveled? Was this merely an instance of the now-cliché NGO hyperbole or "resistance" manufacture in the scramble for attention and enhanced funding from donors, as some from the mine alleged? Or was there more to it? By which social and epistemic processes did such facts of corporate wrongdoing and irresponsibility arise? Through which mechanisms of "awakening," privileged forms of narrations, and relations of knowledge production—and mediation—did claims of the dispossessed come to be set in terms rendered intelligible or compelling to affected local communities and to the "public eye" of the "international community?" Further, how did all of this congeal into an established record? This was a record that could entail considerable legal and financial consequences for the company, in the global amplification and circulation of the award. As we will see, this is a record that also shifted powerful leverage into the hands of some of the dispossessed in their bargaining with the mine in the shadow of the courts, in the shadow of claims that could have been articulated within the formal legal system.

This essay draws upon extensive ethnographic research in Obuasi to examine the complex microhistories of violence and destruction that led to community outrage in this town in Ghana, to the various articulations and narrations through the mediation of civil society advocates, and to the successful nomination of AGA for this award. This exercise provides occasion to examine the broader fraught and contested roles of transnational corporations (TNCs) in effecting territorial rule—variously and unevenly viewed as "legitimate" or "responsible"—through mechanisms of shadow sovereignty within their concessions. Further, this social drama allows for exploration of the role of transnational soft law norms of "corporate best practices" and corporate social responsibility (CSR) in "giving voice" to community protests and articulated dissatisfactions, and in fashioning—and, alternately, undergirding or undermining—corporate territorial rule designs and company image-cleansing campaigns.

Within Obuasi, AGA acts as a "shadow sovereign" within its concession, effecting sovereign-like rule over territories and populations in modes both biopolitical and exceptional, fostering life and also fashioning gradations of death or abandonment. This form of sovereignty is neither formal—a privileged ideal-typical feature of the modernist nation-state—nor is it absolute. Rather, it is relational, always "tentative and emergent"—yet ever present and critical in forms of basic policing, provisioning, and adjudicating, and in deploying decisional violence with varying shades of legitimacy. This concept of shadow sovereignty is akin to recent formulations of "graduated sovereignty,"[5] "patchwork sovereignty,"[6] graying zones of sovereignty,[7] multiple or hybrid sovereignties,[8] or "selective sovereignty"[9]—though selective only in the sense of strategic navigation and qualified purview. Donald Moore was right to note that a volitional inflection of this form—in the sense of people's freely electing to recognize one sovereign over the other—would "ironically smuggle the sovereign self, a fully formed and conscious agent of willful action, into an analytic of agency."[10] People inhabiting worlds governed by shadow sovereigns shuttle in and out of relations of recognition, disavowal, or mere indifference depending on dispositions, circumstances, and changing political and economic winds. Despite the now prevalent accounts of the "denationalization" and the "deterritorialization" of sovereignty, this essay submits that forms of spatial and territorial rule merely have shifted. They have been redrawn and recalibrated to contemporary political economic, geopolitical, and local micropolitical and cultural circumstances. As Moore recently observed, "In Africa as elsewhere, sovereignties have been reterritorialized rather than deterritorialized."[11]

What is more, it is perhaps now clearer than ever how forms of sovereignty—partial, hybrid, selective, shadow—are severable from formal state rule. Despite Michel Foucault's early declarations about the need to "cut off the king's head" in political theory,[12] his development of governmentality and related work on authority and territorial rule have powerfully decentered both power *and* sovereignty from the privileged—and, ordinarily, naturalized—possession of the mythical modern state. As Thomas Blom Hansen and Finn Stepputat argue in their introduction to *Sovereign Bodies*, sovereign power has always been uneven, tentative, an unrealized aspiration of modern states. Yet this is especially so in colonial and postcolonial societies. The narrow circumscription of sovereign rule to formal state authority in political theory has emerged as "a historically contingent and peculiar outcome of the evolution of the modern state system in Europe since the Westphalian peace in 1648."[13] The ideal of a homogenous, perfectly normalized population incarnate in a general will that animates sovereignty has never been an actuality, of course, though the fantasy still holds in thrall much political theory. Hansen and Stepputat compellingly argue that "sovereignty of the state is an aspiration that seeks to create itself in the face of internally fragmented, unevenly distributed and unpredictable configurations of political authority that exercise more or less legitimate violence in a territory."[14]

Broadly speaking, Ghana's sovereign transformations over the past three decades have echoed those throughout much of the global South. Its national political economic prerogatives have been rewritten by structural adjustment reforms that have entailed the privatization of, among other things, the mining industry, which previously was heavily nationalized. This relatively recent disaggregation of the mine and the state, especially as it has unfolded in a century-old mining town such as Obuasi, has rendered the mine predisposed to popular recognition as a "shadow sovereign." For almost a century, leading up to the neoliberal reforms in 1986, the mining company *was* the most visible, palpable, addressable manifestation of the state government for the local population. In fact, it arguably wielded much more social provisioning and policing power, much more coercive might, and much more sway over adjudicatory bodies and proceedings than any other state organ or functioning para-statal body in town.

Given these storied sovereign inheritances in Obuasi—only very recently formally shorn—it is little wonder that shadow sovereign tropes and imaginaries infuse and overdetermine the newly flourishing industry discourse of CSR and its place in contests over the shape and shifting terms of a "social contract" for the company's territory. Likewise, it is unsurprising that denizens of the town continue to clamor for basic government services on the dole of the mine, voicing dissatisfactions in the newly available trump discourse of CSR. These requests—often verging on expectations—cover a panoply of public works and services, from assurances of security and public order, to maintenance of local roads and development of infrastructure, to reliable piped water and expanded electricity grids, to sports league sponsorships and renovated school buildings.

Following the neoliberal reforms, Ghana's gold industry witnessed a surge in foreign direct investment, with a sixfold increase. The gold industry now ranks as the nation's most lucrative, the highest single contributor to foreign exchange earnings. At the same time, Ghanaians seem to be suffering more than ever from severe labor retrenchments, environmental disasters, community displacements, and many other disruptive effects of corporate gold-mining operations. In many ways, the gold-mining industry sits as the signal sovereign dilemma, the paradigmatic "poisoned chalice" in Ghana's neoliberal moment. These tensions are perhaps more acute in Obuasi than anywhere else in the country.

The Golden City and the Blood of the Earth

Obuasi sits about forty miles southwest of Kumasi, the capital of the Ashanti Region. Although accurate census data is elusive, the most recent governmental indications state that there are about 175,000 people who live in the Obuasi municipality. The mine was owned and operated by Ashanti Goldfields Corporation (AGC) from the start of industrial operations in Obuasi in 1897 until 2004, when AGC merged with the global parent company of AngloGold to form AngloGold Ashanti (AGA). It is one of the most plentiful deep-pit mines in Africa. AGA estimates suggest that the mine has generated over thirty million ounces of gold since operations began, and it projects that it may be able to mine an additional nine million ounces in the reserves in the next fifteen to twenty years.[15]

The town lies wholly within the hundred-square-mile concession of AGA, which holds the exclusive rights, by way of a ninety-nine-year lease, to harvest gold beneath the surface within its territory. Obuasi saw the first onset of surface mining in Ghana after it was legalized as part of the first structural adjustment reforms in 1986. The reform logic held that the use of surface mining, with its capital-intensive technology, would render mining more profitable and also help to attract the foreign direct investment to revitalize Ghana's fledgling mining sector. On these narrow economic measures of diversifying industry, expanding operations, and attracting foreign direct investment in mining, the neoliberal governmental reforms and subsequent corporate restructurings were resounding successes—both for AGC and for the nation's gold-mining industry, more generally. Amid this surge in Ghana's gold sector, AGC was one of the largest contributors, on account of its Obuasi operations.[16]

Yet the effects of the structural adjustment reforms on the political structures and local communities most immediately affected by neoliberal mining operations are anything but uncontroversial. Nowhere have debates and conflicts blazed more heatedly, perhaps, than in the communities that have been affected by surface mining, especially where the communities have lost all or most of their farmlands and have suffered severe degradation of their streams. As all operations prior to the 1986 liberalization reforms were underground, with little surface disturbance, villagers could go on farming their surface land with little to no pollution or other disruption. The onset of surface mining brought a considerable loss of farmland, a collection of environmental and health hazards—particularly with cyanide leakages in local water sources—and profound social disruptions to these communities.

AGA has sought to remedy such community fallouts through various explicit CSR ventures. For example, AGA renamed its community outreach campaign "ONE: a culture model." This campaign boasts an ethos of symbiosis and interdependence among community members, the mine, local state politicians, traditional authorities, company investors, and other key "stakeholders."

Community activists often counter such invocations of CSR fidelity by arguing that what AGA is glossing as "CSR" is merely a form of self-serving afterthought—seemingly charitable, but actually aiming to paper over or redress previous legal transgressions. One NGO leader scoffed, amid AGA's intensified CSR campaign following the Public Eye Award: "What is CSR, anyway? Other than a pro-mine PR propaganda campaign? If these companies were following the law, the statutes, and the Constitution, and if they were honoring the communities' human and environmental rights, then what they are calling 'CSR' would not even be necessary."

Another Wacam member from Obuasi added,

> Often times in the previous years, when AGA has reached out to these communities, they have provided them with things that they did not even want, at least over other things they were asking for. For example, one community got a school, which was built with inferior materials and is now not being used. There are large cracks. And when you talk to the community, they didn't even want that. They wanted a clinic and some viable form of alternative livelihoods. But they put up a school, without really even asking the community. And they paint the name of the mine across the side, and they'll be there with photographers, blazing like crazy. Ready to plaster the pictures all over the papers.

Mining companies belonging to the Ghana Chamber of Mines are bound, formally, to participate in CSR and community development as part of the chamber's code of ethics. When civil society groups and community activists—and, at times, customary leaders—have found the mine's compensation, CSR, or other redress gestures inadequate, they invoke such industry obligations and insist that the mine holds key obligations to the affected communities. Oftentimes, the communities' demands have been rather specific, most often centering on the need for jobs—preferably at the mine, or for some sort of viable alternative livelihood. Alongside employment concerns, the community members urgently plead for adequate boreholes to replace contaminated streams, which community members previously used for drinking water. They also often ask for medical clinics, skills-training workshops, school buildings, scholarships for their children's school fees, or start-up capital for small crafts and trades. At times, they ask for resettlement.

The terms of effective and legitimate corporate territorial rule are constantly contested and negotiated within a broader discourse that, on the one hand, draws upon global normative regimes of civil society deliberations and "good governance," and, on the other, remains in keeping with the mine's prior nationalized history—in which community members conceive and debate the mine as a source of shadow sovereign authority and obligation.

Imperiled Chiefs, Compensation Controversies, and Elusive Redress

The central complaints issuing from the communities, which gave force to much of the advocacy that culminated in the Public Eye Award, surrounded the issue of compensation for lands, crops, streams, homes, and livelihoods damaged or destroyed by AGA's surface mining. The nature of the early compensation negotiations in the communities that lost their farmlands in the early and mid-1990s is somewhat debated, though almost all of the members of such communities with whom I spoke during my fieldwork depicted the same basic procedure. The mine arrived to announce that they had to seize the surface land so that they could conduct surface mining. They conferred money and the customary drinks for libations to the chief. Then, before commencing surface mining, the mine would come to negotiate directly with farmers who occupied the surface land. The farmers ordinarily held usufructuary rights that had been conferred by traditional authorities, though at times they held parcels in individual freeholds or in family lands rather than under customary land tenure schemes. The chief would bang the gong to call the farmers to negotiate with the mine. Where it would be too much to negotiate directly with thousands of farmers, the community is supposed to set up a community committee of opinion leaders—elders, churchmen, teachers, professionals, chiefs, and so forth—to preside over the negotiations on behalf of all of the farmers. The constitution of these committees, though an internal community affair, has generated much social unrest and many accusations of shadow dealings, unjust disinheritances, and other wrongdoings.

However, members of these communities repeatedly told me that when the mine arrived to negotiate, they were not given to understand that the compensation the mine was offering was up for negotiation. Most told me that, by and large, the mine merely announced that it would commence operations, and that it had come to compensate the community members at the stated rates, which the landholders almost always found inadequate, at least in retrospect. The community members, most of them peasant farmers who speak little English and read little or none, were then asked to thumbprint English-language documents certifying that they had "negotiated" for compensation and that they had agreed to accept the named amount on the specified date and that they, therefore, disclaim any right to raise the matter again in a court of Ghana. Most community members also say that no one read the document aloud to them, even in English, and that it was never translated into the local dialect of Twi for them.

Further, many emphasized that they were accustomed to the mine's long-running operation as a heavily nationalized enterprise under the Rawlings military regime. One woman from a community that lost all of its farmlands to surface mining in the early 1990s told me that when the mine arrived to announce compensation:

> We wouldn't have dared to question them, to protest what they were telling us they would pay us for the land and crops. We were just emerging from the military regime, when the mine itself was part of the state [over half state-owned]. And then, in those days, the military and police would swiftly silence anyone who questioned or protested the mine or its activities. It was that simple then. We didn't dare question. The ghost of the military regime was still heavily with us, hanging over us, somehow controlling our actions.

The democratic constitution had only recently been put into force, and no one invested much confidence in its integrity or meaning on the ground, if they even knew of it at all. Many in Obuasi-area peasant farming communities told me that they had not even heard of the hallowed national document, until Wacam arrived in the late 1990s and early 2000s. Wacam entered the communities armed with translated copies and announcing news of the peasants' newfound constitutional freedoms and rights as individual humans and as landowners, with fundamental rights and freedoms guaranteed vis-à-vis the mine, the state, and traditional authorities.

At no step in the statutory "negotiation" process that is supposed to take place do Ghanaians with customary alodial, family, or individual ownership of the surface land have the right to object altogether to the surface mining project that would destroy their property and displace or otherwise affect them. Surface owners or occupiers only enjoyed the right to "free prior and informed consultation" (FPIC)—basically, prior notification—and not the more recent proposed right to refuse the project altogether, under "free prior and informed *consent*" doctrines.[17] The right to fair, prompt, and adequate compensation—and to negotiate for it—had been enshrined in the national democratic constitution since its arrival in 1993. However, the early version of the Minerals and Mining Act from the 1986 neoliberal reforms did not contain this language; the act only instructed that the mine *negotiate* and, if the owners or occupiers of the surface land were not content with what the mine was offering, then the Land Valuation Board, a government body, would be called in to perform the valuation procedure. The language from the constitution that requires "fair, prompt, and adequate compensation" for those suffering losses on account of mining activities was later added to the 2006 amendment, the Minerals and Mining Act of 2006, under heavy civil society recommendation that advised the dispelling of this remaining ambiguity between statutory and constitutional law. However, surface mining in Obuasi had ceased in 1998, well before this amended act was passed.

Former AGA officials maintain that the responsibility for setting the compensation rate has rested with a government body, the Land Valuation Board, since 1994. Mine officials who had been working in Obuasi in the 1990s explained that AGA initially negotiated with farmers of the first community to lose farmland, Sansu, directly. But soon after those farmers were compensated, the farmers started to clamor for further compensation, claiming that the mine had cheated them. One former official recalled:

> Then, [we said], the government must come. So, this issue was eventually thrashed at the level of regional administration, and they brought in the Land Valuation Board. When the Land Valuation Board was brought in, from that time on, we were not responsible for providing rates. The Land Valuation Board provides the rates. So, whether it is high or low, the Land Valuation Board has been determining the rates, from 1994 up till now.

If the community members would have known that they could have appealed beyond the Land Valuation Board determination, and if they would have been so inclined, those who remained dissatisfied with the board's valuation figures for compensation could have, by statutory right, appealed to the minister for review of the valuation procedure and negotiation disagreements.

Only after this step, which itself has no statutory timeline and could potentially drag on interminably, could community members then have taken their claims for higher or different forms of compensation to court. However, even if communities had been able at last to take their claims on appeal to the state courts, the court then only would exercise supervisory jurisdiction and evaluate whether the board had adhered to the required technical procedures and negotiations. This remains so even under the 2006 version of the act.

Moreover, the state courts generally do not work for the impacted communities. The courts are either too expensive to access in the first place, or they lack the means—and, often, technical representation—to maintain a lawsuit for the projected ten years or so, a period in which the mining corporations in Ghana generally succeed in miring plaintiffs, bleeding them dry of resources they often scarcely had in the first place. This practice has brought heavy accusations of gross "corporate irresponsibility" from public interest law and mining advocacy organizations involved in the cases. To be sure, if the mines had offered compensation rates acceptable to communities in the first instance, none of these subsequent avenues of redress would be of practical consequence. However, once the state bodies enter the picture, it is difficult not to see these compensation issues as borne not only of dynamics between mines and local communities but also of a bureaucratic and legal quagmire of the neoliberal state. Here, one witnesses political contests, waged by poorer citizens, that must be lodged in adjudicatory venues or adminis-trative appeal domains not designed to offer them effective or adequate redress.

As for customary venues for redress, these are also largely ineffec-tual in such circumstances, as many traditional authorities—especially higher chiefs—have suffered serious legitimacy crises under accusa-tions of collusion or of having been "bought off" by the mine. The ex-tent to which subjects view their chiefs as having been slipped into the pocket of the mine varies, of course, by community. In some cases, the fall has been rather severe. In two large areas that have been acutely af-fected by losses of farmlands to surface mining, the chiefs cannot even return safely to preside over traditional courts, festivals, funerals, or any other chiefly affairs that the offices entail. Some chiefs have even been destooled, or overthrown, though this has been more the exception. Yet even with those who have not (yet) been destooled, they have lost much of their de facto authority. They are seen to have betrayed their subjects and their sacred duties to hold the stool in trust for the ancestors, the liv-ing subjects, and the subjects who are yet to be born or reborn.

Securitization and the Specter of the "Galamseys"

The other critical area of conflict that has fed advocacy and press stories over the years, and that ultimately played a central role in the nomina-tion of AGA for the Public Eye, has been the controversial treatment of galamseys, or local small-scale miners. In Obuasi, galamseys operate in a formally illegal fashion on AGA's very large concession, which spans all of Obuasi and beyond. The forces of the galamseys in town have bur-geoned dramatically in the past two decades, alongside the spread of surface mining, the unfolding of severe retrenchments and the casualiza-tion of formal mine labor, and soaring unemployment. By some local es-timates, there are now around thirty thousand galamseys in town, a fig-ure that towers over AGA's remaining workforce, now hovering around three thousand laborers.

Over the years, there allegedly have been violent and arbitrary—and extrajudicial—crackdowns, beatings, and even killings of galam-seys at the hands of mine security, especially in the days before the 2004 merger between AngloGold and Ashanti Goldfields. Yet these were not only meted out at the hands of AGA's security forces but also, at times, by local state police forces and, periodically, by the state military. The state military periodically has engaged in what it terms an "Operation Flashout" to clear areas of galamseys—and to intimidate them, to loot their homes, to frighten their home communities, and so forth. In one incident in 2006, state military personnel are said to have "swept" several galamseys working illegally on AGA's concession and then to have stripped them naked, bound them at their hands and feet, and driven them through their home villages. Military personnel displayed the miners on the backs of trucks, whipping and beating them in front of their wives, children, kin, and fellow villagers. Intended to serve, it seems, as a deterrent by way of nightmarish spectacle, it bespoke a much deeper rage, insecurity, and attempt at the profound emasculation of the whole enterprise and those who populated it. Many earlier "flashout" operations also are said to have involved the raiding of galamseys' homes for anything of value by military personnel, and attendant intimidation and humiliation of galamseys in front of their families and neighbors.

Among the most disconcerting confirmations of a 2008 independent governmental inquiry into allegations of human rights abuses in mining communities, which was published as a final report of the governmental Commission on Human Rights and Administrative Justice, were such repeated instances of brutality against the galamseys in Obuasi at the hands of the state police, the military, and the mine's private security forces.[18] One highly publicized piece of the report was confirmation that there previously were private detention facilities—functioning akin to "prisons," by allegation—within the mining company compounds, where security personnel deployed various forms of holding, handcuffing, interrogating, and disciplining.[19]

AGA officials, while generally acknowledging such past occurrences, tend to argue in public responses that they have been exaggerated or misrepresented in civil society and journalistic write-ups. For example, AGA responded that the aforementioned detention rooms were merely where mine security officials would hold the apprehended galamsey suspects—in handcuffs, at times—until the local police arrived to take them to the police station, the local jail, or a court. There also was a company history of releasing attack guard dogs on galamsey suspects who had been discovered on the mine's concession. Some allege that attack guard dogs even killed some of the galamseys during their attacks and, often, at least would exact injury. However, this is a practice that AGA claims was only conducted under the corporate predecessor, AGC—and that, long ago, in the early 1990s.

The mine cites the illegal operations of small-scale miners as its highest—and longest standing—threat to the security of mine operations and, sometimes, even to mine laborers. At times, galamseys have arrived at the company's sites, even underground, armed and announcing that they will take over by force, if necessary. Galamseys themselves often say they have no alternative to their labor, facing otherwise destitution and unemployment.

Mining officials tend to dismiss these rationales for galamsey operations as deceptive, their "common refrains." The galamsey phenomenon in Obuasi is multilayered and complex, marked by searing political contests over claims and evidence. Among the more recent battlegrounds, for example, is the mine's blaming galamseys for causing the pollution of vital rivers and streams. Affected communities, usually orchestrated by key civil society groups, often attribute this pollution to the mine itself. Further, the mine contends that it is now the galamseys, often backed by foreign financiers and fronted by local chiefs, who are destroying peasant farms in Obuasi's communities. Mine officials bewail the lack of attention that the local advocacy organizations are paying to this livelihood issue. The advocacy organizations, for their part, counter that the mine is trying to divert them.

Many of these more general claims and particular historical cases are currently being investigated and substantiated by AGA, Wacam, and independent mediators. AGA has stated that it will provide redress where it is established that past incidents indeed occurred. This is part of a larger fact-finding mission in which AGA is engaged—in an effort to rectify many of these legacy issues. All of this appears to be in progress through closed alternative dispute resolution procedures, and none of this has yet been made public.

Conclusion: Redemptive Rule and "Upward Adjustment"

In recent years, mining struggles have registered in national consciousness and helped to generate fiscal reform for the mining industry. Such social turmoil in mining towns has converged with other ill effects of Ghana's neoliberal extractive regime to give rise to Ghana's "upward adjustment" reforms. These were passed in 2012 and significantly tighten Ghana's fiscal regime for the mining sector, rolling back many of the most dramatically liberalizing provisions of the structural adjustment reforms for the industry. These reforms include, among other things, an increase in the corporate taxation rate from 25 to 35 percent, the establishment of a uniform royalty rate of 5 percent (to revise the current customary rate of 3 percent), the imposition of a new windfall profit tax of 10 percent, and—perhaps most significantly for curbing heavy capital flight dynamics—the creation of a uniform capital allowance of 20 percent for a limit of five years, across all companies. This new uniform standard contrasts to capital allowance norms that sometimes had been hovering as high as 80 percent, under which many corporations basically had been operating indefinitely.[20]

In a fascinating ideological shift, and for the first time, even the World Bank and the IMF—signature authors of the neoliberal reforms, of course—are supporting this "upward adjustment," if in slightly more tempered terms. Predictably, mining companies are complaining that these reforms will pose much too onerous costs on their operations and are threatening to withdraw plans for further investment in their operations in the country. In some cases, they even are threatening to halt production.

This "upward adjustment" has resonated with similar reforms that recently have been unfolding across much of the resource-rich global South—enhanced state takings that have been rendered ever-more plausible by soaring global mineral prices and a rapidly increasing demand for raw resources, not least from Chinese buyers.[21] This pattern of upward state takings led to Ernst & Young's 2011 christening of "resource nationalism" as the number one threat to global mining corporations, where it remains. The industry analysts also recently introduced a new itemized threat—"sharing the benefits"—that registered as ninth in the top ten threats to investment.[22] The recent "upward adjustment" trend perhaps augurs or exemplifies the onset of a new epoch in prevailing modes of law and sovereignty, especially in the resource-rich South. These shifts signal a potential move toward much more state-centric—possibly more, possibly less, authoritarian—modes of extraction, accumulation, and governance.

The government of Ghana has pledged to renegotiate the stability agreement contracts it has with two of the three main mining companies operating in Ghana, AGA and Newmont. The agreements immunize these companies from the adverse financial effects of fiscal reforms until the end of their fifteen-year terms. Significantly, however, the risk remains of endless deferral of decisive settlement on renegotiated terms. To date, a year and a half after the renegotiations began, there still has been no final agreement on new contracts.

Meanwhile, in the most affected areas of Obuasi, people continue to wait, halfheartedly. They wait for some news to drop from all of these deliberations to which they have not been directly privy, by and large. They wait for some materialization of the results of all of these "dialogues"—among the mines, the NGOs, the governmental bodies, the consultants, and the lawyers.

In the case of Obuasi—and for Ghana, more broadly—we witness the disaggregation and lateralization of a previously unified sovereign power, to be sure, in line with much recent research.[23] However, in contrast to some formulations, we observe something other than a decisive shift from transcendence to immanence in this new physics of power, and something other than wholly indeterminate, deterritorialized social forms animated by popular masses or rhizomic networks.[24] We also witness something other than exceptional states that entail the complete stripping of symbolic or political entitlement and the rendering of bodies to an unqualified state of "bare life," without signification in the prevailing constitutional order or without the capacity even to be meaningfully sacrificed.[25]

I argue that we see, instead, both the partial unseating and the selective reinscription of "traditional," transcendent forms of authority, as the leaders of these hierarchical shadow sovereign forces deploy forms of authority, power, and legitimacy that, in many ways, mimic the scaffoldings of modern states. In Obuasi, intensely local processes have underwritten this shift, in part. Yet these emergent CSR struggles and shadow sovereign formations also clearly partake of transformations wrought within the broader dynamics of contemporary capitalism, including the selective retreat of the state and the denationalization of industry; the casualization of labor forces and soaring unemployment; heavy executive policing in the names of the sanctity of "rule of law" property concessions and of corporate purview cast as "national interest"; and the resurgence of prominent forms of "private indirect government," particularly in extractive realms—a phenomenon that courses with the added material weight and affective charge of pronounced colonial echoes.[26]

While these sovereign transformations have generated situations in which much power and effective authority has been concentrated in the mine's shadow rule, the social dramas of the Public Eye Award and of related contests in Obuasi also bear witness to the power of advocacy groups such as Wacam in bringing a critical public gaze upon the mine. In this way, the Public Eye has illuminated manifold injuries and complexes of violence in the shadows of the mine's realm, however partially. The campaign succeeded, at least, in bringing the mine to negotiation tables with members of dispossessed communities to begin to draw plans for redress. In this way, Wacam and other mining advocacy organizations have assumed forms of shadow rule in their own right—tabulating, provisioning, policing, adjudicating, broadcasting, and world-making. Even still, the extractive histories to be recast or laid to rest through these ongoing negotiations—and the futures foretold for shadow rule and resource governance—remain to be seen.

Notes

1. About the Public Eye Awards, available at http://publiceye.ch/en/about-the -public-eye-awards/, last accessed May 25, 2014.

2. The same term *sika*, in Twi, is used to denote gold, money, and wealth. Speakers routinely employ the term to denote any of the three. One may also hear "*sika kra*," meaning "soul's gold." Such usages index gold's sacred status, its dual signification and manifestation of one aspect of *Nyame*. This usage also signals the sacred form of property that gold constitutes—and the fact that it traditionally, under Akan customary laws, belongs to the divine royal authorities of the territory in which it is found. See, generally, Eva L. R. Meyerowitz, *The Sacred State of the Akan* (London: Faber and Faber, 1953); Ivor Wilks, *Forests of Gold: Essays on the Akan and the Kingdom of Asante* (Athens: Ohio University Press, 1993).

3. In fact, until 2009, AGA was holding large annual sacrifices at its six principal shaft openings. This phenomenon is detailed and analyzed at length in Lauren Coyle, "Sovereigns of the Golden Twilight: Law, Land, and Sacrificial Labor in Ghana" (PhD diss., University of Chicago, 2014).

4. Richard Ellimah, Re: Press Statement by Hon. Edward Ennin in Reaction to AngloGold Ashanti's 2010 Public Eye Award, February 21, 2011, available at http://www.modernghana.com/news/317368/1/re-press-statement-by-hon -edward-ennin-in-reaction.html.

5. Aihwa Ong, *Neoliberalism as Exception: Mutations in Citizenship and Sovereignty* (Durham, NC: Duke University Press, 2006).

6. John L. Comaroff and Jean Comaroff, "Introduction: Law and Disorder in

the Postcolony," in *Law and Disorder in the Postcolony*, ed. John L. Comaroff and Jean Comaroff (Chicago: University of Chicago Press, 2006), 1–16.

7. Elizabeth Povinelli, *Economies of Abandonment: Social Belonging and Endurance in Late Liberalism* (Durham, NC: Duke University Press, 2011); Charles Piot, *Nostalgia for the Future: West Africa after the Cold War* (Chicago: University of Chicago Press, 2010); Janet Roitman, *Fiscal Disobedience: An Anthropology of Economic Regulation in Central Africa* (Princeton, NJ: Princeton University Press, 2005).

8. Thomas Blom Hansen and Finn Stepputat, eds., *Sovereign Bodies: Citizens, Migrants, and States in the Postcolonial World* (Princeton, NJ: Princeton University Press, 2005). See also Thomas Blom Hansen and Finn Stepputat, "Sovereignty Revisited," *Annual Review of Anthropology* 35 (2006): 295–315.

9. Donald Moore, *Suffering for Territory: Race, Place, and Power in Zimbabwe* (Durham, NC: Duke University Press, 2005); Rebecca Hardin, "Concessionary Politics: Property, Patronage, and Political Rivalry in Central African Forest Management," *Current Anthropology* 52, no. 3 (2011): S113–S125.

10. Moore, *Suffering for Territory*, 220.

11. Ibid., 233. See also Brenda Chalfin, *Neoliberal Frontiers: An Ethnography of Sovereignty in West Africa* (Chicago: University of Chicago Press, 2010); Jean Comaroff and John Comaroff, *Theory from the South; or, How Euro-America Is Evolving toward Africa* (Boulder, CO: Paradigm, 2012); James Ferguson, "Seeing Like an Oil Company: Space, Security, and Global Capital in Neoliberal Africa," *American Anthropologist* 107, no. 3 (2005): 377–82; James Ferguson, *Global Shadows: Africa in the Neoliberal World Order* (Durham, NC: Duke University Press, 2006); Michael Watts, "Resource Curse? Governmentality, Oil, and Power in the Niger Delta, Nigeria," *Geopolitics* 9, no. 1 (2004): 50–80.

12. Michel Foucault, *Power/Knowledge: Selected Interviews and Other Writings, 1972–1977*, ed. Colin Gordon (New York: Knopf Doubleday, 1980), 121.

13. Hansen and Stepputat, *Sovereign Bodies*, 3. See also Jens Bartelson, *A Genealogy of Sovereignty* (Cambridge: Cambridge University Press, 1995); Peter Gratton, *The State of Sovereignty: Lessons from the Political Fictions of Modernity* (Albany: State University of New York Press, 2012); James Ferguson and Akhil Gupta, "Spatializing States: Toward an Ethnography of Neoliberal Governmentality," *American Ethnologist* 29, no. 4 (2002): 981–1002.

14. Hansen and Stepputat elaborate that these myriad forms of sovereignty can assume quite various manifestations in their performative dimensions. Hansen and Stepputat, *Sovereign Bodies*, 3.

15. Edward S. Ayensu, *Ashanti Gold: The African Legacy of the World's Most Precious Metal* (London: Marshall, 1997).

16. World Bank, "Ghana: Mining Sector Rehabilitation Project (Credit 1921-GH) and Mining Sector Development and Environment Project (Credit 2743-

GH)," Project Performance Assessment Report, Operation Evaluations De-
partment, July 1, 2003; Thomas M. Akabzaa, J. S. Seyire, and K. Afriyie, *The
Glittering Façade: Effects of Mining Activities on Obuasi and Its Surrounding
Communities* (Accra, Ghana: Third World Network–Africa, 2008); Emmanuel
Ababio Ofosu-Mensah, "Gold Mining and the Socio-Economic Development of
Obuasi in Adanse," *African Journal of History and Culture* 3, no. 4 (2011): 54–64.

17. This latter right recently was inscribed in the current draft of a proposed
regional mining sector framework for the Economic Community of West African States. It also is gaining momentum across compulsory-acquisition-of-land
reforms in Latin America. See, e.g., César Rodríguez-Garavito, "Ethnicity.gov:
Global Governance, Indigenous Peoples, and the Right to Prior Consultation
in Social Minefields," *Indiana Journal of Global Legal Studies* 18, no. 1 (2011):
263–305.

18. Commission on Human Rights and Administrative Justice (CHRAJ,
Ghana), "The State of Human Rights in Mining Communities in Ghana" (2008),
available at http://www.chrajghana.org/. UNDP provided the funding for the
commission's research for this report.

19. Ibid.

20. National Coalition on Mining (NCOM), Ghana, "Statement by National
Coalition on Mining on 2012 Budget: Proceed with Further Reforms in the Mining Sector," November 21, 2011, available at http://twnafrica.org.

21. There also are growing alliances at supranational levels, within bodies such as the United Nations Economic Commission on Africa and the policy
units of the African Union, the Economic Community of West African States,
and the Southern African Development Community, all of which are aiming to
push cognate mining sector reforms for countries within their regional purviews.
The pan-African Africa Mining Vision also has been gaining much force in public policy and civil society debates in Ghana and elsewhere in Africa in recent
years.

22. Ernst & Young, "Business Risks Facing Mining and Metals 2012–2013,"
available at http://www.ey.com/Publication/vwLUAssets/Business-risk-facing
-mining-and-metals-2012-2013/$FILE/Business-risk-facing-mining-and-metals
-2012-2013.pdf.

23. See also Stuart Kirsch, "Indigenous Movements and the Risks of Counterglobalization: Tracking the Campaign against Papua New Guinea's Ok Tedi
Mine," *American Ethnologist* 34, no. (2007): 303–21; Anna Tsing, *Friction: An
Ethnography of Global Connection* (Princeton, NJ: Princeton University Press,
2005).

24. Michael Hardt and Antonio Negri, *Empire* (Cambridge, MA: Harvard
University Press, 2000); Michael Hardt and Antonio Negri, *Multitude: War and
Democracy in the Age of Empire* (New York: Penguin Press, 2004).

25. Giorgio Agamben, *Homo Sacer: Sovereign Power and Bare Life (Homo Sacer I)*, trans. Daniel Heller-Roazen (Stanford, CA: Stanford University Press, 1998); Giorgio Agamben, *State of Exception (Homo Sacer II, 1)*, trans. Kevin Attell (Chicago: University of Chicago Press, 2005).

26. Chalfin, *Neoliberal Frontiers*; Christian Lund, ed., *Twilight Institutions: Public Authority and Local Politics in Africa* (Malden, MA: Wiley-Blackwell, 2007); Gareth Austin, *Labour, Land and Capital in Ghana: From Slavery to Free Labour in Asante, 1807–1956* (Rochester, NY: University of Rochester Press, 2005); Comaroff and Comaroff, *Theory from the South*; Achille Mbembe, *On the Postcolony* (Berkeley: University of California Press, 2001); John Kelly, "The Other Leviathans: Corporate Investment and the Construction of a Sugar Company," in *White and Deadly: Sugar and Colonialism*, ed. Pal Ahluwadia, Bill Ashcroft, and Roger Knight (Commack, NY: Nova Science Publishers, 1999), 95–134.

CHAPTER FIFTEEN

Corporate Social Responsibility and Latecomer Industrialization in Nigeria

Richard Joseph
Kelly Spence
Abimbola Agboluaje

The principles of corporate social responsibility, as noted in the introduction to this volume, derived from a concern for extreme imbalances in the distribution of wealth generated by networks of production and finance. Of the many definitions of corporate social responsibility (CSR), one of them, cited by Charlotte Walker-Said, is pertinent to contemporary Nigeria: "the continuing commitment by business to behave ethically and contribute to economic development while improving the quality of life of the workforce and their families as well as the local community and society at large." CSR reflects the evolution of human rights to include not only economic rights but also "humanitarianism." The current humanitarian and interventionist character of the human rights agenda is relevant to the slow pace of Nigeria's industrialization.

In Nigeria, multinational companies and national firms have usually approached CSR from the perspective of palliative humanitarianism. This approach is reflected in the discourse of a wide range of stakeholders: government, the media, civil society groups, and prominent citizens. Businesses in Nigeria tend to engage the government to further their interests as individual owners rather than society as a whole. There is an obvious tension, as private returns are not aligned with social returns.[1] In the historic context of a state-dominated economy, businesspeople are far more concerned with securing patronage from individuals in government than being advocates of policy or governance change. Yet the CSR agenda in Nigeria, and in other African countries, is evolving to include fostering an enabling environment for private sector growth alongside the usual range of human rights and societal concerns. In Nigeria as elsewhere, CSR is a contentious area, especially with regard to the periodic exposés of misconduct by multinational firms, from Shell to Halliburton to Siemens. The greatest responsibility of all businesses in Nigeria, whether national or multinational, is to be effective in what they are meant to do: expand production, serve customers, and generate profits. To accomplish these goals, however, they must overcome many instances of market and government failure that characterize the Nigerian landscape.[2]

Overcoming Corporate Social Irresponsibility

Corporate social responsibility in an oil-exporting country such as Nigeria is overshadowed by what could be called corporate social irresponsibility (CSI), a phenomenon that particularly afflicts mineral-exporting countries. In this chapter we will focus on efforts to develop a manufacturing sector that is responsible in the sense of being productive, and not just extractive, and that also contributes to reducing governance and social welfare deficits.[3] While assessing progress along these two tracks, the deep shadow cast by CSI cannot be overlooked.

The term *tollgate society* was coined to refer to the innumerable bribery transactions that occur. Individuals entrusted to perform an act based on governmental authority can establish an arbitrary toll to be paid before the operation is carried out. In a World Bank study widely reported in the Nigerian media, it is estimated that 80 percent of Nigerian businesses pay bribes to government officers.[4] This study, conducted in twenty-six of Nigeria's thirty-six states, arrived at percentages for the value of contracts that are paid as illicit inducements: formal sector firms paid more than microenterprises, manufacturers handed over larger bribes (6.7 percent) than service providers (3.9 percent), and percentages were determined of what these payments added to the balance sheet of firms depending on whether they operated in the formal or informal sector.

At the upper echelon of the tollgate society, the level of corruption is virtually limitless. Cecilia Ibru, a bank managing director convicted in October 2010 of corrupt practices, had ninety-four personal properties in Nigeria and other countries confiscated along with numerous bank deposits and other forms of wealth.[5] Former governor James Ibori of Rivers State, accused of stealing $250 million dollars in public funds, was convicted in April 2012 of money laundering in the United Kingdom and sentenced to thirteen years and fined $79 million. When the federal government decided to remove the subsidy on commercial sales of refined petroleum in January 2012—much of it imported because of the dilapidated state of Nigeria's refineries—the national strike that ensued provoked investigations that revealed the extraordinary level of corruption this program nurtured. A discrepancy of more than $4 billion a year was uncovered between the amount of motor fuel subsidized by the government and actual consumption.[6] Alexandra Gillies of the Revenue Watch Institute reports that "in 2011, the subsidy on gasoline cost the government over $9 billion, more than the entire federal government capital budget and about double the subsidy's cost in 2010."[7] Dozens of companies were created just to take advantage of the arbitrage between the imported price of refined petroleum and prices the government subsidized. On top of its highly inefficient national petroleum company, a bogus industry had emerged devoted solely to dunning the government both for oil delivered to end users and oil neither bought nor sold.[8]

Much focus on CSR (and CSI) in Nigeria has been devoted to its oil industry. A few notable examples will be mentioned. After a long review, the US Supreme Court declined jurisdiction in the case of *Kiobel v. Royal Dutch Petroleum* concerning the extrajudicial killing, torture, and other crimes committed by the Nigerian government in the mid-1990s. The court ruled on April 17, 2013, that the oil company could not be held liable under the Alien Tort Statute of 1789. Nevertheless, the amount of expert attention and litigation this case elicited raised the threshold of awareness about CSR. Had minority opinion among the justices prevailed, the implications for CSR and past corporate misconduct would have been momentous. When Albert J. Stanley, the former head of the engineering and construction firm KBR (a subsidiary of Halliburton) was sentenced along with "middleman" Jeffrey Tessler for the payment of bribes amounting to $180 million to Nigerian government officials to secure $6 billion in contracts for building liquefied natural gas facilities, that case added to a long list of similar revelations involving other multinational firms and their dealings in Nigeria.[9]

All major companies in Nigeria now have CSR programs, many of them involving the delivery of charitable benefits to specific categories of citizens or organizations. Because they have been targets of much criti cism, as a consequence of environmental degradation caused by their activities in the Niger Delta, multinational oil companies have developed the most extensive and sustained ameliorative activities. Many Nigerians in the affected areas have benefited from education, health, water, and other community development projects. Some unique CSR programs have emerged from the modern corporate sector. An important initiative was the creation in 2010 of a CSR center in the Lagos Business School (LBS) by Etisalat, a multinational telecommunications company. Since many companies sponsor Nigerian senior executives of the major Nigerian firms to pursue training courses at the LBS, this center has the opportunity to refine a CSR methodology appropriate for Nigeria, and also to impart deeper awareness and more effective methods throughout Nigerian public and private institutions.

Late Industrialization: Obstacles and Opportunities

The opening up of African economies to greater private sector investments, by local entrepreneurs and multinational companies since the 1980s, has enhanced the importance of making CSR relevant to the transformations underway. Although Nigeria has experienced economic growth of over 7 percent for the past decade, this growth has been accompanied by a steady rise in unemployment and poverty. And while the country has earned $600 billion from petroleum exports since 1973, it "cannot guarantee any of the basic necessities to the citizens: food, water, good roads, electricity, education, health."[10] According to the *African Economic Outlook*, a prime reason for growth without development in Nigeria is "the dilapidated state of infrastructure and the overdependence on the oil and gas industry."[11] Nigerian businesses must contend with an anemic electricity, water, and transportation infrastructure. They are therefore forced to create their own "ministates" by building roads, supplying their own electricity, and arranging their own security.

Compounding these infrastructural challenges are many governance and institutional deficits, such as the unharmonized and often corrupt tax regime. At state and local levels, excess taxes and levies are often imposed without services provided in return. There is widespread tax evasion because business and private citizens believe that taxes will be embezzled. They also feel they can get away with not paying taxes or underpaying them. Some improvements have been made at the federal level and in Lagos State, the largest of Nigeria's thirty-six states and a pacesetter in governance reforms. However, the inadequate taxation system remains a crucial barrier to improving physical infrastructure and social services.

Business firms are usually unable to pass the extra cost of managing their "ministates" on to the consumer because of widespread poverty. Nigerian consumers often prefer to purchase cheaper Chinese-made goods. When the business community cannot engage effectively in creating an enabling business environment, not just their activities are adversely affected but also their capacity to improve the life condition of the population.

The share of Africa's manufacturing in GDP has been stagnant since 1960. It is surprising to note that in the early 1970s this share was greater in sub-Saharan Africa than in Southeast Asia.[12] Manufacturing and industrialization generally are more powerful engines of economic growth than other sectors.[13] Osita Ogbu concurs: "no other sector is more important than manufacturing in developing an economy, providing quality employment and wages, and reducing poverty."[14] The urgent need for robust and sustained employment-generating growth in Africa must therefore be brought more centrally into the discourse on CSR.[15]

Roughly two-thirds of Africa's population is under the age of twenty-four and many are unemployed or underemployed. With population growth expected to be 2.2 percent in the next twenty-five years, Célestin Monga contends that considerable responsibility will fall on the private sector to generate the needed employment opportunities. To accommodate the high rate of population growth, seven to ten million jobs must be produced *annually* in sub-Saharan Africa over an extended period. The chart below captures the limited structural transformation in Africa over four decades, 1965–2005:[16]

The development of a robust manufacturing sector in Nigeria is therefore a social as well as economic imperative. Despite the country's size and resource endowments, it has a poverty profile little different from that of its neighbors, with 61 percent of the population living below the poverty line.[17] Nigeria is also faced with profound demographic challenges. The fertility rate of 6.4 in 1982 declined in four decades to

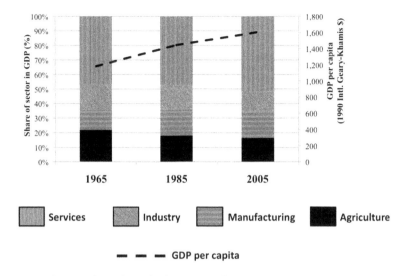

FIGURE 1 Structural transformation in Africa, 1965–2005

only 5.7.[18] In the largely Islamic northern states, besieged by terrorist and intercommunal violence, the rate is substantially higher. Nigeria's population, now estimated at 170 million, could rise to 430 million by mid-century, the third largest in the world after China and India.[19] With a population growing by over 300,000 annually, and a pronounced youth bulge, industrialization and rapid job creation in Nigeria are paramount. However, as can be seen in the chart below, the proportion of manufacturing in Nigeria approximates the African mean. It is well below the country's potential considering its extensive financial, energy, and human resources.

Chukwuma Charles Soludo, a former governor of Nigeria's Central Bank, contends that "the manufacturing sector is largely comatose and declined from a share of 7 percent of GDP in the 1970s to 4 percent currently." "Our manufacturers," he added, "are fighting a losing battle against the armada of imports from cheaper and more productive locations abroad."[20] For comparison, the share of the manufacturing sector to GDP is 20 percent in Brazil and 34 percent in China. Nigeria's development failure therefore reflects, to an important degree, a failure to industrialize. The economic growth recently experienced (notably in telecommunications and financial services) does not reflect the structural changes that would alter the composition of its exports (still

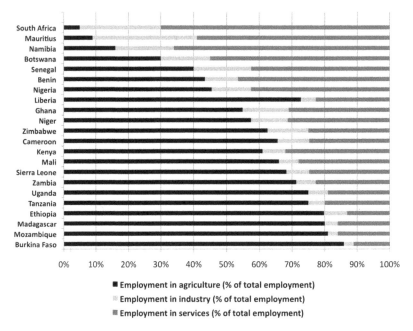

FIGURE 2 Employment in Africa by sector

primarily mineral and agricultural) and generate high-value employment expansion. Nigeria is caught in a dire trap. "As the size of the economy has increased, the share of the workforce in gainful employment has declined."[21]

Nigeria is caught in a syndrome that is evident in much of the continent. According to Homi Kharas and Julie Biau, "Africa is growing fast but transforming slowly." "In spite of impressive growth," they continue, "the structure of most of sub-Saharan African economies has evolved little in the past 40 years, with a poorly diversified export base, limited industrialization and technological progress. . . . In many African economies, manufacturing—the sector that has led rapid development in East Asia—is declining as a share of GDP."[22] Nigeria, despite its abundant human and material resources, demonstrates key aspects of this syndrome. Why has Nigeria failed to build an administrative and physical infrastructure that can support the growth of manufacturing, and what roles can businesses play in helping overcome these challenges? These, we contend, are core aspects of CSR in a late-developing country.

Nigeria has consistently maintained economic policies that encouraged consumption at the expense of production, a tendency that facilitates corruption. A list of obstacles to be overcome includes deficient infrastructures of electricity, transportation, and water; pervasive corruption and rent-seeking; policies that encourage massive corruption, such as the high petroleum subsidy; duplication of state agencies and government positions with unclear mandates; high inflation and bank-lending rates; policy inconsistency and insular political party culture; weak and predatory bureaucracy and collusive regulatory agencies; inadequate education and worker skills; pervasive physical insecurity; and popular distrust of public and private sector leaders.

What the Nigerian experience has also shown is the interconnection between inadequate economic policies, corruption, and state weakness. Without proactive CSR practices, and the forging of a long-term vision for the business sector, Nigeria's entrepreneurs will continue to focus on their activities as traders. This trend contributes to low job growth, the steady expansion of the informal economy, and an undiversified import-based economy. It also deepens poverty and income inequality. The *African Economic Outlook*—compiled by the African Development Bank, the Organization of Economic Cooperation and Development (OECD), and the UN Economic Commission for Africa—has identified the following challenges to resource mobilization for economic growth in Nigeria: the excessive number of institutions involved and the overlap of functions among the three tiers of government, the multiplicity and duplication of taxes, obsolete tax laws, and laborious documentation procedures. Government units, especially at state and local levels, have been slow to implement tax reforms that could improve the ease of doing business. They are often unaware how to enact business-friendly tax legislation. An environment that favors opacity and corruption over transparency and accountability further encourages the pursuit of short-term gains.

Business Associations and Corporate Social Responsibility

Business associations can serve as the nexus between business and civil society and promote CSR dialogues. According to Charlotte Walker-Said, business associations are the vehicles through which "business and society interface." Despite their long history, Nigerian business associations have acquired little capacity to influence policy and combat the challenges around CSR and latecomer industrialization. In many instances at both national and state levels, Nigerian business associations are behind the governmental curve on reform issues. These associations often focus more on convening trade fairs than listening to their members, responding to their needs, providing member services and policy advocacy, and engaging effectively with the government.

The Manufacturers Association of Nigeria (MAN), established in 1971, is one of the country's largest business associations. Its mission is to work in close cooperation with the "organized private sector," the government, and other stakeholders to create an enabling environment for industrial development, growth, and prosperity. Its current membership of about two thousand companies is spread throughout the country's six geopolitical zones. Despite MAN's size and support, it continues to demonstrate weak institutional capacity, strategic thinking, research, and policy advocacy skills. At a crucial point in Nigeria's manufacturing sector's history, MAN is insufficiently active in promoting governance reform and conducting advocacy campaigns. The organization reflects the same governance challenges as state institutions: the sway of personal interests, nepotism, and low remuneration. Most important is the lack of a vision and strategy for driving policy changes. Moreover, individuals who are overly careful about offending the government often lead the organization.

Rather than enlightening the public on the need for wider, deeper, and more consistent reforms, MAN has often sought protection from liberalization policies, which either slowed the reforms or created new avenues for corruption. Neither MAN nor any other business association has designed a strategy or program regarding key reform issues. These include the successful completion of power sector reform, which has included substantial privatization of government power firms; the liberalization of the opaque and corrupt oil sector through the passage of a Petroleum Industry Bill; and the removal of the petroleum subsidy, which has been a source of enormous corruption and fiscal stress. While important progress has been made on key aspects of power sector reform, action on the Petroleum Industry Bill has stalled. The government could have made more progress by working closely with media and civil society organizations. Manufacturing remains dominated by midsize firms unaccustomed to organizing and investing resources to advance their interests. For most of the 1990s and the early 2000s, MAN's advocacy has aligned more with the antireform positions of the labor unions and populist media. Manufacturers continue to demand targeted government interventions and palliatives such as tariff protection or import bans. A vision has not been developed regarding the improvement of government economic policy, administrative and political practices, and creating a favorable environment for investment and growth. In 2009, the US-based Center for International Private Enterprise (CIPE) supported MAN in the design and execution of a project on multiple taxation.[23] While the project highlighted the severe limitations of MAN and many other Nigerian business associations, it also illustrated the untapped potential for effecting systemic change.[24]

Why the focus on taxation? For the manufacturing sector, tax policy plays a crucial role in enabling manufacturers to thrive and compete in a global economy. In Nigeria, overly complex and poorly harmonized tax policies and collection mechanisms have been a major constraint on the country's economic growth. More taxes are often demanded of companies because of a corrupt and redundant system. A well-structured and transparent taxation system would contribute not only to an improved business environment but also to democratic governance. Unfortunately, most government officials at state and local levels in Nigeria do not understand the benefits of harmonizing taxation policies and tax-collecting mechanisms. As the commissioner of economic planning and budgets of Lagos State, Ben Akabueze, stated: "Every once in a while, local government just wakes up and decides to introduce new taxes without regard to whether or not they already exist."[25] Multiple taxation has therefore made the cost of doing business in Nigeria seemingly prohibitive. It also serves as a disincentive to both local and foreign investors, inducing firms to relocate to more business-friendly countries such as Ghana. The most significant revelation of the rebased GDP is that Nigeria has one of the lowest ratios of taxation to GDP in the world. Businesses often save significantly on levied taxes by paying off government tax authorities, a practice more prevalent among local than Western and multinational firms. In the case of Lagos State, a 2012 tax law spelled out which taxes were collected by the state government and which by local governments. It has been effective in reducing multiple taxation and the extortion that accompanies it. In this regard, CSR requires an activist government that can counter efforts by businesspeople to suborn civil servants and other officials.

In the project with CIPE, MAN conducted research on taxes and levies at the national, state, and local levels to identify which taxes were being imposed multiple times; researched illegal tax collection practices; and surveyed and interviewed local and state government officials and business leaders to acquire a better understanding of multiple taxation and how it affects businesses in various parts of the country.[26] Based on their research, MAN also drafted a policy paper that outlined (a) taxation laws in each state and the specific taxes that each level of government has the legal authority to collect; (b) the practical application of taxation policy detailing the incidence of illegal taxes, modes of collection, and revenue lost from corrupt collection practices; and (c) the impact of multiple taxation on businesses and how it discourages local and foreign investment. Finally, MAN educated the business community on how to pay taxes properly to minimize the use of coercion and physical threats by local tax collectors to impose illegal taxes. MAN's efforts aimed to enhance the capacity of local- and state-level government officials to understand tax policies and how they affect the business community. While there were limitations in MAN's capacity as well as that of many government officials to effect systemic change, this type of initiative demonstrates how business, government, and other actors can cooperate to improve economic growth and governmental accountability.

State-Level Private Sector Coalition Building

Corporate social responsibility, when implemented through business associations, can assume different forms and yield a variety of results. Nigeria's thirty-six states receive monthly financial allocations from the Consolidated Revenue Fund. However, state governments "often act as if they have no responsibility for any economic activity at the state level."[27] In addition, state legislators usually display little understanding of how to craft policies that will improve manufacturing and business in their states, and also about the policy-making process in general. Few legislators have any experience in business. In seeking to advance their industries' growth and promote job creation and poverty alleviation, Nigerian manufacturers and business associations must contend with these realities. They consequently need to engage state and local legislators more effectively in efforts to improve industrialization and poverty reduction policies.

Although much of Nigeria's industry is located along the Lagos–Ibadan Corridor, there are pockets of manufacturing elsewhere in the

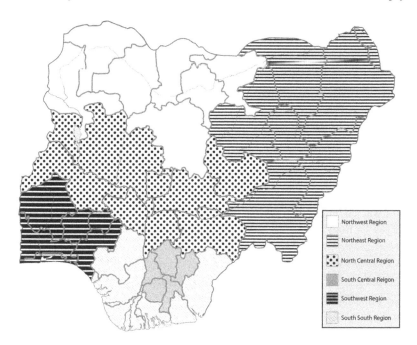

MAP I State-level private sector coalition building: Nigeria geopolitical zones

country. In addition, there are several free trade zones operated by the government, private entities, and public-private partnerships. They host companies engaged in manufacturing, trading, oil and gas distribution, and other industries. These companies benefit from special taxation rules and duty-free imports. Yet these zones are hampered by the same infrastructural challenges mentioned above. Manufacturing and business must be expanded throughout the country to generate jobs and economic development in the poorer regions of the country. These objectives can only be met if the business community is able to communicate effectively with state and local governments about what is needed to expand growth and job creation. In addition, state and local governments must be receptive to private sector policy recommendations and willing to engage in dialogue. The project activities discussed below show the concrete steps that were pursued to improve the operating environment for manufacturers, businesses, and ordinary citizens.

We will briefly summarize specific experiences in one of Nigeria's six geopolitical zones, that of north central. Manufacturers' associations have created coalitions with other business and professional associations in the six states in this zone: the Plateau Coalition of Business and Professional Associations (PLACOBPA), the Benue Coalition of Business and Professional Associations (BENCOBPA), the Nasarawa Coalition of Business and Professional Associations (NACOBPA), the Kogi Coalition of Business and Professional Associations (KOCOBPA), the Kwara Coalition of Business and Professional Associations (KWACOBPA), and the Niger Coalition of Business and Professional Association (NICOBPA). Prior to the creation of these coalitions, the business community was fragmented. Each business or sector approached legislators separately in search of favors. Once established and trained, each coalition was encouraged to shape its advocacy work to the particular challenges in their states. In some states, legislators never convene public hearings and have even allowed the printing presses that produce public records to fall into disrepair. As a result, in many states there has been no dialogue between the public and the business sectors on improving industrialization and job creation. State and local legislators are often unaware of the struggles of the private sector, while the private sector has had little experience crafting its messages and advocacy strategies.

The creation of coalitions in each of the six states and subsequent public-private dialogues have had positive outcomes. The Benue House of Assembly sought the input of the Benue Chamber of Commerce and passed a bill to privatize defunct state-owned enterprises. In Nasarawa State, NACOBPA's efforts led to a 7.5 million naira intervention (US$47,468) by the Nasarawa state government to improve the power and water supply to the largest rice processing plant in the state, and also purchased and installed transformers in rice milling areas throughout the state capital, Lafia. This project has generated more reliable work for hundreds of workers. In Kogi State, the Kogi Coalition of Business and Professional Associations (KOCOBPA) created a forum for dialogue with public sector leaders to discuss economic growth. A central issue was the poor condition of infrastructure. The coalition also worked with government officials representing the Ministries of Works, Housing, and Water Resources, and the Power Holding Company of Nigeria to discuss solutions to infrastructural challenges of limited power supply, bad roads, and poor water supply.

In both Kogi and Kwara States, the coalitions convened regular meetings with key ministries from each of the state's executive branches. In these meetings, the participants sought to identify the factors that hinder

the state's economic development, as well as those that restrict cooperation between the public and private sectors. The two sectors have since
made commitments to work more closely to enact the necessary reforms,
such as the liberalization of land administration, reforming state-wide
tax administration, and computerizing the land acquisition process.

In southeastern Nigeria, progress has been made in crafting CSR
practices that allow "business to behave ethically and contribute to economic development while improving the quality of life of the workforce
and their families as well as the local community and society at large."[28]
This progress has been achieved through coalition building among manufacturers, business, and professional associations. With the Enugu
Chamber of Commerce playing the role of catalyst, the Enugu Coalition of Business and Professional Associations (ECOBPA) was formed.
ECOBPA drew up a list of issues affecting the business environment
in which insecurity and unharmonized taxation were again at the top.
To tackle these issues, ECOBPA launched a statewide advocacy campaign on the issue of multiple taxation, and a regional advocacy campaign to address the negative impact of poor security on businesses. A
series of high-level meetings took place in Enugu with a public-private
roundtable involving the Enugu State Speaker of the House and other
high-level state government representatives. The meetings and roundtable helped the government better understand the factors that hindered
the business community in Enugu. They informed ECOBPA members
about the steps that the government was taking to streamline the state's
taxation processes such as developing an electronic system for adminis-
tering taxes. As a result of ECOBPA's advocacy efforts, the Enugu State
government announced the creation of a taxation commission and invited ECOBPA to have a seat on it.

In the course of these reviews, it was discovered that close to 80 percent of the taxes the local governments were collecting was illegal. The
Enugu government decided to publish a list of taxes and implement a
sensitization program to inform people what they should be paying.
Businesses were encouraged to question tax collectors about the taxes
being collected. The government also promised to freeze the tax rate
for two years and allow businesses to pay in installments. As a result of
these efforts, there was a 400 percent increase in tax revenues for the
government after eight months. In addition, ECOBPA turned its attention to security, hosting a summit that attracted over 250 participants
from seven Nigerian states in the southeast and south-south zones. The

summit addressed such topics as investing in an insecure environment, sustaining business operations in southeastern Nigeria, the high crime rate, and combating armed robbery and kidnapping.

Representatives of the coalition took the issue to the national level, meeting with the Nigerian national inspector general of police regarding the opportunities for bribery caused by roadblocks in the area. As a result of these efforts, the police roadblocks—more often used for collecting bribes than enforcing security—were reduced from sixty-five to fifteen along the hundred-kilometer trading corridor between Enugu and Onitsha, thereby allowing over many businesses and manufacturers to move their goods more efficiently, cheaply, and securely. In addition, police patrols have increased, reducing the likelihood of kidnapping and robbery of prominent businesspersons. What these initiatives demonstrate is the painstaking work that must be done in Nigeria in state and local governments to overcome the obstacles to building an efficient manufacturing sector, and which also advances measures to improve the physical security of citizens.

CSR and Effective Policy Intervention

The most severe weakness of Nigerian business organizations is the lack of a strategy on governance impediments to investment and economic growth, and the design of programs with impact assessment tools to address them. Who, it could be asked, would provide the leadership of a more effective and coherent CSR approach in Nigeria? The most obvious candidate is MAN given the central importance of industrialization. MAN has branches in almost every state and local government area and could therefore pursue and coordinate CSR initiatives at all levels of the federation. Another organization that could contribute to new CSR thinking would be the Nigerian Economic Support Group (NESG). With appropriate leadership, MAN and NESG can play complementary roles in the formulating and implementing of a comprehensive CSR agenda.

The NESG was founded during the period of renewed military rule, December 1983 to May 1999. The main driver, Ernest Shonekan, served for many years as the CEO of a leading conglomerate, the United Africa Company, whose existence dates back a century. In the mid-1980s,

Shonekan attended a conference in Nairobi, Kenya, on Tripartite Partnership for Development (public and private sectors and NGOs) sponsored by the Agha Khan Foundation. Perceiving the need for business engagement with the government on policy issues, he created the Enabling Environment Forum (EEF) in 1987 with other Nigerians who had attended the conference, such as Alhaji Abubakar Alhaji, then secretary to the government and finance minister. The EEF marked the beginning of more assertive policy engagement by the private sector. It evolved into the Nigerian Economic Summit Group in 1994, the first Nigerian think tank that includes membership from the private sector. Its flagship event is the annual Nigerian Economic Summit.

Despite the wide range of financial resources on which it draws, the NESG, similar to MAN, suffers from low institutional capacity. Its central mandate is to conduct policy dialogues with the government. The president of the Nigerian Federation and several ministers attend its annual summit, and ministers tap it for policy ideas. Ministers with a reformist agenda can partner with the NESG to promote their views in the hope of swaying the government. The NESG contends that its dialogue with successive governments has resulted in important reforms, such as the repeal of the Nigerian Enterprises Promotion Decree and the Exchange Control Act 1962. These were replaced by the Nigerian Enterprises Promotion Act and the Foreign Exchange Act, both of 1995. They eliminated controls on foreign investment and liberalized the foreign exchange market. The NESG also attributes the liberalization of the telecommunications sector and the setting up of the Infrastructure Concession Regulatory Commission to its advocacy.

The limitation of this "dialogue" is underlined by the discontinuation of key reforms such as the power sector liberalization during the administration of President Shehu Yar'Adua (2007–10). The NESG lacks effective influence. The reforms it advocates are not rooted in wider social networks and are often little understood by the media. It lacks a plan for follow-up action when reforms are reversed or are poorly implemented. Nigerian governments are often willing to make use of the NESG to burnish their proreform credentials. Because the NESG maintains close ties with the government, it rarely voices critical opinions. Moreover, the fact that senior NESG officials often move on to government posts tempers their willingness to challenge and pressure governments.

Another limitation is that manufacturers are often distrustful of the

NESG. When it was founded, it was regarded as a lobby that served the interests of the multinationals. Its policy commission on manufacturing is inactive because manufacturers have refused to join it. Another criticism of the NESG is that it is too close to the government to be effective. Many high-ranking founding members no longer participate in its programs. Another key weakness the NESG shares with other organizations such as MAN is that its publications and research output are poorly disseminated. Unlike the products of foreign think tanks, they seldom become the basis for public debate. What this review suggests is that Nigeria is endowed with associations that can lead the robust and dual-tracked CSR initiatives described in this chapter if adjustments are made to their outlook and structures. NESG's comparative advantage is that it can focus on big-picture policy changes that can have a systemic effect, for example, petroleum industry regulation, power sector reform, and fiscal reforms, while MAN has the presence throughout the federation to advance their implementation. The case studies described above demonstrate the role that business organizations could play in addressing policy and governance issues. Success in tackling concrete concerns such as multiple taxation can encourage the members of these groups to continue reforms of benefit to their businesses and society as a whole.[29] Their impact would be even greater if civil society organizations (CSO) and the media, which tend to have greater reach and social support but are usually antireform, are incorporated in evidence-based strategic advocacy programs. Nigeria has a vibrant CSO community, which emerged as human/civil rights groups especially during the period of prolonged military rule, 1983–99. The media could partner with the coalitions to educate and inform the government of the reforms needed to effect poverty alleviation and economic growth. According to a CSO activist, however, "manufacturers have not reached out to civil society organizations and have done little to mainstream their issues."[30]

Conclusion

The final version of this chapter was completed while Nigeria was simultaneously in the global media for a contrasting series of events: the kidnapping of hundreds of young women attributed to the terrorist group Boko Haram; bombing incidents in the capital, Abuja; and the hosting in the same city of the World Economic Forum on Africa, May 7–9, 2014, attended by leaders of many governments and international agencies. Nigeria was therefore touting itself as a leader in economic growth and development that depend on enhanced business entrepreneurship while insecurity and discord sent the opposite image of Nigeria as a place to do business.

As discussed here, Nigerian businesses, including manufacturers, engage in a constant struggle for survival and to advance their short-term interests. The advancement of human rights, democracy, rule of law, and economic development through policy advocacy is not seen as a priority.[31] In this regard, they differ little from their counterparts in other countries. What we have suggested is that CSR should be an important component of the new wave of economic activity in Africa. Other African commentators are alluding to new thinking on CSR, as reflected in a statement by a South African entrepreneur, Nicholas Maweni. He called attention to the efforts of a "number of large international companies to help the small business sector." "It's almost become," he stated, "like corporate social responsibility. It is happening in countries that are going through a second wave of economic transformation. It's happening in Ghana, Kenya and Uganda for example."[32] We would respond that it is not "like CSR." Rather, it *is* an essential component of CSR and latecomer industrialization in Nigeria and other African countries.

Greater success will depend on the ability of the relevant organizations and their leadership to combine strategies based on "elite knowledge sharing" and those based on "popular knowledge dissemination." The latter refers to the "dialogue" approach business associations favor while the former refers to an approach that concentrates on educating the media, civil society organizations, and the wider public on reform issues. The CIPE-supported case studies demonstrate the possibility of combining an elite knowledge-sharing strategy with a knowledge-dissemination approach. The Enugu Chamber of Commerce case showed that business policy interventions could assist governments in monitoring the activities of their own staff, while also serving as mechanisms through which the government could gain greater understanding of the needs of businesses. The achievements of the Enugu Chamber of Commerce demonstrate the potential for enlisting business organizations in such interventions.

This chapter has dealt with a number of paradoxes in Nigeria, a situation familiar to observers and students of this country in many contexts. While it is the arena of much corporate social irresponsibility, it is also a country in which important efforts are being made to design appropriate, and sometimes pioneering, CSR programs. We also drew on the work of a US-based organization, CIPE, to show the efforts being made, in partnership with Nigerian associations and government institutions, to confront the persistent impediments business enterprises face in local contexts. Our study has shown how key organizations such as MAN, NESG, and the Lagos State Chamber of Commerce would be more effective if they collaborated on the major issues confronting Nigeria in the business and related social sectors.

The central paradox to be confronted, as stated at the outset, is that Nigeria's high levels of income from mineral exports, and even the upswing in foreign direct investment, are not reflected in either employment growth or poverty reduction. Bridging that gap must be an essential component of CSR pursued along two tracks: assisting businesses to be effective, productive, and globally competitive; and encouraging them to work with government and civil society organizations to reduce the country's governance and social problems. As demonstrated in presentations made during the World Economic Forum, Nigeria, although a leader in oil and gas production in Africa, is among the laggards in providing adequate electricity for its citizens and business enterprises. After tens of billions of dollars have been invested in improving the power sector, the federal government has now privatized large components of it. Yet paradoxical as it may sound, Nigeria is exploring the option of importing electric power from the Democratic Republic of Congo, a poster state for dysfunctional and corrupt governance.

It is easy to be cynical and even pessimistic about Nigeria. But cynicism and pessimism can be costly if it means that a country destined to be the third most populous nation in the world remains stuck in a poverty track and experiences repetitive political and social upheavals. While elucidating the immense challenges, we hope to have shown how corporate social responsibility is implicated in the pursuit of economic and social progress in this complex nation. CSR in late-developing countries such as Nigeria must include the improvement of productivity, employment, and incomes, which can only be achieved through the emergence of more effective and dynamic business enterprises that coordinate their activities effectively with government agencies, business associations, and civil society and media groups.

Notes

1. Akbar Noman and Joseph E. Stiglitz, "Strategies for African Development," in *Good Growth and Governance in Africa: Rethinking Development Strategies*, ed. Akbar Noman et al. (Oxford and New York: Oxford University Press, 2012), 3–47.

2. Richard Joseph, "Economic Transformation and Developmental Governance in Nigeria: The Promise of the Obama Era," Brookings Institution, May 21, 2009, http://www.brookings.edu/research/speeches/2009/05/21-nigeria-joseph.

3. On extractive versus inclusive and productive political economies, see Daron Acemoglu and James A. Robinson, *Why Nations Fail?: The Origins of Power, Prosperity, and Poverty* (New York: Crown Publishers, 2012).

4. http://allafrica.com/stories/201208170215.html.

5. Davidson Iriekpen, "Cecilia Ibru Pleads Guilty, Jailed Six Months," *AllAfrica*, October 8, 2010, http://allafrica.com/stories/201010090007.html.

6. James Jukwey, "Nigeria Investigates $4 Billion Fuel Subsidy Fraud," *Reuters*, January 19, 2012, http://www.reuters.com/article/2012/01/19/us-nigeria-fuel-scam-idUSTRE80I1R220120119.

7. Alexandra Gilles, "Nigeria's Chance for Reform," *Huffington Post*, last modified January 13, 2012, http://www.huffingtonpost.com/alexandra-gillies/nigerias-chance-for-refor_b_1204853.html.

8. Nigeria seems trapped in webs of kleptocracy described in such studies as Jean-François Bayart, Stephen Ellis, and Beatrice Hibou, *The Criminalization of the State in Africa* (Bloomington: Indiana University Press, 1999); Ricardo Soares de Oliveira, *Oil and Politics in the Gulf of Guinea* (New York: Columbia University Press, 2007).

9. Clifford Krauss, "Former KBR Executive Pleads Guilty to Bribery," *New York Times*, last modified September 3, 2008, http://www.nytimes.com/2008/09/04/business/04bribe.html.

10. Chukwuma Charles Soludo, "Nigeria: Where Is the New Economy?" *ThisDay* (Nigeria), August 20, 2012.

11. "African Economic Outlook: 2012," *African Economic Outlook*, http://www.africaneconomicoutlook.org/fileadmin/uploads/PAGES-%20Pocket%20Edition%20AEO2012-EN.pdf.

12. Matsuo Watanabe and Atsushi Hanatani, "Issues in Africa's Industrial Policy Process," in Noman et al., *Good Growth and Governance in Africa*, 376. Célestin Monga similarly contends that the passage to sustained growth and high-income status has usually been via industrialization: "Implications and Opportunities of Increasing Wage Costs in Asia for African Reindustrialization," presented at the International Economic Association, World Bank, and United

Nations Industrial Development Organization Roundtable on New Thinking on Industrial Policy: Implications for Africa, Pretoria, South Africa, July 3–4, 2012.

13. Robert H. Wade, "How Can Low-Income Countries Accelerate Their Catch-Up with High-Income Countries? The Case for Open-Economy Industrial Policy," in Noman et al., *Good Growth and Governance in Africa*, 255.

14. Osita Ogbu, "Toward Inclusive Growth in Nigeria," Brookings Institution, http://www.brookings.edu/~/media/research/files/papers/2012/6/growth% 20nigeria%200gbu/06_growth_nigeria.pdf.

15. For relevant discussions, see Tim Kelsall, *Business, Politics, and the State in Africa: Challenging the Orthodoxies of Growth and Transformation* (London and New York: Zed Press, 2013); Homi Kharas and Julie Biau, "Depth in Africa's Transformation," http://www.brookings.edu/blogs/up-front/posts/2014/04/07 -africa-transformation-kharas; and Richard Joseph, "Africa's Third Liberation," http://africaplus.wordpress.com/2014/04/03/africas-third-liberation-transitions-to -inclusive-growth-and-developmental-governance/.

16. These statistics and two charts are drawn, with permission, from Monga, "Implications and Opportunities."

17. In fact, the poverty rate has been increasing in Nigeria while dropping on average in sub-Saharan Africa. According to Nigeria's National Bureau of Statistics, 61 percent of Nigerians earn less than $1 per day. In February 2012, the World Bank announced that for the first time poverty in Africa had declined below 50 percent, using the $1.25 per day rate. See Joe Brock, "Nigerian Poverty Rising Despite Economic Growth," Reuters, http://www.reuters.com/ article/2012/02/13/us-nigeria-poverty-idUSTRE81C0KR20120213; Annie Lowrey, "Dire Poverty Falls Despite Global Slump, Report Finds," *New York Times*, last modified March 6, 2012, http://www.nytimes.com/2012/03/07/world/extreme -poverty-down-despite-recession-world-bank-data-show.html.

18. Xan Rice, "Nigeria: Stymied by Culture and Faith," *Financial Times*, last modified July 7, 2012, http://www.ft.com/intl/cms/s/0/1bf2ceaa-c12e-11e1-8179 -00144feabdc0.html#axzz2z7U22pXq.

19. Ibid.

20. Charles Chukwuma Soludo, "Nigeria: Where Is the New Economy?" *ThisDay* (Nigeria). August 20, 2012. The rebasing of GDP has moved the manufacturing percentage to just under 7 percent.

21. Festus Akanbi, "Telecoms, Banking Are Slower at Creating Jobs," *ThisDay* (Nigeria), April 1, 2012.

22. Kharas and Biau, "Depth in Africa's Transformation."

23. All views expressed here are those of the authors and do not represent those of CIPE.

24. MAN also received funding from the World Bank's Small Medium Enterprise Department to conduct a study of Nigeria's energy and transport in-

frastructure; to build capacity to improve nonsubscription, fee-based membership services; and for the creation of a resource center. It has also received grants from the International Finance Corporation (IFC) and collaborated with other international organizations such as the United Nations Development Program (UNDP) and the United Nations Industrial Development Organization (UNIDO).

25. Personal interview with Kelly Spence.

26. "Principles of Tax Policy," National Association of Manufacturers, last modified winter 2012, http://www.nam.org/Issues/Official-Policy-Positions/Tax -Technology-Domestic-Economic-Policy/TTDEP-01-Tax-Policy.aspx#101.

27. Ogbu, "Toward Inclusive Growth in Nigeria."

28. Phil Watts and Lord Holme, "Corporate Social Responsibility: Meeting Changing Expectations," World Business Council for Sustainable Development Report, 3.

29. This is especially so given the perception of ineffectiveness and exploitation for personal and political purposes.

30. Personal interview (A. Agboluaje), Coordinator, Centre for Constitutionalism and De-Militarisation, Dr. Sylvester Akhiane, May 2012.

31. According to Pat Utomi, a political economist, civic activist, and politician, Nigerian businesses engage in hypocrisy by refusing to support social initiatives promoting good governance because they do not want to be seen as political. Yet they eagerly support individuals in government and exploit relationships with them for profit. Many businesspersons tread carefully because they are often involved in infractions that can be used against them if they are seen as too critical of government.

32. Russell Hotten, "Africa: Where Everyone Wants to Be an Entrepreneur," BBC News, http://www.bbc.co.uk/news/business-16723791.

Final Thoughts and Acknowledgments

John D. Kelly and Charlotte Walker-Said

It is easier to be satisfied with the progress made by intellectual work when the agenda is reasonable and we can accept that there is only gradual enlightenment. But as argued in the preface, things are different when we are called to confront political questions more directly, when the agenda touches on what is to be done.

At the end of this endeavor, we must ask again: Can codes of corporate social responsibility solve the massive problems attending efforts to make real the promise of human rights? Can corporate social responsibility make a positive difference in the world? Is it the best means to enlist corporate capitalist agency into the advancement of human rights agendas? If we think of this project as a collective essay in Montaigne's original sense, think of it as an effort, an attempt, a practical and moral experiment seeking what our collected reason can do, it matters which of these three questions we are essaying to answer. Reading across the papers we leave the siloes so seamlessly constituted by each individual discipline. The anthropologists are remarkable in their realism, and also in their ethical outrage, but not so focused on the practical follow-through and dilemmas in enactment of new policy. They are clearer that something must be done, than how to make new solutions work. Their colleagues in the legal field at the end of the day demonstrate a radically complementary talent, events turned seamlessly into cases that illustrate failures and successes of larger-scale approaches, the necessities metamorphosing from what might be done, to how the capacity to narrate complexity was compromised in favor of the ability to identify proximate, practical dilemmas. Penal or financial penalties? Which jurisdictions? We also hear from historians and political scientists who understand the importance of social critique but are also able to give a sense of perspective on how reflexive knowledge about corporate responsibility has been created over the twentieth century and how the execution of CSR policies and mandates have stood up for or opposed strategies of accountability and reform.

Problems both particular and general are clarified. But it matters, here in the end, which question measures our task, as we seek a sense of where we are. Obviously, massive problems are not going to melt under the light generated by a single volume, and CSR codes are not poised by themselves to make global human rights a reality. And on the other hand, it is too easy to accept positive gestures as sufficient when we know what we know about the larger trajectories of the world, the geography of hope and the geography of anger. We hope this book clarifies, perhaps in different ways for different audiences, where we are in the assessment of corporate social responsibility codes as a tool for the advancement of human rights. If some want to debate whether they can work, while others pursue how to make them work better, both groups can find the state of their art in this collection. If Africa, for obvious reasons, is your analytical and ethical focus, this volume is particularly well ordered to push the core questions. But it also is a resource for information about a wide range of legal outcomes in many other locations, CSR implementations and their consequences strongly argued across the global North and South.

Are corporate codes of conduct the best way to refashion corporations into forces advancing human rights? For several kinds of readers the question is impossible to take seriously. Readers for whom the evil is ineradicable in corporate pursuit of profit, who see corporate actions always constituting exploitation, will likely have no hope for any future organized with large sway to corporate actions. And readers who find in economic development the very definition of advancing good, who see corporations as the hardest-working engines of change, will have no anxiety over outcomes, let alone apperception of trenchant, tragic anger. For everyone in between the stakes are higher.

It was for the exploration of this middle ground that this project was launched. Any project like this has myriad roots, but in this case there is one main line, the research program of the Human Rights Program of the University of Chicago. The Human Rights Program aims to work on the cutting edge of the most challenging human rights questions of our time—promoting scholarship as well as real-life engagement with human rights problems through its undergraduate internship program and funded postbaccalaureate fellowships. The passion of its directors Michael Geyer and now Mark Bradley, and leaders Susan Gzesh and John Kelly, as well as its board, guides the curricular agenda and research program of the program, which has explored the most serious current human rights challenges in the present day, including statelessness, terrorism, torture, state failure, humanitarianism, and not least, corporate social responsibility.

The project for this volume developed rapidly and collaboratively from an initial conference in 2011 to an intensive workshop in 2012, with the authors of this volume participating in dialogue across disciplines. Thanks are due to Sarah Moberg for all her work in organizing and facilitating the original and secondary conferences. From these meetings, a coherent conversation emerged, from which this volume takes form. John Kelly entered the project precisely at this juncture. The University of Chicago Human Rights Program, under his direction in 2011–12, backed the project of organizing a writing seminar and supporting an initiative to organize a cross-disciplinary group of thinkers to present findings on the latest and most up-to-date results of CSR initiatives, which would be joined in a published work. Walker-Said and Kelly brought the project to the University of Chicago Press in the summer of 2012, and deeply appreciate the efforts of Priya Nelson, David Brent, anonymous reviewers, and the very professional staff of the press for all of their help and support in making the volume a reality.

In the end, this book presents the question: knowing what we know now, can CSR do meaningful work in the service of human rights? In the face of all the evidence here, it is clear that there is no one answer. It is clear, however, that CSR, like human rights, can act as a chameleon, adapting to cultures, political movements, and economic philosophies that are ascendant in a given moment. Critically, the absence of cogent alternatives to CSR also speaks loudly. David Scott has pointed out, for a postcolonial studies audience, that it is no longer clear what the concept of overcoming Western power means anymore. So also, it becomes increasingly difficult to seriously imagine a global landscape without the active good and evil of capitalist corporations organizing significant human activities. We believe firmly that the human rights literature needs to deal with its hard cases, to investigate the real practices associated with human rights interventions, mandates, alibis, and reforms in the realm of all the major institution-types of contemporary global society. For good reasons most human rights literature focuses on states and NGOs, with their sovereign duties and moral agendas. How to figure the place of corporations in the advancement of human rights remains most urgent. Can the lawyers resolve how to best make CSR codes work? Do the anthropologists, in their most mordant forays into behind-the-scenes relationships, find the more telling truths? Our final thought is less that these discussions resolve the question than that they show us, clearly, where the best available social science addressing the problematics of CSR can take us. In fact the question of the future of CSR is still open, and the need still urgent for insight into its real consequences.

The editors have left it to each chapter author to express their own acknowledgments within their chapters. We too have personal debts and observations to record. Charlotte Walker-Said would first like to thank Michael Geyer, Mark Bradley, and Susan Gzesh for giving her the opportunity to join the Human Rights Program at the University of Chicago as a postdoctoral researcher and lecturer, and thereby collaborate in the program's important work. She would also like to thank her family and her husband, Maher Walker-Said, for their sensitive and insightful perspectives on the human rights challenges of the current day. John Kelly also wants to thank some wonderful backstage interlocutors. For their independence of mind and insights into academic choices he thanks his daughters, particularly the one in Chicago, Nory, also a participant on her own terms in Chicago's Human Rights Program. And he thanks his wife Martha Kaplan, overburdened, charismatic professor and faculty leader at her own institution, Vassar College, for her patience, her unerring good sense, her sharp eyes, and her moral center.

Above all, thanks are owed to Richard and Ann Pozen. The Pozens have funded student and faculty research generously and observantly, taking a highly intellectual program dominated by real insight and focused objectives and crafting a vehicle for advanced research that faces few limits. Human rights research at the University of Chicago is currently pursuing many important questions with innovative methods and developing many ongoing projects. Because of the generosity of the Pozens, Chicago now sponsors human rights research and teaching from undergraduate to postgraduate levels that should make a difference. We hope this volume supported by the Pozen endowment might kindle the further discussion that these most important topics deserve.

Bibliography

Abdelal, Rawi. *Capital Rules: The Construction of Global Finance.* Cambridge, MA: Harvard University Press, 2009.

Abouharb, M. Rodwan, and David Cingranelli. *Human Rights and Structural Adjustment.* Cambridge: Cambridge University Press, 2007.

Abrahamsen, Rita. "Blair's Africa: The Politics of Securitization and Fear." *Alternatives: Global, Local, Political* 30, no. 1 (2005): 55–80.

Acemoglu, Daron, and James Robinson. *Why Nations Fail: The Origins of Power, Prosperity, and Poverty.* New York: Crown Business, 2012.

Adler, Nancy J. *From Boston to Beijing: Managing with a World View.* 1st ed. Cincinnati, OH: Cengage Learning, 2001.

———. "Global Companies, Global Society: There Is a Better Way." *Journal of Management Inquiry* 11, no. 3 (2002): 255–60.

Agamben, Giorgio. *Homo Sacer: Sovereign Power and Bare Life (Homo Sacer I).* Translated by Daniel Heller-Roazen. Stanford, CA: Stanford University Press, 1998.

———. *State of Exception (Homo Sacer II, 1).* Translated by Kevin Attell. Chicago: University of Chicago Press, 2005.

Agier, Michel. *Managing the Undesirables.* New York: Polity Press, 2011.

Aguilera, Ruth V., Deborah E. Rupp, Cynthia A. Williams, and Jyoti Ganapathi. "Putting the S Back in Corporate Social Responsibility: A Multilevel Theory of Social Change in Organizations." *Academy of Management Review* 32, no. 3 (2007): 836–63.

Akabzaa, Thomas M., J. S. Seyire, and K. Afriyie. *The Glittering Façade: Effects of Mining Activities on Obuasi and Its Surrounding Communities.* Accra, Ghana: Third World Network—Africa, 2008.

Ali, Saleem H., and Julia Marton-LeFevre. *Peace Parks: Conservation and Conflict Resolution.* Cambridge, MA: MIT Press, 2007.

Althusser, Louis. "Ideology and Ideological State Apparatuses: Notes Towards an Investigation." In *The Anthropology of the State: A Reader*, edited by Aradhana Sharma and Akhil Gupta, 86–111. Oxford: Blackwell, 2006.

Amnesty International. *Injustice Incorporated: Advancing the Right to Remedy for Corporate Abuses of Human Rights.* London: Amnesty International, 2014.

Anidjar, Gil. "The Meaning of Life." *Critical Inquiry* 37, no. 4 (2011): 697–723.

Antoni, Giacomo Degli, and Lorenzo Sacconi. "Modeling Cognitive Social Capital and Corporate Social Responsibility as Preconditions for Sustainable Networks of Relations." In *Social Capital, Corporate Social Responsibility, Economic Behaviour, and Performance*, edited by Lorenzo Sacconi and Giacomo Degli Antoni, 161–242. New York: Palgrave Macmillan, 2011.

Appadurai, Arjun. "Grassroots Globalization and the Research Imagination." *Public Culture* 12, no. 1 (2000): 1–19.

Arendt, Hannah. *On Violence.* New York: Harcourt, Brace and World, 1969.

Asmus, Peter, Hank Cauley, and Katharine Maroney. "Turning Conflict into Cooperation." *Stanford Social Innovation Review* (Fall 2006): 52–61.

Attfield, Robin, Johan Hattingh, and Manamela Matshabaphala. "Sustainable Development, Sustainable Livelihoods, and Land Reform in South Africa: A Conceptual and Ethical Inquiry." *Third World Quarterly* 25, no. 2 (2004): 405–21.

Austin, Gareth. *Labour, Land, and Capital in Ghana: From Slavery to Free Labour in Asante, 1807–1956.* Rochester, NY: University of Rochester Press, 2005.

Ayensu, Edward S. *Ashanti Gold: The African Legacy of the World's Most Precious Metal.* London: Marshall, 1997.

Bakan, Joel. *The Corporation: The Pathological Pursuit of Power.* New York: Penguin, 2004.

Ballard, Chris, and Glenn Banks. "Resource Wars: The Anthropology of Mining." *Annual Review of Anthropology* 32 (2003): 287–313.

Bannerjee, Arhit, and Esther Duflo. *Poor Economics: A Radical Rethinking of the Way to Fight Global Poverty.* New York: PublicAffairs, 2011.

Bansal, Pratima, and Kendall Roth. "Why Companies Go Green: A Model of Ecological Responsiveness." *Academy of Management Journal* 43 (2000): 717–36.

Banuri, Tariq, and Erika Spanger-Siegfried. "The Global Compact and the Human Economy." *Journal of Human Development* 2, no. 1 (2001): 7–17.

Barnoya, Joaquin, and Stanton A. Glantz. "The Tobacco Industry's Worldwide ETS Consultants Project: European and Asian Components." *European Journal of Public Health* 16, no. 1 (2006): 69–77.

Barrios, Cristina. "Fighting Piracy in the Gulf of Guinea: Offshore and Onshore." *EU Institute for Security Studies* 20 (May 2013): 1–4.

Bartelson, Jens. *A Genealogy of Sovereignty.* Cambridge: Cambridge University Press, 1995.

Bates, Robert. *When Things Fall Apart: State Failure in Late-Century Africa.* Cambridge: Cambridge University Press, 1998.

Bayart, Jean-François, Stephen Ellis, and Beatrice Hibou. *The Criminalization of the State in Africa.* Bloomington: Indiana University Press, 1999.

Beamish, Thomas D. *Silent Spill: The Organization of an Industrial Crisis.* Cambridge, MA: MIT Press, 2002.

Beck, Jim, Otodo Kede, Frederic Medjo, Susan Minnemeyer, Roger Ngoufo, Lawrence Ayenika Nsoyuni, and Maria Jacoba Van de Pol. *Interactive Forestry Atlas of Cameroon.* World Resources Institute, Global Forest Watch, 2006.

Bendell, Jem. "In Whose Name? The Accountability of Corporate Social Responsibility." *Development in Practice* 15, no. 3–4 (2005): 362–74.

Benjamin, Walter. *The Arcades Project.* Translated by Howard Eiland and Kevin Mclaughlin. Cambridge, MA: Belknap Press of Harvard University Press, 2002.

Benson, Peter. *Tobacco Capitalism: Growers, Migrant Workers, and the Changing Face of a Global Industry.* Princeton, NJ: Princeton University Press, 2011.

Benson, Peter, and Stuart Kirsch. "Capitalism and the Politics of Resignation." *Current Anthropology* 51, no. 4 (2010): 459–86.

———. "Corporate Oxymorons." *Dialectical Anthropology* 34, no. 1 (2010): 45–48.

Bernstein, S., and B. Cashore. "Can Non-state Global Governance Be Legitimate? An Analytical Framework." *Regulation and Governance* 1, no. 4 (2007): 341–71.

Bettencourt, Luis M. A., and Jasleen Kuar. "Evolution and Structure of Sustainability Science." *Proceedings of the National Academy of Sciences of the United States of America* 108, no. 49 (2011): 19,540–45.

Bishop, Toby J., and Frank E. Hydoski. *Corporate Resiliency: Managing the Growing Risk of Fraud and Corruption.* Hoboken, NJ: Wiley, 2009.

Black, Bernard, and Anna Tarassova. "Institutional Reform in Transition: A Case Study of Russia." *Supreme Court Economic Review* 10 (2003): 211–78.

Blair, Margaret, and Lynn Stout. "A Team Production Theory of Corporate Law." *Virginia Law Review* 85 (1999): 247–328.

Blowfield, Mike. "ETI: A Multi-stakeholder Approach." In *Corporate Responsibility and Labour Rights: Codes of Conduct in the Global Economy*, edited by Rhys Jenkins, Ruth Pearson, and Gill Seyfang, 184–95. London: Earthscan, 2002.

Bloxham, Donald. *Genocide on Trial.* Oxford: Oxford University Press, 2001.

Blumberg, Phillip. *The Multinational Challenge to Corporation Law: The*

Search for a New Corporate Personality. Oxford: Oxford University Press: 1993.

Blumenstyk, Goldie. "Mining Company Involved in Environmental Disaster Now Advises Sustainability Institute at U. of Michigan." *Chronicle of Higher Education* 54, no. 15 (2007): A22.

Bocking, Stephen. *Nature's Experts: Science, Politics, and the Environment.* New Brunswick, NJ: Rutgers University Press, 2004.

Bohnet, Iris, Bruno Frey, and Steffen Huck. "More Order with Less Law: On Contract Enforcement, Trust, and Crowding." *American Political Science Review* 95 (2001): 131–44.

Borgwardt, Elizabeth. *A New Deal for the World: America's Vision for Human Rights.* Cambridge, MA: Belknap Press of Harvard University Press, 2005.

Borkin, Joseph. *The Crime and Punishment of I. G. Farben.* New York: Free Press, 1978.

Bower, Tom. *Blind Eye to Murder: Britain, America, and the Purging of Nazi Germany—A Pledge Betrayed.* London: William Collins and Sons, 1981.

Brainbridge, Stephen M. *Corporation Law and Economics.* St. Paul, MN: Foundation Press, 2002.

Brammer, Steven, Andrew Millington, and Bruce Rayton. "The Contribution of Corporate Social Responsibility to Organizational Commitment." *International Journal of Human Resource Management* 18 (2007): 1701–19.

Branch, Adam. "Neither Liberal nor Peaceful? Practices of 'Global Justice' by the ICC." In *A Liberal Peace? The Problems and Practices of Peacebuilding,* edited by Susanna Campbell, David Chandler, and Meera Sabaratnam, 121–37. London: Zed Books, 2011.

Brandt, Allan. *The Cigarette Century: The Rise, Fall, and Deadly Persistence of the Product That Defined America.* New York: Basic Books, 2007.

Braudel, Fernand. *Capitalism and Material Life, 1400–1800.* New York: Harper-Collins, 1973.

———. *The Structures of Everyday Life: Civilization and Capitalism, Fifteenth to Eighteenth Century.* Vol. 1. New York: Harper and Row, 1982.

Bridge, Maurice, and Angus Wong. "Consenting Adults: Changes to the Principle of Free, Prior, and Informed Consent Are Changing the Way in Which Firms Engage Communities." *Mining, People, and the Environment* (July 2011): 12–15.

Brinkerhoff, Jennifer M. "Global Public Policy, Partnership, and the World Commission on Dams." *Public Administration Review* 62, no. 3 (2002): 324–36.

Brown, Halina Szejnwald, Martin de Jong, and Teodorina Lessidrenska. "The Rise of Global Reporting Initiative (GRI) as a Case of Institutional Entrepreneurship." *Environmental Politics* 18, no. 2 (2009): 182–200.

Buchholtz, Ann K., Jill A. Brown, and Kareem M. Shabana. "Corporate Governance and Corporate Social Responsibility." In *The Oxford Handbook of Corporate Social Responsibility*, edited by Andrew Crane, Abagail McWilliams, Dirk Matten, Jeremy Moon, and Donald S. Siegel, 327–45. Oxford: Oxford University Press, 2008.

Bush, Jonathan A. "The Prehistory of Corporations and Conspiracy in International Criminal Law: What Nuremberg Really Said." *Columbia Law Review* 109, no. 5 (2009): 1094–262.

Butler, Henry. "The Contractual Theory of the Corporation." *George Mason University Law Review* 11 (1989): 99.

Calhoun, Craig. "The Imperative to Reduce Suffering: Charity, Progress, and Emergencies in the Field of Humanitarian Action." In *Humanitarianism in Question: Politics, Power, Ethics*, edited by Michael Barnett and Thomas G. Weiss, 73–97. Ithaca, NY: Cornell University Press, 2008.

Campbell, Kevin, and Douglas Vick. "Disclosure Law and the Market for Corporate Social Responsibility." In *The New Corporate Accountability*, edited by Doreen McBarnet, Aurora Voiculescu, and Tom Campbell, 241–78. Cambridge: Cambridge University Press, 2007.

Carroll, Archie. "The Pyramid of Corporate Social Responsibility: Toward the Moral Management of Organizational Stakeholders." *Business Horizons*, July–August 1991, 39–48.

——. "A Three-Dimensional Conceptual Model of Corporate Performance." *Academy of Management Review* 4 (1979): 497–505.

Carson, Rachel. *Silent Spring*. New York: Houghton Mifflin, 1962.

Cassese, Antonio. *International Criminal Law*. New York: Oxford University Press, 2008.

Chalfin, Brenda. *Neoliberal Frontiers: An Ethnography of Sovereignty in West Africa*. Chicago: University of Chicago Press, 2010.

Childress, Donald Earl, III. "The Alien Tort Statute, Federalism, and the Next Wave of International Law Litigation." *Georgetown Law Journal* 100 (2012): 709–57.

Chomsky, Noam. *Failed States: The Abuse of Power and the Assault on Democracy*. New York: Holt, 2007.

Chomsky, Noam, and Robert W. McChesney. *Profit over People: Neoliberalism and Global Order*. New York: Seven Stories Press, 1999.

Chukwuone, N. A., C. N. Ukwe, A. Onugu, and C. A. Ibe. "Valuing the Guinea Current Large Marine Ecosystem: Estimates of Direct Output Impact of Relevant Marine Activities." *Ocean and Coastal Management* 52, no. 3 (2009): 189–96.

Cohen, Lizabeth. *A Consumer's Republic: The Politics of Mass Consumption in Postwar America*. New York: Vintage, 2003.

Collier, Paul. *The Bottom Billion: Why the Poorest Countries Are Failing and What Can Be Done about It*. Oxford: Oxford University Press, 2008.

——. "Rebellion as a Quasi-Criminal Activity." *Journal of Conflict Resolution* 44, no. 6 (2000): 839–53.

Comaroff, Jean, and John L. Comaroff. *Millennial Capitalism and the Culture of Neoliberalism*. Durham, NC: Duke University Press, 2001.

——. *Theory from the South; or, How Euro-America Is Evolving toward Africa*. Boulder, CO: Paradigm, 2012.

Comaroff, John L., and Jean Comaroff. "Introduction: Law and Disorder in the Postcolony." In *Law and Disorder in the Postcolony*, edited by John L. Comaroff and Jean Comaroff, 1–16. Chicago: University of Chicago Press, 2006.

Conca, Ken. *Environmental Peacemaking*. Baltimore: Johns Hopkins University Press, 2002.

Connor, Tim. "Time to Scale Up Cooperation? Trade Unions, NGOs, and the International Antisweatshop Movement." *Development in Practice* 14, no. 1–2 (2004): 61–70.

Conroy, Michael E. *Branded! How the "Certification Revolution" Is Transforming Global Corporations*. Gabriola, BC: New Society Publishers, 2007.

Conway, Martin. "Justice in Postwar Belgium: Popular Passions and Political Realities." In *The Politics of Retribution of Europe: World War II and Its Aftermath*, edited by István Deák, Jan T. Gross, and Tony Judt, 133–56. Princeton, NJ: Princeton University Press, 2000.

Cooper, Frederick. "Networks, Moral Discourse, and History." In *Intervention and Transnationalism in Africa: Global-Local Networks of Power*, edited by Thomas M. Callaghy, Ronald Kassimir, and Robert Latham, 23–46. Cambridge: Cambridge University Press, 2001.

Cooper, Frederick, and Ann Laura Stoler. *Tensions of Empire: Colonial Cultures in a Bourgeois World*. Berkeley: University of California Press, 1997.

Coumans, Catherine. "Occupying Spaces Created by Conflict: Anthropologists, Development NGOs, Responsible Investment, and Mining." *Current Anthropology* 52, no. S3 (2011): S29–S43.

Courtemanche, Charles, and Art Carden. "Supersizing Supercenters? The Impact of Wal-Mart Supercenters on Body Mass Index and Obesity." *Journal of Urban Economics* 69, no. 2 (2011): 165–81.

Coyle, Lauren. "Sovereigns of the Golden Twilight: Law, Land, and Sacrificial Labor in Ghana." PhD diss., University of Chicago, 2014.

Crane, Andrew, Abagail McWilliams, Dirk Matten, Jeremy Moon, and Donald Siegel. "The Corporate Social Responsibility Agenda." In *The Oxford Handbook of Corporate Social Responsibility*, edited by Andrew Crane, Abagail McWilliams, Dirk Matten, Jeremy Moon, and Donald S. Siegel, 3–18. Oxford: Oxford University Press, 2008.

——, eds. *The Oxford Handbook of Corporate Social Responsibility*. Oxford: Oxford University Press, 2009.

Crone, T. J., and M. Tolstoy. "Magnitude of the 2010 Gulf of Mexico Oil Leak." *Science* 330, no. 6004 (2010): 634.

Daddieh, Cyril K., and Kidane Mengisteab. *State Building and Democratization in Africa: Faith, Hope, and Realities.* New York: Praeger, 1999.

Davis, James H., F. David Schoorman, and Lex Donaldson. "Toward a Stewardship Theory of Management." *Academy of Management Review* 22 (1997): 20–47.

De Kuijper, Mia. *Profit Power Economics: A New Competitive Strategy for Creating Sustainable Wealth.* Oxford: Oxford University Press, 2009.

Debord, Guy. *Society of the Spectacle.* New York: Black and Red, 2000.

Deci, Edward. *Intrinsic Motivation.* Dordrecht: Plenum Publishing, 1975.

Deleuze, Gilles. *Nietzsche and Philosophy.* New York: Columbia University Press, 1983.

Deva, Surya, and David Bilchitz. *Human Rights Obligations of Business: Beyond the Corporate Responsibility to Respect?* Cambridge: Cambridge University Press, 2013.

Devlin, Lawrence. *Chief of Station, Congo: A Memoir of 1960–1967.* New York: PublicAffairs, 2008.

Dewey, John. *Human Nature and Conduct: An Introduction to Social Psychology.* New York: Cosimo, 2007.

Dickinson, Laura A. *Outsourcing War and Peace.* New Haven, CT: Yale University Press, 2011.

Dingwerth, Klaus. "North-South Parity in Global Governance: The Affirmative Procedures of the Forest Stewardship Council." *Global Governance: A Review of Multilateralism and International Organizations* 14, no. 1 (2008): 53–72.

———. "Private Transnational Governance and the Developing World: A Comparative Perspective." *International Studies Quarterly* 52 no. 3 (2008): 607–34.

Dombret, Andreas, and Otto Lucius. *Stability of the Financial System: Illusion or Feasible Concept?* Cheltenham, UK: Edward Elgar Publishing, 2013.

Donaldson, Thomas, and Thomas Dunfee. *Ties That Bind: A Social Contracts Approach to Business Ethics.* Cambridge, MA: Harvard Business Press, 1999.

Dorfman, Lori, Andrew Cheyne, Lissy C. Friedman, Asiya Wadud, and Mark Gottlieb. "Soda and Tobacco Industry Corporate Social Responsibility Campaigns: How Do They Compare?" *PLoS Medicine* 9, no. 6 (2012): e1001241.

Dower, John W. *Embracing Defeat: Japan in the Wake of World War II.* New York: W. W. Norton, 2000.

Duncan, Luce, and Raiffa Howard. *Games and Decisions.* New York: Dover, 1957.

Easterly, William. *The Tyranny of Experts: Economists, Dictators, and the Forgotten Rights of the Poor.* New York: Basic Books, 2014.

Eccles, Robert, Michael P. Krzus, and Don Tapscott. *One Report: Integrated Reporting for a Sustainable Strategy.* Hoboken, NJ: Wiley, 2010.

Edwards, Andres, and David Orr. *The Sustainability Revolution: Portrait of a Paradigm Shift.* Gabriola, BC: New Society Publishers, 2005.

Elhauge, Einer. "Sacrificing Corporate Profits in the Public Interest." *New York University Law Review* 80 (2005): 733–869.

Elkington, John. "Enter the Triple Bottom Line." In *The Triple Bottom Line: Does It All Add Up?,* edited by Adrian Henriques and Julie Richardson, 1–16. London: Earthscan Publications, 2004.

Fairchild, Amy, and James Colgrove. "Out of the Ashes: The Life, Death, and Rebirth of the 'Safer' Cigarette in the United States." *American Journal of Public Health* 94, no. 2 (2004): 192–204.

Fassin, Didier. *Humanitarian Reason: A Moral History of the Present.* Berkeley: University of California Press, 2012.

Feher, Michel, Yates McKee, and Gaëlle Krikorian, eds. *Nongovernmental Politics.* New York: Zone Books, 2007.

Feld, Lars, and Bruno Frey. "Trust Breeds Trust: How Taxpayers Are Treated." *Economics of Governance* 3 (2002): 87–99.

Felice, William F. *The Global New Deal: Economic and Social Human Rights in World Politics.* Lanham, MD: Rowman and Littlefield, 2010.

Ferencz, Benjamin B. *Less Than Slaves: Jewish Forced Labor and the Quest for Compensation.* Bloomington: Indiana University Press, 2002.

Ferguson, James. *Global Shadows: Africa in the Neoliberal World Order.* Durham, NC: Duke University Press, 2006.

——. "Seeing like an Oil Company: Space, Security, and Global Capital in Neoliberal Africa." *American Anthropologist* 107, no. 3 (2005): 377–82.

——. "The Uses of Neoliberalism." *Antipode* 41 (January 1, 2010): 166–84.

Ferguson, James, and Akhil Gupta. "Spatializing States: Toward an Ethnography of Neoliberal Governmentality." *American Ethnologist* 29, no. 4 (2002): 981–1002.

Filer, Colin, Glenn Banks, and John Burton. "The Fragmentation of Responsibilities in the Melanesian Mining Sector." In *Earth Matters: Indigenous Peoples, Extractive Industries, and Corporate Social Responsibility,* edited by Ciaran O'Faircheallaigh and Saleem Ali, 163–79. Sheffield, UK: Greenleaf, 2008.

Finnemore, Martha. "Rules of War and Wars of Rules: The International Red Cross and the Restraint of State Violence." In *Constructing World Culture: International Governmental Organizations since 1875,* edited by John Boli and George M. Thomas, 149–65. Stanford CA: Stanford University Press, 1999.

Forman, Shepard, and Derk Segaar. "New Coalitions for Global Governance: The Changing Dynamics of Multilateralism." *Global Governance: A Review of Multilateralism and International Organizations* 12, no. 2 (2006): 205–25.

Forsyth, David. *Human Rights in International Relations*. Cambridge: Cambridge University Press, 2000.

Fortun, Kim. "Remembering Bhopal, Refiguring Liability," *Interventions: International Journal of Postcolonial Studies* 2, no. 2 (2000): 187–98.

Foster, Robert L. *Coca-Globalization: Following Soft Drinks from New York to New Guinea*. London: Palgrave McMillan, 2008.

Foucault, Michel. *Power/Knowledge: Selected Interviews and Other Writings, 1972–1977*. Edited by Colin Gordon. New York: Knopf Doubleday, 1980.

Fraenkel, Ernst. *Military Occupation and the Rule of Law: Occupational Government in the Rhineland, 1918–1923*. Oxford: Oxford University Press, 1944.

Frank, Thomas. *The Conquest of Cool: Business Culture, Counterculture, and the Rise of Hip Consumerism*. Chicago: University of Chicago Press, 1998.

Freeman, Bennett, Maria B. Pica, and Christopher N. Camponovo. "A New Approach to Corporate Responsibility: The Voluntary Principles on Security and Human Rights." *Hastings International and Comparative Law Review* 24, no. 3 (2001): 423–50.

Freeman, R. Edward. *Strategic Management: A Stakeholder Approach*. Cambridge: Cambridge University Press, 1984.

Frei, Norbert. *Adenauer's Germany and the Nazi Past*. New York: Columbia University Press, 2002.

Frey, Bruno. *Not Just for the Money: An Economic Theory of Personal Motivation*. Cheltenham, UK; Brookfield, VT: Edward Elgar Publishing, 1997.

Friedlander, Henry. "The Judiciary and Nazi Crimes in Postwar Germany." *Simon Wiesenthal Center Annual* 1 (1984): 27–44.

———. "Nazi Crimes and the German Law." In *Nazi Crimes and the Law*, edited by Nathan Stoltzfus and Henry Friedlander, 15–33. Washington, DC: German Historical Institute, 2008.

Friedman, Lissy S. "Philip Morris's Website and Television Commercials Use New Language to Mislead the Public into Believing It Has Changed Its Stance on Smoking and Disease." *Tobacco Control* 16 (2007): 6–9.

Friedman, Milton. *Capitalism and Freedom*. Chicago: University of Chicago Press, 1962.

———. "The Social Responsibility of Business Is to Increase Its Profits." *New York Times Magazine*, September 13, 1970.

Frynas, J. George. "The False Developmental Promise of Corporate Social Responsibility: Evidence from Multinational Oil Companies." *International Affairs* 81, no. 3 (2005): 581–98.

Fukuyama, Francis. *Trust: The Social Virtues and the Creation of Prosperity*. New York: Free Press, 1995.

Fuller, Lon L. "Positivism and Fidelity to Law: A Reply to Professor Hart." *Harvard Law Review* 71, no. 4 (1958): 630–72.

Gauthier, David. *Morals by Agreement*. Oxford: Oxford University Press, 1986.

Gillette, Philip. "American Capital in the Contest for Soviet Oil, 1920–23." *Soviet Studies* 24 (1973): 477–90.

Givel, Michael. "FDA Legislation." *Tobacco Control* 16 (2007): 217–18.

Gledhill, John. *The Enron Scandal: Global Corporation against Society*. New York: Berghahn Books, 2004.

Global Witness. *Do No Harm: A Guide for Companies Sourcing from the DRC*. London: Global Witness, 2010.

Gneezy, Uri, and Aldo Rustichini. "A Fine Is a Price." *Journal of Legal Studies* 29 (2000): 1–17.

Goodman, Michael B. "Restoring Trust in American Business: The Struggle to Change Perception." *Journal of Business Strategy* 26, no. 4 (2005): 29–37.

Goodman, Ryan, and Derek Jinks. *Socializing States: Promoting Human Rights through International Law*. Oxford: Oxford University Press, 2013.

Gratton, Peter. *The State of Sovereignty: Lessons from the Political Fictions of Modernity*. Albany: State University of New York Press, 2012.

Greenfield, Kent. "Ultra Vires Lives! A Stakeholder Analysis of Corporate Illegality (With Notes on How Corporate Law Could Reinforce International Law Norms)." *Virginia Law Review* 87 (2001): 1316–18.

Greig, Alastair, David Hulme, and Mark Turner. *Challenging Global Inequality: Development Theory and Practice in the 21st Century*. New York: Palgrave Macmillan, 2007.

Habib, Irfan. "Potentialities of Capitalistic Development in the Economy of Mughal India." *Journal of Economic History* 29, no. 1 (1969): 32–78.

Hanlon, Gerard. "Rethinking Corporate Social Responsibility and the Role of the Firm." In *The Oxford Handbook of Corporate Social Responsibility*, edited by Andrew Crane, Dirk Matten, Abagail McWilliams, Jeremy Moon, and Donald Siegel, 156–72. Oxford: Oxford University Press, 2008.

Hansen, Thomas Blom, and Finn Stepputat, eds. *Sovereign Bodies: Citizens, Migrants, and States in the Postcolonial World*. Princeton, NJ: Princeton University Press, 2005.

———. "Sovereignty Revisited." *Annual Review of Anthropology* 35 (2006): 295–315.

Hansen, Valerie. *Negotiating Daily Life in Traditional China: How Ordinary People Used Contracts, 600–1400*. New Haven, CT: Yale University Press, 1995.

Hardin, Rebecca. "Concessionary Politics: Property, Patronage, and Political Rivalry in Central African Forest Management." *Current Anthropology* 52, no. 3 (2011): S113–S125.

Hardt, Michael, and Antonio Negri. *Empire*. Cambridge, MA: Harvard University Press, 2000.

———. *Multitude: War and Democracy in the Age of Empire*. New York: Penguin, 2004.

Harris, Patricia Sowell. *None of Us Is as Good as All of Us: How McDonald's Prospers by Embracing Inclusion and Diversity*. London: Wiley, 2009.

Hart, H. L. A. "Positivism and the Separation of Law and Morals." *Harvard Law Review* 71, no. 4 (1958): 593–629.

Hartmann, Thom. *Unequal Protection: How Corporations Became "People"— and How You Can Fight Back*. San Francisco: Berrett-Koehler, 2010.

Harvey, David. *A Brief History of Neoliberalism*. Oxford; New York: Oxford University Press, 2005.

Hatekar, Neeraj. "Farmers and Markets in the Pre-Colonial Deccan: The Plausibility of Economic Growth in Traditional Society." *Past and Present* 178 (February 1, 2003): 116–47.

Hatsukami, Dorothy K., Jack E. Henningfield, and Michael Kotlyar. "Harm Reduction Approaches to Reducing Tobacco-Related Mortality. *Annual Review of Public Health* 25 (2004): 377–95.

Hayek, Friedrich. *The Road to Serfdom*. Chicago: University of Chicago Press, 1944.

Hayes, Peter. "The Degussa AG and the Holocaust." In *Lessons and Legacies: The Holocaust and Justice*, edited by Ronald Smelser, 140–77. Evanston, IL: Northwestern University Press, 2002.

———. *From Cooperation to Complicity: Degussa in the Third Reich*. Cambridge: Cambridge University Press, 2004.

———. *Industry and Ideology: IG Farben in the Nazi Era*. Cambridge: Cambridge University Press, 1987.

Heckman, James, Alan B. Krueger, and Benjamin Friedman. *Inequality in America: What Role for Human Capital Policies?* Cambridge, MA: MIT Press, 2005.

Heller, Kevin Jon. *The Nuremberg Military Tribunals and the Origins of International Criminal Law*. Oxford: Oxford University Press, 2011.

Ho, Karen. *Liquidated: An Ethnography of Wall Street*. Durham, NC: Duke University Press, 2009.

Hoffman, Andrew J. *From Heresy to Dogma: An Institutional History of Corporate Environmentalism*. San Francisco: New Lexington Press, 1997.

Hopgood, Stephen. *The Endtimes of Human Rights*. Ithaca, NY: Cornell University Press, 2013.

Hopkins, David. *Corporate Social Responsibility and International Development: Is Business the Solution?* London: Routledge, 2008.

Hopwood, Anthony, Jeffery Unerman, and Jessica Fries. *Accounting for Sustainability: Practical Insights*. London: Earthscan, 2010.

Hughes, Alex, Neil Wrigley, and Martin Buttle. "Global Production Networks, Ethical Campaigning, and the Embeddedness of Responsible Governance." *Journal of Economic Geography* 8, no. 3 (2008): 345–67.

Humes, Edward. *Eco Barons: The Dreamers, Schemers, and Millionaires Who Are Saving Our Planet.* New York: HarperCollins, 2009.

Humphreys, David. "From Corporate Social Responsibility to the Democratic Regulation of Transnational Corporations." *International Journal of Environmental, Cultural, Social and Economic Sustainability* 5, no. 4 (2009): 207–18.

Humphreys, Macartan, Jeffrey D. Sachs, and Joseph E. Stiglitz. *Escaping the Resource Curse.* New York: Columbia University Press, 2007.

Huyse, Luc. "The Criminal Justice System as a Political Actor in Regime Transitions: The Case of Belgium, 1944–50." In *The Politics of Retribution of Europe: World War II and Its Aftermath*, edited by István Deák, Jan T. Gross, and Tony Judt, 157–72. Princeton, NJ: Princeton University Press, 2000.

Ignatieff, Michael. *Human Rights as Politics and Idolatry.* Princeton, NJ: Princeton University Press, 2001.

Ikenson, Daniel J. *A Compromise to Advance the Trade Agenda: Purge Negotiations of Investor-State Dispute Settlement.* Washington, DC: Cato Institute, 2014.

International Commission on Intervention and State Sovereignty. *The Responsibility to Protect: Report of the International Commission on Intervention and State Sovereignty.* Ottawa: International Development Research Centre, 2001.

Irwin, Douglas. *Free Trade under Fire.* Princeton, NJ: Princeton University Press, 2009.

Jacobs, James, and Frank Anechiarico. *The Pursuit of Absolute Integrity: How Corruption Control Makes Government Ineffective.* Chicago: University of Chicago Press, 1996.

James, Harold. *The Creation and Destruction of Value: The Globalization Cycle.* 1st ed. Cambridge, MA: Harvard University Press, 2009.

Jensen, Michael. "Value Maximization, Stakeholder Theory, and the Corporate Objective Function." *Business Ethics Quarterly* 12 (2002): 235–56.

Jensen, Michael, and William Meckling. "Theory of the Firm: Managerial Behavior, Agency Costs, and Ownership Structure." *Journal of Financial Economics* 3 (1976): 305–60.

Johnson, Jennifer. "Public-Private-Public Convergence: How the Private Actor Can Shape Public International Labor Standards." *Brooklyn Journal of International Law* 24 (1998): 291–356.

Joseph, Richard A. *Radical Nationalism in Cameroon: Social Origins of the U.P.C. Rebellion.* Oxford: Oxford University Press, 1977.

Kaeb, Caroline, and David Scheffer. "The Paradox of Kiobel in Europe." *American Journal of International Law* 107 (2013): 852–57.

Kaldor, Mary. "In Defence of New Wars." *Stability* 2, no. 1 (2013): 1–16.

———. *New and Old Wars: Organized Violence in a Global Era*. Palo Alto, CA: Stanford University Press, 2006.

Kalyvas, Stathis. "'New' and 'Old' Civil Wars: A Valid Distinction?" *World Politics* 54, no. 1 (2001): 99–118.

Kaplan, Rami, and David L. Levy. "Corporate Social Responsibility and Theories of Global Governance: Strategic Contestation in Global Issue Arenas." In *The Oxford Handbook of Corporate Social Responsibility*, edited by Andrew Crane, Dirk Matten, Abagail McWilliams, Jeremy Moon, and Donald Siegel, 432–51. Oxford: Oxford University Press, 2008.

Karlan, Dean, and Jacob Appel. *More Than Good Intentions: How a New Economics Is Helping to Solve Global Poverty*. New York: Dutton, 2011.

Kates, Robert W. "What Kind of Science Is Sustainability Science?" *Proceedings of the National Academy of Sciences of the United States of America* 108, no. 49 (2011): 19,449–50.

Katz, Donald. *Just Do It: The Nike Spirit in the Corporate World*. Avon, MA: Adams Media, 1995.

Keck, Margaret E., and Kathryn Sikkink. *Activists beyond Borders: Advocacy Networks in International Politics*. Ithaca, NY: Cornell University Press, 1998.

Keen, David. *Useful Enemies: When Waging Wars Is More Important Than Winning Them*. New Haven, CT: Yale University Press, 2012.

Keenan, Jeremy H. "Chad-Cameroon Oil Pipeline: World Bank and Exxon-Mobil in 'Last Chance Saloon.'" *Review of African Political Economy* 32, nos. 104–5 (2005): 395–405.

———. "Demystifying Africa's Security." *Review of African Political Economy* 35, no. 118 (2008): 634–44.

Kelly, John. "The Other Leviathans: Corporate Investment and the Construction of a Sugar Company." In *White and Deadly: Sugar and Colonialism*, edited by Pal Ahluwadia, Bill Ashcroft, and Roger Knight, 95–134. Commack, NY: Nova Science Publishers, 1999.

Kent, John. *America, the UN, and Decolonization: Cold War Conflict in the Congo*. New York: Routledge, 2011.

Kerr, Michael, Richard Janda, and Chip Pitts, eds. *Corporate Social Responsibility: A Legal Analysis*. Markham, ON: LexisNexis, 2009.

Kiernan, Matthew. *Investing in a Sustainable World: Why GREEN Is the New Color of Money on Wall Street*. New York: Amacom, 2008.

Kiernan, V. G. "Foreign Mercenaries and Absolute Monarchy." In *Crisis in Europe, 1560–1660*. Edited by Trevor Aston, 117–40. Abingdon: Routledge, 2011.

Kinley, David, and Junko Tadaki. "From Talk to Walk: The Emergence of Human Rights Responsibilities for Corporations at International Law." *Virginia Journal of International Law* 44 (2004): 931–57.

Kirsch, Stuart. "Anthropology and Advocacy: A Case Study of the Campaign against the Ok Tedi Mine." *Critique of Anthropology* 22, no. 2 (2002): 175–200.

———. "Indigenous Movements and the Risks of Counterglobalization: Tracking the Campaign against Papua New Guinea's Ok Tedi Mine." *American Ethnologist* 34, no. 2 (2007): 303–21.

———. *Mining Capitalism: Dialectical Relations between Corporations and Their Critics.* Berkeley: University of California Press, 2014.

———. *Reverse Anthropology: Indigenous Analysis of Social and Environmental Relations in New Guinea.* Stanford, CA: Stanford University Press, 2006.

———. "Sustainable Mining." *Dialectical Anthropology* 34, no. 1 (2010): 87–93.

Klein, Naomi. *The Shock Doctrine.* London: Penguin, 2007.

Koechlin, Lucy, and Richard Calland. "Standard Setting at the Cutting Edge: An Evidence-Based Typology for Multi-Stakeholder Initiatives." In *Non-State Actors as Standard-Setters,* edited by Anne Peters, Lucy Koechlin, Till Förster, and Gretta Fenner Zinkernagel, 83–102. Cambridge: Cambridge University Press, 2009.

Kotler, Philip, and Nancy Lee. *Corporate Social Responsibility: Doing the Most Good for Your Company and Your Cause.* New York: Wiley, 2004.

Krasner, Stephen D. "Structural Causes and Regime Consequences: Regimes as Intervening Variables." In *International Regimes,* edited by Stephen D. Krasner, 1–21. Ithaca, NY: Cornell University Press, 1983.

Kriger, Norma. *Zimbabwe's Guerrilla War: Peasant Voices.* New York: Cambridge University Press, 1992.

Krippner, Greta R. *Capitalizing on Crisis: The Political Origins of the Rise of Finance.* Cambridge, MA: Harvard University Press, 2012.

Kubů, Eduard, and Jan Kuklík Jr. "Reluctant Restitution: The Restitution of Jewish Property in the Bohemian Lands after the Second World War." In *Robbery and Restitution: The Conflict over Jewish Property in Europe,* edited by Martin Dean, Constantin Goschler, and Philipp Ther, 223–39. New York: Berghahn Books, 2007.

Langan, Mark. "Private Sector Development as Poverty and Strategic Discourse: PSD in the Political Economy of EU-Africa Trade Relations." *Journal of Modern African Studies* 49, no. 1 (2011): 83–113.

Lapavitsas, Costas "Financialised Capitalism: Crisis and Financial Expropriation." *Historical Materialism* 17, no. 2 (2009): 114–48.

Lauren, Paul Gordon. "A Human Rights Lens on U.S. History: Human Rights at Home and Human Rights Abroad." In *Bringing Human Rights Home: A History of Human Rights in the United States,* edited by Cynthia Soohoo,

Catherine Albisa, and Martha F. Davis, 9–30. Philadelphia: University of Pennsylvania Press, 2009.

Lauterpacht, Hersch. *International Law and Human Rights.* New York: Garland, 1973.

Le Billon, Philippe. *Wars of Plunder: Conflicts, Profits, and the Politics of Resources.* Oxford: Oxford University Press, 2013.

Leary, Virginia A. "The WTO and the Social Clause: Post- Singapore." *European Journal of International Law* 8, no. 1. (1997): 118–22.

Leith, Denise. *The Politics of Power: Freeport in Suharto's Indonesia.* Honolulu: University of Hawai'i Press, 2003.

Lepper, Mark, and David Greene. *The Hidden Costs of Rewards: New Perspectives on the Psychology of Human Motivation.* Hillsdale, NJ: L. Erlbaum Associates, 1978.

Lessig, Lawrence. *Republic, Lost: How Money Corrupts Congress—and a Plan to Stop It.* New York: Twelve, 2011.

Levitt, Justin. "Confronting the Impact of Citizens United." *Yale Law and Policy Review* 29 (2010): 217–26.

Li, Tania Murray. *The Will to Improve: Governmentality, Development, and the Practice of Politics.* Durham, NC: Duke University Press, 2007.

Liebenthal, Andres, Roland Michelitsch, and Ethel Tarazona. *Extractive Industries and Sustainable Development: An Evaluation of the World Bank Group's Experience.* Washington, DC: World Bank Publications, 2005.

Lindgreen, Adam, and Valerie Swaen. "Corporate Social Responsibility." *International Journal of Management Reviews* 12 (2010): 1–7.

Lindner, Stephan H. *Inside IG Farben: Hoechst during the Third Reich.* Cambridge: Cambridge University Press, 2008.

Lo, Marieme. "Revisiting the Chad-Cameroon Pipeline Compensation Modality, Local Communities' Discontent, and Accountability Mechanisms." *Canadian Journal of Development Studies* 30, nos. 1–2 (2010): 153–74.

Locke, Richard. *The Promise and Limits of Private Power.* Cambridge: Cambridge University Press, 2013.

Lonkila, Markku. "Post-Soviet Russia: A Society of Networks?" In *Russia: More Different Than Most?*, edited by Markku Kangaspuro, 99–112. Helsinki: Kikimora Publications, 2001.

Lund, Christian, ed. *Twilight Institutions: Public Authority and Local Politics in Africa.* Hoboken, NJ: Wiley-Blackwell, 2007.

M'baye, Kéba. "Le Droit du Développement comme un Droit de l'Homme." *Revue des Droits de l'Homme* 5 (1972): 503–34.

MacPherson, Darcy L. "Criminal Liability of Partnerships: Constitutional and Practical Impediments." *Manitoba Law Journal* 33, no. 2 (2010): 329–90.

Maddison, Angus. *The World Economy: A Millennial Perspective.* Paris: OECD, 2001.

Maguire, Peter. *Law and War: An American Story.* New York: Columbia University Press, 2000.

Maignan, Isabelle, and David A. Ralston. "Corporate Social Responsibility in Europe and the U.S.: Insights from Businesses' Self-Presentations." *Journal of International Business Studies* 33 (2002): 497–514.

Małowist, M. "The Social and Economic Stability of the Western Sudan in the Middle Ages." *Past and Present* 33 (April 1, 1966): 3–15.

Mamdani, Mahmood. *Citizen and Subject: Contemporary Africa and the Legacy of Late Colonialism.* Princeton, NJ: Princeton University Press, 1996.

———. *Saviors and Survivors: Darfur, Politics, and the War on Terror.* New York: Pantheon Books, 2009.

Marchand, Roland. *Creating the Corporate Soul: The Rise of Public Relations and Corporate Imagery in American Big Business.* Berkeley: University of California Press, 1998.

Marks, Susan. "Four Human Rights Myths." LSE Legal Studies Working Paper. London School of Economics and Political Science (LSE), September 4, 2012.

Marrus, Michael R., ed. *The Nuremberg War Crimes Trial, 1945–46.* Boston: Bedford Books, 1997.

Matten, Dirk, and Andrew Crane. "Corporate Citizenship: Toward an Extended Theoretical Conceptualization." *Academy of Management Review* 30 (2005): 166–79.

Max, D. T. "Green Is Good." *New Yorker,* May 12, 2014.

Mayer, Carl. "Personalizing the Impersonal: Corporations and the Bill of Rights." *Hastings Law Journal* 41 (March 1990): 577–667.

Mazower, Mark. *Governing the World: The History of an Idea, 1815 to the Present.* New York: Penguin, 2012.

Mbembe, Achille. *On the Postcolony.* Berkeley: University of California Press, 2001.

McBarnet, Doreen, and Marina Kurkchiyan. "Corporate Social Responsibility through Contractual Control? Global Supply Chains and 'Other-Regulation.'" In *The New Corporate Accountability,* edited by Doreen McBarnet, Aurora Voiculescu, and Tom Campbell, 59–92. Cambridge: Cambridge University Press, 2007.

McBarnet, Doreen, Aurora Voiculescu, and Tom Campbell. *The New Corporate Accountability.* Cambridge: Cambridge University Press, 2007.

McCully, Patrick. "The Use of a Trilateral Network: An Activist's Perspective on the Formation of the World Commission on Dams." *American University Law Review* 16, no. 6 (2001): 1453–75.

McDaniel, Patricia A., and Ruth E. Malone. 2005. "Understanding Philip Morris's Pursuit of U.S. Government Regulation of Tobacco." *Tobacco Control* 14 (2005): 193–200.

McDaniel, Patricia A., Elizabeth A. Smith, and Ruth E. Malone. "Philip Morris's Project Sunrise: Weakening Tobacco Control by Working with It." *Tobacco Control* 15 (2006): 215–23.

McGee, Brant. "The Community Referendum: Participatory Democracy and the Right to Free, Prior, and Informed Consent to Development." *Berkeley Journal of International Law* 27, no. 2 (2009): 570–635.

McTaggart, James M. *Value Imperative: Managing for Superior Shareholder Returns.* New York: Free Press, 1994.

McWilliams, James E. *American Pests: The Losing War on Insects from Colonial Times to DDT.* New York: Columbia University Press, 2008.

Meister, Robert. *After Evil: A Politics of Human Rights.* New York: Columbia University Press, 2011.

Mendelsohn, John. *Trial by Document: The Use of Seized Records in the United States Proceedings at Nürnberg.* New York: Garland Publishing, 1988.

Mettraux, Guénaël. *The Law of Command Responsibility.* Oxford: Oxford University Press, 2009.

Meyerowitz, Eva L. R. *The Sacred State of the Akan.* London: Faber and Faber, 1953.

Mitchell, Lawrence E. *Corporate Irresponsibility: America's Newest Export.* New Haven, CT: Yale University Press, 2001.

———. *The Speculation Economy: How Finance Triumphed over Industry.* Vol. 2. San Francisco: Berrett-Koehler, 2007.

Mitchell, Ronald K., Bradley R. Agle, and Donna J. Wood. "Toward a Theory of Stakeholder Identification and Salience: Defining the Principle of Who and What Really Counts." *Academy of Management Review* 22, no. 4 (1997): 853–86.

Mitchell, Timothy. *Carbon Democracy: Political Power in the Age of Oil.* New York: Verso, 2011.

Monbiot, George. *Captive State: The Corporate Takeover of Britain.* London: Pan, 2001.

Monshipouri, Mahmood, Claude Welch Jr., and Evan Kennedy. "Multinational Corporations and the Ethics of Global Responsibility." In *Human Rights in the World Community: Issues and Action,* edited by Richard Pierre Claude and Burns Weston, 434–45. Philadelphia: University of Pennsylvania Press, 2006.

Moon, Jeremy, and David Vogel. "Corporate Social Responsibility, Government, and Civil Society." In *The Oxford Handbook of Corporate Social Responsibility,* edited by Andrew Crane, Abagail McWilliams, Dirk Matten, Jeremy Moon, and Donald Siegel, 303–26. Oxford: Oxford University Press, 2008.

Moore, Donald. *Suffering for Territory: Race, Place, and Power in Zimbabwe.* Durham, NC: Duke University Press, 2005.

Mosse, David. *Cultivating Development: An Ethnography of Aid Policy and Practice*. London: Pluto Press, 2004.

Moyn, Samuel. "Human Rights and 'Neoliberalism.'" *Humanitarianism and Human Rights*, December 9, 2013. http://hhr.hypotheses.org/215.

——. *The Last Utopia*. Cambridge, MA: Belknap Press of Harvard University Press, 2010.

Muchlinski, Peter. *Multinational Enterprises and the Law*. New York: Oxford University Press, 2007.

Negri, Antonio. "The Specter's Smile." In *Ghostly Demarcations: A Symposium on Jacques Derrida's Specters of Marx*, edited by Michael Sprinker, 5–16. New York: Verso, 1999.

Nestle, Marion. *Food Politics: How the Food Industry Influences Nutrition and Health*. Berkeley: University of California Press, 2007.

Newton, Michael A., and Casey Kuhlman. "Why Criminal Culpability Should Follow the Critical Path: Reframing the Theory of 'Effective Control.'" *Netherlands Yearbook of International Law* 40 (2009): 3–73.

Noman, Akbar, and Joseph E. Stiglitz. "Strategies for African Development." In *Good Growth and Governance in Africa: Rethinking Development Strategies*, edited by Akbar Noman, Kwesi Botchwey, Howard Stein, and Joseph E. Stiglitz, 3–47. Oxford: Oxford University Press, 2012.

Ofosu-Mensah, Emmanuel Ababio. "Gold Mining and the Socio-Economic Development of Obuasi in Adanse." *African Journal of History and Culture* 3, no. 4 (2011): 54–64.

Oliveira, Ricardo Soares de. *Oil and Politics in the Gulf of Guinea*. New York: Columbia University Press, 2007.

Ong, Aihwa. *Neoliberalism as Exception: Mutations in Citizenship and Sovereignty*. Durham, NC: Duke University Press, 2006.

Onuoha, Godwin. "Energy and Security in the Gulf of Guinea: A Nigerian Perspective." *South African Journal of International Affairs* 16, no. 2 (2009): 245–64.

Oreskes, Naomi, and Erik M. Conway. *Merchants of Doubt: How a Handful of Scientists Obscured the Truth on Issues from Tobacco Smoke to Global Warming*. New York: Bloomsbury Press, 2010.

O'Rourke, Dara. "Market Movements: Nongovernmental Organization Strategies to Influence Global Production and Consumption." *Journal of Industrial Ecology* 9, no. 1–2 (2005): 115–28.

Otañez, Marty G., and Stanton A. Glantz. "Social Responsibility in Tobacco Production? Tobacco Companies' Use of Green Supply Chains to Obscure the Real Costs of Tobacco Farming." *Tobacco Control* 20 (2011): 403–11.

Otañez, Marty G., Hadii Mamudu, and Stanton A. Glantz. "Global Leaf Companies Control the Tobacco Market in Malawi." *Tobacco Control* 16 (2007): 261–69.

Ougaard, Morten. "Instituting the Power to Do Good? The CSR Movement and Global Governance." In *International Political Economy Yearbook*, edited by Christopher May, 227–47. New York: Lynne Rienner Publishers, 2006.

Overbeck, Henk, Klaus Dingwerth, Philipp Pattberg, and Daniel Compagnon. "Forum: Global Governance: Decline or Maturation of an Academic Concept?" *International Studies Review* 12 (2010): 696.

Phillips, Hugh. "From a Bolshevik to a British Subject: The Early Years of Maksim Litvinov." *Slavic Review* 48, no. 3 (1989): 388–98.

Pierce, John P. "Harm Reduction or Harm Maintenance?" *Nicotine and Tobacco Research* (supplement) 2 (2002): 53.

Piketty, Thomas. *Capital in the Twenty-First Century*. Cambridge, MA: Harvard University Press, 2014.

Piot, Charles. *Nostalgia for the Future: West Africa after the Cold War*. Chicago: University of Chicago Press, 2010.

Pistor, Katharina. "On the Plasticity of Corporate Form." *Complexity and Institutions: Markets, Norms, and Corporations*, 2012, 173–88.

Pitcher, M. Anne. *Party Politics and Economic Reform in Africa's Democracies*. Cambridge: Cambridge University Press, 2012.

Pogge, Thomas. *World Poverty and Human Rights*. Malden, MA: Polity, 2002.

Pollay, R. W., and T. Dewhirst. "The Dark Side of Marketing Seemingly 'Light' Cigarettes: Successful Images and Failed Fact." *Tobacco Control* 11 (2002): 18–31.

Porter, Michael, and Mark Kramer. "The Big Idea: Creating Shared Value; How to Reinvent Capitalism—and Unleash a Wave of Innovation and Growth." *Harvard Business Review*, January–February 2011, 5.

Porter, Michael, and Claas van der Linde. "Toward a New Conception of the Environment-Competitiveness Relationship." *Journal of Economic Perspectives* 9, no. 4 (1995): 97–118.

Povinelli, Elizabeth. *Economies of Abandonment: Social Belonging and Endurance in Late Liberalism*. Durham, NC: Duke University Press, 2011.

Power, Michael. *The Audit Society: Rituals of Verification*. Oxford: Oxford University Press, 1997.

Poynder, John, ed. *Literary Extracts*. 1st ed. London: John Hatchard and Son, 1844.

Prahalad, C. K., and Yves Doz. *The Multinational Mission: Balancing Local Demands and Global Vision*. New York: Free Press, 1999.

Proctor, Robert N. "Tobacco and the Global Lung Cancer Epidemic." *Nature Reviews Cancer* 1, no. 1 (2001): 82–86.

Rajak, Dinah. *In Good Company: An Anatomy of Corporate Social Responsibility*. Stanford, CA: Stanford University Press, 2011.

———. "Theatres of Virtue: Collaboration, Consensus, and the Social Life of Corporate Social Responsibility." *Focaal* 60 (2011): 9–20.

Raman, K. Ravi, and Ronnie D. Lipschutz. *Corporate Social Responsibility: Comparative Critiques*. New York: Palgrave Macmillan, 2010.

Ratner, Stephen. "Corporations and Human Rights: A Theory of Legal Responsibility." *Yale Law Journal* 111 (2001): 461–546.

Rawls, John. *A Theory of Justice*. Cambridge, MA: Belknap Press of Harvard University Press, 1971.

Reed, Darryl. "Resource Extraction Industries in Developing Countries." *Journal of Business Ethics* 39 (2002): 199–226.

Ricoeur, Paul. *Freud and Philosophy: An Essay on Interpretation*. New Haven, CT: Yale University Press, 1970.

Rittberger, Volker, Martin Nettesheim, and Carmen Huckel. *Authority in the Global Political Economy*. New York: Palgrave Macmillan, 2008.

Roberts, John. "The Manufacture of Corporate Social Responsibility: Constructing Corporate Sensibility." *Organization* 10, no. 2 (2003): 249–65.

Roberts, Mary Louise. "Gender, Consumption, and Commodity Culture." *American Historical Review* 103, no. 3 (1998): 817–44.

Rodríguez-Garavito, César. "Ethnicity.gov: Global Governance, Indigenous Peoples, and the Right to Prior Consultation in Social Minefields." *Indiana Journal of Global Legal Studies* 18, no. 1 (2011): 263–305.

Roitman, Janet. *Fiscal Disobedience: An Anthropology of Economic Regulation in Central Africa*. Princeton, NJ: Princeton University Press, 2005.

Rose, Nikolas. *Powers of Freedom*. Cambridge: Cambridge University Press, 1999.

Rosenblum, Peter. "Pipeline Politics in Chad." *Current History* 99, no. 637 (2000): 195–99.

Rosenblum, Peter, and Susan Maples. *Contracts Confidential: Ending Secret Deals in the Extractives Industry*. New York: Revenue Watch Institute, 2009.

Ross, Michael. "What Do We Know about Natural Resources and Civil Wars?" *Journal of Peace Research* 41, no. 3 (2004): 337–56.

Rousseau, Jean-Jacques. *On the Social Contract*. Indianapolis: Hackett, 1988.

Rousso, Henry. *The Vichy Syndrome: History and Memory in France since 1944*. Cambridge, MA: Harvard University Press, 1991.

Ruggie, John G. "Business and Human Rights: The Evolving International Agenda." *American Journal of International Law* 101, no. 4 (2007): 819–40.

Runge, Jurgen, and James Shikwati. *Geological Resources and Good Governance in Sub-Saharan Africa: Holistic Approaches to Transparency and Sustainable Development in the Extractive Sector*. Boca Raton, FL: CRC Press, 2011.

Rupp, Deborah E., Jyoti Ganapathi, Ruth V. Aguilera, and Cynthia A. Williams. "Employee Reactions to Corporate Social Responsibility: An Organizational Justice Framework." *Journal of Organizational Behavior* 27 (2006): 537–43.

Rutherford, Danilyn. *Laughing at Leviathan: Sovereignty and Audience in West Papua*. Chicago: University of Chicago Press, 2012.

Sacconi, Lorenzo. "Corporate Social Responsibility (CSR) as a Model of 'Extended' Corporate Governance: An Explanation Based on the Economic Theories of Social Contract, Reputation and Reciprocal Conformism." In *Reframing Self-Regulation in European Private Law*, edited by Fabrizio Cafaggi, 289–34. Alphen aan den Rijn, Netherlands: Kluwer Law International, 2006.

Sacconi, Lorenzo, Marco Faillo, and Stefania Ottone. "Contractarian Compliance and the 'Sense of Justice': A Behavioral Conformity Model and Its Experimental Support." *Analyse and Kritik* 1 (2011): 273–310.

Sachs, Jeffrey. *The End of Poverty: Economic Possibilities for Our Time*. New York: Penguin, 2005.

Santos, Boaventura de Sousa, ed. *Another Knowledge Is Possible: Beyond Northern Epistemologies*. New York: Verso, 2007.

——. *Democratizing Democracy: Beyond the Liberal Democratic Canon*. New York: Verso, 2007.

Sassen, Saskia. *Territory, Authority, Rights: From Medieval to Global Assemblages*. Princeton, NJ: Princeton University Press, 2006.

Sawyer, Suzana. *Crude Chronicles: Indians, Multinational Oil, and Neoliberalism in Ecuador*. Durham, NC: Duke University Press, 2004.

Scheffer, David. *All the Missing Souls: A Personal History of the War Crimes Tribunals*. Princeton, NJ: Princeton University Press, 2012.

——. "Genocide and Atrocity Crimes." *Genocide Studies and Prevention* 1 (2006): 229–50.

——. "Introductory Note to Military Commissions Act of 2006." *International Legal Materials* 45 (2006): 1241–75.

Scheffer, David, and Caroline Kaeb. "The Five Levels of CSR Compliance: The Resiliency of Corporate Liability under the Alien Tort Statute and the Case for a Counterattack Strategy in Compliance Theory." *Berkeley Journal of International Law* 29 (2011): 334–97.

Schmidheiny, Stephan. *Changing Course: A Global Business Perspective on Development and the Environment*. Cambridge, MA: MIT Press, 1992.

Schoenberger, Karl. *Levi's Children: Coming to Terms with Human Rights in the Global Marketplace*. New York: Grove Press, 2001.

Schrijver, Nico. *Sovereignty over Natural Resources: Balancing Rights and Duties*. New York: Cambridge University Press, 1997.

Schulz, Wolfgang, and Thorsten Held. *Regulated Self-Regulation as a Form of Modern Government: An Analysis of Case Studies from Media and Telecommunications Law*. Eastleigh, UK: John Libbey, 2004.

Schwartz, Mark, and Archie Carroll. "Corporate Social Responsibility: A Three-Domain Approach." *Business Ethics Quarterly* 13 (2003): 505–6.

Scott, James C. *Seeing Like a State: How Certain Schemes to Improve the Human Condition Have Failed.* New Haven, CT: Yale University Press, 1999.

Scott, W. Richard. "Symbols and Organizations: From Barnard to the Institutionalists." In *Organization Theory: From Chester Barnard to the Present and Beyond*, edited by Oliver E. Williamson, 38–55. Oxford: Oxford University Press, 1995.

Seagle, Caroline. "Inverting the Impacts: Mining, Conservation, and Sustainability Claims Near the Rio Tinto/QQM Ilmenite Mine in Southeast Madagascar." *Journal of Peasant Studies* 39, no. 2 (2012): 447–77.

Sellström, Tor. *Sweden and National Liberation in Southern Africa: Solidarity and Assistance, 1970–1994.* Uppsala: Nordiska Afrikainstituteten, 2002.

Sen, Amartya. "Choice, Ordering, and Morality." In *Practical Reason*, edited by Stephan Körner, 66–79. Oxford: Blackwell, 1974.

———. *Development as Freedom.* Cambridge, MA: Harvard University Press, 1999.

———. "Human Rights and the Limits of Law." *Cardozo Law Review* 27, no. 6 (2006): 2919.

Sengupta, Arjun. "The Right to Development." In *Human Rights in the World Community*, edited by Richard Pierre Claude and Burns H. Weston, 249–61. Philadelphia: University of Pennsylvania Press, 2006.

Shamir, Ronen. "Between Self-Regulation and the Alien Tort Claims Act: On the Contested Concept of Corporate Social Responsibility." *Law and Society Review* 38, no. 4 (2004): 635–64.

———. "Capitalism, Governance, and Authority: The Case of Corporate Social Responsibility." *Annual Review of Law and Social Science* 6 (2010): 531–53.

Shaw, Randy. *Reclaiming America: Nike, Clean Air, and the New National Activism.* Berkeley: University of California Press, 1999.

Shiffman, Saul, Joe G. Gitchell, Kenneth E. Warner, John Slade, Jack E. Henningfield, and John M. Pinney. "Tobacco Harm Reduction: Conceptual Structure and Nomenclature for Analysis and Research." *Nicotine and Tobacco Research* 4, supp. 2 (2002): S113–S129.

Siegel, Michael. "Food and Drug Administration Regulation of Tobacco: Snatching Defeat from the Jaws of Victory." *Tobacco Control* 13 (2004): 439–41.

Silverstein, Michael. "Shifters, Linguistic Categories, and Cultural Description." In *Meaning in Anthropology*, edited by Keith Basso and Henry Selby, 11–55. Albuquerque: University of New Mexico Press, 1976.

Simma, Bruno. "Foreign Investment Arbitration: A Place for Human Rights?" *International and Comparative Law Quarterly* 60, no. 3 (2011): 573–96.

Simon, John G., Charles W. Power, and Jon P. Gunnemann. *The Ethical Investor: Universities and Corporate Responsibility.* New Haven, CT: Yale University Press, 1972.

Singer, P. W. "The Ultimate Military Entrepreneur." *Military History Quarterly*, Spring 2003, 6–15.

Slaughter, Anne-Marie. "A Liberal Theory of International Law." *American Society of International Law Proceedings* 94 (2000): 240–49.

———. *A New World Order*. Princeton, NJ: Princeton University Press, 2005.

Smillie, Ian. "Natural Resources: Diamonds and Human Security." In *Globalization and Security: Social and Cultural Aspects*, edited by G. Honor Fagan and Ronaldo Munck, 239–56. Santa Barbara, CA: ABC-CLIO, 2009.

Smith, Elizabeth A., and Ruth E. Malone. "Altria Means Tobacco: Philip Morris's Identity Crisis." *American Journal of Public Health* 93, no. 4 (2003): 553–56.

———. "Thinking the 'Unthinkable': Why Philip Morris Considered Quitting." *Tobacco Control* 12, no. 2 (2003): 208–13.

Smith, James Howard. *Bewitching Development: Witchcraft and the Reinvention of Development in Neoliberal Kenya*. Chicago: University of Chicago Press, 2008.

Snider, Laureen. "The Sociology of Corporate Crime: An Obituary." *Theoretical Criminology* 4, no. 2 (2000): 169–206.

Social Funds. "Merrill Lynch Fund Participant Pioneers Divestment Resolution." July 27, 2000. http://www.socialfunds.com/news/save.cgi?sfArticleId=321.

Spar, Deborah. "The Spotlight and the Bottom Line: How Multinationals Export Human Rights." *Foreign Affairs* 77, no. 2 (1998): 7–12.

Spence, Roy M., and Haley Rushing. *It's Not What You Sell, It's What You Stand For: Why Every Extraordinary Business Is Drive by Purpose*. New York: Portfolio Hardcover, 2009.

Springer, Jonathan D. "Corporate Constituency Statutes: Hollow Hopes and False Fears." *Annual Survey of American Law* 85 (1999): 85–124.

Stearns, Peter. *Consumerism in World History: The Global Transformation of Desire*. London: Routledge, 2006.

Stephens, Beth. "Corporate Liability: Enforcing Human Rights through Domestic Litigation." *Hastings Journal of International and Comparative Law* 24 (2001): 408–9.

———. "Judicial Deference and the Unreasonable Views of the Bush Administration." *Brooklyn Journal of International Law* 33 (2008): 773, 813–18.

———. "Translating Filártiga: A Comparative and International Law Analysis of Domestic Remedies for International Human Rights Violations." *Yale Journal of International Law* 27 (2002): 1–58.

Stewart, James G. *Corporate War Crimes: Prosecuting the Pillage of Natural Resources*. New York: Open Society Institute, n.d.

———. "A Pragmatic Critique of Corporate Criminal Theory: Lessons from the Extremity." *New Criminal Law Review* 16 (2013): 261–99.

Stout, Lynn. *Cultivating Conscience: How Good Laws Make Good People*. Princeton, NJ: Princeton University Press, 2010.

Strathern, Marilyn. "Introduction: New Accountabilities." In *Audit Cultures: Anthropological Studies in Accountability, Ethics, and the Academy*, edited by Marilyn Strathern, 1–19. New York: Routledge, 2000.

———. "The Tyranny of Transparency." *British Journal of Educational Research* 26, no. 3 (2000): 309–21.

Strauss, Leo. "The Spirit of Hobbes's Political Philosophy." In *Hobbes Studies*, edited by K. C. Brown, 12–13. Oxford: Basil Blackwell, 1965.

Suchman, M. C. "Managing Legitimacy: Strategic and Institutional Approaches." *Academy of Management Review* 20, no. 3 (1995): 571–610.

Sunstein, Cass. "Social Norms and Roles." *Columbia Law Review* 96 (1996): 903–68.

Sutton, Antony. *Western Technology and Soviet Economic Development, 1917 to 1930*. Stanford, CA: Hoover Institution on War, Revolution, and Peace, 1968.

Swanson, Diane L. "Top Managers as Drivers for Corporate Social Responsibility." In *The Oxford Handbook of Corporate Social Responsibility*, edited by Andrew Crane, Abagail McWilliams, Dirk Matten, Jeremy Moon, and Donald Siegel, 227–48. Oxford: Oxford University Press, 2008.

Swart, Bert. "International Trends towards Establishing Some Form of Punishment for Corporations." *Journal of International Criminal Justice*, 2008, 947–79.

Szablowski, David. *Transnational Law and Local Struggles: Mining, Communities, and the World Bank*. Portland, OR: Hart Publishing, 2007.

Szczypka, Glen, Melanie A. Wakefield, Sherry Emery, Yvonne M. Terry-McElrath, Brian R. Flay, and Frank J. Chaloupka. "Working to Make an Image: An Analysis of Three Philip Morris Corporate Media Campaigns." *Tobacco Control* 16 (2007): 344–50.

Tamm, Ingrid J. *Diamonds in Peace and War: Severing the Conflict-Diamond Connection*. Report 30.Cambridge, MA: World Peace Foundation, 2002.

Taylor, Telford. *Final Report to the Secretary of the Army on the Nuernberg War Crimes Trials under Control Council Law No. 10*. Washington, DC: Government Printing Office, 1949.

———. "The Nazis Go Free: Justice and Mercy or Misguided Expediency?" *Nation* 172, no. 8 (1951): 170–72.

Terretta, Meredith. *Nation of Outlaws, State of Violence: Nationalism, Grassfields Tradition, and State-Building in Cameroon*. Athens: Ohio University Press, 2014.

Thomson, Janice. *Mercenaries, Pirates, and Sovereigns: State-Building and Extraterritorial Violence in Early Modern Europe*. Princeton, NJ: Princeton University Press, 1996.

Thompson, Robert, Anita Ramasastry, and Mark Taylor. "Translating Unocal: The Expanding Web of Liability for Business Entities Implicated in International Crimes." *George Washington International Law Review* 40 (2009): 841–902.

Thrasher, J. F., J. Niederdeppe, M. C. Farrelly, K. C. Davis, K. M. Ribisl, and

M. L. Haviland. "The Impact of Anti-Tobacco Industry Prevention Messages in Tobacco Producing Regions: Evidence from the US Truth Campaign." *Tobacco Control* 13 (2004): 283–90.

Tignor, Robert L. *W. Arthur Lewis and the Birth of Development Economics.* Princeton, NJ: Princeton University Press, 2006.

Tilley, Helen. *Africa as a Living Laboratory: Empire, Development, and the Problem of Scientific Knowledge, 1870–1950.* Chicago: University of Chicago Press, 2011.

Topa, Giuseppe, Alain Karsenty, Carole Megevand, and Laurent Debroux. *Forêts tropicales humides du Cameroun: Une décennie de réformes.* Washington, DC: La Banque Mondiale, 2010.

Torgler, Benno. "Tax Morale and Direct Democracy." *European Journal of Political Economy* 21 (2005): 525–31.

Tsing, Anna Lowenhaupt. *Friction: An Ethnography of Global Connection.* Princeton, NJ: Princeton University Press, 2004.

Ukiwo, U. "From Pirates to Militants: A Historical Perspective on Anti-State and Anti-Oil Company Mobilization among the Ijaw of Warri, Western Niger Delta." *African Affairs* 106, no. 425 (2007): 587–610.

Ukwe, C. N., and C. A. Ibe. "A Regional Collaborative Approach in Transboundary Pollution Management in the Guinea Current Region of Western Africa." *Ocean and Coastal Management* 53 (2010): 493–506.

United Nations Environment Programme Finance Initiative. *Sustainability Metrics: Translation and Impact on Property Investment and Management.* UNEP FI Property Working Group Report. United Nations, May 2014.

Urciuoli, Bonnie. "Entextualizing Diversity." *Language and Communication* 30 (2010): 48–57.

———. "Excellence, Leadership, Skills, Diversity: Marketing Liberal Arts Education." *Language and Communication* 23 (2003): 385–408.

———. "Skills and Selves in the New Workplace." *American Ethnologist* 35, no. 2 (2008): 211–28.

Utting, Peter. "CSR and Equality." *Third World Quarterly* 28, no. 4 (2007): 697–712.

Valentine, Sean, and Gary Fleischman. "Ethics Programs, Perceived Corporate Social Responsibility, and Job Satisfaction." *Journal of Business Ethics* 77 (2008): 159–72.

Van den Herik, Larissa, and Daniella Dam-de Jong. "Revitalizing the Antique War Crime of Pillage: The Potential and Pitfalls of Using International Criminal Law to Address Illegal Resource Extraction during Armed Conflict." *Criminal Law Forum* 15 (2011): 266–71.

Vogel, David, and Brookings Institution. *The Market for Virtue: The Potential and Limits of Corporate Social Responsibility.* Washington, DC: Brookings Institution Press, 2006.

Waddell, Steve. *Societal Learning and Change*. Austin, TX: Greenleaf Publishing, 2005.

Waddock, Sandra A., and Samuel B. Graves. "The Corporate Social Performance—Financial Performance Link." *Strategic Management Journal* 18, no. 4 (1997): 303–19.

Ward, Barbara, and René J. Dubos. *Only One Earth: The Care and Maintenance of a Small Planet*. New York: W. W. Norton, 1972.

Watkins, Michael, Mickey Edwards, and Usha Thakrar. *Winning the Influence Game: What Every Business Leader Should Know about Government*. New York: Wiley, 2001.

Watts, Michael. "Resource Curse? Governmentality, Oil, and Power in the Niger Delta, Nigeria." *Geopolitics* 9, no. 1 (2004): 50–80.

Webb, Kernaghan, and Andrew Morrison. "The Law and Voluntary Codes: Examining the 'Tangled Web.'" In *Voluntary Codes: Private Governance, the Public Interest, and Innovation*, edited by Kernaghan Webb, 125–52. Ottawa: School of Public Policy and Administration, Carleton University, 2004.

Weinmann, Martin, ed. *Das nationalsozialistische Lagersystem (CCP)*. Frankfurt am Main: Zweitausendeins, 1990.

Weinstein, Jeremy. *Inside Rebellion: The Politics of Insurgent Violence*. New York: Cambridge University Press, 2007.

Welker, Marina, and David Wood. "Shareholder Activism and Alienation." *Current Anthropology* 52, no. S3 (2011): S57–S69.

Wells, Celia. *Corporations and Criminal Responsibility*. New York: Oxford University Press, 2001.

Wheeler, David, and Maria Sillanpaa. *The Stakeholder Corporation: A Blueprint for Maximising Shareholder Value*. London: Pitman, 1997.

Whelan, Daniel J. *Indivisible Human Rights: A History*. Philadelphia: University of Pennsylvania Press, 2010.

Wilburn, Kathleen M., and Ralph Wilburn. "Achieving Social License to Operate Using Stakeholder Theory." *Journal of International Business Ethics* 4, no. 2 (2011): 3–16.

Wilks, Ivor. *Forests of Gold: Essays on the Akan and the Kingdom of Asante*. Athens: Ohio University Press, 1993.

Wilson, Richard. *The Politics of Truth and Reconciliation in South Africa: Legitimizing the Post-Apartheid State*. Cambridge: Cambridge University Press, 2001.

Witte, Jan Martin, Wolfgang H. Reinicke, and Thorsten Benner. "Beyond Multilateralism: Global Public Policy Networks." *International Politics and Society* 2 (2000): 176–88.

World Business Council for Sustainable Development. *The Business Case for Sustainable Development*. Geneva: WBCSD Publications, 2001.

———. *Environmental Performance and Shareholder Value*. Geneva: WBCSD Publications, 1997.

World Health Organization. *WHO Report on the Global Tobacco Epidemic, 2008: The MPOWER Package*. Geneva: World Health Organization, 2008.

Wouters, Jan, and Leen Chanet. "Corporate Human Rights Responsibility: A European Perspective." *Northwestern Journal of International Human Rights* 6 (2008): 262–303.

Wright, Gwendolyn. *The Politics of Design in French Colonial Urbanism*. Chicago: University of Chicago Press, 1991.

Wu, Timothy, and Yong-Sung Kang. "Criminal Liability for the Actions of Subordinates—the Doctrine of Command Responsibility and Its Analogues in United States Law." *Harvard International Law Journal* 38 (1997): 272–97.

Wynhoven, Ursula, and Yousuf Aftab. "Why We Volunteer: Corporate Responsibility, Human Rights and the UN Global Compact." *In-House Defense Quarterly*, Winter 2013, 44–70.

Yergin, Daniel, and Joseph Stanislaw. *The Commanding Heights: The Battle for the World Economy*. New York: Free Press, 2002.

Zalik, Anna. "The Niger Delta: Petro-Violence and Partnership Development." *Review of African Political Economy* 31, no. 101 (2004): 410–24.

———. "The Peace of the Graveyard: The Voluntary Principles on Security and Human Rights in the Niger Delta." In *Global Regulation: Managing Crises after the Imperial Turn*, edited by Kees van der Pijl, Libby Assassi, and Duncan Wigan, 111–27. New York: Palgrave Macmillan, 2004.

Index

Obuasi, Ghana, 297–301, 303–14
OECD Guidelines for Multinational Enterprises, 114–15
Ogbu, Osita, 322
oil and gas industries: ameliorative activities, 321; auditability issues, 73–87; climate change and, 66; consumer relations, 96; environmental concerns, 37–38, 45, 74, 81–87, 92, 297; foreign concessions in Soviet Union, 260; human rights violations, 160–64, 237; lawsuits against, 153–54, 156–64; merging of public and private interests, 76–78; pipelines, 38–39, 81, 83–84; transparency initiatives, 39–40, 43–44, 47, 72–87; voluntary compliance, 75–78, 118, 215. *See also* extractive industries; *and specific companies*
Ojdanić, Dragoljub, 165
Ojokwu, Chukwuemeka, 78
Okonta, Ike, 80
Ok Tedi copper and gold mine, 93–94, 96–97, 99, 104
Olson, Mancur, 291
Open Society Institute, 39
Opium Wars, 127
Organization for Economic Cooperation and Development (OECD), 4–5, 40, 229–30n44, 246–47, 278
Organization of African Unity, 263–64
organized crime, armed conflicts and, 263, 272
Otañez, Marty, 64
Ottone, Stefania, 200, 201
outsourcing, 34–36
Oxfam, 39, 76
Oxfam-America, 298

PACT, 41
Palestinian Liberation Organization (PLO), 264
Panama, 89n21
Papua New Guinea, 93–94, 96–97
"penny a pound" initiative, 42, 47
PepsiCo, 66, 237
Perišić, Momčilo, 166
Peru, 98
Peters, Gerhard, 140
Petroleum Industry Bill (Nigeria), 326
Philip Morris: CSR initiatives, 58–62, 64–

65; Marlboro Man campaign, 56–57; "Project Sunrise" campaign, 57–60; supply chain monitoring, 64–65; WHO treaty and, 63–64
Picard, Michèle, 166–67
Piketty, Thomas, 285
pillage and plunder, 129, 130; corporate collusion, 262, 268–69; corruption contrasted with, 271, 289; foreign concessions and, 261
Pinochet, Alberto, 184
Piore, Michael, 51n33
Pistor, Katharina, 46
Pitcher, M. Anne, 289
Plateau Coalition of Business and Professional Associations (PLACOBPA), 330
Pohl, Oswald, 132
poison gas manufacture, 129, 139
politics of space, 97, 98
politics of time, 97–99
Porter, Michael, 238, 241; "Toward a New Conception of the Environment-Competitiveness Relationship" (with van der Linde), 23–24n26
"Porter hypothesis," 24n26
Posner, Richard, 162
poverty problems and alleviation, 5, 10, 103–5, 321, 322–23, 336, 338n17
Power, Michael, 74
Presbyterian Church of Sudan v. Talisman Energy case, 156–60, 165, 193, 206n4
Prince of Wales Business Leaders Forum, 76
"prisoner's dilemma," 198–99, 201
private sector development (PSD), 10, 22n14
privatization: mining industry and, 96; politics and, 295n42; social responsibility and, 8–9. *See also* neoliberalism
profit, concept of, 236
propaganda campaigns, 40–41, 47, 56–57, 66–67, 304–5
property rights, 130, 134–35, 305–9. *See also* environmental concerns
Prosecutor v. Perišić case, 166–68
Prosecutor v. Šainović et al. case, 168–69
"Public Eye Award," 297–300, 304, 305–9, 314
public health issues, 66; corporate philanthropy, 102–3; individual choice and,

voluntary initiatives (*continued*)
239–41; transparency and, 234–35; UN
Global Compact as case study, 243–49;
virtues of, 232–49
"Voluntary Principles on Security and
Human Rights" (VP), 38, 41, 42, 74,
75–78, 118, 215, 234; signatories to, 75–
76, 77, 78

Wacam, 298–300, 304–5, 307, 311, 314
Walker-Said, Charlotte, ix, xiv, 318, 325
Wallenstein, Albrecht von, 177–78
Walmart, 42, 47, 66
war crimes, 129, 130, 154, 175, 178, 186,
259–60, 262, 264, 272. *See also* Interna-
tional Criminal Court (ICC); Nurem-
berg trials (1945–49)
Warri crisis, 76
Weber, Max: "Politics as a Vocation" lec-
ture, xii–xiii; *The Protestant Ethic and
the Spirit of Capitalism,* xiii; "Science
as a Vocation" lecture, xii
West Papua, 38, 105
Westphalia, Peace of (1648), 178
White, Allen, 216
Wildlife Conservation Society, 286
Williams, Cynthia W., 46; "Engage, Em-
bed, Embellish" (with Conley), 52n43
Wilson, John, 79–80
Wilson, Woodrow, x, xiii
Wiwa v. Shell case, 80–81
Wolfensohn, James, 39
Worker Rights Consortium (WRC), 35, 37,
42, 218
World Bank: in Africa, 312, 319; Global
Environmental Facility, 84–85; in-
digenous rights movement and, 98–

100; Manibeli Declaration and, 226n9;
multistakeholder initiatives, 215; "Performance Standards," 42; Small Me-
dium Enterprise Department, 338–
39n24; Structural Adjustment Credit II
and III, 286; sustainability initiatives,
278, 283–84; West African pipeline
support, 38–39
World Business Council for Sustainable
Development, 2, 283
World Commission on Dams, 215
World Commission on Environment and
Development, 283, 290
World Economic Forum on Africa, 334–
35, 336
World Health Organization: Tobacco Con-
trol Convention, 54, 62–64
World Organization for Human Rights
USA, 224
World Summit on Sustainable Develop-
ment (WSSD), 103–4, 283
World Trade Organization, 35–36
World Wildlife Fund, 286
Wouters, Jan: "Corporate Human Rights
Responsibility" (with Chanet), 207n15
WuDunn, Sheryl, 46–47

Yahoo!'s Business and Human Rights Pro-
gram, 115
Yar'Adua, Shehu, 333
Young, Andrew, 35
Yugoslavia Tribunal, 155–56, 159, 164, 165–
69, 181, 262
Yum Brands, 42

Zambia, 273
Zyklon B (Tesch) Case, 139, 179

Lightning Source UK Ltd.
Milton Keynes UK
UKHW01f1534150618

324308UK00002B/184/P